NATURE AND CIVILIZATION

THE
LOYOLA UNIVERSITY SERIES
IN POLITICAL ANALYSIS

1977

NATURE AND CIVILIZATION:
Some Implications For Politics

MULFORD Q. SIBLEY

University of Minnesota

F. E. PEACOCK PUBLISHERS, INC.

ITASCA, ILLINOIS 60143

FOR

My Dear Wife Marjorie
and
My Wonderful Children Muriel and Martin

Table of Contents

CONTENTS

CONTENTS

CONTENTS

Series Editor's Preface

In 1968, the Political Science Department at Loyola University of Chicago, under the sponsorship of the university, initiated the Loyola Lectures in Political Analysis. The rationale for the series was the perceived need to provide a verbal and literary forum for contemporary political philosophers. No limits on subject matter were prescribed. The only requirement was that the guest lecturers address themselves to modern political questions from a normative perspective.

Professor Henry S. Kariel, from the University of Hawaii, was the series's inaugural lecturer. The subsequent publication of his lectures, entitled *Open Systems: Arenas for Political Action,* published by F. E. Peacock Publishers, Inc., was widely and enthusiastically accepted. One commentator described it as "a seminal book for the '70s."

A variety of delays prevented resumption of the series on a regular basis until 1973, when Professor Mulford Q. Sibley, of the University of Minnesota, presented his lectures. The present volume is the result of those lectures, the second in our series, and an indication of the continued originality of insight which has and will mark these presentations. Additional publications from the lecture series will follow soon, the result of presentations made by Professor Eugene F. Miller, University of Georgia, and Professor Christian Bay, University of Toronto.

Mulford Q. Sibley requires no introduction to scholars of political philosophy. Furthermore, his written and active espousal of various principles and contemporary causes has earned him the well-deserved recognition of the general public, beyond the confines of the academic community. He has proven again and again his dedication to his students, to his scholarly profession, and most importantly, his commitment to the ideal that the marketplace of the modern philosopher involves communication with persons at all levels.

All of us associated with the Loyola Series are especially pleased, therefore, by the publication of *Nature and Civilization,* for it means that a wider audience will be able to share with us Professor Sibley's perception and scholarship. Unfortunately, we cannot share or adequately convey the profound gratitude which we at Loyola University feel toward the person himself, who so enriched our lives during his stay with us.

RICHARD SHELLY HARTIGAN
Editor, Lecture Series Director

Preface

It is never easy to justify another book, particularly in the social sciences and social thought. So much is being published that it would be surprising if any one person could read more than a tiny fraction, even within a narrowly circumscribed field, of everything that is already available. Moreover, so much that is hailed as new is not really new, if one knows the history of thought.

Why, then, the present volume?

It seemed to me that, in view of recent interest in environmental and technological-ecological issues, there might be room for a book which would consider these and similar questions within a framework, particularly of political philosophy, which is broader than usual.

My intention is to provide not a highly technical discussion but rather one which will help establish a perspective on the never-ending puzzle of man's relation to Nature and civilization. I also hope to underline the fact that the issues were not born yesterday but instead are part of the whole warp and woof of human history.

Critics will probably contend that many questions are treated too briefly. My reply is that the purpose of the book is not to examine problems exhaustively but rather, within the context, to point to possible positions, to be suggestive, and to provide a kind of bird's-eye view. The reader, I trust, will acquire at least the sketch of a vision; a vision which he can then proceed to question in terms of his or her own perspective. In this way, a dialogue will be initiated that might conceivably bear good fruit.

That dialogue has been going on within me. At times, I take on the role of a critic who might attack my formulation. Then I reply to myself as critic. The dialogue seems to be never-ending. But this is the nature of political discussion. And both blunders and insights may contribute to the debate.

I wish to thank Professor Richard Hartigan for his always warm encouragement. Without his confidence and patience, it would have been much more difficult to complete this book.

MULFORD Q. SIBLEY

ONE

The Problem:
Nature, Human Nature,
and Civilization

AN IMPORTANT characteristic of the past 300 to 400 years has been the attempt to know things through breaking down wholes into parts. So-called mechanist views have maintained that wholes are indeed simply the sums of their parts; that wholes are not organic and do not shape their parts. Some have even adopted a kind of reductionism — that, for example, complex experiences such as the ethical and political could be explained as ultimately merely psychological, or biological, or chemical, or physical. Associated with such views has been the idea of "scientific materialism," which seems to suggest that only the material, sensual, and observable world is "real" and "objective" and therefore worthy of study. Other supposed realms of experience are to be examined by methods appropriate for the objective analysis of "matter." "Inner" experience is thought of as purely subjective and therefore either unreal or at least an inferior type of reality. The notion of humanity as a universal is often cast out, just as the Socratic idea of the soul as a substance, and therefore as immortal, retreats.

Accompanying notions of this kind has been a powerful tendency to the radical specialization of labor. Recognized occupations have multiplied almost infinitely. In agriculture, we are no longer general farmers but growers of a particular type of soybeans, for example. In medicine, we may specialize in the kidneys or heart or spleen, sometimes seeming to forget

1

that these are parts of a larger organism which perhaps is not understandable except in light of the whole. In public policy, we often consider issues segmentally, as if one form of transport or communication, for example, could be rationally considered apart from others.

In light of this, it is not surprising that academic fields have been profoundly affected. Within any given discipline, the accent is often on extreme specialization: thus we become specialists on Portuguese history from 1801 to 1810 or on the early life of Wilkie Collins. In the process, the more general questions, such as those turning on what Reinhold Niebuhr characterized as the "nature and destiny of man,"[1] have often receded; and men like the late Arnold Toynbee, who, in *A Study of History,* sought a bird's-eye vision of the human experience, not infrequently find themselves criticized by the specialists.

Some versions of philosophy have sought to discard whole segments of what used to be regarded as "philosophy" on the ground that the questions they discussed were "meaningless." In political science, there has been a marked proclivity, particularly since World War II, for tossing out or at least reducing the importance of the issues students of politics used to raise.

As for psychology, writers like B. F. Skinner develop a "behavioralism" which restricts the area of study to those things that can supposedly be observed, thus rejecting many of the issues which earlier psychologists thought of as significant. One gathers that man is simply an animal who can be completely programmed and whose agonizing doubts and paradoxes can be eliminated.[2] Of Skinner's philosophy, Floyd Matson has observed: "A theoretical system restricted so rigidly to observables can have no place for concepts dealing with psychic events or inner states, and its author Skinner promptly banished as irrelevant such archaic terms as 'meaning,' 'intent,' and 'understanding.'"[3]

At the same time, it has become more and more apparent, particularly during the past generation, that this segmentation of life, and what we might call this reductionism, whether at the level of the ivory tower or in public policy, cannot cope with either the academic or the practical problems that confront us. At the academic level, for example, the specialties of yesteryear, carefully developed and often reified, are breaking down. Chemistry and biology reach out to each other, and something called "biochemistry" is born. Astrophysics indicates the ways in which astronomy is related to physics and physics to astronomy. Physicists long ago helped undermine simplistic scientific materialism; and they, with some philosophers, began to question the sharp distinction between subjective and objective. Physicists, above all, are often most sensitive to the problem of even defining the "physical"; and some of them, in the never-ending quest to account for the behavior of the physical universe, are now

2

postulating principles which bring them astonishingly close, in both concept and terminology, to the ideas of sophisticated parapsychologists. Thus a very well-known physicist suggests that behind so-called "matter" is a kind of "psi" quality, and some speak of "psychons." "Scientific materialism" has disappeared for many. In a recent semipopular work, Arthur Koestler has dramatized this tendency for theories of physics and conceptions of parapsychology to parallel each other and converge.[4] Even in the social sciences, it should be clear that many of the so-called disciplines which their adherents might think had been ordained by God himself are rather arbitrary. Thus we see emerging such studies as political sociology, social psychology, or an inquiry which is about as sweeping as we can imagine—so-called futurology, which, whatever else it may do, certainly aspires to some kind of holistic vision.

In the practical world, too, there is a growing awareness that physicians must comprehend the human being as a whole if they are to understand the diseases of his parts. The so-called ecological crisis has alerted us once more to people's interrelatedness to one another and to their close connections with the nonhuman. The civil rights crisis of the 1960s dramatized not only the ways in which discrimination against blacks also diminishes whites, but also the fact that many other types of irrational discrimination exist—against children, against women, against homosexuals. And in the 1970s, the specter of food shortages, a commonplace in many parts of the world, began to hover over even the so-called developed nations, making all increasingly aware that their fates are inextricably bound up with those of the less affluent segments of mankind. Temporarily, at least, we have become more cognizant—whether economically or otherwise—of William Blake's aphorism in *Auguries of Innocence.*

> A dog starved at his master's gate
> Predicts the ruin of the State.

Perhaps in this context we can look forward, too, to the reinvigoration of political philosophy, which the Loyola series is doing so much to encourage. For political philosophy, in its ancient classical sense, has been concerned with seeing man not only "scientifically"—as if he were the sum total of his physical, psychological, and spiritual parts—but also holistically and teleologically. Political philosophy in this sense has sought to account for man not only in terms of his simpler or more primitive "motions" but also in light of what he can and should become. In its most comprehensive view, political philosophy has tended to understand "politics" as man's conscious and deliberate efforts to control, direct, and order his collective life. In this sense political philosophy would be the study of the metaphysical foundations for such efforts, the existential factors which have to be considered in carrying out the attempts, the limits within which the endeavors have to be contained, and the purposes and goals of the endeavors. Any studies casting light on these issues would be grist for the mill of the political philosopher.

Thus the political philosopher would see specific issues of policy formulation within the context of a broad assessment of both man's beginnings and his potentialities and duties. Political philosophy would seek to comprehend not only man's origins but also where he is and ought to be going. It would try to understand him not only as a species aspiring to the development of conscious collective control but also as a being individualized in the eccentricities of personality. It would endeavor to see him in his relation not only to the gods but also the beasts and flowers. It would understand that only by viewing him in this rather universal context could it come to grips with specific issues of policy.

It is some such notion of political philosophy that we shall be using in the chapters to follow. The broad categories within which we shall view important issues of politics have been given to us by the history of political philosophy itself. These categories are nature, human nature, and civilization. We shall examine them in their relations to one another and to the problems of politics which are goading modern man.

In carrying out the general theme, we seek in this present chapter to define in very broad terms the relation of nature, human nature, and civilization to one another and to political problems. Subsequent chapters will spell out in greater detail how these underlying questions are reflected in and affect specific issues in politics.

The Meaning and Uses of Nature

The history of political philosophy can be written in terms of the meanings and uses of the term "nature."[5] In ancient times, *physis,* as the Greeks termed it, was used to designate the general patterns of action and reaction which men discerned in the "physical" universe. In intimate association with the ancient inquiry into the relation of permanence to change and of the one to the many, the "physicists" sought the "one" which might be said to be at the foundation of things. Then the problem was to discern how the one became the many, how unity became diversity. How was the one connected to the many? There were hypotheses of evolution. As people reflected on their social and political experience, too, the problem of *physis* entered, as they asked what their relation was to the changes disturbing the social order. Originally, it was "natural" to obey custom and the ways of the fathers and "unnatural" to disobey them. That which was

4

custom and therefore natural was also "good." Later, however, as custom's role as regulator became undermined, it had to stand up to the claimed authority of the political ruler, whose decrees might violate custom (as in Sophocles's *Antigone*). Hence the individual was compelled to decide which was "right" and, therefore, presumably natural.

Meanwhile, the notion of natural as involving specific implicit purposes had arisen. The "nature" of the eye was to see, the "nature" of an acorn was to become an oak, the "nature" of man was to be political and rational. Notions of this kind were spelled out explicitly and were both implicit and sometimes explicit in Socrates, Plato, and Aristotle.

Physis became *natura* with the Latins and played an important role in speculations both about animal, plant, and primitive human life and about the essence or substance of things in general. *Natura* was sometimes identified with the primitive or undeveloped form of a thing (as in "uncivilized" human nature) and sometimes as the developed form (as when one spoke of an ideally developed human being or wise man). In law, *natura* became a standard for jurists: When a statute or decree was ambiguous or incomplete, they turned to *natura* for guidance as to how the ambiguity should be overcome or the decree could be made complete.[6] In this context, the term sometimes referred to what a thing was in its primitive sense and sometimes to what it might become teleologically. When the Epicurean Lucretius, in the first century B.C., came to deal with the principles of psychology, physics, ethics, and politics, he used the term "the nature of things."[7]

Gradually the idea of Natural Law arose, built around various alternative ideas of nature. In the Middle Ages, the myth of the Fall of Man described man's natural state, from which in a sense he had "fallen" into civilization with its institutions of property, the State, and servile subordination. In early modern times, "states of nature" (some were secularized versions of the Edenic state, while others differed from it) were postulated by political philosophers like John Locke, Thomas Hobbes, Jean Jacques Rousseau, and Thomas Jefferson.[8] In the 19th century, much was made of nature by the devotees of natural science, who not only thought they had discovered descriptive "laws" stating the regularities of nature but also, in some cases, believed that there was a relation between these descriptive principles and the necessary prescriptions for ethics and politics.[9]

Throughout the history of the term's various meanings, "natural" has evoked attitudes of approval, while "unnatural" has been a kind of reverse value-laden word — when a situation, action, or person is termed unnatural, we are supposed to get a signal that it or he or she is evil or vile.

While there have thus been many permutations and uses of nature, we shall be employing it, by and large, in three basic and sometimes interrelated senses: (1) as indicating everything in the nonhuman realm which is regarded as being more primitive than man in the scale of things; (2) as referring to that which is fundamental or characteristic about a thing, species, or individual; and (3) as designating a postulated or actual primitive state of man in which he is very close to nonhuman Nature and has not yet entered civilization. In this sense, we often speak of states of Nature. Meanings which appear to be different from or modifications of these three fundamental points of departure can be discerned from the context.

In the first sense, trees and rocks, planets and beasts would be part of Nature. They would be distinguished in greater or lesser degree (depending on one's outlook) from man, on the one hand, and from heavenly beings and God, on the other. Presumably angels would not be part of Nature in this sense, for traditionally they have been conceived to be in some sense higher than man in the hierarchy of the universe (pure forms, in the language of St. Thomas Aquinas),[10] although the very attempt to differentiate between higher and lower involves value judgments of an ultimate sort.

Nonhuman Nature, then, would include both animate and inanimate things thought of as less developed than man. Any movement having as its effect sharper and sharper differentiations of man from Nature, with the former becoming less immediately dependent on the latter, would presumably be advancing the "civilized" as against the Natural. On the other hand, when Count Leo Tolstoy bids us return to "Nature,"[11] he obviously wishes to reverse those tendencies in existence which have widened the gap between human life and animals, flowers, and closeness to the land. When William Wordsworth and the so-called Nature mystics eulogize Nature, they would appear to be employing the word in roughly the same way. When we speak of the natural scientist we are usually referring to one who studies Nature in this sense of the term, by contrast with the social scientist who studies man. When some thinkers refer to the relation between God and Nature, they have in mind this definition, although sometimes they virtually merge human nature in Nature.

What are some of the implications of the notion of Nature conceived as nonhuman and nonangelic? As a kind of ideal type, it would seem to be characterized by life cycles which are relatively fixed. Things come into being, exist for a time, and then disintegrate and change form—the energy first reflected as a rock, or flower, or beast is simply transformed into a different guise, and the flower or rock or beast is no more. The "thing" does not learn appreciably from experience, and social inheritance is sketchy, even though not entirely absent. Thus we say that there is a sameness in

Nature; there is no "history." To be sure, very limited learning takes place, particularly among some of the beasts (much more than we used to believe), but it would seem to be so little, by comparison with the capacity of man, as to be relatively unimportant.

In Nature thus conceived, things are moved by pushes from the outside. Except perhaps in some very embryonic sense, they are not self-moving. They are acted upon but do not act. They behave in response to wind and storms and sunshine and rather rigid instinct. They do not "conduct" themselves or, if they do (modern physics has important observations to make on the alleged indeterminacy of ultimate particles), it is at a very elemental level. To be sure, there are changes during the course of time; but these alterations tend to be blind and to proceed with a kind of glacial slowness. There are occasional tempests or "sports" or mutations during the course of biological evolution, but they are far less frequent than the turmoil often associated with social changes in human history. Even when outlooks of this kind are criticized, as they are by such neo-Lamarckians as the eminent biologist Sir Alister Hardy, the biological changes trail far behind the pace of historical mutations. Although Hardy's hypothesis of species telepathy as a factor in biological adaptation is a striking way to combat the idea of chance evolution, it does not challenge the general contrast between Nature and human nature.[12]

This picture, of course, is an overall portrayal which does not consider important distinctions within the Nature thus conceived. There are, for example, significant distinctions between rocks and plants and between plants and animals. At stake here is the very meaning of "life" and the significance of its appearance in the evolution of things. We should not slight these differences. Nevertheless, the general history of political thought indicates that in the category of Nature, compared to human nature, these internal differences are less significant than the characteristics that unite. At a minimum, Nature is a kind of provisional category.

Whether one's image is of "Nature red in tooth and claw" — as our Victorian ancestors used to say — or of relatively nonviolent mutual adjustment, rocks and stones and flowers and beasts are apparently not bothered about how they should relate to one another. Species and individual are somehow made compatible with each other through the natural forces which move both. Many species may disappear in the process, to be sure; but there is no one to pass judgment on the scheme as a whole, to pronounce whether it is good or bad. It simply *is*. It is a reflection of the "cosmic order" of things, by contrast with historical or political orders.[13]

In Nature (as we continue this ideal typical analysis) there is little or no consciousness on the part of its members. The individual stone does not conceive itself to be separate from other stones — as far as we can tell, it does not conceive anything. The "meanest flower" which gave Wordsworth "thoughts that do often lie too deep for tears"[14] could neither laugh nor cry at him. What human beings perceive as the individual entities of Nature — the separate stones, flowers, and beasts — do not themselves have any awareness of their individuality; or, if they do, it is at so primitive a level as not to count.

The absence of consciousness in Nature implies that the dichotomies we so often take for granted — freedom v. coercion; individual v. species; chaos v. order, and so on — do not exist. While the human mind may impute such conflicts to nonhuman, nonangelic creatures, the process of doing so is a kind of anthropomorphization of Nature, just as we tend to anthropomorphize the gods. Some of this may be inevitable and quite understandable, but we always should be aware of what we are doing. We often tend to think of the nonhuman in human terms.

A second significant usage of the term "nature" is to designate that which is fundamental or characteristic about a thing, species, or individual. Thus we speak of the nature of the stars, or rocks, or animal life, or human existence, or angels, or Gods. We might speak of the "nature of Nature," meaning by this expression the basic characteristics which seem to set off Nature from human nature or the nature of angels. There have, of course, been various versions of the nature of Nature and the nature of human nature. Aristotle speaks of the nature of the eye, of the ear, of man as a whole, and so on. We can talk about the nature of number, of cold, and of sunshine.

Classically, there have been two ways of understanding the nature of a thing or person or group. In the first way, its nature is grasped by taking it apart and analyzing it into its basic constituents, somewhat as one might say that the nature of the watch is to be discovered by examining the watchworks in detail. Hobbes attempts to get at the nature of man by going back to his primitive "motions," which are conceived to be physical, and he uses the analysis of the watch as his model for viewing the nature of human nature. Hobbes furthermore specifically excludes imputed purpose (what Aristotle called "final cause") in giving his account of the nature of man. For, he argues, final causation is a kind of ghost.[15]

The other way of discovering the nature of a thing is to center on its *telos,* or goal or purpose. While this approach would not exclude a breaking down into parts (physical, psychological, or otherwise), it would stress the notion that the whole is an entity that itself shapes the parts. Thus while from one point of view the nature of the eye consists of the fibers, chemical factors, and most minute physical particles of which it is composed, in a more fundamental sense the nature of the eye can only be grasped if we ask ourselves what its purpose may be. Its fibers, chemistry, and physics take on significance only when we ask what they are *for:* the purpose of the eye is to see. Similarly, according to this view, the nature of anything can be understood only by asking what end it serves. Criticizing mechanistic conceptions of life, the biologist Albert Szent-Gyoergyi suggests that function precedes mechanism — that, for example, man first had to wish to say something *before* his physiological speech center could develop; the desire to communicate preceded the structure which enabled him to communicate.[16]

What sets man off from other creatures? If we can discover the answer to this question, we shall have an important clue to his "nature." But we can find the answer, the teleologist and "vitalist" say, only by discovering implicit purpose and not merely by breaking up man into biological and psychological "parts."

Both "scientific" and "teleological" interpretations, we shall contend, are essential if we are to give an adequate account of Nature and of man, although it is probably true that as one moves from nonliving to living things, the teleological approach to the nature of things takes on greater significance.[17]

As for the third usage of the term "nature," it has obvious affinities with the first two. A "state of Nature" suggests closeness to or participation in nonhuman Nature as well as a way of looking at man in terms of his origins or primitive condition. But the assumed nature of nonhuman Nature or of states of Nature will vary, depending on the particular political philosopher.

In general, when speaking of the nonhuman realm or of supposed states of Nature, we shall use a capital *N*. When only the second usage discussed above is involved, a small *n* will be employed.

It is unfortunate that the term "nature" has designated so many things in the history of thought. But if understood in its various contexts, its meanings should become relatively clear, and it is difficult to imagine how its use could be dispensed with, since it has become so much a part of the warp and woof of what we call moral and political philosophy. As a term of reference, whether as Nature or as nature, it would seem to be indispensable unless we attempt to sever all our ties to the past.

The Nature of Human Nature

While there are many social scientists who criticize or even ridicule the idea that there is a human nature transcending the various cultures which have characterized both "primitive" and historical experience, a major tradition of political philosophy sees the conception as central to any thinking about the political world. As David Bidney puts it,

Culture . . . is not the only or primary factor in human experience; it is but one essential condition of human experience. The other pole or dimension of reality is that of nature, cosmic and human, which provides human experience with a common frame of reference and enables man to correlate his cultural constructs with the coercive power of nature and his own individual and social needs and desires.[18]

This is essentially the position we shall take.

How, then, are we to assess the nature of human nature? Several years ago a colleague of mine, an economist, was asked for advice by a student as to how he could study human nature. He asked the professor whether he should take a good many psychology courses in order to pursue his interest. After thinking a moment about the question, my friend said:

No, I should advise you not to take many courses in psychology. That is no way to study human nature. The psychologist may tell you about rats and mazes and conditioned reflexes and positive reinforcement, but his ability as an orthodox psychologist to tell you about human nature is severely limited. If you wish to learn about it, study the great novels or examine the writings of the political philosophers or of the religious sages.

Perhaps the professor was being hyperbolical in his response — for surely both experimental and clinical psychologists can help us enormously to understand human nature — but he was right in the sense that *merely* academic psychology is not enough. Modern psychology tends to aspire to the scientific mode of explanation and to depreciate the teleological. It sometimes seems to think that human nature is simply Nature and that human beings can be studied precisely as we study natural objects. It has frequently lost sight of the sense in which the whole of a human personality is more than the sum total of its parts — the way in which the whole is shaping the parts, in which the human being is a living soul setting in motion events and in principle cannot be wholly explained simply as the result of other events. Psychology tends to forget that from this point of view, we can never know the human being simply through academic analysis but must have direct experience of him or her. Human personality is more like an artistic rendition of a Beethoven symphony than it is like a piece of clockwork.

Academic psychology for a long time, too, has discounted introspection as a mode of understanding human nature; yet there are dimensions of the soul which can only be comprehended in this way. By comparing introspections about feelings and direct perceptions of oneself with one another, one is endeavoring to understand in an immediate sense the motions of the soul which the behavioralist can at best get at only indirectly, through experiments. Thus by comparing the experiences of some religious mystics with those of others, we gain some insight into levels of consciousness. And consciousness itself is best apprehended by the so-called subjective approach which psychological science tends to spurn.

To be sure, there have been political philosophers who have adopted essentially the position of "scientific" psychology. Earlier we mentioned Hobbes, who purports to cast out all teleological modes of explanation and to see mind as material movements within the brain. While we should not identify this position with that of "scientific" psychology, it certainly has affinities with some aspects of the modern study.

In the Hobbesian approach, human nature tends to be reduced to the merely Natural. While man's memory and imagination appear to set him apart from Nature, these supposed hallmarks of human nature are only enormous exaggerations of tendencies which exist in Nature. Under the veneer of civilization one will find a fearful animal who has to be forced to appear to love his neighbor if he himself is to get the better of his neighbor. One can interpret civilization from this point of view as a kind of gigantic fraud or hypocrisy, even though it be regarded as in some sense "necessary."

Whatever one's description of Nature and of primitive human nature may be — whether a state of innocence and spontaneous harmony, as in the traditional Christian view and, to some degree, in Rousseau's perspective, or a world that is nasty, brutish, and short or "red in tooth and claw" — "civilized" human beings have always been intrigued by their relation to both Nature and primitive human nature. Their ties have been obvious, and the relation of Nature to the primitively human (as against the "civilized") has been part of the problem. On the one hand, political thinkers have sought to identify human nature with Nature, although they might differ in the attributes they assign to Nature. On the other hand, they have sometimes seen human beings as virtually transcending Nature and taking on characteristics attributed to God.

When they conceive of human beings as wholly in Nature, they are so impressed by the affinities of man with rocks and flowers and beasts — and all this before Darwin and the Darwinians — that they cannot understand how human beings can possibly rise above Nature. Any characteristics that supposedly set man off sharply from Nature they have attempted to explain away — even though, ironically, in the act of doing so they are behaving as no rat or flower ever did. To some who attempt to explain man as simply a part of Nature, the regularities presumably present in the evolution of species can somehow be transformed into *prescriptions* for what human beings *ought or ought not to do,* ethically and politically. Thus many so-called Social Darwinists sought to provide ethical and political guidance to a perplexed generation by citing the presumed facts of the struggle for survival in biological evolution: What governed biological change must also rule social development, both descriptively and, somehow, prescriptively as well. Much of the literature they produced is a rather naive effort to derive an *ought* from an *is.*[19]

When we become perplexed by the apparently insuperably difficult issues confronting us in political life, we at times would like to see man as simply an expression of a Nature which allows the individual little if any freedom. With Mark Twain, in his more pessimistic moments, we would desperately like to say: "Whatsoever a man is, is due to his *make,* and to the *influences* brought to bear upon it by his heredities, his habitat, his associations. He is moved, directed, COMMANDED, by *exterior* influences—*solely.* He *originates* nothing, not even a thought. . . ."[20] We hesitate to face the maze of ethics and politics; we would like to deny Aristotle's dictum that this is a realm where "things could be other than they are." We often try to deny the liberty which traditional political philosophy has seen as one of the hallmarks of the nature of human nature. As Erich Fromm pointed out long ago, we frequently seek to escape from freedom.[21] We are forever wishing to deny what many of our prophets have told us — that in some sense, we are divine and creative and not merely part of a more or less "determined" Nature.

On the other hand, some conceptions of human nature are so impressed by the supposedly divine qualities present in humanity that they tend to see it as going far beyond Nature and, in some sense, almost completely rising above its constraints, so that man is no longer affected by the limitations of the Natural world or by the brutishness and wastefulness which are often said to characterize it. In this view, man has the capacity to transcend the circumscriptions of Nature and perhaps the parameters of historic human nature. As he develops his technology, for instance, he is in effect preparing the way for a time when he can virtually dispense with his natural body (that which ties him to Nature) and put on bodies that are much more efficient than the one he is discarding. Already he can put on wings and fly, attach himself to machines which can travel for thousands of miles under the ocean, and far exceed anything in Nature when wresting foodstuffs from the earth. He now stands on the verge of "conquering" the heavens through space machines. People, as the late H. G. Wells suggested in the title of one of his novels, can literally become "like Gods."[22] They can create a human world which will largely sever their traditional ties to Nature and produce a certainty and security which they have never had

12

before. As Eugene Zamiatin sees this aspiration in his famous novel *We*,[23] they will modify the bodies they have inherited from beasts, cut themselves off from the messy and ragged aspects of Nature, and, through their dictator the Well-Doer, completely control their collective destiny (even though their individualities may be destroyed). In many of the conceptions of "progress" which J. B. Bury has taught us to associate with characteristically modern views of man,[24] the notion that "politics" itself could be transcended has been present.[25]

The psychological attractiveness of the notion that human beings can completely escape from Nature owes not a little to the ubiquitous human quest for assurance. The gods are presumably quite secure in their positions, so if people could believe themselves to be gods, they should acquire a like security. It is the nature of the gods, presumably, to play fixed tunes on harps which never wear out or need repair. Just as some thinkers have sought to portray man as *simply* a part of Nature and hence accordingly characterized by the presumed certainties associated with Nature (such as instinct and absence of the necessity for choice), so others, motivated by a similar search, have sought to picture him as *simply* divine. In the first type of quest, man seeks to tell himself that, like the beasts and flowers, he dies a physical death which ends all but at least provides a kind of certainty. Like the beasts and flowers, too, he sees himself as really lacking in freedom, despite appearances to the contrary; and this becomes a basis for undermining his ever-present insecurity. At the opposite pole, where man seeks to repudiate his ties to Nature by stressing his divinity, he loses his sense of finiteness while at the same time assuring himself that his divine creativity can never be used for evil or destruction.

Whether man takes the one road or the other, he is endeavoring to deny that he is in some sense *both* beastlike and godlike. With one side of his being, he sees this. But so horrified is he by its implications and uncertainties that he frequently seeks to escape them through complete identification with either Nature or divinity. If he faces up to the apparent fact that he is in some peculiar sense *both* natural and divine, he is plagued by the disquietudes inevitably accompanying that situation. How can he both die and be immortal? How can he be determined, in a certain sense, and yet be free? How can he really face up to problems of ethical and political choice but at the same time recognize that many of his choices will be tragic and that all will be made in the absence of adequate information? How can he live amidst the ambiguities and paradoxes of human history, which seem to be peculiar to him?

These are the kinds of questions we are reluctant as human beings to encounter. The very fact that we are *both* Natural and divine is the root of many of our psychological, ethical, and political problems. As Alexander Pope put it in his well-known lines, man is

> Placed on this isthmus of a middle state,
> A being darkly wise, and rudely great;
> With too much knowledge for the skeptic side,
> With too much weakness for the stoic's pride,
> He hangs between; in doubt to act or rest;
> In doubt to deem himself a god, or beast;
> In doubt his mind or body to prefer;
> Born but to die, and reasoning but to err;
>
> Created half to rise, and half to fall;
> Great lord of all things, yet a prey to all;
> Sole judge of truth, in endless error hurled;
> The glory, jest, and riddle of the world![26]

If one takes this view of human nature — which will be both the point of departure and the point of return in our discussion — human paradoxes and contradictions and tragedies are traceable to man's location on this "isthmus of a middle state." The indecisive Hamlets of this world occupy the same position. Because human beings are neither merely beasts nor merely gods, their uncertainties are compounded, their doubts never really completely resolvable, their anxieties often acute, and their freedom well-nigh unbearable. Out of this situation arise some of the most profound issues of religion and politics.

Whereas the beasts and the rocks are in greater or lesser degrees extensions of the cosmic order, thrown up by it and governed by it but not appreciably (or only passively) shaping it, human beings are partly naked and alone, called upon to make decisions though they often reject the call and are ill-equipped to carry the decisions out. Several years ago an actress with psychological problems was quoted as saying that she "had the emotions of a woman but the mind and body of a child." So it is with man: He has many of the notes of divinity and yet at the same time is closely connected with the mortality and severe limitations characteristic of Nature. In a sense, the defenders of the doctrine that Christ is perfectly divine and perfectly human have an easier task in vindicating their position than do those who say that humanity is limited by the constraints of Nature on the one hand, while transcending a number of those constraints on the other.

Long ago, of course, the Biblical writers recognized the paradox of man's position in the universe. Job suggested that man "fadeth as the flower,"[27] but the writer of one of the Psalms replied that man "is a little lower than the angels."[28] Both are right, yet it is not easy to understand how they can be.

This perspective on human nature is particularly difficult to accept when we think of its full implications. Given his divinelike attributes, man possesses imagination, memory, ingenuity, and the capacity for at least in some measure transforming the Natural world; but because these attributes are attached to a being who can act for other than divine ends, human action may escape the self-imposed limits characteristic of God. If God is omnipotent but at the same time good, his goodness must be an expression of a nature which might have acted contrary to itself but rationally chose not to do so. Or we may think of God as perfectly good and deliberately using his omnipotence to restrain himself from doing certain things which he might, in the absence of his goodness, have been tempted to do. For example, he saw that it would be good for man to have freedom; but the condition of man's possessing freedom was that God would limit the degree to which, under certain circumstances, God would utilize his own undoubted power.

Man, by contrast, has certain attributes of divinity — he lives partly in a timeless dimension, can will, can imagine, and can choose — yet he has a kind of fatal flaw in that his judgments are limited by his frustrating position in Nature and by the fact that he can and often does choose the evil, even when he knows (or seems to know) what a desirable course of action might be. God, once he decides that a given course of action is good, proceeds to will the good — there is no conflict between the decision and the capacity and will to carry it out. Thus once God decided to create the world as an expression of his goodness, he hastened to get to work. This is a quality in which man is often lacking, however, and one of the factors that must be taken into account when we assess his potentialities as an ethical and political being. St. Paul's analysis of himself may be taken to typify the condition of man in general: "The things which I know I should do, I do not do; the things which I know I should not do, those I do."[29] And he goes on to say that this makes him wretched but that he has to recognize his condition frankly.

Man's plight in the middle state, in other words, is not merely that he certainly errs but that even when he presumably does not err, he often finds himself blocked from carrying out what he knows to be right. A kind of irrational rebellion (or perhaps we can say an inertia) exists within him. Often the supposedly divine qualities of memory, imagination, rationality, and creativity are distorted and warped in such ways that they are used to destroy himself, his fellow human beings, and the Nature upon which all are dependent. To be sure, there are those who will argue that this is a misconstruing of man's nature: If he truly *knows* what he should do, it may be contended, he will do it; the problem is not one of will but of whether he *really* knows. But this view, it would seem, is inadequate to account for many human acts or failures to act: St. Paul would appear to be more nearly right when he argues that in at least many instances (although obviously not in all) there is a radical gulf between the knowledge we possess and the will to act under its guidance. It is an important factor to be considered as we make judgments and predictions about human conduct, whether individual or collective.

Given this notion of existential human nature, the evil acts of human history (those that appear to be nihilistic and destructive of both man and Nature, reflecting what Freud calls the Death Instinct[30]) are not "beastly," as they are sometimes described, but rather "human." They are deeds which the beasts are utterly incapable of performing, given their very narrow range of imagination, the rigid patterns which govern them, and the absence of flexibility in adapting means to ends. Only human beings are capable of organizing and executing an Auschwitz or a Hiroshima. Only human beings have the potentiality for the systematic torture so characteristic of many nations in the 20th-century world.[31] Only human beings can contemplate and defend such atrocious and outrageous policies as supposedly necessary "strategies of terror." Only a human being could have been a Napoleon, taking pride in his genius for destruction and littering the world with millions of corpses. Likewise, only human beings could submit themselves in obedience to a Napoleon, allowing him to disrupt their lives and even to plot their deaths in the name of something called "glory."

By the same token, of course, only human beings appear to be capable of the many dimensions of love. To be sure, God's love for the world is infinite and no doubt far exceeds that of man. But in a sense, man's love is more startling, since it is in such close juxtaposition to his potential hate and to his frequent tendency to destruction. While the beasts, too, exhibit many attributes of love, in them its scope is severely constrained by their rather narrow range of memory, imagination, and potentialities for communication. Love in Nature, moreover, tends to be merely reciprocal; while there may be a few exceptions, the kind of love represented by returning kindness for hatred (if indeed we can use those terms at all) does not seem to be present.

The great lovers in history — Buddha, Jesus, St. Francis, and many others — are not "beastly" but rather "human." And in a sense, their merit (if we can legitimately use the term) is greater than the merit of God, for to become great lovers they had to struggle with another side of their natures which bade them embrace destruction and death. Thus while it is surely just to characterize the acts of a Hitler or Napoleon or Tamerlane as distinctively "human" — and not divine or beastly — William Blake also was indubitably right when he observed:

> To Mercy, Pity, Peace, and Love
> All pray in their distress;
> And to these virtues of delight
> Return their thankfulness.
>
> .   .   .
>
> For Mercy has a human heart,
> Pity a human face,
> And Love, the human form divine,
> And Peace, the human dress.[32]

While Blake ends this poem by saying "Where Mercy, Love, and Pity dwell/There God is dwelling, too," from the viewpoint of our assessment this love in man, although indubitably having a divine quality, exists in quite a different context from that of the company of angels, for it coexists with the very real possibility (and often the probability) of hate, destruction, and rebellion against reason. We are told in the myth of the fall of Lucifer and his colleagues that once they had departed from Heaven the remaining angels developed a closely knit community in which they mutually reinforced one another in their determination not to fall. Being close to the source of good and far away from that of evil, they are necessarily removed from the constant temptations of man, in whom good and evil, love and hate are closely juxtaposed.[33]

Civilization and Its Perturbations

Thus far we have been dealing with human nature rather abstractly as a kind of marriage between divine and Natural qualities in which the compound resulting becomes neither divine nor Natural, but something which somehow goes beyond both, often distorting and sometimes transforming both the divine and the Natural. Hence while the limitations of language force us to describe man as both divine and Natural, the commingling of the two in human existence and history can in a sense be thought of as transmuting man into a being *neither* divine nor Natural. He is, as it were, a peculiar compound — not a mixture — of that which is *both* Natural and divine and that which is *neither* Natural nor divine.

From time to time we have been referring to "history" and to civilization. Our propositions about man have been ambiguous in that at points we have seemed to be commenting on man as a being taken out of the concrete episodes of history and at other points we have illustrated our propositions by adverting to history. In a sense, this ambiguity has been deliberate, for we wish to suggest that the ties which link man to Nature or prehistory (as an ideal type) always must be seen in the context of the development of civilization.

A distinction must also be made between culture and civilization. Human societies in all stages of development have a culture of some type — patterns and ways of doing things, common world outlooks and attitudes, and so on — but not all cultures are "civilized."[34] Civilized cultures arise as the importance of cities becomes greater, consciousness of individuality is magnified, writing and record keeping take on a greater centrality, the arts and sciences develop more complexity and subtlety, and ordering by mere wont and custom ceases to be as significant as it was. Although the Marxist concept of a rather simple linear development from "primitive" to "nonprimitive" cultures is now suspect by many,[35] still it seems significant in principle to contrast largely preliterate, less differentiated, less urbanized cultures and societies with those that are relatively literate, sharply differentiated in terms of division of labor, and highly urbanized. There is an important distinction in pattern between "gathering" and early agricultural societies on the one hand and commercial, industrial, and urbanized cultures associated with sizable cities on the other. When we have considered all that we can about the complexity of thought of many preliterate cultures, we must still insist that there is a sharp distinction to be made between a society of highly complex technology and all that tends to go with it and a culture of relatively undeveloped technology. Although the Aztec and Inca civilizations, to be sure, did not possess certain types of technology which we have come to think of as indispensable (the wheel, for instance), still, overall, they are surely to be placed in a category rather different from that of societies of nomadic tribesmen.

In sum, we are emphasizing here ideal typical differences, which are suggested by certain existential distinctions between noncivilized ways of life and those that we term civilized. Neither term is intended to be pejorative: We are neither condemning nor approving either way of human existence. We are suggesting, however, that the noncivilized is closer to Nature and that as one approaches the pole of the civilized, ties to Nature become more indirect and less immediate. Certainly this is the framework in which much political thought has been cast.

The very term "civilization" is redolent etymologically of the development of "politics" as a human activity. The words we connect with civilization — derivatives of Latin and Greek words for "city" or associated terms

— give us clues as to what we have historically meant by the concept. Thus we have "polity," which signifies the framework within which public decisions are to be made; "civic," which designates matters of concern to the city; "urban," having to do with the city; "urbane," which signifies politeness or polish; "civil," which indicates courtesy in approaching and dealing with other human beings in the life of the city or of civilization; "policy," which is, of course, central to politics, one of the hallmarks of civilization; and "police," agents for maintaining the order of the city and of civilization.[36]

Civilization moves away from primitive Nature but in so doing allows man (to some degree and within limits) to become what he is potentially capable of becoming and "ought" to become. In Aristotelean terms, man potentially exists in primitive Nature but becomes fully human, under certain conditions, only in civilization. He has always been potentially civilized and therefore political, but this potentiality cannot be actualized except in the city and in civilization. The oak is potential in the acorn and the acorn is a kind of primitive oak. Man is, in one sense, as William Cullen Bryant puts it, "a brother to the insensible rock/And to the sluggish clod, which the rude swain/Turns with his plow, and treads upon."[37] Unlike the insensible rock and the sluggish clod, however, there is within man a very powerful tendency to get beyond primitive Nature and therefore to become more fully human. Ralph Waldo Emerson sees even purely Natural things as endeavoring to be human — "And, striving to be man, the worm/Mounts through all the spires of form."[38]

The expression of this quest — a flowing out of potential human nature — is what we call civilization. By contrast with at least one version of the ideal type of precivilized state, it is characterized by class divisions, relatively rapid change, and extreme conflict. Some of its conflicts erupt in a violence far beyond that of precivilized culture, let alone that of Nature; others are within the soul and become perhaps more excruciatingly painful than those of groups and states. In civilization, irony, tragedy, paradox, and comedy are commingled, and the dynamics of the process are customarily referred to as human history.

Civilization and History

If man in the abstract has been a central problem to himself, a vital part of this problem has been his assessment of the civilized condition. Just as he has been torn between thinking of himself as primarily a beast and conceiving of his essence as being godlike, so has he been divided in his evaluation of civilization. While civilization may be an expression of his potentiality as a human being, by that very fact it appears to enhance *both* the aspect of humanity which loves, reasons, and constructs *and* the dimension which tends to hate, to be irrational, and to destroy.

This assessment has a long history; here we need only be reminded of it. In Book II of the *Republic,* Plato suggests the problem when he contrasts life under conditions of limited division of labor with the tendency to complexity which sets in as human beings attempt to express their "humanity." On the one hand there is a kind of "city of pigs," with low-level division of labor, few material wants, slight or no expression of the arts and sciences, no cities, and only a faint development of the political. At the other extreme there is fever-heat development of the division of labor, almost limitless material wants and desires, a vast growth of the arts and sciences, multiplication of cities, enormous expansion of commerce and the money system, and imperialism and war. The question is raised as to whether man is truly human in either state. In the city of pigs, his potentialities for the development of reason are forestalled, while in the luxurious state the economic forces and techniques which his development engenders so completely capture him that his potentialities for rationality and control of his own destiny are equally frustrated. In a sense, the idea of justice in the *Republic* is one which bids us avoid both the city of pigs and the fever-heat economy, development, and technology of the luxurious state.[39]

The problem of civilization is posed at many points in the Bible. On the one hand, there is evidence of a keen awareness of man's peculiar place in the universe, as reflected in his capacity everywhere to construct civilization. On the other hand, there is an equally profound consciousness of the dilemmas and conflicts which always seem to be connected with civilization.

The first tendency is reflected in those passages of Genesis which tell us that man was placed on this earth to subdue and control the beasts, birds, and fish.[40] There is a kind of awe about the rise of cities, as exhibited in the story of Cain's founding of the first city, the account of the Tower of Babel, and the idealization of Jerusalem as an epitome of the sacred city. The development of political institutions, too, is seen as one of humanity's great achievements — in the story of Joseph, for instance, and in the great respect often shown for the united monarchy under Saul, David, and Solomon. The tradition of the wisdom of Solomon was associated with the supposedly sophisticated wisdom necessary for a considerable development of civilization and increased emphasis on political ordering.

Yet there also runs through the Bible a kind of despair about civilization and all its works. Thus the founder of the first city, Cain, was also the first murderer, and crime apparently was peculiarly associated with civilization.[41] And, according to Josephus, Cain was likewise the inventor of private property, an institution intimately bound up with the exploitation of man by man. Whether or not murder and private property are in fact developed or accentuated by civilization, of course, is not really the issue. The point is rather that relatively late students of ancient Hebrew civilization thought that this was true.

While the Hebrews stood in awe of the very old Egyptian civilization and in some respects sought to emulate it, they saw it, too, as the symbol of many of the evils which afflicted them. Was it not Egyptian civilization which idolized human creations, which invented the horrible war chariot, and which was responsible for terrible forms of slavery? Then, too, while there was a certain pride in the Hebrew monarchy, this attitude was frequently mingled with fear, hatred, and mistrust; premonarchical days were seen as much closer to Nature and in some sense, therefore, as nearer to Yahweh. Although the city of Jerusalem was, to be sure, a noble creation, still the cry "to your tents, O Israel!" evoked supposed memories of a day that was simpler, more just, and both more "natural" and human. Thus Samuel, possibly observing the behavior of non-Hebrew kings, is represented as very reluctant to sanction the monarchy in the first place, predicting dire consequences if centralized political institutions should be established:

> This will be the procedure of the king who shall reign over you: he will take your sons and appoint them for himself for his chariots and his horsemen. . . . He will take your daughters for perfumers, for cooks, and for bakers. He will take the best of your fields and your vineyards and your olive orchards, and give them to his servants. . . . He will take your male and female slaves, and the best of your cattle and your asses, and make use of them for his work. He will take a tenth of your flocks; and you yourselves will become his slaves. Then you will cry out on that day because of your king whom you will have chosen for yourselves; but the Lord will not answer you on that day.[42]

Yahweh is represented, too, as telling Samuel that in establishing a monarchy, the people will be rejecting God. Nevertheless, the Lord allows the monarchy to be established.

Similar criticisms are advanced throughout the Old Testament. In the story of Nathan, Bathsheba, and David,[43] when the king takes the wife of Uriah the Hittite and sends Uriah to die in battle, he is roundly denounced by the prophet Nathan, who sees in this act the tendency for wealth and power holders of all kinds to aggrandize themselves at the expense of justice. When King Solomon dies and is succeeded by his son Rehoboam, there is some hope that his oppressions will be alleviated, but Rehoboam dashes these hopes with a speech to the delegation visiting him: "My father has chastised you with whips but I will chastise you with scorpions."[44] In the interpretation of the Biblical writer, this confirms the worst fears of Samuel: When one departs from a more primitive Nature and from decentralized tribalism, one inevitably subjects oneself to the arbitrary power of men. Throughout much of the prophetic movement in ancient Israel, similar motifs can be found — from Amos and Micah in the eighth century B.C. to Jeremiah in the seventh and sixth. One infers from reading some of the prophets (although not all of them) that the supposed precivilized state is much more just and in conformity with the will of God than the state arising out of commerce and cities, which has the inevitable tendency to be associated with the establishment of centralized political authority and power.

Nor are these ambivalences about the civilized condition confined to the ancient world. Indeed, they appear to be ubiquitous in every age. In our day, for instance, much of the so-called youth revolt has centered on a repudiation of what its leaders see as the tendency of complex civilization to make wealth an end, to lose human beings in the mazes of advanced division of labor, to "dehumanize" the individual, and to undermine moral integrity. In American history, notoriously, the city has been suspect in the Jeffersonian tradition, and moral virtue has been seen as largely confined to the presumed simplicities of country living. When I was growing up in Oklahoma and the process of urbanization was being accentuated, Governor "Alfalfa Bill" Murray proposed the passage of a law whch would require all legislators to live in a dormitory attended only by women of very mature age, for, said the governor, as legislators came in from the country to live in Oklahoma City for the legislative session, they needed to be protected against the temptations of the urban environment — against civilization.

To understand man's praise of and dubiety about civilization (enthusiasms and questions which are amply reflected in political philosophy), we might note how the civilized state both reflects Nature and human nature and also tends to shape and control them. The city, symbol of civilization, reflects the fact that as man moves from the hunting to the pastoral to the agricultural to the commercial stages, he proceeds from relatively simple division of labor — at first primarily biological and sexual — to a much more involved state. Both Aristotle and Marx suggest that as trade and commerce seriously lessen the predominance of agriculture, direct-use values tend to be overshadowed by exchange values. Money economies are hallmarks of the civilized state, and with the eclipse of direct barter, money values emerge as central. Selling at a high price in money terms has no necessary connection with the supply of what human beings need, and "demand" comes to be associated with the possession of money. Thus no matter how badly a man is starving or how inadequate his shelter, if he does not possess the indispensable money he cannot demand the fulfillment of his needs.

In civilization, man becomes less directly dependent on the vagaries of Nature — weather, for example, and crop failures — for he can in some measure counteract these fortuitous circumstances through technology and social planning, as in ancient Egypt. In so doing, however, he tends to substitute the vagaries of man (in the form of rulers and manipulators of techniques) for those of Nature. The market arises as a reflection of economic interdependence. Material goods tend to increase as man moves from gathering to agricultural to commercial to industrial cultures, but problems in their distribution cause serious tensions among human beings, and enormously important ethical and political problems arise.

With the growth of cities (demographically, greater concentrations of populations) as centers of commerce, a relatively few individuals begin to have the economic wherewithal to develop the arts and sciences. They are encouraged and assisted by the intellectual stimulation so often characteristic of cities, for the city, from one point of view, is a congeries of rapidly and constantly interacting minds.[45] The shepherd meditates in a rather solitary way, his companions being merely his sheep, his dogs, the stones and grasslands about him, and the usually clear sky. He is impressed by the awesomeness of Nature.[46] In cities, by contrast, the meditators are brought together, stimulating one another, but as they are several steps removed from constant contact with Nature, they find it less awesome and tend to see it as subject to human domination. In the large, pollution-filled city, even Kant's "starry heavens above" may be almost blotted out, whatever may have happened to the German philosopher's "moral law within."

The relative importance of communication increases, of course, with civilization. Language, although always changing, alters even more rapidly in the context of city life (Latin, for example, apparently underwent its most rapid transformations in the large cities of the late Roman Empire, remaining relatively more stable in the villages and remote countryside). The development of philosophical and scientific inquiry is both the fruit of a more complex division of labor and the root of a still more complex division. Those extensions of man's body that we may term physical technology result both from a basic curiosity and from the intellectual stimulus associated with the rise of civilization and the life of the city.

But while human beings become more and more interdependent economically, they often tend to be pulled apart in social terms and world views. Occupational specialization promotes a diversity of perspectives, as has long been recognized, and class stratification — based both on differential income distribution and diversity of occupation — has a tendency to break down older forms of community. Such phenomena as "alienation" (in its many meanings) are highly characteristic of civilization. A given human being's circle of acquaintanceships may grow, but the intensity of his relationships may well decline. As groups unite and what Benjamin Nelson calls "others" supposedly become "brothers," intimacy is undermined and the strength of personal bonds tends to erode.[47]

Under these general circumstances, it is not surprising that a considerable degree of social instability is often a result of civilization. The movement to cities and hence to civilization is characterized by an attenuation of custom. In the relatively small village community or clan, or even in the wandering tribe, the ways of the fathers are to a considerable degree determinative; they take on a sacred character and tend to govern a major part of life. Custom, a mixture of incremental "adjustment," accident, and unconscious slow adaptation, becomes to the precivilized state what instinct and native tendencies are to nonhuman Nature. Custom reflects man's implicit quest for certainty and his ever-present tendency to invest something with divine characteristics. In the ideal type of precivilized community (which is not, of course, ever completely exemplified existentially), custom is a kind of social cement which none can question, and it tends to rule in both the public and the private realms. But this tends to be changed as the nonurban culture gives way to the city; what Walter Bagehot called the "cake of custom"[48] breaks up, and the area of the sacred becomes somewhat more confined. The market and commerce are ruthless in the way they treat custom, corroding even its most unquestioned aspects. Traders have little respect for many taboos, so long as they can turn a profitable exchange, and with commerce in goods comes commerce in ideas. More things become subject to question and open to criticism, abetted by the development of philosophy and science.

Although no existential society is or has been ever wholly sacred or nonsacred, with civilization differences in degree become differences in kind. Thus if we compare the relatively "primitive" Athens of the eighth century B.C. with the Athens of Pericles in the fifth century, we find the breakdown of settled tradition one of the most significant phenomena. Similarly, if we contrast medieval London with, let us say, the London of the 19th century, a distinguishing characteristic was the far greater tendency of the former to rely on mere tradition or wont as guiding factors in the life of the town; by the 19th century, "tradition's chains" had become much weaker, the individual was freer (at least in one sense of that ambiguous term), and the degree of uncertainty about right and wrong had been greatly accentuated.

With the decline of custom and tradition as governing factors (we should emphasize that they do not disappear but rather become more limited as ruling powers), the tendency to relatively rapid social change is accentuated. Men and women become aware, both spontaneously and under the goading of their philosophers and scientists, of the general problem of permanence and change. They view it in the context of Nature, and increasingly they see it in the framework of human nature. As the realm of the sacred is narrowed, human consciousness becomes increasingly perturbed by change and by the turbulence so often associated with it. It is as if human beings had lost their anchorage. If there is little or nothing that is permanent, where, then, do I find my identification? What is the essential "I"?

While we have been dealing here largely with ideal typology, it should not be assumed that our propositions are always remote from existence. The contrast between Nature and primitive human nature, on the one hand, and civilization, on the other, was sharply reflected when the period of the Judges ended and the Hebrew monarchy began.[49] It was exemplified, too, as early as the eighth century B.C. in Greece, when Hesiod testified to the breakdown of the primitive, the erosion of the ways of the fathers expressed in custom, and the lack of guidance for youth.[50] During the seventh and sixth centuries B.C. the crisis was exacerbated. Another illustration can be found in the breakdown of medieval customary ways associated with the revival of commerce and the growth of cities, when things that had hitherto been taken for granted came to be questioned, and men found themselves puzzled about where to turn for guidance.[51] In our own day, we see a similar paradigm reflected when relatively isolated, nonurban communities, such as Harlan County, Kentucky, find the old custom-laden ways being eroded by the introduction of mechanical technology — violence increases, for example, and men tend to associate the violence with the questioning attitudes that accompany the innovations brought by industry.

In the development of our personal lives, as Hegel long ago suggested, there would appear to be an analogous movement. If we are born into a stable family, the patterns of conduct expected of us are usually taken for granted, and we find our security in the customs of family life as interpreted by our parents. But the family, in a sense, is conspiring against us, for the security it affords prepares us for expulsion into the uncertainties of society at large. As we grow into that society, moreover, we see ourselves as individuals apart from our families. We question what was formerly taken for granted and often feel ourselves alienated from our parents and siblings. We desperately search for new forms of certainty in a society dominated by the marketplace, with its emphasis on material things and competition for scarce goods. We are now out of the relatively sacred security of the family and acutely conscious of our individualities and of our separation from others. How can we remain individuals and yet overcome the insecurities and uncertainties inevitably associated with our feeling of isolation and lack of guidance? Although we may seek to resolve this question in some measure by founding families of our own, we cannot really return to those of our childhood, for we are no longer children — despite our frequent yearning to go back to that seeming bliss.

While we should beware of pressing analogies too far, within a measure this picture of our experience as individuals is in some degree applicable to the movement from primitive human nature to human nature in civilization. "Individuality," so to speak, is enhanced as custom erodes, commerce expands, class conflict arises, the sciences and the arts flourish, cities multiply, and organized warfare (so characteristic of civilization) reveals all its ghastly characteristics. Under these circumstances, the individual, who has just been born, so to speak, is puzzled and uncertain. The very economic interdependence so characteristic of the civilized state tends to pull him away from his fellows socially. The same division of labor which enables him to produce more material goods places him at the mercy of impersonal economic forces which he does not seem to be able to control. The very city where he is in much closer physical proximity to other human beings seems often to increase his psychological distance from them. Improvements in his tools or techniques, while bettering his material lot, force him to adjust his life to the requirements of the techniques.

Although he now has a freedom of maneuver unknown in primitive human nature, he is often at a loss as to how to use that freedom, for he has neither the relatively rigid instincts possessed by the beasts of Nature nor the fixed, customary patterns which gave him a certain security before he became "civilized." Although the arts and sciences have apparently increased his knowledge and skills and perhaps lengthened his life expectancy, with every step in their development has frequently come a new spiritual insecurity. By their very nature these developments lead men to question accepted premises and thus constantly to change the paradigms and myths within which human beings live, and move, and have their being. Sometimes, however, they endeavor to restore their security and to destroy their painful freedom through various forms of authoritarianism or totalitarianism.

Finally, while human nature, as we have said, is in one of its aspects firmly implanted in Nature, the development of civilization tends to remove and isolate us from our roots and in the process undermines the humility which comes from awareness of our kinship to the rocks, flowers,

26

and beasts. As the humility declines we tend to think of ourselves as gods, only to be awakened too late by our stupidities.

These, then, are some of the paradoxes and problems which arise as primitive human nature moves into civilization. If we see the movement as one from undeveloped human nature to more "actualized" forms, this interpretation has to be heavily qualified and explained. This is so because of the very contradictions that tend (other things being equal) to be present in civilization. If war and peace, supreme love and supreme hatred, freedom from primitive rigidities and noxious slavery to man, boundless kindness and unmitigated cruelty — if these are some of the reflections of developed human nature, then one must ask whether the apparent fissions, so dramatized by civilization, are final, or whether the contradictions can be overcome.

In Thomas Gray's "Elegy Written in a Country Church-Yard," the poet describes the simple, rather unsophisticated countrymen whose remains lie in the cemetery:

> Their lot forbade: nor circumscribed alone
> Their growing virtues, but their crimes confined;
> Forbade to wade through slaughter to a throne,
> And shut the gates of mercy on mankind.

Here Gray seems to be suggesting, as have we, that civilization appears to reveal in macrocosm and to dramatize both the "virtues" — love, concern, reason, unselfishness — and the "crimes" — selfishness, hate, war — of mankind. Those buried in the country churchyard, being less civilized, were limited in both. They did not "wade through slaughter to a throne," in part because the opportunity did not arise in the village close to Nature. On the other hand, their field for the exercise of the virtues was also very circumscribed: they could not, for example, be multimillionaire philanthropists affecting all areas of the globe and having an impact on perhaps millions of human beings. Gray would seem to be right, on any reading of human history.

The problem, however, is whether this is the whole truth. Are there potentials within man and his civilization which will enable him to integrate his life so that the fissions and contradictions can be transcended? Can he be the individual he became with the decline of the primitive and yet belong to a genuine community? Can he etch on his consciousness the fact that he is in Nature, thus preserving his humility and his sense of reality, while at the same time he lives in a civilization which tends to separate him from Nature and often does violence to it? Can he and should he attempt to restore the ideal-type order present in customary governance, or should he seek a new ordering which, while preserving the elements of civilization, will yet overcome the apparent chaos so characteristic of much past history? Can he eliminate the tendencies to organized, violent conflict in history, while recognizing and preserving nonviolent forms of conflict which are inseparable from the arts and sciences and from individuality itself? Can he preserve the material gains associated with the division of labor while transcending the tendencies to social fissions that accompany it? Can he make the economic forces released by civilized life less blind so that they will only serve and not dominate man? Can he, while developing the technology so intimately associated with human nature in civilization, prevent its imperatives from controlling him for their own ends? Can he create, while avoiding idolization of his creations, thus preventing enslavement by them?

Man's practical effort to answer questions of this type in the context of civilization is what many would call politics. Having moved away in part from both Nature and primitive human nature, he also leaves the collective orderings central to those ideal types: the orderings of sheer external determinism, relatively rigid native tendencies, or immemorial, unconsciously developed wont and custom. The challenge of civilization and of the human history which is the reflection of its dynamisms is whether man can substitute political orderings and directions — conscious, deliberate orderings — for the predeliberate orderings characteristic of Nature and primitive human nature. This is a particularly acute challenge when we remember that the more complex a civilization becomes — in terms of division of labor, development of technology, growth of science and the arts — the fewer are the segments of collective life that are readily amenable to nonpolitical orderings. Thus modern civilization is particularly confronted by the political challenge, precisely because of the distance it has gone from Nature.

It is appropriate, then, that we devote the next chapter to spelling out the political challenge, particularly in the context of modern times.

Notes

1   Reinhold Niebuhr, *The Nature and Destiny of Man: A Christian Interpretation*, 2 vols. (New York: Scribner's, 1940), p. 41. For another perspective, see Arthur O. Lovejoy, *Reflections on Human Nature* (Baltimore: Johns Hopkins Press, 1961).

2   See B. F. Skinner, *Beyond Freedom and Dignity* (New York: Alfred A. Knopf, 1971).

3   Floyd Matson, *The Broken Image* (New York: G. Braziller, 1964), p. 54.

4   See Arthur Koestler, *The Roots of Coincidence* (New York: Random House,

1972). For an examination of similar themes, note Sir John C. Eccles, *Facing Reality: Philosophical Adventures by a Brain Scientist* (Heidelberg: Springer-Verlag, 1970), particularly ch. 10, in which Eccles treats of "The Brain and the Soul." Peter A. French, ed., in *Philosophers in Wonderland: Philosophy and Psychical Research* (St. Paul: Llewellyn Publications, 1975), brings together essays by Immanuel Kant, H. F. Saltmarsh, Michael Scriven, H. H. Price, C. D. Broad, and others. Matson, in *The Broken Image*, mourns what he calls the "broken image" of man that is attributable to materialistic world views. One of the more sophisticated recent works which discusses the relation of physics to psi phenomena is by the mathematician John Taylor, in *Superminds* (New York: Viking Press, 1975).

5   And, one might add, in terms of the idea of the "primitive," which is often associated with some uses of "nature." For the relation of the primitive to "nature" and other conceptions in ancient times, see, for example, Arthur O. Lovejoy and George Boas, *Primitivism and Related Ideas in Antiquity* (Baltimore: Johns Hopkins Press, 1935). Consult also Edwyn Bevan, *Stoics and Sceptics* (New York: Barnes and Noble, 1913).

The Cynics, observe Lovejoy and Boas, seem to have used "nature" in at least four senses: (1) as anything which does not involve art, (2) as a characterization of a primeval age, (3) as desires which are spontaneous and instinctive, and (4) as moral codes, laws, and customs considered permissible by any particular people. *Primitivism and Related Ideas,* p. 120.

For a comprehensive philosophical approach to the conception of nature, see R. G. Collingwood, *The Idea of Nature* (Oxford: Clarendon, 1945). See also Collingwood, *The Idea of History* (Oxford: Clarendon, 1946).

6   See A. P. D'Entreves, *The Natural Law* (London: Oxford, 1955).

7   Lucretius, *De Rerum Natura*, translated as *On the Nature of Things.* For an English translation, see Whitney J. Oates, ed., *The Stoic and Epicurean Philosophers* (New York: Random House, 1940), pp. 69–219.

8   The Declaration of Independence, whose thought owes so much to John Locke, speaks of "unalienable rights" and of "Nature and Nature's God."

9   And thus Herbert Spencer, in *Man versus the State* (New York: D. Appleton, 1884) seems to hold that because the tendency of social evolution is from "status to contract" and toward the elimination of state controls, all political philosophies (such as those of revised 19th-century liberalism) that advocated state "intervention" in the economic order somehow contravened "Nature."

10   In *Contra Gentes*, II, 42, St. Thomas speaks of angels as "intellectual natures, at the peak of creation." They are "substances . . . without matter: they rank below the first substance, which is God, and above human souls united to bodies." *Contra Gentes*, II, 91.

11   See particularly Tolstoy's *My Religion,* trans. Huntington Smith (New York: Thomas Y. Crowell, 1885), pp. 182–90, where much of his attack on what he thinks of as the corrupting influence of civilization is summarized. Civilization is said to cut us off from Nature; deprive us of the joys of physical labor; dissolve the family, in that men are dominated by the quest for "worldly success" and hence cut

themselves off from domestic pleasures; rob us of unrestricted intercourse with all classes of human beings (through the development of class structures); and impair bodily health through pollution, luxurious and harmful food, and the virtual elimination of physical toil.

12   See Sir Alister Hardy, *The Living Stream: Evolution and Man* (New York: Harper & Row, 1965).

13   On the relation of cosmic to political orders at the dawn of political thought, see particularly Eric Voegelin, *Order and History: Israel and Revelation* (Baton Rouge: Louisiana State University Press, 1956).

14   William Wordsworth, "Ode, Intimations of Immortality from Recollections of Early Childhood."

15   See particularly Thomas Hobbes, *Leviathan,* Parts III and IV.

16   Albert Szent-Gyoergyi, "Drive in Living Matter to Perfect Itself," reprinted from the *Graduate Faculty Newsletter of Columbia University* and the *Journal of Individual Psychology; Synthesis,* Spring 1974, p. 22.

17   Cf. C. E. M. Joad, *Guide to the Philosophy of Morals and Politics* (New York: Random House, 1937), particularly pp. 25-35. Interpreting Socrates's mode of explaining human beings teleologically, Joad comments: "You will extend this mode of interpretation to all human psychological experiences, seeing even in our most elementary physical desires some traces, however faint, of aspirations to higher things. As opposed to those of an animal they are never, you will say, *purely* physical. Secondly, it is only in so far as human beings act teleologically, seeking by a distinctively human form of activity to achieve ends appropriate to man, that they will realize their full nature; that they become, in other words, entirely human" (p. 34).

18   David Bidney, "The Philosophical Presuppositions of Cultural Relativism and Cultural Absolutism," in Leo Ward, ed., *Ethics and the Social Sciences* (South Bend, Ind.: University of Notre Dame Press, 1959), p. 68.

19   They seemed not to take to heart the suggestion of T. H. Huxley that man's ethical standards must presuppose a revolt against "Nature," as understood in its "red in tooth and claw" sense. See Huxley's *Evolution and Ethics* (New York: Appleton, 1896).

20   Mark Twain, "What Is Man?" in Charles Neider, ed., *The Complete Essays of Mark Twain* (Garden City, N.Y.: Doubleday, 1963), p. 337.

21   Erich Fromm, *Escape from Freedom* (New York: Farrar & Rinehart, 1941).

22   H. G. Wells, *Men Like Gods* (New York: Macmillan, 1923).

23   Eugene Zamiatin, *We,* trans. Gregory Zilboorg (New York: Dutton, 1924).

24   J. B. Bury, *The Idea of Progress* (London: Macmillan & Co., 1920).

25   Cf. Eric Voegelin, *The New Science of Politics* (Chicago: University of Chicago Press, 1952).

26   Alexander Pope, *Essay on Man,* Epistle II.

27   Job, XIV:1-2; 7-9.

28   Psalms, VIII:3-8.

29   Romans, VII:15-24.

30   See Sigmund Freud, *Civilization and Its Discontents,* trans. James Strachey (New York: W. W. Norton & Co., 1962).

31   See, for example, Amnesty International, *Report on Torture* (New York: Farrar, Straus & Giroux, 1975). The *Report* observes of the period since World War II: "Never has there been a stronger or more universal consensus on the total inadmissibility of the practice of torture: at the same time the practice of torture has reached epidemic proportions" (p. 31).

32   William Blake, "The Divine Image," in Geoffrey Keynes, ed., *Poetry and Prose of William Blake* (London: Nonesuch Press, 1939), p. 58.

33   This seemed to be St. Augustine's interpretation in the *City of God.*

34   Our use of the term "civilization" is akin to that of Arnold Toynbee, who divides "intelligible fields of study" into primitive societies on the one hand and civilizations on the other. Primitive societies are much more numerous than civilizations but are "restricted to relatively narrow geographical areas and embrace relatively small numbers of human beings." Civilizations, by contrast, embrace large numbers of human beings over wide geographical areas. See Arnold J. Toynbee, *A Study of History,* abridgement of vols. I–VI by D. C. Somervell (New York: Oxford University Press, 1947), p. 35.

Freud's definition of civilization as "the whole sum of the achievements and the regulations which distinguish our lives from those of our animal ancestors" is broader than Toynbee's and seems to make little distinction between culture in general and civilization. As we use the term, civilization is a particular type of culture.

For the general nature of culture, see, for example, Clark Wissler, *Man and Culture* (New York: Crowell, 1923); Leonard T. Hobhouse, G. C. Wheeler, and M. Ginsberg, *The Material Culture and Social Institutions of the Simpler Peoples* (London: Chapman & Hall's, 1930); and Clyde Kluckhohn, *Mirror for Man: The Relation of Anthropology to Modern Life* (New York: McGraw-Hill Book Co., 1949).

35   The early Marxists seemed to value Lewis Henry Morgan's *Ancient Society* as a portrayal of "primitive" culture everywhere, and the characteristics of primitive culture were contrasted with such features of nonprimitive cultures as private property. Aside from the fact that many modern scholars question the accuracy of Morgan's portrayal at certain points, typical Marxist interpretations of history seem to be far too neat and uncomplicated. For an analysis of Marx's conception of history, see M. M. Bober, *Karl Marx's Interpretation of History* (Cambridge, Mass.: Harvard University Press, 1946).

36⁻   The close association of "civilization" with "politics" and the "State" has bothered some, particularly those who think of the State as primarily repressive. In a recent work, for example, Elman Service seems to suggest that the State is not needed to promote and advance civilization. See his *Origins of the State and Civilization* (New York: Norton, 1975).

37   William Cullen Bryant, "Thanatopsis."

38   Attached to Emerson's essay, *Nature.*

39   Book II of the *Republic* is, of course, difficult to interpret; for at points Plato seems to be suggesting that the primitive "city" — or the city of pigs — is better than the luxurious. Yet he postulates a considerable economic development in the very structure of the *Republic*. The key, it seems to me, lies in his rejection of *both* the primitive and the accident-dominated luxurious state. Perhaps he is suggesting that if he were asked to choose between the city of pigs and the luxurious state, uncontrolled and undirected by deliberation, he would select the former.

40   In Genesis, I:26, God is represented as making man "in our image" and as giving him "dominion over the fish of the sea, and over the fowl of the air, and over the cattle, and over all the earth, and over every creeping thing that creepeth upon the earth." And Psalms, VIII:6-8 says: "Thou madest him to have dominion over the works of thy hands; thou hast put all things under his feet; all sheep and oxen, yea, and the beasts of the field, the fowl of the air, and the fish of the sea, and whatsoever passeth through the paths of the seas."

41   Genesis, IV:17.

42   I Samuel, VIII:10-19.

43   II Samuel, XI, and XII:1-25.

44   I Kings, XII:14. Rehoboam is represented as taking the advice of the "young men" and rejecting the counsel of the elders, who suggested that he be a "servant" to his people.

45   For a brief elaboration of some of the characteristics of modern urban life, see Louis Wirth, "The Urban Way of Life," *American Journal of Sociology*, July 1938, pp. 1-24.

46   As in Psalm XIX, which begins "The heavens declare the glory of God; and the firmament sheweth his handywork."

47   Benjamin N. Nelson, *The Idea of Usury* (Princeton, N.J.: Princeton University Press, 1949), particularly pp. 135-37. Observes Nelson: "The road from clan comradeship to universal society is beset with hazards. When two communities merge and two sets of others become one set of brothers, a price is generally paid. The price . . . is an attenuation of the love which had held each set together."

48   Walter Bagehot, *Physics and Politics* (New York: D. Appleton, 1973).

49   This is epitomized in Judges, XXI:25: "In those days there was no king in Israel: every man did that which was right in his own eyes."

50   Hesiod, *Works and Days,* ed. T. A. Sinclair (New York: Macmillan Co., 1932).

51   This would seem to be illustrated in Charles Reade's great novel *The Cloister and the Hearth* (New York: G. Munro, 1878).

TWO

Nature, Civilization, and the Political Imperative

WE HAVE ATTEMPTED to distinguish between Nature and human nature and to relate both to questions about the development of civilization. Our discussion has been general and suggestive, opening up the possibility of the varying interpretations which will be referred to in this and subsequent chapters. While we rejected the notion that there is no such thing as a universal human nature — whether regarded in terms of its origins or its implicit goals — we did suggest that the limits on human nature are rather broad, at least in all probability, and that what aspects of human nature are to be emphasized depend on the degree to which deliberation and developing consciousness can organize and control the structures of civilization. As human nature in its primitive sense is engulfed by civilization, the possibilities of enormous constructive endeavor and of equally great destructive power are released. The very freedom man acquires is fraught with ambiguity: on the one hand he fears it, while on the other he thinks of it as indispensable to his being a person. Released from the thralldom of wont or custom and from the extreme constraints imposed by very restricted material resources and a severely limited life span, human beings are forced to seek guidance for the use of their freedom.

In other terms, the problems of ethics and politics emerge. However one

33

conceives primitive human nature — whether, for example, as in the Christian myth, as a state of innocence; or, in another version, as one of constant war; or as a custombound community — the burdens and joys of freedom begin to make their appearance as it is transcended. Freedom is associated with development of consciousness or awareness — with knowledge of self and awareness of others — and therefore with the very origin of the notion that civilization is a problem or series of problems. That is to say, in an ideal-type Nature, presumably guided by God or instinct or custom, neither freedom nor ethical-political issues would exist. It is only when these systems of guidance break down that both freedom and moral-political questions emerge. In a sense, the more sensitive and many-faceted the consciousness, the more acute will be the problems: as consciousness broadens and deepens, alternatives appear to multiply, so that what originally seemed to be an either-or conundrum will turn out to be a question which might have eight or ten possible answers. Using the mythology of the fall of man, the only question faced by Adam and Eve was whether or not to eat of the fruit of the Tree. But once the fruit was eaten, possible choices seemingly became endless; and which were matters of right, wrong, or indifference became a question potentially fraught with enormous subtlety.

Broadly speaking, the ethical problem became: What should we do, or how should we conduct ourselves in relation to our fellow human beings? The political issue was similar: How should we deliberately order and control our collective affairs to ensure the good life? Both questions suggest that the history which is born with the decline of the primitive tends to release dynamic forces that are, other things being equal, directionless and blind. People have somehow to take these directionless and blind forces or dynamic factors and shape them to ends which they themselves determine. In their personal relations — insofar as they can — they seek to establish standards for interpersonal governance. But personal relations always exist in a framework or context of some kind — of biological instinct, of custom, of the market, and so on — and the political problem becomes that of shaping this context deliberately, rather than allowing it to be molded simply by instinct or rigid custom or the blind forces of the market. The raw materials of history, so to speak, are the Aristotelean "matter" — or unformed stuff — out of which man seeks to develop order or to advance the good life which, at least according to Aristotle, is potential in his nature.

The political quest assumes that we can no longer rely on predeliberative factors for ordering, for, from the beginning, man's potential has been to be free and therefore to be responsible for creating his own order. This is, in part at least, what we have meant by that very slippery term "rationality." As the order of mere wont and instinct is transcended and man enters history, he confronts the problems — in greater or lesser degree — of what we call politics.

While custom, native tendencies, and similar factors continue to play enormous roles, once we cross the line which separates what we are calling primitive human nature from civilized human nature, the political challenge continues to grow. The further man moves from Nature and primitive human nature, the more ubiquitous does it become. With every advance in civilization comes an enlargement of the dimensions and problems of politics. With the speed-up of social change so characteristic of civilization arises a corresponding magnification of the apparent demands for political ordering.

Modern civilization accentuates the political challenge, for never before in history have we witnessed in more extreme form the breakdown of those elements that we have associated with primitive ordering. We can say, perhaps, that one of the first views of modern civilization is to be found in Francis Bacon's utopian vision during the early part of the 17th century.[1] There it seems to be assumed that if only human beings will turn to "empirical" modes of understanding the universe, the secrets of Nature will be unlocked and with them the key to human technological development will be found. The wonders of mechanical inventions are revealed: submarines, airplanes, weather observation towers, and many others. Implicitly, it is asserted that with technological development will come not only an abundance of material goods but also both moral and political progress. When the Royal Society was chartered in 1662, it was supposed to be modeled on Bacon's vision, its purpose being the encouragement of both pure and applied sciences. To be sure, the so-called Industrial Revolution did not come until much later, but the Royal Society symbolized the spirit of the new age. Although conservatives like Jonathan Swift might bitterly protest that spirit and satirize scientific experimentation,[2] their attacks were but a minor countereddy in the stream which was to lead to the late 18th-century technological revolution.

Let us be a bit more explicit about the political challenges of modern times by first considering the ways in which traditional nonpolitical governance declined; second, describing briefly significant political problems which became accentuated with the development of modern civilization; third, suggesting possible alternative responses to the political challenges, in the context of the Nature-civilization question and the central problem of justice; and fourth, stating the general notion of justice which will govern our discussion. In subsequent chapters we shall examine each of the major specific challenges and subject it to closer analysis and judgment, in light of the varied responses and of the idea of justice.

The Explosion of Modern Times and the Decline of Customary Orderings

After 1662, several factors contributed to the decline of customary orderings and to the eruption of political challenges. They were an expansion of commerce even greater than in the previous century, the development of science, the growth of the technological imperative, and the almost limitless explosion of industrial culture. While events of this magnitude were originally confined to Western civilization, they promise in the latter part of the 20th century to engulf the world in their rather blind and heedless embrace.

As was noted in the previous chapter, commercial development always undermines nonpolitical levels of ordering. But modern commercialism, which began at the close of the Middle Ages, represented an explosion in which differences in degree became distinctions in kind — by comparison, let us say, with the development of commerce and piracy in preclassical and classical Greece.[3] The medieval cake of custom was corroded as voyages to the Indies and to the Americas pushed trading values to the forefront and compelled men and women of diverse cultures to intermingle and to compare notes. St. Sir Thomas More's *Utopia* (1516) reflected what was to become a common set of themes under commercial capitalism: the search by merchants for quick profit, the study of comparative cultures (reminding one of that ancient gossip Herodotus), the breakdown of customary land allotments, the growth of cities,[4] the apparent increase in crime, the undermining of traditional systems of law, and the development of increasingly sharp criticism of what hitherto had been regarded as sacred. These are, of course, features of any expansion of commerce, but they were particularly acute in the 16th and 17th centuries.

By sapping the foundations of traditional culture, the expansion of commerce helped create an atmosphere in which man began to think that other forms of society were conceivable. Thus the 16th, 17th, and 18th centuries were above all characterized by the revival of utopian thought. When well-established ways of governance decline, men feel compelled to speculate about alternatives. A custombound society in which the political domain is strictly circumscribed will tend to be lacking in utopian speculation. But as the old orderings begin to crumble at an accelerating rate, a minority of human beings — albeit a rather small minority — will evince a renewed interest in proposals for deliberate, or political, orderings. As many a 19th-century thinker might have put it, man's political consciousness expands, and with the broadening of that consciousness there is an accentuation, too, of the difficulties of political speculation.

The rise of science was probably even more basic in shaping the political challenge. Since the 17th century, that development has tended to be according to geometric progression. Now, however the dynamics and definitions of modern science may be viewed, at a minimum they reflect fairly rapid shifts in what Thomas Kuhn has popularized as "paradigms."[5] Older scientific paradigms were relatively stable, as was the unconsciously developed custom which largely governed the relations of mankind. However, from the 17th century to our own day, nothing seems to be permanent in the rapidly shifting perspectives associated with what is regarded as the most developed of the "empirical" sciences, physics. The physics of the 17th century — which many now think of as naive — is superseded by that of the earlier 19th, which in turn is transcended by that of the late 19th and early 20th; and then come the Einsteinian and post-Einsteinian frameworks of our own day. It is possible to become so impressed by these shifts that we sometimes wonder whether the physics of our day is any longer even "physical," when some of its practitioners speak in terms of psychons or of subatomic particles like the neutrino, which has neither mass nor magnetic field. But then we recall that physics itself is derived from a Greek word meaning Nature and that Nature could embrace both "material" and "nonmaterial" things.[6]

Now the political implication of the relatively rapid changes in scientific world-views lies in the fact that politics both reflects the generally rapid departure from primitive human nature and in turn contributes to the widespread uncertainty about possibilities of deliberately guiding man's collective life. Scientific change is part of that ubiquitous acceleration of social change which exacerbates the problems of deliberate collective ordering. When nothing seems to be certain, let alone sacred — whether immemorial custom or scientific frameworks — the problem of grounding any political ordering on something that is supposedly known is almost infinitely magnified.

It is significant, for example, that shifts in scientific frameworks are accompanied by a dissolution of the old securities apparently embodied in classical views of natural law. From the 17th to the 20th centuries our uncertainties about guiding our policy decisions seem to have increased, and with this acceleration there often appears a tendency to identify might with right, as is reflected in Hobbes-like views. The sheer range of apparent political choices seems to defy what the critics have charged was the overly simplified or even naive categories of natural law thinking.

But it has been the practical results of scientific inquiry which have been most momentous in developing characteristically modern political challenges. Nothing is more important than man's tool-making capacity in promoting social changes and in breaking down sacred societies. This has been true historically, but it is even more significant today and in modern times generally. Mechanical and other forms of technique are, of course, very closely tied in with the level of commerce and the development of scientific paradigms. Commerce, by broadening horizons, tends to stimulate curiosity and the comparative study of cultures; and curiosity and the comparative examination of cultures in turn are vital factors in evoking the development of techniques. Here again, modern civilization differs from previous ones not in principle but in degree; but the difference in degree seemingly approaches a difference in kind.

At first, technological development appears to be very unorganized and often to be the result of serendipity; by our day, however, its growth is organized and man's faith in it has become overwhelming. It is simply assumed by modern man that technological development is desirable. Indeed, as the old faiths and securities decline, about the only certainty which remains (and ought to remain, according to much modern thought) is scientific and technological change. As we shall emphasize later on, this faith has taken on overtones of an idolatrous religion, creating many of the problems always engendered by idolatry.

As part of the faith, the notion of the "conquest of Nature" occupies a central position. While, as we have seen earlier, the conception of man dominating Nature and using it for his own ends is a very ancient one,[7] the supposed leap taken by science in the 17th and 18th centuries leads people to believe that their manipulations of the natural world can be virtually complete. The Biblical faith in domination of Nature had been heavily qualified by great dubiety concerning man's capacity to avoid domination by his own creations. The prophets were as worried, in other words, by the idolization of technique and social institutions as they were about making Nature sacred. Neither Nature nor human inventions were to take the place of the invisible Lord.

With the onset of modernity, however, came a faith in the conquest of Nature which was increasingly emancipated from the Biblical doubts. Before modern times (in the Middle Ages, for instance), the expression "in accordance with Nature" meant that Nature (whether nonhuman or human, whether in its primitivist or its teleological sense) imposed severe limits on man who was, after all, simply a creature himself. With growth of faith in applied science, however, "unlocking the secrets of Nature" frequently signified for some a kind of rape in which the victim did not resist. And the rapist himself was not subject to any penalty.

But however we evaluate the precise influence of modern technology, there can be little question about its corrosive effect on governance by wont and custom. Technological change has so many ramifications for social change in general and so many "side effects" that no sooner do we think we are unconsciously building a new custom to take account of new technology than the custom in embryo is utterly disrupted again by technological innovation. In the old days of relatively slow technological change, we might count on new patterns of customs to develop which would take account of the alterations produced by relatively slight modifications in the plow or in ways of building houses or in methods of excavating stone. But in our day, the new customs are often stillborn. We either allow the changes to take place without an attempt at conscious, overall collective direction, or we have to tackle the problem deliberately, through politics. We can no longer count on custom, so to speak, to fill the vacuum.

Finally, modern civilization has been characterized by what many have called an industrialist culture. To be sure, some claim now that we are moving into what is variously termed a "superindustrial" or a "postmodern" or a "postindustrial" age. But for our purposes, generally speaking, "industrialist culture" or "industrialist civilization" will be sufficiently descriptive.[8] Industrialist culture is, of course, intimately associated with the technological explosion and, like that explosion, it illustrates in dramatic form what happens when man moves rapidly away from Nature and primitive human nature. In fact, and speaking very broadly and tentatively, industrialist culture might be said to be an existential illustration of what Plato referred to in Book II of the *Republic* as the uncontrolled, undirected "luxurious state." Like the luxurious state ideal type, the industrialist culture represents a vast development of complex division of labor and an almost unimaginable proliferation of material goods. While the modern spirit repeats that it wishes to "understand" Nature, by and large that understanding is for a purpose — to exploit and manipulate Nature in order to make it yield material abundance. In fact, material abundance often appears to become almost the chief end of industrialist culture. As Wordsworth said at the outset of the machine age:

> Getting and spending, we lay waste our powers;
> Little we see in nature that is ours.[9]

The myth systems we associate with industrialist culture embody mankind's own expectations of what industrialism will do. It will release man from hard work; increase leisure; remove him yet further from the dirtiness of Nature; and emancipate him from the superstitions associated with primitive human nature.[10] For many — although they differ about how this will be done precisely — it will eliminate "politics."

But whatever else an industrial culture may or may not do, it would seem, initially at least, to magnify greatly the political problem. Like the complex technology with which it is so intimately connected, industrialism tends to destroy everything which in the past was regarded as sacred — as Marx and Engels recognize in the *Communist Manifesto*. Traditional family forms, sex relations, religious beliefs, and the expectations men and women have of one another — all are subject to erosion. To be sure, industrialism will search for its own sacred objects and thus impose limits on the degree to which those subject to its aegis allow themselves to speculate politically. But granting this, it still remains true that methods of nonpolitical ordering which hitherto have dominated are literally riddled by the onset of industrialist culture.

Thus a very substantial segment of life becomes potentially subject to methods of political rather than nonpolitical direction. Labor which has been minutely divided must somehow be coordinated again, and even decisions to allow market forces to do the coordinating are political in nature. When decisions take the form of provision for formal organization, as over against market coordination, the issue of deliberately controlling the bureaucratic coordinators arises. The phenomena connected with bureaucracy are, of course, as old as civilization, but they become particularly acute in modern industrialist culture, with the sheer multiplication of bureaucrats, the frightening complexities involved in meshing the many threads of collective life, and the accelerated tendency of the bureaucracy to set up ends of its own which escape community control. With the apparent decline of the nuclear family, more and more of its traditional functions are taken over by political bodies such as school boards. In preindustrialist civilization, to be sure, there was always a political sphere (indeed, it is a hallmark of any civilization), but that arena in modern times has been enormously magnified. Thus in ancient civilization political issues tended to turn on such questions as military defense, public works, and irrigation. But with modern technology, economy, interdependence, and almost constant social change, it is difficult to see any limits in principle on the range of the political.

We rightly say (although sometimes whether we fully understand its implications is doubtful) that life tends increasingly to be "politicized." This may be interpreted in one sense as meaning that more and more aspects of existence can be legitimately regarded as having a collective or "public" character. If we accept close economic interdependence as a given, for instance, then our economic lives will inevitably take on a public significance that they might not have had in a culture of low-level division of labor. Thus joint withholding of labor, or a strike, could affect millions of human beings and be of incalculable potential importance for those charged with the responsibility of deliberating about public affairs. In a world made crowded in part by health measures which have flowed from the progress of science, whether or not to have children can quite normally become a political issue. Even the selling of one's house, which used to be invested with the sacred character of disposing of purely "private" property, now comes to be endowed with a partially public character insofar as we accept the legal prohibition of sales that are based on racial considerations. Can suicide in the modern world be regarded as a purely private act? It is at least questionable.

There is a second sense, too, in which the word "politicized" may be used. Not only do more and more of our activities assume a public or collective character, but it is increasingly impossible to take account of that character without resorting to deliberate — or political — modes of ordering. Tradition or custom in the old days could constitute modes of governing the public as well as the private arena, and methods, too, of distinguishing between the two spheres. Today, however, incipient traditions and customs are nipped in the bud, so to speak, by constant alterations in human relations connected in large measure with technological change. In these circumstances, almost constant legislating — a political act — appears to many to be required. Law as custom gives way to law as legislation and executive decree; the common law, with its slow accretions through time, measurably retreats and statutory law tends to usurp its place.

But as more and more of the ordering process seems to involve politics, questions about consciousness of values, short-run versus long-run considerations, and the problems of forecasting assume greater and greater significance. In societies where politics are less central, collective awareness of value priorities may not be so important, since people are called upon to deliberate about collective affairs with only moderate frequency and over a narrower range of subjects. In cultures where constant revision of legislation seems to be an imperative, however, the ideal of rationality entails an enormously acute awareness of value hierarchies.

The long-run against short-run considerations which are inevitably involved in political decisions create particularly acute issues, whatever the form of governance. If it is decided by deliberation not to make a decision on a given issue, or if the issue is simply ignored, a decision is, nevertheless, made: it is a decision simply to allow "social forces" to have their way. If decisions are postponed, this, too, involves the making of at least a negative decision. It is in light of these propositions that one must see the short-run versus long-run question. The short-run consequences of a given positive decision, let us say, would result in greater immediate material prosperity, but the long-run consequences of the same decision would tend to deprive the next generation of clean air or adequate water supplies. To

41

make the decision on the basis of long-run consequences might, moreover, erode political support for the decision maker. Since unborn children do not vote, there is always the temptation in politics to ground decisions on short-term consequences, even though it may be well known that long-run results could be disastrous. Alternatively, refusal to make a decision would in effect be a decision to allow accident or adventitious circumstances to rule.

The great debate about slavery and the slave trade from the time of the Constitutional Convention of 1787 will illustrate some of these notions. While many of the Founding Fathers were concerned about both issues, they feared that making positive decisions to circumscribe the institutions immediately would impair the chances of the Constitution's being approved. Hence they settled for a 20-year period of grace for the slave trade and did nothing to check slavery itself. Many believed, in fact, that a formal decision preparing the way for the abolition of slavery was unnecessary, since in their judgment the institution was already being eroded by economic and other factors. Then came the invention of the cotton gin, however, and with it renewed hopes for gain by slaveholders. "Accident" began to legislate to strengthen the institution of slavery, and it became increasingly difficult, psychologically and politically, to legislate by deliberation against the institution, particularly after the 1830s. The matter, of course, became enmeshed with constitutional and sectional issues, and the possibility of avoiding violence (given prevalent assumptions) declined drastically. Throughout the whole period from 1787 to the Civil War, there was a kind of dialogue going on between the legislation of deliberation (Missouri Compromise, Compromise of 1850, and so on) and the legislation of accident (growth in power and wealth of slaveholders, the development of industry in the North, and similar factors). While in the early thirties the possibility of compensated emancipation could still be calmly discussed in the South, by the fifties this was virtually barred, thus narrowing the options for controlling events through peaceful deliberation.

Or note some examples from the 20th century. Notoriously, politicians often seek to remain in power by refusing to face honestly and openly the necessity for increased taxes. So they postpone the day of reckoning by contriving financial gimmicks of various kinds which give the appearance (but not the reality) of balancing the budget. Many perhaps know that the financial legerdemain cannot last forever, that the day of judgment will come. But, like Louis XV and other politicians in 18th-century France, they in effect say "After me, the deluge." Thus Congress and the President refused to levy adequate taxes to fund an admittedly unpopular Vietnam War. Had they raised additional revenue, perhaps opposition to the war would have been greatly exacerbated. But their failure to legislate through deliberation also had its enormous price, for the Great Inflation of the midseventies was partially attributable to the underfinancing of the war: here again, absence of positive deliberate legislation opened the way for the legislation of accident. Failure to tax deliberately was a factor in gigantic and unfair taxation through inflation.

Let us take another 20th-century illustration. Over the course of many years, neither Congress nor most local legislative bodies had grappled positively with the peculiarities of the gigantic urban complexes of the United States. Mounds of statistics, to be sure, were available about in-migration, out-migration, the decline of the central cities, and similar subjects, but the implications for legislation did not seem to be fully grasped. Thus neither the State of New York nor New York City faced its financial problems without equivocation, Congress having set the example for them. Positive and adequate consideration of economic and financial issues was continually postponed. Legislation at national, state, and local levels was avoided; difficult issues turning on the interdependence of the modern world were evaded. Despite a history of this kind, some seemed to be surprised when New York City appeared suddenly to be on the verge of bankruptcy in the fall of 1975. Failure to legislate positively and intelligently at national, state, and local levels led to the domination of legislation by accident or by banks and similar institutions.

But the failure to grapple with issues by public deliberate legislation is understandable when we consider the difficulty of weighing long-term consequences of given acts, which entails the problem of forecasting. Immediate consequences of decisions, while by no means always easy to determine, are still fairly simple to judge, compared with long-term forecasts. Thus the immediate consequences of a war are in some measure easy to assess: usually social solidarity in a nation is accentuated, and of course there is great destruction of lives and material goods. But beyond very immediate short-run consequences, the long-run impact of any public and deliberate legislative decision is problematical. All decisions in a complex civilization affect, directly or indirectly, most facets of life. Yet we can never foretell precisely how they will affect those facets. We will indubitably be governed, either through accident or through legislation by deliberation; but often, with the best will in the world, what we may intend in deliberate legislation may be belied by its apparent long-run consequences.

The history of civilization is filled with decisions which purported to effect one result only to bring about its reverse. Even if we accept the view that controlling predominant economic interests endeavor to shape public policy for their own particular ends or interests, it does not follow that they can discover what specific decisions will bring about those ends. In fact, much political history is, as Reinhold Niebuhr long ago pointed out, "ironical,"[11] in that statesmen were not wise enough to be able to implement their intentions and also not prescient enough to prevent fulfillment of just the opposite of their intentions.

Political challenges of these types become sharper as division of labor advances, economic interdependence is magnified, and the imperatives of coordination make themselves felt to an even greater degree. The history of complex civilizations has hitherto been one in which the challenges were only imperfectly perceived or, where perception was greater, in which the response was inadequate to save the civilization from disintegration. Cyclical theories of politics are based in part on a recognition of this imperfect perception or inadequate response.[12] The challenge to human imagination, ingenuity, and understanding becomes so great, in fact, that there is always a gulf between the apparent imperatives of political ordering and man's capacity to cope with those imperatives. His inability to cope has been indicated by rising crime rates, civil wars, sharp and destructive changes in the economy, and similar phenomena.

The challenges of modern times are perhaps the greatest of all.

Eruption Points

These propositions about modern civilization and its accompanying technological development, proliferation of science, and undermining of nonpolitical controls can be more specifically illustrated by reference to four issues which dramatize the political challenges of civilization, and particularly of modern civilization. Here we refer briefly to these questions — (1) authority, coercion, and freedom; (2) technology; (3) the economy; and (4) the problems of utopia — reserving for later chapters a more complete discussion.

Authority, Coercion, and Freedom

Modern civilization illustrates a point we have already suggested — that as man moves from Nature to primitive human nature to civilization, his range of choices is initially enlarged, but at the same time he is challenged by new tendencies to restrict his choices and his scope of supposed freedom. When he lives close to nonhuman Nature or under conditions of primitive human nature, he is constrained (depending on one's view of the "natural" state) by weather, erratic animals, direct limitations of God, shortness of life, or rigid custom. When he enters civilization, he often appears to be "freer" but finds himself increasingly constrained by the often

44

arbitrary operations of the marketplace, the restraints of bureaucratic organization, and the impersonalism of large size and scale. While he often enters modern civilization with glowing hopes for enlarged freedom from death and the frustrations it involves, the very nature of that civilization often seems to threaten the whole human race with death. Although modern civilization is intimately associated historically with the theory and ideology of democracy — with its emphasis on liberty, equality, and fraternity — it often appears to dramatize even more fully than premodern civilization that most human beings either cannot or will not commit themselves to the kinds of activities that democracy makes imperative. Thus in our day perhaps as large a proportion of mankind as ever lives under despotic or near-despotic nondemocratic regimes. While modern political theory has above all been concerned with the problem of reconciling individual freedom with organization (at least since Rousseau),[13] many of us legitimately ask whether it has succeeded in doing so; and the tentative suggestions that political theory has been able to make have often not been taken seriously by practical politicians.

Although a major stream of recent political thought sees history as the story of freedom,[14] modern industrial and "postindustrial" man confronts the 21st century under a double menace: that both his freedom and his life will be wiped out by a lack of adequate natural resources or by war, or, assuming that he continues to live, that the presumed needs of the culture and its accompanying political organization will so restrict his freedom that the concept itself will have little congruity with social and political reality.

Involved in modern civilization, as in all civilizations, is also the issue of coercion and violence. Both are obviously related to the problem of authority and freedom, but precisely how they are connected and their exact relationship to concepts of Nature and civilization will be shaped by the particular framework one brings to their study.

Technology

Whatever one's particular view of Nature and human nature, it would seem clear that the technological question must be central in any conceptualization of the problems of civilization. The challenge of political ordering in our day demands that we somehow come to grips with the question of what we are to do with the tools we have spawned. There is a tendency, too, to wish to find the solution of all questions (ethical, political, cultural) in techniques: Thus, if technology creates what we regard as problems for the human condition, the answer, we tend to say, lies in new technology. If the Nature from which man sprang comes to be exploited almost to the vanishing point by man's techniques, the answer — and this has been seriously proposed — is for human beings deliberately to go off into space (through improved technology) in order to discover an unspoiled Nature elsewhere.

Technology tends to be seen in much modern thought as the instrument that will emancipate man from the erratic and often arbitrary and cruel characteristics of Nature. Less commonly has modern man examined the costs of technology. So impressed has he been with its supposed benefits that he has frequently pushed aside those critics who from the beginning have uttered warning cries. In some measure, so-called advanced civilized man has so committed himself to complexity in technology that the question arises as to whether, even if he should decide that he wishes to call a halt, it is not already too late to do so.

The politics of technology becomes the problem of the degree to which we are able to, or should deliberately control and order its introduction and development. This is in turn connected with the tendency of modern civilization to make a sacred object of technology, thus limiting the degree to which we can deliberate collectively about it. In the same context, we raise the question of what a "democratic" solution for the problem of technology might be.

The Politics of the Economy

A third enormously significant issue posed by modern civilization is that of the economy. Even if one does not adopt a primarily economic interpretation of political history, the question of the economy is always highly important. It becomes particularly so because, with the release of enormous energies following the decline of medieval civilization and the growth of commerce and industry, and with the concomitant technology, there is a tendency for purely economic forces to run away with all of life. When they were freed in considerable measure from the constraints of both the nonpolitical and the political governance of the Middle Ages, economic forces — which in and by themselves are "blind" — tended to dominate all of life. Given the fact that the segments of life were increasingly regarded as autonomous, economic factors were often seen as simply a part of Nature and not to be controlled politically by man. The realm of the political was restricted in thought at the very time that essentially political challenges became greater than ever.

Much of the history of modern political thought has turned on this curious anomaly. In the 19th century, the exponents of laissez-faire provided the ideology which sought to justify the autonomy of the economic realm, and even after they were seriously challenged by Marxists, later liberals, and non-Marxian socialists, their assumptions lingered on, under the curious rubric of "free enterprise." Basically, too, although the defenders of laissez-faire were increasingly pressed by their critics, at least one of their propositions tended to be accepted even by their most caustic enemies — the notion that economic and technological progress betokened progress in every realm of life. Sometimes the economic appeared to be so central that other forms of progress were not even taken seriously. The whole problem of distributive justice, for example, which Aristotle had made so central in his system, often receded in importance; it was frequently assumed that somehow if gross national product were increased, issues of distribution would almost automatically be resolved.

In our day, of course, it is widely recognized that economic issues must be seen not only in terms of the systems of national states but also in relation to the world as a whole. The very technological and economic factors that pose such challenges to modern politics also tend to compel us to see these challenges in world rather than in national terms — thus almost infinitely magnifying their complexity.

The Problem of Utopia Building

Political discussion which simply breaks down or analyzes the challenges of modern politics is not enough. It must also attempt to provide a constructive vision of where modern man should and can go. It must see the several strands of political analysis in relation to one another and to the ideal. It must, in short, once more engage in the task of utopia building.

This has not been a popular endeavor in our day. The fetish of "incremental" change and the fear of what Sir Karl Popper calls "wholesale social engineering"[15] — not to speak of the obvious ways in which the modern State has tended often to denigrate human personality — produced a reaction to the literary construction of utopias or ideal communities, which was so important in the first three centuries of modern development. Quite understandably, too, the existential distortion of Marxist goals by societies claiming to be Marxist and the development of Fascist dictatorships have made many wary of projecting yet other forms of organization which, once implemented, would in all likelihood be distorted. Modern man, seemingly trapped by the organizations he had spawned, revolted in terror against all attempts to imagine a more nearly ideal society.

Despite this understandable revulsion against the formulation of utopian schemes, the student of politics has an obligation not only to explain

47

and criticize but also to propose and explicate ideals. We need more utopian visions, not fewer. For if politics be that activity through which man seeks consciously and deliberately to order and control his collective life, then one of the salient questions in all politics must be: Order and control for what ends? Without utopian visions these ends cannot be stated as wholes; and even a discussion of means and strategies will be clouded unless ends are at least relatively clear.

Since we are dealing with modern politics in relation to Nature, human nature, and civilization, moreover, it is important to point out that the formulation of utopias is perhaps one of man's most distinctively "human" capacities and responsibilities. It represents a central exercise of his freedom as he moves from Nature and primitive human nature to civilization, and it is preeminently political since it epitomizes the fact that the political task is a holistic one involving evaluations and judgments of human life as a whole, as well as analyses of past experience and the development of strategies.

The Responses: Paradigms of Political Thought

In the remaining chapters of this volume we shall be treating our own responses to the eruption points characteristic of civilization, particularly of modern civilization. But these responses must be seen against the background of certain major paradigms under which the problems of Nature, human nature, and civilization have been treated. Within each paradigm we shall remind ourselves of the peculiar meanings given or attributed to Nature and the alternative conceptions of human nature and civilization. While all systems of political philosophy treat these themes either explicitly or implicitly, their specific conceptualizations may differ markedly. We should, moreover, in reminding ourselves of the responses, remember that in some contexts Nature is taken literally as an existential situation, whereas in others it seems to be simply an analytical construct to lay bare the problems of politics. In some, moreover, Nature is used in its primitivist sense, while in others it represents the object teleologically conceived.

In all the paradigms civilization is contrasted with nonhuman Nature, and in all of them human nature is distinguished from Nature, at least in some degree. In all, too, the question stated in the first chapter — whether man might or can be understood completely by methods characteristic of the study of nonhuman Nature — would seem to be at least impliedly raised. Is man in some way reducible to Nature in its nonhuman sense, despite appearances to the contrary, or is he potentially a god? As we turn

48

to the paradigms, these are the kinds of questions we should ask ourselves, particularly in the context of the issues so dramatized by modern civilization. Here we note five responses.

1. Nature and primitive human nature are viewed as states to be suppressed if man is to avoid violent death at the hands of his neighbor, but civilization is seen as an artifact based on agreement maintained by force. There is no telos for man, however — no *summum bonum*.

2. Nature and primitive human nature are conceived as basically harmonious, with freedom central and coercion rare. Civilization, then, is largely a matter of convenience: It is designed to make a bit more certain what was basically a beneficent situation.

3. Because Nature and primitive human nature are fundamentally nonviolent and beneficent, the further we move away from them, the more we distort and mangle essential humanity. Civilization is thus evaluated as a corrupting influence, and its institutions inevitably reflect this corruption.

4. Another position seems to suggest that there are two types of harmony between the opposite poles of individuality and community: there is a primitive Natural harmony which is broken up by civilization, and civilization, in turn, disrupts Nature and primitive human nature, thus inflicting mankind with misery. But out of all this misery may arise a new and more sophisticated harmony — one for which civilization has been a preparation.

5. The nature of man is such, in a teleological sense, that neither justice nor harmony will be discovered unless one recognizes both the value and the evil in Nature, primitive human nature, and civilization. Both primitive human nature and civilization, when taken alone, impair the possibility of justice, a resolution of the problem of freedom and coercion, and a surmounting of the issues posed for politics by technology and the economy.

In the sections below we shall comment on these alternative frameworks.

Civilization against Nature

The first position we can associate with Hobbes-like views. Civilization and its institutions are seen preeminently as suppressing man's primitive nature, at least ostensibly. Through consciously and unconsciously developed mythologies, we hold down our basic fear of our neighbor and pretend to love him. We even covenant with those whom we fear to relent in our hatreds, so that we can somehow survive a longer period of time. Gradually, a body of so-called laws of nature is developed to state maxims of expediency which seem to be necessary if we are to express our passions, while avoiding the attacks of others on our lives. Thus the principles of the Sermon on the Mount, far from reflecting man's social proclivities, are seen as exemplifying his antisocial nature: When they tell us to love one another, to turn the other cheek, to judge not that we be not judged, and so on, they are expressions of the fear that unless we at least appear to act in these ways, we shall be done to death by others.

While we should beware of equating the two, something very much like this will also be found in the Freudian analysis. Desire to express one's id is almost boundless, until it comes up against the almost equally boundless desires of others. And desire, somewhat as in St. Augustine, is above all reflected in sexual lust. To avoid the destruction which would undoubtedly ensue if ids pressed their desires endlessly, a kind of superego arises which represents the desire of all to survive. Despite this factor, however, we are still seeking to express our desires without limit. Now, however, we consciously strive to balance our desires against the built-in superego, which represents maxims of expediency. Through our egos, we try to act so that we can have our cake and eat it too — the ego in this sense being the calculating, scheming, planning side of our selves. Civilization is the fruit of this scheming, and underneath all its elaborate pretenses will be found the basic raw thrusts of individuals who resent their suppression and are forever seeking to transcend the boundaries established by morality and political institutions. Religion itself is part of the system of rationalizations whereby we tell ourselves and others that what we do is for the benefit of mankind, whereas in reality, and beneath the conventions of civilized human nature, we are seeking to express our own individual pleasure principle to the maximum degree.[16] In a somewhat different version of his conception, Freud suggests that there is a kind of natural Death Instinct, or Thanatos, which is at war with Eros, or a type of natural, life-enhancing tendency which presumably is related to the id on its constructive rather than its destructive side.[17] Interpreted in this way, our primitively natural desires have two facets, one of which, sublimated (through what Hobbes might have called the Contract which ended the state of Nature), leads us to create the structures of civilization, while the other works to tear down those structures.

To be sure, the raw natural stuff which both Freud and Hobbes postulate differs in character within the two frameworks of the paradigm — in one, it is the libido; in the other, the desire to inflate the self and to dominate. Nevertheless, in both versions it is this material which is repressed or sublimated. In both, moreover, nonteleological explanations of man — those that attempt to understand him by analyzing him into his primitive elements — are uppermost.

In many derivatives of this first reaction to the dilemmas of politics, the implication is that the further we move away from Nature and the primitive, the better. Science, the arts, and political institutions, unnatural as they are, take man from Nature in general and are presumably insulating him from the death which is ever present in the primitive state. Logically, this perspective would seem to be saying that the more we remove ourselves from Nature and primitive human nature, the less likely we are to meet death, and particularly violent death. Hence the greater the complexity of division of labor, technology, and the economy — and the more impressive the amount of organized violence at the command of the society — the less will be the likelihood that our physical existence will be wiped out.

Yet there is a curious apparent contradiction in the more specifically Hobbist version of this paradigm. On the one hand, it purports to be taking us away from a Nature which is "nasty, brutish, and short." On the other hand, it allows the individual to be the judge of when the agent of civilization, the sovereign, is threatening him with death — and for the individual to be a judge in his own cause is, of course, a characteristic of Nature. Moreover, if a group of individuals can successfully overthrow a given ruler, his legitimacy is ipso facto destroyed. This would seem to equate "right" with "might," which is also a hallmark of the Nature from which the group has ostensibly escaped.

Freud-like versions of this view often reflect a similar ambivalence. On the one hand, they seek to explain how direct expressions of the id are repressed or at least strictly limited. Thus in one interpretation, both the natural expression of sexual desire and that side of the passions which represents the tendency to sheer destruction are suppressed. The implication is that there is a kind of war going on between the structures of civilization and the free-flowing, spontaneous individual who would otherwise exist. The individual is mangled in the process, since repression and sublimation are unnatural. One can never be certain, to be sure, whether this is simply an explanation or whether the view would likewise be that the procedures for mangling are justified. Insofar as there is also an element of justification, the implication is that it is desirable to be "unnatural." On the other hand, there is a clear recognition by Freud himself of the tendency for repression and sublimation to produce violent reactions in the form of personality disorders, civil violence, and war. In his later years, as is well known, he seemed to be very pessimistic about the prospects for eliminating war in human affairs, since it was, as it were, the price paid for civilization.[18]

In some expressions of Freud-like conceptions (for example, in Herbert Marcuse at one point in his evolution and in Norman O. Brown),[19] it seems

51

to be suggested that the repressive structures of civilization will in the end lead to their own demise (for instance, the production of endless quantities of material goods will wipe out scarcity and hence competition). When that stage is reached, man can once more "play." His spontaneity will be released from the constraints and mangling of history, yet the "good" results of those constraints — science, material abundance, the arts — will remain. This notion obviously has affinities with Marxism. Hobbes-like views have no such optimism, apparently seeing hypocrisy and organized suppression and overt war (between rulers and ruled) as never-ending concomitants of the civilization which they seemingly exalt.

In the civilization-against-Nature outlook, too, the emphasis is on a never-ending quest for the expression of impulses. There seems to be no supreme good in which we can be emancipated from the dominance of primitive desire. Both ruler and ruled are dominated by it, however much their aggressions may be encrusted over by rationalizations, conventions, and the claimed "justice" of civilization. While the desires may be sublimated and destructive tendencies may be curtailed, they are forever likely to erupt in their Natural forms. Reason, as classically understood, is an illusion, as is the religion which historically has suggested that the soul can find rest in God, thus releasing itself from the incessant and restless heaping of desire on desire.

It is easy to see how a perspective of this kind (while historically at least as old as the positions of Thrasymachus and Glaucon in the *Republic*) could win widespread support in the culture of the past 300 years, where the whole notion of man dominating Nature — carrying on a kind of war against it — is closely associated with modern civilization's enormous strides in ostensibly taking us away from the primitive. Nonhuman Nature must be conquered and primitive human nature suppressed. Although this creates enormous difficulties, human beings must become reconciled to it, unnatural as it may be.

Nature as Basically Harmonious and a Model for Civilization

This perspective is often associated in modern political thought with Locke-like conceptions. It sees the nature of the State of Nature as fundamentally harmonious, in the sense that men are close to nonhuman Nature, and in their relations with one another they spontaneously recognize and usually (although by no means always) observe one another's rights as revealed to them in the laws of "Nature" and of "Nature's God." Moreover, even before the development of formal civil society, men had begun to carry on commerce with one another and to divide the earth among themselves. Formal civilization is designed for convenience, to make a bit more certain and less erratic the conditions of precivilized human nature; for while man is usually peaceful in Nature, still there are occasions when gusts of passion or his own uncertainties lead to breaches of the harmony. While he usually understands what Nature and Nature's God demand of him, sometimes his calmness and understanding are eclipsed. In the state of Nature, moreover, each is the judge of his own actions; and while in the majority of cases, perhaps, each is fair in applying the directly perceived laws of Nature, there are times when this self-judgment needs to be supplemented and corrected by others. When civil society is formed, then, it is established for very limited purposes, and the gulf between Nature and primitive human nature, on the one hand, and civilization, on the other, is narrow and does not reflect a kind of "war."

It is small wonder that responses of this kind often gave rise to doctrines of very limited rule or even of anarchism.[20] In the days before the great industrialist explosion of the 18th century, the conception of automatic harmony of economic forces — or laissez-faire — had strong affinities with this position. To be sure, many of those who held it — like Jefferson — argued that "in harmony with Nature" meant in harmony with relatively undeveloped civilization, a civilization of small towns and agrarianism rather than industrialism. But whatever the particular permutation, the response, by contrast with a Hobbes-like perspective, held that a relatively beneficent Nature's "laws" could somehow be a guide to man in his quest for justice under civilization. Civilization was not quite the traumatic event that it became in the first view. Natural Rights, as in the Declaration of Independence, were associated with the primitive state of Nature and constituted the standards for civilization. While the view was highly "individualistic" and hence contrary to classical Platonic-Aristotelean positions, and although it could hardly be said to embrace a teleology, there was about it the flavor of a kind of Aristotelean middle way.

Civilization as Inevitably Corrupting

By contrast with the second paradigm, which sees a relative harmony among Nature, primitive human nature, and civilization, at least under certain conditions, the third outlook is a root-and-branch repudiation of civilization. We immediately think of Rousseau in this connection; and, indeed, in one of his many sides he does appear to be saying that civilization is inevitably corrupting, and that we should return to a kind of innocent and spontaneous state of Nature.[21] But if we take Rousseau's political philosophy as a whole, he seems to see no possibility of returning to Nature. His task instead is to seek the form of civilization which will be "legitimate" and in which the freedom supposedly characteristic of the state of Nature will be restored at a different level. The *Social Contract* is an effort to spell out the conditions under which this legitimacy can arise, and by whose standards all previous civilizations can be condemned.[22]

In ancient times the view that civilization is inevitably corrupting was best represented in Greece by the Cynics[23] and in Eastern thought, perhaps, by Lao-tze.[24] In modern Western thought, its best and most consistent exemplar is probably Leo Tolstoy. Although not all exponents of the general view that civilization is inevitably corrupting would agree with the specifics of Tolstoy, still his position might well stand for the perspective as a whole.

Unlike some defenders of Nature and the primitive, who spurn certain aspects of civilization while seeking to maintain others, Tolstoy is relatively consistent in rejecting the whole complex of what he regards as civilized life. William Godwin sought to repudiate law and the State as aspects of civilization, but at the same time he envisioned an enlightened development of science, technology, and the economy.[25] Tolstoy, by contrast, sees law and the State as reflections of a whole network of institutions and practices which must be undercut if the anticivilization goal is to be attained. The idea of progress in civilization, he seems to contend, is like saying that we can advance by committing evil.

Tolstoy-like rejections of civilization — and particularly of modern civilization, in which the political challenge is magnified almost infinitely — are often religious in character and refer back to the long-standing disquietudes of many Christians with coercion of any kind. Tolstoy himself roots his views in his own emphatically held interpretation of Christianity. Basically, as he argues in such novels as *Resurrection* and elsewhere,[26] all the institutions and practices of modern civilization are incompatible with the Christian ethic of simplicity, nonviolence, and brotherly love. When the State conscripts us for war, this is simply a reflection of a whole complex of practices built upon involved division of labor which have the effect of discouraging individual responsibility and blinding us to the destructive consequences of a technological and industrialized culture. Man is reduced to his highly specialized social roles and in the process is diminished.

The State as the agent of civilization becomes essentially a device whereby the rich enhance their riches and exploit the poor through the overt violence of war or the covert violence of exploitation. As civilization becomes increasingly complex, moreover, human beings in the city are cut off from direct contact with nonhuman Nature and are thus deprived of that which is indispensable for their growth as human beings. Civilization, far from freeing human beings, stimulates the passions which enslave them — their sexual lusts, their unlimited desires for material things, their spiritual arrogance, and their violence. Through complex division of labor, moreover, human beings can plausibly relieve themselves of personal responsibility for the most outrageous acts (outrageous in terms of the Gospel ethic). Thus the executioner can blame the judge for his killing a man, since he is simply obeying authority and not initiating the killing himself; the factory worker can disclaim responsibility for the poisons in the food he helps can, since he is simply an unimportant unit in a whole factory complex; and the soldier can reject moral responsibility for his wholesale slaughter by pleading that he was forced to be a soldier.

Nor do Marxist and socialist politics provide answers, according to this paradigm; for Marxism and socialism strengthen the very tendencies that enhance civilization. To be sure, Marxists promise that after a period of accentuated State coercion, the engines of State restrictions, including the army and civil service, will wither away. But how can they wither away, Tolstoy-like thinkers ask, when the conditions of which they are the expressions — complex division of labor, highly developed machine technology, the decline of personal responsibility, and unnatural stimulation of human lusts — are proliferated?

The only answer, Tolstoy concludes, lies in a repudiation of civilization, root and branch — a return to the primitive, with only sketchy division of labor, a livelihood based on hand labor, and a life characterized by personal relations rather than impersonal bureaucracy. In such a situation, human beings would once more live in intimate relations with the beasts and plants, and their spiritual life would be renewed by their closeness to the soil. Physically, too, their existence would reflect the values of proximity to Nature — air and water pollution would drastically decline, artificial and adulterated foods would be no more, and physical labor would do far more for health than all the boasted physicians of civilization.

The framework suggested here is, of course, a revival in all its essentials of Plato's simple and nonluxurious state in Book II of the *Republic*. It resembles Hobbes-like outlooks in that it sees civilization as an artifact, one of whose central characteristics is coercion of all kinds, but it sharply differentiates its position from Hobbes-like views in its evaluation of Nature and the primitive as basically harmonious and life-enhancing. There are, of course, affinities with Locke-like perspectives insofar as the Tolstoyan position would stress a normal harmony in Nature and the primitive; but contrary to the interpretation in Locke-like notions, the supposed insecurities of Nature are barely recognized. Many versions of Locke would be reconcilable with a kind of selective civilizing process — a minimal State, for instance — but at the same time a vast proliferation of technology and commerce and the arts. For Tolstoy-like views, we cannot have it both ways: once we embark on the processes of civilization, and particularly of modern civilization, which has pressed division of labor to the utmost, all the characteristics of civilization must be accepted — a coercive State and law, impersonalism, a proliferating bureaucracy, a decline of personal responsibility, and what might be called a degenerate aesthetic.

Civilization as Preparation for Justice and Sophisticated Harmony

In this paradigm, Nature and pristine human nature are seen as relatively harmonious, but it is the harmony of innocence rather than of experience. Civilization disrupts the harmony with its class struggles, violence, political manipulations, and disquietudes. But out of civilization as we have known it can or will emerge a posthistorical state in which a new harmony can or will arise. For this more sophisticated reconciliation, political authority, the State, and civilization generally will have acted as a kind of preparation or discipline. Civilization is seen as a half-way house between a naive, spontaneous, and uncivilized humanity on the one hand and a warless, propertyless, and liberated society on the other.

There are, of course, several versions of this viewpoint, the differences among them turning in some measure on whether the society of the envisioned third stage is inevitable or merely possible. There are also divergencies about the degree to which the third stage can be realized on earth or must be postponed to some other sphere of existence. Then, too, while some think of the final epoch as primarily or partly a human achievement, others would assign a decisive role to divine Grace which uses civilization and the disciplines of the State as its instruments. To some, the transition from the second to the third phase is relatively smooth; to others, catastrophic events are its signs and portents.

Up to the second stage, that of historic civilization, this view agrees in part with the civilization-as-corrupting perspective. But it would differ sharply with the latter in its evaluation of the potentialities of the second stage. The civilization-as-corrupting paradigm sees the development of civilization as producing only more of the same; the civilization-as-preparation view, by contrast, sees factors in historic civilization, or designs in the God who is the Lord of civilization, which will eventually enable man to transcend its supposedly deleterious aspects.

In the historical conceptions of many of the Hebrew prophets one can find anticipations of the civilization-as-preparation view. Eighth century B.C. figures like Amos, Micah, and others, as well as later prophets such as Jeremiah and the second Isaiah, looked back with some longing to a more primitive human nature, one in which there was no monarchy and where simplicity and direct attachment to Yahweh reigned supreme. In their denunciations of the civilizations of their times, they saw the accomplishments of urban life as always tainted by corruption of power and by exploitation. Nevertheless, they apparently thought that the class and international struggles which we associate with the very words "history" and "civilization" would educate humanity and enable it to achieve a warless and classless world.[27]

In what came to be an orthodox Christian version of this perspective, the harmony of Nature was harmony with God; but it gave way, through Adam's and Eve's sin, to the disharmonies, conflicts, and freedoms of civilization. In Nature, there was no private property and the State, if it existed at all (it did not exist for the Augustinian but did for the Thomist), was noncoercive. In the Fall of Man, which had been anticipated by a war in Heaven, Nature is left behind, and men are no longer under the direct day-to-day guidance of the Lord.[28] Instead, they must make their own decisions and are forever blundering, erring, and rebelling against what they know to be morally right. Their worst excesses are limited by State and property institutions (State and property institutions arising out of sin, following the Augustinian version; State institutions present in Nature but taking on coercion after sin, according to the Thomist view, with property "added" to Nature), in the providence of God. In varying degrees, though, civilization exhibits destructive as well as constructive tendencies. Nevertheless, through Divine Grace and, in the Thomist version, a considerable modicum of human reason, paradise can be regained, but only in a state of existence beyond this earth. The Augustinian expressions of this drama are throughout much harsher than the Thomist, particularly in the role assigned to human reason, but the general paradigm is reflected in both. Thus Father Thomas Gilby, in his study of Thomist thought,[29] suggests that for St. Thomas political history is a kind of middle stage between "Community" on the one hand (a kind of pre-historic ordering through wont and custom, in which human "personality" is only latent) and "Society" on the other, which is characterized by "association without organization" and full development of autonomous personality. Society in all its dimensions is, of course, fully attained only in Heaven.

In unorthodox and chiliastic versions of the Christian view, the third stage can (and in some cases will) be achieved on earth and is not reserved for postmortal existence.[30] Here modern views of inevitable "progress" are anticipated.

Certain interpretations of Rousseau would have him fit this paradigm. His state of Nature is one of innocence, spontaneity, and simplicity. Although he is a bit uncertain and contradictory as to how and why men leave Nature, he thinks he is clear as to how they can "legitimize" the civilized state. Although most historic civilization has been tainted by a destruction of the freedom characteristic of Nature, a higher level of freedom — moral liberty — is possible under conditions in which a genuine general will is developed in civilization. In the city of Rousseau's dreams, one can be free and yet belong fully to others; property rights are no longer disruptive; and in conforming to communal authority, one is obeying only oneself.[31]

Rousseau's perspective on the paradigm does not suggest any inevitability, but only possibility. His vision contends that the presumed values of civilization can be combined with an elimination of its destructive tendencies. "Legitimacy" for him has the connotation of establishing a condition in which the freedom of innocence will be transmuted into the autonomy of fully self-conscious moral beings and in which the entailments of a community of moral beings will not conflict with their individual liberties. The State remains, fully reconciling freedom with authority.

In Marxism, the third stage on earth is not only possible but — as in chiliastic Christian views — inevitable. Marx, Engels, and Lenin seem to be united in seeing the history of civilization as enlarging human consciousness through the very class struggles which ultimately are to be transcended. Civilization, as in Hegel, is an enlargement of subjective consciousness through the dialectic, objective events and struggles interacting with subjective factors. As in many of the Hebrew prophets, the very civilizations which are denounced for their crimes are preparing the way for a resolution of their contradictions. The ruling classes, in their endeavors to preserve their power and privileges, are in reality laying the groundwork for their own demise. Marxism, in its several facets, manages to combine ancient prophetic and apocalyptic perspectives.

The paradigm which sees civilization as preparation for justice and harmony is also reflected to some extent in such 19th-century outlooks as that of Herbert Spencer. In Spencer's so-called liberalism,[32] the movement from status to contract is viewed as a liberating of the human personality, even though in the process thousands of persons suffer and die (as in the Marxist version) because they are unable to compete. Out of all this suffering and violent coercion will emerge a kind of super-man who, because of his enormous psychological, intellectual, and physical strength, will compete on equal terms with his similarly endowed fellow human beings, thus reflecting a kind of balance of power in which the State will virtually wither away. Civilization will not be repudiated, as in Tolstoy-like perspectives, but will rather lead to human beings who, while emancipated from the thralldom of State and law, will yet share the material abundance produced by modern technology and a modern economy.

Both Marxist and Spencerian views differ from orthodox Christian versions of the paradigm in that they appear to adhere to the notion of "progress." While orthodox Christian approaches see "paradise regained" as giving significance and meaning to the history of civilization (in St.

58

Augustine, in the conflict of the two cities, with divinely elected citizens of God destined eventually to dwell in the transhistorical pure city; in St. Thomas, with the idea of the pure city helping to shape existential polities), they do not envision the third stage as actually being attained on earth. Positions like those of Marx and Spencer, by contrast, foresee just that — an earthly consummation. Despite all the overwhelming evidence that industrial civilization has been characterized by often-magnified coercion, exploitation, class conflict, gross disparities in income and power, and other hallmarks which are regarded as evil, Marx and Spencer think that these characteristics can or will in the end be transcended, since historic civilization is itself preparing the way for its own demise, in which its evil features will be wiped out and only its good ones will remain.

The Classical Paradigm

A fifth possible response to the political imperatives of modern civilization is what we are terming the "classical" paradigm. With its point of departure in the Platonic-Aristotelean outlook, it obviously repudiates the notion that civilization is forced on man simply by fear. It likewise rejects the conception that primitive Nature is some kind of model which can guide us in political deliberations; the view that we ought to or can reject civilization for Nature; and the position that historic civilization by its very existence points to its own transcendence in posthistoric life (although the marriage of Aristotle to Christianity performed by St. Thomas surely indicates that efforts to think in terms of overall paradigms will always do injustice to particular political philosophies). The classical view tends to doubt the notion often held in Hebrew-Christian thought that history has significance and reflects an overall design. To the degree that the classical position is retained in modern culture, it patently repudiates the notion of inevitable historical progress, as that idea is understood in its many modern versions, including the Marxist.

In its positive outlook, the classical paradigm suggests that man cannot be comprehended merely in terms of the primitive Nature from which he came but must also, and more importantly, be seen through the goals implicit in his nature, teleologically understood. He is a creature, to be sure, of subatomic particles, atoms, chemical compounds, "drives," and animal lusts; but there is also working within him a telos or end which cannot be reduced to any or all of these and which represents him as the kind of whole that is more than the sum of all its possible parts. This end, which has been defined as that of being rational and political, is shaping existential man somewhat as the not-yet-attained oak tree is shaping the acorn, or, to change the figure, somewhat as the "idea" of victory is shaping the athlete, even though the victory may never be made "actual." Rationality and politics distinguish teleological man from beasts and plants.

Man cannot be understood by reducing him to his primitive elements. He can only be grasped by transcending those primitive elements and by asking what he is implicitly striving to become. Working within even primitive Nature is the idea of developed human nature, which requires civilization to make it actual. Yet at the same time, civilization, if undirected through deliberate rational collective planning, can frustrate man's teleological nature. To return to primitive Nature is to repudiate our collective telos as human beings; but to see the technological and economic processes of civilization as autonomous factors to which human beings ought to adjust is equally to spurn our telos as human beings.

Many nonclassical paradigms tend to respond to the political challenges of modern civilization by seeking, through various devices, to repudiate politics, at least ultimately. In one way or another, views like those of Tolstoy, Spencer, and even, in the end, Marx seek an answer in the rejection of conscious deliberation about man's collective affairs. The classical paradigm, by contrast, understands the process of deliberation and conscious direction of collective matters, as of so-called private affairs, to be the element which is most distinctively human about human beings. Man cannot repudiate all this without repudiating his humanity. Nor can he basically escape it, except momentarily. He cannot restore his childhood, nor should he wish to do so.

The classical paradigm would see the contradictions and paradoxes of complex civilization, to which we called attention at the conclusion of the first chapter, as challenges to be met through politics. Looked at from this perspective, politics is the process whereby man seeks to integrate the factors of civilization around the idea of the Good. As Plato suggests in Book II of the *Republic,* economic, social, aesthetic, and other aspects of human existence, left to themselves, are often at war with one another; and the greater the complexity of the civilization, the more this tends to be true. Only politics, or conscious deliberation and action about human collective affairs, can hope to subordinate all these aspects of the human situation to the essence of the Good. By taking account of both primitive nature and human nature considered teleologically, we can, through deliberation, develop an integrated human nature. It will not, however, arise automatically or unconsciously, any more than an adult human being's personal life can be adequately integrated without deliberation and thought.

Out of considerations like these grew the concept of Natural Law, which may be thought of, at least in part, as one expression of the classical view. But it is important to distinguish its classical version from similarly designated conceptions associated with modern thought since Hobbes. Although exponents of classical views were by no means united in their interpretation of the contents of Natural Law, there was widespread agreement as to how the term "Nature" was to be employed. With but few exceptions, its exponents thought of it as referring both to nature in its primitive sense of raw passion and instinct and to teleological nature conceived as those imputed or inferred or intuited purposes distinctive of man. Natural Law represented an effort to state the limits, possibilities, and imperatives of both primitive and teleological nature when seen in the context of humanity; and while the conception was only embryonic in Plato and Aristotle and emerged in rather different form in Stoic and medieval Christian interpretations, still all versions agreed that its principles were somehow associated with reason and with the effort to establish rational principles for individual and collective human conduct.

Of course, Natural Law applied to all creation, but when used as guidance for deliberation about human affairs, it had to be adapted both to the side of humanity that united it with the beasts and to the aspect that differentiated it from nonhuman creation. Natural Law, referring to the beasts and to beastlike aspects of humanity, was descriptive and hypothetical: It attempted to state, for example, what beasts in fact tended to do when deprived of food or when isolated from members of the opposite sex or under other specified conditions. Similarly, human beings could be described in these primitively natural terms. But there were aspects of the human being which could not be treated simply in descriptive terms, for human nature was such that it embraced the possibility of freedom and moral choice: in "practical philosophy," as Aristotle put it, things could be other than they were. Hence, Natural Law as applied to humanity must also treat of prescriptive questions, and prescriptive propositions were related to man's teleological nature — what he might and ought to become. There was a supreme Good for human nature, and this was the Good which ought to determine all priorities in establishing prescriptive principles.

By contrast with classic-like conceptions of this kind, Hobbes-like versions of the so-called laws of Nature explicitly denied the existence of a supreme good and admitted the existence of only a supreme evil. The laws of Nature themselves were rooted wholly in a primitive Nature which was conceived to be a constant war of men and women against one another. In effect, the laws of Nature described in this fashion sought to indicate how such moral commands as love for one another could be "explained" in terms of the primitive psychology of fear.

Hobbist-type views of the laws of Nature (and their spiritual descendants in many Social Darwinist versions of the 19th century) should thus be carefully differentiated from the Natural Law associated with such thinkers as St. Thomas Aquinas. St. Thomas, while heavily indebted to Hebraic views of history, also sought to embody Aristotle-like views of nature conceived teleologically in his political philosophy.

The Responses and the Problem of Justice in Civilization

Several times we have suggested that the civilized state inevitably gives rise to the question of what principles are to guide us in political direction and control. Gone is the guidance of the gods (at least in a direct sense); and the guidance of custom, tradition, and instinct becomes less and less sure and more sketchy. The search for guidance in the ethical and political realm we often call the quest for a definition of justice (or righteousness) and its implications.

Now each of the paradigmatic or ideal-type responses to the problem of Nature and civilization has its own rather characteristic response to the central question of justice. Let us note briefly the attitude of each and conclude with an evaluation.

The implications of the civilization-against-Nature paradigm are that justice is purely conventional; that its meaning varies from culture to culture; that there are no rational standards by which we can judge the justice of alternative cultures; and that suppression, force, and violence must inevitably characterize all civilizations, as convention and "culture" strive to hold in check unnaturally an appetitive or sexually lustful power-seeking man.

In other terms, Hobbes-like views revive and expand the positions taken by Thrasymachus and Glaucon in Plato's *Republic,* with Thrasymachus suggesting that righteousness is simply the "interest" of the stronger and Glaucon maintaining that it is a kind of compromise between the inherent, limitless appetites of each, on the one hand, and the fear of retaliation by others, on the other hand. Justice is either the will of the stronger or else a convention by which we seek, under cover of a supposedly universal, rational principle, both to hide and to defend our own self-interest. In Nature "justice" is sheer physical and psychological force; and while there may be a kind of balance of power in Nature, it is constantly being disturbed by massacres and chaotic manipulations of various types. Civilization and the State, which supposedly bring an end to this situation, are nevertheless still grounded on superior power; except that now, by contrast with Nature, there is an overwhelming concentration of power which normally holds at bay the natural tendency of individual men to wish to dominate and to express their material and power interests without let or hindrance. Since there is no supreme good but only the supreme evil of violent death, definitions of justice by the rulers of society cannot be questioned from the vantage point of any universal standard. Any perspective or view — providing its exponents are successful in the manipulation of force, the use of symbols of government, and the gaining of acquiescence — is "just." The regime may be socialist, liberal, autocratic, democratic, or communist and still be just. Truth, beauty, and goodness are what the predominant forces in society say they are: there is no universal standard.

The view which considers Nature as basically harmonious and civilization as not too great a leap — the Locke-like paradigm — postulates mutual general recognition of rights in Nature and thus seeks to vindicate, so to speak, both Nature and civilization. The basic principles are present in Nature — respect for life, liberty, and estate — and civilization is seen simply as an undergirder of those rights. The more effectively the civilization seeks the guidance of Nature as thus defined, the more just it will be. The rights themselves arise prior to political society. Thus while the state of Nature ought not to be restored, its central, original principles, recognized spontaneously by men even in Nature, should and can be applied to guide complex civilization.

In the paradigm which sees civilization as corrupt, civilization and State are positive hindrances to the attainment of justice, which was present in the state of Nature and regarded as a combination of good fellowship, spontaneity, and very low division of labor. Justice for "civilized man" is defined as the attempt to restore this order by undermining the structures of civilization. The implications of this position are that it is possible to transcend the ubiquitous tensions and conflicts of civilization — individual-community fission, technological values v. human values, and economic man against social and ethical man — by supposedly simpler modes of existence. The reverse of this is that with every step in the supposed advance of civilization, the possibilities of justice correspondingly diminish.

In the view which sees civilization as preparation for justice, civilization as known historically has always been unjust, but at the same time its very injustice is paving the way for justice. And justice itself, in many expressions of this paradigm, consists of the elimination of all coercion of man by man, distribution of goods according to need, and the wiping out of any conflict between individuality and community. Freedom and authority are completely reconciled, and there are no longer apparent tensions between and among liberty, equality, and fraternity. In many versions of the type, the consummation of justice in heaven or on earth, is seen as inevitable, although men can hasten it by their ethical and political choices in civilization.

The classical paradigm tends to see justice as a mean between the extremes of primitive Nature, on the one hand, and civilization pushed to the extremes of division of labor, complex cities, and technological development, on the other. Primitive Nature is rejected because it frustrates man's teleological nature, which is defined as "political." At the same time, any limitless movement away from primitive Nature is attacked because it, too, would destroy the possibilities of man's political nature. This *via media* view would tend, too, to see justice in the soul and justice in the society as two sides of the same coin, both to be effected when each soul is performing that which it can do best. This position, as well as the second perspective and some versions of the fourth, would emphasize that standards for justice are not grounded in mere emotion, but rather can be vindicated by reason. The meaning of the fulfillment of human nature — or its teleological actualization — can be defined and explicated and defended, and there is a *summum bonum* which, contrary to the first paradigm, is not arbitrary or a mere ghost. It is one which exalts spiritual and intellectual values, with the desire for honor or prestige or material goods placed in a strictly secondary position.

Anyone who thinks about the attainment of justice in modern civilization must come to grips with the basic propositions of all five paradigms. All have something to tell us not only about Nature and human nature but also about the way we think. From time to time, in all probability, all of us have taken every position, for they are points in a dialogue which has been going on constantly since the beginning of political philosophy.

We can briefly epitomize each view by saying that for civilization-against-Nature positions, justice is a chimera, if by that term is meant some natural characteristic of the universe; or if it does exist, it is not discoverable by man. Like religion in the Freudian version, it is always a rationalization of self-interest. For Nature-as-model outlooks, on the contrary, its meaning can be understood prior to the formation of political society: its principles can be and are grasped even before the rise of civilization. For the civilization-as-corrupting perspective, civilization and the State always represent a departure from justice. For the fourth position, justice in some sense existed in a primitive natural state, was clouded in civilization, but may — and, in some views will — be reattained at a more sophisticated level. For the classical paradigm, justice is to be found in a kind of middle position between primitive Nature and sophisticated civilization allowed to develop without limit. It consists essentially of every person doing the thing he can best do which contributes to the whole, with the ruling principle always to be the intellectual or contemplative; and the norms of justice can be discovered through reason.

The nature of political philosophy, as we have suggested, is such that no one ideal type can embrace all the normative reality, and this is preeminently true of the attempt to define justice. Although there has sometimes been an almost vitriolic controversy in recent years about the values of classical as against nonclassical perspectives,[33] our position here is that every outlook has something to contribute in the many-sided effort to develop defensible standards for politics, even though much of our basic outlook in this book will be rooted in what we have called the classical paradigm.

The General Notion of Justice

We conclude this chapter with a sketch of the general notion of justice that will be central in the remaining chapters. More detailed implications will be spelled out in the context of specific issues. Here we consider and comment on (1) the issue of universality and justice, (2) the problem of stating the starting points and major propositions, (3) the relation of rational to empirical elements, and (4) the place of justice in the Nature-civilization framework.

The Issue of Universality and Justice

We side with the classical paradigm in holding that justice (or righteousness) is more than "conventional" or a matter of arbitrary definition by the sovereign. When we search for the substance of justice, we are endeavoring to discover principles which transcend cultural differentiations. While our statements may in varying degrees be colored by class or self-interest, still we are often genuinely seeking to grasp the universal. And to some extent we can succeed.

The value of Hobbes-like and similar views is, of course, that they call attention to the ease with which we can delude ourselves into believing that we have indeed discovered universal norms. But such views go too far when they claim that justice is merely the interest of the stronger or simply convention.

We can, moreover, defend moral principles rationally, just as propositions about science can be vindicated. In each case, to be sure, we must begin with certain statements which are assumed to be true (e.g., in ethics, "Material goods ought never to become an end but always only a means"; in mathematics, "Things equal to the same thing are equal to each other") and then, through logic and references to experience, reason from them. But the process would seem to be similar in both the realm of "fact" and that of "value." In both domains, propositions regarded as basic are "intuited" or "revealed" or "self-evident."

Starting Points

If this is so, what starting points are we to formulate in our reasoning about justice? We begin by assuming that human beings are incomplete or unfulfilled existentially and that this accounts for their quest for the "right" or the "just": They are dissatisfied with their personal lives and with their communities. How did they become separated from the "right" and the "just"? We do not know, but the mythology of mankind has endeavored to give various answers (the Fall of Man, some of the Platonic myths, and so on). However the separation occurred, it seems to be a fact. The issue, then, is to discover primary "ought" propositions, from which we can, given logic combined with empirical investigation, derive specific advice on what we should do about our personal lives and communities.

These "ought" propositions at the primary level are revealed or intuited or self-evident (although the supposed revelations or intuitions may, of course, be objectively mistaken). But the process of intuition in discovering starting points for discussion of justice is not, or ought not to be, a solitary one: We exchange experiences of primary values and value hierarchies with our fellow human beings and as a result refine our statements, hopefully making them clearer (for much turns on precision of language). We ask: "Is it not true?" and if we do not gain reinforcement from others, we may begin to doubt the exact formulation of our original statements. Discovery of points of departure is thus both individual and social. We generally hope to keep the basic starting points as few as possible, expecting to derive other propositions from these few.

What are some of the interrelated and sometimes overlapping starting points for the discussion to follow? Among them, we suggest these:

1. Human beings should be rational.
2. Human beings can fulfill themselves only in communities of various kinds.
3. The idea of fairness, as John Rawls[34] and others have suggested, is akin to that of justice.
4. Rendering what is due to ourselves, to others, to communities of human beings, and to God is at the heart of justice.
5. A just society ought to recognize three dimensions of the human being: (1) as unique, (2) as needing for fulfillment close relations with

some but not with all, (3) as striving, at the same time and in some sense, to identify with the whole human race.

6. No person should be regarded simply as a means but always as an end. This would exclude all violence against persons.
7. There are various gradations of goods, and material goods ought always to be subordinate to those of the spirit and the intellect.
8. The burden of proof must be on those who would permit inequalities among human beings.
9. It is better, as Socrates maintained, to suffer injustice than to commit it.

Many of these propositions may seem vague, and we shall attempt to elaborate their meaning later on. We shall see the modern revolutionary slogan, "Liberty, equality, fraternity," as seeking to epitomize many dimensions of justice, including that of distributive justice. In drawing out the meaning of such notions and in working out propositions subsidiary to these primary statements, we hope to become more concrete.

Rational-Empirical Relationships

The subsidiary principles will, of course, depend in many instances upon specific empirical assessments which may help us exclude certain means in our pursuit of ends. In the working out of detailed standards, the moral and the technical must be married. Max Weber distinguishes between the "ethic of ultimate ends" and the "ethic of responsibility," meaning by the former that we should act in specific ways regardless of consequences and by the latter that we should always weigh consequences.[35] We are contending, of course, that both ethics must be used within the context of our framework. Both the statement "I shall do right though the heavens fall" and the asseveration "The rightness of an act can be determined only by examining its consequences" are wrong when taken alone — the former because it seems to divorce "right" from any results for human beings, however horrible; the latter because it appears to ignore standards by which to judge consequences and also because it seems to forget that remote consequences can but rarely be assessed.

Throughout any discussion of the "empirical" dimensions of justice, we should keep in mind two ancient statements: "The end justifies the means" and "The means shape the ends." It sometimes seems to be assumed that if one accepts the former one must reject the latter.[36] Actually, they should be examined together; each is valid, but only when seen in the context of the other. Some goods, as Aristotle observed, ought to be pursued as ends in themselves, others only as means to further ends, while some are perhaps both goods in themselves and also desirable as means to other ends. We seek many ends and use many alternative means; but in pursuing some ends, the means we use may set up ends contradictory to the ones we are ostensibly pursuing. To be sure, if a given means will lead to an end that we think desirable, then the means is "justified"; but at the same time we should make certain that the means does not also lead, by its very nature, to other ends which contradict the complex of ends we have in mind. "Ends and means on earth are so entangled," one thinker has said, "that choosing one we choose the other, too. Each different path brings different ends in view."

All this is something like the discussion of what we call the side effects resulting from the use of certain drugs. The drugs may attain the end we have in mind but also bring about ends that we did not intend and which, indeed, may often undermine our broad objectives.

Logic and empirical investigation go hand in hand as we seek to spell out the implications of justice for the political order, beginning with premises which themselves are taken for granted. But we should always remember, too, that the conclusions drawn from empirical investigation are often very unclear and confusing. We might be able, at best, to predict the immediate outcome of a given decision, but the long-run consequences are usually beyond us, in any strict empirical sense. Thus the immediate results of the Vietnam War were rather clear — destruction, death, and social disorganization. But how could one show — empirically — that the long-run consequences would be "good," as the defenders of the war claimed they would be?

The Place of Justice in the Nature-Civilization Framework

Finally, how do these principles fit into the Nature-civilization framework? They obviously follow the classical paradigm at many points — in assuming man's rational potentiality, for instance, and in contending that he can be himself only in community. Implicit, too, is the notion associated with the classical view that, while some development from primitive Nature is essential for man to fulfill himself, a point can be reached where the civilization becomes so complex, and the difficulties of keeping material goods instrumental for spiritual ends become so great, and the problems of predicting consequences become so enormous, that the possibilities of political man are undermined. Thus fulfillment of man's teleological nature requires a deliberately contrived stopping point in the movement away from primitive Nature through civilization.

In certain of its other emphases, the notion of justice we are suggesting appears to resemble nonclassical views. Thus in its stress on freedom of intellectual, spiritual, and aesthetic expression it is closer, perhaps, to a Lockean or modern liberal framework than to the classical. While it is certainly not Tolstoyan, it would not be unsympathetic to a kind of modified Tolstoyanism — one in which an effort is made to reverse, to a limited degree, certain of the developments of modern civilization.

Any framework such as we are proposing must, of course, respond to the question of whether we are to take Nature literally or "historically," or whether, on the other hand, it is simply an analytical device whereby we imagine what man would be without civilization and then seek to show what he would be most likely to do, or perhaps should do with a blank slate, if he had to construct civilization from the ground up. The second interpretation is that of John Rawls in his recent treatise on justice.[37] Actually, whether we take the first or the second interpretation would seem not to make a great deal of difference. Natural Rights thinkers like Locke apparently took "state of Nature" as in some sense literal, yet this did not prevent their using the conceptions as a way of seeking to justify certain aspects of civilization. In the case of Plato's famous Book II, he seems to have seen the movement from primitive Nature to civilization primarily as a psychological and logical account of what might happen to human beings as they construct civilization.

This, then, is a very rough sketch of the terms in which we shall view the problem of justice. It is very rough at this point because to fill it out would be to anticipate the discussion of the subsequent chapters. Its purpose has been to suggest the terms of reference we shall use. The details will have to await an examination of the questions of freedom, equality, and fraternity and of coercion and violence as they develop in civilization, particularly in modern civilization. The first of these issues is the topic of Chapter 3, and the second is considered in Chapter 4.

Notes

1 Francis Bacon, *New Atlantis* (Oxford: Clarendon Press, 1915).

2 In *Gulliver's Travels* (London: Printed for Benjamin Motte, 1726), Swift uses the "Voyage to Laputa" to attack what he conceives to be the scientists of his day, who engage in all types of allegedly impractical experiments. Basically, he is directing his shafts at the Royal Society.

3 Alfred Zimmern, in *The Greek Commonwealth* (Oxford: Clarendon Press, 1911), stresses the degree to which the expansion of commerce and development of piracy contributed to the rise of political consciousness in ancient Greece. Often

closely connected with each other, they reflected the breakdown of the old order of custom and, for many, underlined the need for deliberate or political ordering.

4 In works like *The Culture of Cities* (New York: Harcourt, 1938), Lewis Mumford stresses the relation of urban growth historically to such factors as commerce, the development of weapons technology, and intellectual curiosity associated with voyages of discovery. The growth of cities can be regarded perhaps as both cause and effect: they expanded in connection with many other factors but were themselves responsible in some measure for stimulating those factors.

5 Thomas Kuhn, in *The Structure of Scientific Revolutions*, 2nd ed. (Chicago: University of Chicago Press, 1970), perhaps did not suggest a completely new hypothesis, but he did manage to give wide currency to a view which in effect criticizes the notion that the history of science is "cumulative" in any simple way.

6 A point stressed recently in Arthur Koestler's *The Roots of Coincidence* (New York: Random House, 1972).

7 See Genesis, I:28, where God is represented as telling man to be fruitful and multiply and to subdue the earth.

8 Writers who endeavor to describe either what is supposedly happening after industrialism or what will happen after it are sometimes confusing and often contradictory; and the terms they use to designate the allegedly new age differ from one another. Thus A. F. Organski speaks of the "politics of abundance" in the *The Stages of Political Development* (New York: Alfred A. Knopf, 1965). Kenneth Boulding talks of "post-civilization," by which he apparently means a period when society is controlled by the consciousness that it is based on knowledge; one, too, in which there is growing dominance of social over individual self-consciousness. See Boulding's *The Meaning of the Twentieth Century: The Great Transition* (New York: Harper & Row, 1964), p. 2. In *Future Shock* (New York: Bantam Books, 1971), Alvin Toffler simply says "super-industrial" society. Daniel Bell made current the expression "post-industrial society" in *The Coming of Post Industrial Society: A Venture in Social Forecasting* (New York: Basic Books, 1973) and elsewhere. He terms this culture a "knowledge society" (p. 212) and gives it a number of other characteristics as well, including a decline in the proportion of direct industrial workers and a growth of "service" occupations.

For our purposes in the text, we prefer to speak of "industrialism" or perhaps of "advanced industrial civilization," while admitting that the industrial technological culture of the last part of the 20th century is not precisely what we termed industrialism in 1900. Despite the changes which modern high-technology civilization has undergone, however, many of its fundamental features remain the same.

9 William Wordsworth's sonnet "The World Is Too Much with Us."

10 Much of 19-century thought turns on this theme. Thus Herbert Spencer sharply contrasts industrialism with military-feudal society, suggesting that with the former, peace and harmony will arise and human beings will be enlightened. Auguste Comte, too, regards the regime of industrial civilization as transcending, through positivism, merely "theological" and "metaphysical" thinking. See Auguste Comte, *The Positive Philosophy*, Eng. trans. (New York: W. Gowans,

1868). And in Alfred Tennyson's great poem "Locksley Hall," we find the optimism so often associated with the belief in an inevitable progress connected with industrialist civilization: the conflicts of the age, as with Marx, herald the elimination of all violence:

> Till the war-drum throbbed no longer, and the battle-flags were furled
> In the Parliament of man, the Federation of the world.

11   See Reinhold Niebuhr, *The Irony of American History* (New York: Scribner's, 1952).

12   Of course, there is a tendency for many cyclical theories of politics to go beyond this and to say that mankind can *never* adequately perceive the situation or respond effectively. Then, too, most conceptions of the cyclical view give a large role to fortune. Characteristics of this kind are to be found in Aristotle (*Politics*), Polybius (*Universal History*), and Machiavelli (*Discourses on Titus Livius* and *The Prince*).

13   See Bertrand Russell, *Freedom versus Organization* (New York: W. W. Norton, 1934). Nicholas Berdyaev is also concerned with the problem in his many works. See, for example, his *Slavery and Freedom* (London: BLES, 1943).

14   This has certainly been true of the Hegelian stream and is reflected in, for example, Benedetto Croce's *History as the Story of Liberty* (London: G. Allen & Unwin, 1941).

15   Popper may be regarded as one of the leading critics of overall, general planning. Throughout *The Open Society and Its Enemies* (London: G. Routledge, 1945), in the context of the political philosophies of Plato, Hegel, and Marx, he warns us of man's limitations in planning and suggests that to attempt thoroughgoing planning is to prepare the way for dictatorship. Similar notes are struck in Friedrich von Hayek, *The Road to Serfdom* (Chicago: University of Chicago Press, 1944) and Ludwig von Mises, *Omnipotent Government* (New Haven, Conn.: Yale University Press, 1944).

16   At one point, Freud observes of religion: "Its technique consists in depressing the value of life and distorting the picture of the real world in a delusional manner — which presupposes an intimidation of the intelligence." And he goes on to speak of religion fixing individuals in a "state of psychical infantilism." *Civilization and Its Discontents,* trans. James Strachey (New York: W. W. Norton & Co., 1962), pp. 31, 32.

17   But Freud often seems to suggest that Thanatos is a more powerful force and is with difficulty held in check.

18   See Freud's comments in Albert Einstein and Sigmund Freud, *Why War?* (Paris: International Institute of Intellectual Co-operation, League of Nations, 1933).

19   See Norman O. Brown, *Life against Death* (New York: Random House, 1959) and *Love's Body* (New York: Random House, 1966). In Brown, we have the suggestion that civilization has been compelled until modern times to engage in strict repression of the "play" aspects of man, but that with the ultimate liberation to be expected from modern civilization through its technology, men and women

will once more play with one another and thus get beyond the repressions of centuries.

20   Thus John Locke, on one of his sides, is sometimes said to be the great inspirer of American political institutions, with their doctrines of very limited rule, and, from another point of view, the intellectual ancestor of William Godwin's *Political Justice* (1793), which is generally regarded as an anarchist classic. Godwin himself traced the intellectual origins of *Political Justice* to Locke's doctrine of the *tabula rasa,* which held that at birth each human being is a kind of blank slate and thus almost infinitely malleable.

21   Thus in his first and second *Discourses,* he seems to exalt the supposedly innocent life of Nature and to bemoan the corruptions of civilization, even while he attempts to account for the fact that mankind somehow left that life for the hardships and divisions and class conflicts of civilization.

22   The "moral freedom" which the individual supposedly attains in *The Social Contract* is gained in exchange for the "natural freedom" of the primitive community. At the same time, Rousseau seems to be clear that historical civilizations and historical "states" have lacked the legitimacy supposedly reflected in the community of *The Social Contract.* The conditions for discovery of the general will are rigorous: a relatively simple society; strictly limited material wants; absence of severely competing special interests; restricted territory and population. Few if any historical communities have embodied these conditions, and hence *The Social Contract* from this point of view can be looked upon as a "utopia."

23   See Eduard Zeller, *The Stoics, Epicureans, and Skeptics,* Eng. trans. (London: Longmans, Green, 1870).

24   *Tao-te-King,* Eng. trans. (London: Kegan Paul, Trench, Truebner, 1898).

25   *Enquiry into Political Justice,* 2 vols. (London: Printed for G. G. J. and J. Robinson, 1793).

26   See Leo Tolstoy, *Resurrection,* trans. Louise Maude (New York: Grosset, 1899) and *The Kingdom of God Is within You* (London: Oxford University Press, 1946).

27   For a modern interpretation which touches on prophetic theory, see John Macmurray, *The Clue to History* (London: Student Christian Movement Press, 1938).

28   There is a parallel to the myth of the fall of man in the Platonic myth of the Age of Cronus versus the Age of Zeus. In the Age of Cronus, Cronus controls the universe, including men, directly. But eventually Cronus "lets go" and the Age of Zeus arrives: in it, both universe and men are "on their own," and problems of human choice arise. See Plato's *Statesman.*

29   Thomas Gilby, *Between Community and Society* (London: Longmans Green, 1953).

30   This was a characteristic view of the medieval Joachimites, followers of Joachim of Flora. Eric Voegelin sees in them the beginnings of the modern "idea of progress." See Eric Voegelin, *The New Science of Politics* (Chicago: University of Chicago Press, 1952).

31   Of course, the implication is that he is obeying only what might be called his "true self," rather than what some call the "false self," which is unaware of its real relation to the whole — an anticipation of Hegel.

32   Thus in *Man versus the State* (New York: D. Appleton, 1884), as well as in other works, Spencer tends to oppose political authority to "man" and to see "progress" as emancipation from political authority. "Progress" consists in basing all human relations on contracts rather than on the "status" so closely associated etymologically and historically with the "State."

33   This is reflected in part in the debate about Plato's political theory. On one side, which stresses the value of Plato's thought and argues that he is not a political "totalitarian," one will find, for example, John Wild in *Plato's Theory of Man* (Cambridge, Mass.: Harvard University Press, 1946) and *Plato's Modern Enemies and the Theory of Natural Law* (Chicago: University of Chicago Press, 1953); Ronald Levinson, *In Defense of Plato* (Cambridge, Mass.: Harvard University Press, 1953); and Leo Strauss on Plato in Joseph Cropsey, ed., *History of Political Philosophy* (Chicago: Rand McNally & Co., 1963). On the other side, which tends to see the influence of Plato as unfortunate and often looks upon him as a "totalitarian," will be arrayed such writers as Alban Winspear, *The Genesis of Plato's Thought* (New York: Dryden Press, 1940); Richard H. S. Crossman, *Plato Today*, rev. ed. (London: Allen & Unwin, 1959); and, of course, Sir Karl Popper in *The Open Society and Its Enemies: The Spell of Plato* (London: Routledge & Sons, 1945).

34   See John Rawls, *Theory of Justice* (Cambridge, Mass.: Harvard University Press, 1971).

35   See H. H. Gerth amd C. Wright Mills, trans. and eds., *From Max Weber: Essays in Sociology* (New York: Oxford University Press, 1946), pp. 228-35.

36   Thus Max Lerner, in *Ideas for the Ice Age* (New York: Viking, 1941), asks if ends do not justify means, what does? If the notion that the end justifies the means is accompanied by the observation that means also shape the ends, there would seem to be no objection to the statement.

37   Rawls, *Theory of Justice.*

THREE

On Justice:
The Idea of Liberty,
Equality, and Fraternity

IN THE PRECEDING CHAPTER we stressed the ways in which modern civilization, even more than previous ones, dramatizes the political imperative. We suggested that the issues of freedom, technology, the economy, and utopia building are four primary eruption points for that imperative, outlined five ways of responding to these issues within the ambit of the Nature-civilization problem, and examined the idea of justice in the light of these five approaches. We also presented the conception of justice we shall be using and supporting, the specific implications of which will be discussed as we deal with the primary eruption points of politics in modern civilization.

In this chapter we inquire into the general notion of freedom in relation to conceptions of equality and fraternity and show how our conception of justice bears on the idea.

General Conceptions of Freedom and Coercion

In general, moving from primitive Nature to civilization is never wholly a story of developing from coercion to freedom or freedom to coercion, but rather a matter of types and levels of both freedom and coercion. This has been recognized by many political philosophers, from Plato to modern thinkers. Whatever one's precise postulations about Nature and primitive human nature, some types of both freedom and coercion are present; and whatever one's exact analysis of modern civilization may be, the tension between freedom and coercion remains. In Nature and primitive human nature, for example, all would agree that freedom from bureaucracy is a hallmark; but at the same time, the constraints imposed by weather, insects, and similar phenomena are — unless we accept a literal version of Eden — ubiquitous.

In modern civilization, coercive elements of all kinds are reflected in industrial and State bureaucracy and in organization generally. But the development of technology and the arts has made less pressing the constraints of weather, insects, and other natural phenomena. In many primitive societies one is not even conscious that one is being constrained; for the reign of unconscious or customary ordering (or, in the myth of Eden or Plato's myth of Cronus,[1] the direct reign of God) is so universal that awareness of individuality is at a relatively low level. In modern civilization, by contrast, we tend to become far more aware of the ways through which we are restrained, of the dichotomy between the "I" and the "other," and of the conscious and deliberate restrictions on our thought or conduct which are reflected in legislation and decrees. We become enormously introspective and, as Carl Jung puts it, are forever "searching" for our souls.[2] In many primitive societies, the notion of private property — particularly in land — is attenuated or absent, and so is the idea that one can "do what one likes with one's own." In modern civilization, freedom is often associated with the idea of private property; and even where the notion is ideologically depreciated, as in the Soviet Union, the contrast between property and its absence is heightened by the fact that limitations on property have been introduced deliberately.

In the primitive society, the utilization of violent coercion, while present, is relatively unorganized and is carried on with rather simple techniques; one is usually free from the threat of a Belsen or a Hiroshima, although it ought always to be remembered that large-scale destruction has also taken place in cultures that are far less developed technologically than is the culture characteristic of industrial civilization.[3] In modern times, however, violent coercion can be on a much larger scale and is carried on with all the devilish ingenuity for which man has been equipped through the arts and sciences. While populations in large portions of given areas could be and were destroyed in previous generations (some one third to one half of the people of Germany are said to have died during the Thirty Years War in the 17th century), modern civilization makes possible equally great destruction for mankind as a whole. Primitive mankind might conceivably have been obliterated by widespread disease, although even this would presumably have been severely limited because of the isolation of human groups from one another. But it is characteristic of modern civilization that the universal destruction of both freedom and life is now made possible, if not probable, by the free development of the arts and sciences and by the skills in organization which accompany complex civilization.

The very idea of freedom as against coercion becomes more involved with the development of civilization. As a primitive, one is presumably narrowly limited in one's conceptions to more or less obvious examples: freedom to use a waterhole for one's cattle, for example, or the threat of coercion from a personal or tribal enemy. It is of the nature of civilization that as our intellectual vistas widen, with the development of learning and the decline of the sacred society, both the possibilities of freedom and the potentialities for violent coercion broaden and deepen. This is another way of saying that the political challenge broadens and deepens, dramatizing the issue of whether mankind can meet it.

Personhood and the Group

As Nature and primitive human nature are left behind, the potentialities for what Jacques Maritain calls personhood[4] grow. Awareness of individual goals apart from those of the group becomes more acute. The figure of the 14th century B.C. Ikhnaton in ancient Egypt represents, according to Breasted, the "first individual" in history. With increasing consciousness of personhood, however, our confusions also are likely to grow. We become so impressed by individual uniqueness that we may forget that that uniqueness is itself dependent on the nourishment of the group. The piratical, egoistical elements in each of us are released and, unguided by God, tradition, custom, or animal instinct, we prey on other individuals. Thus individual power and glory are exalted, as with Thrasymachus and Hobbes, and Ayn Rand.[5]

Contrariwise, our consciousness may lead us to be so aware of the social basis of personhood that it becomes all too easy to say that our seeming uniqueness is an illusion. We conceive of ourselves as being simply extensions of the group, subject to its determinism. Psychologically, we often seek refuge in the group, for we fear our uniqueness. Just as some students of human personality believe that we often yearn to return to the womb, so it can be suggested that at times we endeavor to deny that we are in any sense individual beings not bound to a group.

Thus one aberration leads to what some have called the theory and practice of social atomism, while the other tends to some extreme versions of organicism as a social outlook. Both social atomism and radical interpretations of organicism are inadequate as accounts of human personality and of the problems of freedom which accompany it.

A more nearly complete view of personhood would see it as always rooted in the group and finding the group as essential for its fulfillment, yet at the same time as transcending the group and having legitimate ends and purposes of its own upon which the group has no legitimate claim. In other terms, the indestructible human soul develops its personhood in the community of souls. But while the group is a necessary condition, it is not a sufficient condition for personhood.

Let us place this conception of personhood within the context of modern physical and biological theories. According to much modern physics, every unit of the physical world is unlike every other unit in some respects, although obviously the differences between atom and atom, or particle and particle, may be very infinitesimal. As we move from physics to biology, what might be called the degree of uniqueness increases: That is to say, for example, differences between and among animals of a given species are far greater than differences between and among molecules or atoms or particles. By the time we have reached the human species, differences in degree have become magnified enormously.[6]

But this is only one side of the coin. The other is the sense in which the group, too, is a reality, whether at the most primitive level or in the human species. According to Sir Alister Hardy, the eminent biologist, in every animal species there may be something of what we might call a group mind, built up through telepathic communications among members of the species. The experiences of one member of the species, Hardy appears to contend, may be subconsciously signaled by telepathy to other members, who may thus modify their behavior accordingly. Perhaps there is a kind of psychic pool which may be tapped by all or parts of the species and to which all members contribute. While individuality is still real, it must be seen against the background of the psychic lake from which individuals can draw.[7]

As is well known, the late Carl Jung, the renowned psychologist, developed the notion of a racial memory which could be reflected in dreams and through a near-universal symbolism. Like the psychic telepathic pool of Hardy, Jung's conception emphasizes that the individuality which we so often prize is itself stimulated and encouraged by a whole which goes beyond individual differentiation. While this may sound "mystical" and rather vague, we should not forget that almost any formulation attempting to express adequately the numerous dimensions related to the problem of the "one" and the "many" will also sound vague. Moreover, many scientists other than Jung and Hardy feel compelled to resort to not dissimilar language. Thus Oliver Sacks, a neuropsychologist, has maintained that "Our consciousness is like a flame or a fountain, rising up from infinite depths. . . . We are vessels or funnels for what lies beyond us. . . . Nature achieves self-consciousness through us."[8]

The organicist view of human personality, then, is right to the degree that it assumes the teleologically natural character of a kind of biological, psychic, and social community of human beings and to the extent, too, that it suggests the indispensability of genuine human community for the development of personality. Those versions of organicism are wrong, however, that seem to contend that personality is simply the "product" of society. Personality can be creative. It can innovate and shape the world, and this implies that it can bring into existence things and thoughts out of "nothing."

But this does not imply that all personalities under all existential or historical conditions are in fact creative. Most are probably not what they ought to be or can be. They are divorced from what they should be and often are not even aware that this is so.

The problem, then, is for every person, as he or she gains self-awareness, to discover the ways in which justice or righteousness can be attained for himself or herself in the context of his or her multifarious relations with groups. Contrariwise, the issue confronted by the group is equally acute: how to make certain that the individual, who is both a product of groups and in some sense independent of them, is given what rightfully belongs to him or her, while the general good of the group is simultaneously assured. We postulate that humanity in its infancy had a low level of awareness or consciousness about the distinction between potential personality and the life of the group, just as the biological infant during the first period of its life is hardly aware of any differentiation between itself and the "other." As consciousness develops, whether in civilization as a whole or in individual lives, awareness of differentiation expands, and with it the search for norms which can guide both individual and collective life. In the beginning, the individual perceives himself as undifferentiated from others, so that issues of "freedom" and "justice" cannot arise; and likewise in a hypothetical primitive humanity, the individual is lost in the group. With the development of the person, on the one hand, and of civilization, on the other, consciousness of differentiation enlarges, and with it awareness of such issues as justice, liberty, equality, and fraternity. This is another way of saying that, whether in the life of the individual or of humanity, with growing awareness of differentiation comes increasingly involved consciousness of issues in ethics and politics.

But with awareness of differentiation and of the major issues in ethics and politics comes a search for solutions of the questions which are raised. No sooner are we conscious that the "I" is not identical with the "other" than we also see that we are seeking to discover their right or just relationships — issues which could not arise before awareness of differentiation. Within each developing soul, two questions emerge:

1. How can I relate the disparate and often conflicting aspects of myself to one another and to the whole which potentially I can become?
2. How can I bridge the gulf between myself and the others without which I could not be myself and then relate myself and the others to the whole which is the collectivity?

For ants, presumably, such questions do not arise; for human beings, they become central. They are posed because human beings in civilization are in many senses free. Their consciousness of these issues is both the root and the fruit of freedom.

The five paradigms noted in the preceding chapter all attempt, in their diverse ways, to address themselves to questions of this kind. Each has a different emphasis. In the view which pits civilization against Nature, it is because we fear one another in Nature and are obsessed and dominated by primitive passions that we establish civilization; the State, as the organ of civilization, represents an attempt to avoid violent death but itself reflects simply predominant power. In the view which sees Nature as a model for civilization, the root of justice and freedom in civilization lies in following the laws of a Nature in which individuality and the whole are already basically reconciled. In the civilization-as-corrupting paradigm, it is denied that civilization contributes to freedom in any sense (even though, paradoxically, the discovery of this supposed fact was attributable to highly civilized and literate men). In the civilization-as-preparation model, developing consciousness first of differentiation and then of the problems of ethics and politics either will or can lead to an ultimate resolution of all the tensions. For the classical paradigm, problems of social ordering and the ordering of the soul are obverse sides of the same coin; and the just state and just soul arise together, but only in the context of recognizing a strict hierarchy of goods. Absent is the notion, found in the civilization-as-preparation model, that humanity will inevitably or can completely attain the goal. Individual thinkers like St. Thomas Aquinas obviously reflect in part both civilization-as-preparation and classical models. Thus Thomas may be interpreted as suggesting that civilization is a kind of intermediate step between the primitive, in which free personhood is frustrated, and the teleologically natural idea of full personhood, which is seeking to impress itself on the existential world. He seems to open the way for what will later be called "progress" but does not really envision consummation of the goal on earth.

The view we are espousing here has elements of the civilization-as-preparation paradigm but is perhaps more nearly akin to the classical view. Civilization is the fruit of man's teleological nature and is foreshadowed as he emerges from Nature. The pattern of civilization, so to speak, is one first of consciousness of differentiation, then of exploration of various notions of freedom, and, in connection with ethics and politics, the effort through justice to make whole (holy, healthy) the human soul and, simultaneously, the collectivity of souls. Righteousness and integrity (integration; oneness) in the soul cannot be completely attained until we achieve justice in the social order; and by the same token, justice in the social order is not gained without at least an embryonic righteousness in individual souls or groups of souls. As awareness grows, so do possibilities for justice. But just as we must move away from Nature to become human, so a too-complex civilization will impair the possibilities for achievement of justice in souls and in societies.

As awareness develops and we seek to transcend mere consciousness of differentiation by discovering justice in soul and society, it becomes evident that the soul cannot perfect itself, nor can the society become just (in the general sense of the preceding chapter), unless three minimal conditions are met: first, the person's uniqueness must be recognized both by himself and by the state; second, full acknowledgement must be made of the sense in which personal development toward righteousness is dependent on differentiating self from others through a diversity of groups and associations; and finally, we ought to see that neither soul nor humanity can become just unless the soul's kinship with all other souls is fully understood.

First, every soul is, as Emerson once observed, "an unique." Whether in existence or potentially, there has been no one like me or like you, there is no one like me or you, and there will be no one like me or you. As we noted earlier, while we cannot become human beings except in groups of human beings, there is something about each of us which cannot be attributed to others: our existence in human society is not sufficient to account for what we are or can be or ought to be. Whether or not we connect this with the idea of some eternal and indestructible soul at the center of every human being, we reject the notion, implicit in some forms of organicism, that there is not an "I" which lies beyond all historical social groupings. Political justice requires that this be recognized but, as we shall see more fully in the following chapter, historical states are forever tending to deny this quality of uniqueness, the extreme example being modern totalitarianism. Any polity which utilizes its options in civilization to deny scope for this uniqueness is by definition unjust.

Second, every person, to become his ideal and just self, must be recognized as requiring for his fulfillment a relationship to many types of diverse groups, in some of which he will be setting himself off from other human beings. Although we are not simply group products, we cannot find our true identities unless we experience existence in a variety of groupings — economic, social, religious, national. Here again, many states historically have sought to suppress this dimension of human personality, which is also an attribute of what we call "freedom." States have been as suspicious of diverse groupings and associations as they have been of unique individuals. In ancient Rome, even burial societies were looked upon with suspicion, on the ground that they might compete with the state for allegiance. In the United States, during the period of McCarthyism, even the most innocent societies or associations were investigated or penetrated by the FBI. In the United States, too, we have been almost obsessed by fear of language and cultural differentiation and have sought, through the public education system, to provide a kind of uniformity. And much political history is the story of empires or kingdoms seeking to crush idiosyncratic national or religious groupings within them. Perhaps we can think of this tendency to suppression as representing vestiges of the ideal of tribal uniformity. But however we account for it, there can be no doubt about its existence. In terms of giving full and consistent recognition to pluralism of groupings, political mankind is still in its infancy. And unfortunately, as we note later, the greater the complexity of civilization, the more ubiquitous seem to be the pressures to uniformity.

Finally, there is a sense in which we cannot be our true selves unless we somehow are closely tied to all human beings. While we are by our teleological natures like no other human beings in some respects, and like some human beings but not others in other respects, we are like and require all human beings in still other relations. In terms of the classical paradigm, working within us is the idea or the "form" of universal humanity. Humanity in this sense is not simply an abstraction derived after examining individual "human" beings. Rather it is a natural end by which we are defined in our ideal sense. Each of us is existentially only a partial human being when measured by what he might or ought to become. The idea of humanity is one which differentiates the human species from others: potentially, in other words, we are rational, creative, free (in the meanings we explore below), just, and appreciators of the world of beauty; and the idea of humanity is seeking its way with us, not to command us but rather to goad us and to ask questions to which we must respond. The idea suggests universality. Politically, of course, the idea of humanity has yet to be realized, for there are few organs through which the conception of universalism can express itself. We are still divided by warring nation-states, each a kind of jealous god repelled by the universal god and seeking to become the sole divinity for groups and individuals within its borders.

Justice, then, in part, would imply full ethical, legal, and political

81

recognition of individual uniqueness, group pluralism, and universalism. Without acknowledgement of all three dimensions, fulfillment of the human soul is frustrated, and its freedom is impaired.

We can imagine an hypothetical Nature in which uniqueness, group pluralism, and human unity are reconciled and automatically assured. In civilization, however, fortunately or unfortunately, this cannot be: Human beings are thrown on their own resources to bring about and maintain the reconciliation. To the degree that they succeed, they have attained at least one dimension of justice. To the extent that they fail, they are confronted with such phenomena as alienation, violence, war, and, in general, what Plato termed political "illness." The reverse of this political illness would be a community of souls in which personality as unique would no longer be at odds with personality as pluralistically social or with personality as ecumenical.

This, then, is the general context within which the problem of justice and freedom arises in civilization. Personality is freed from the gods and custom and instinct, only to find itself puzzled by how it ought to order itself. The issue is posed by civilization; the answer must be found by political reflection.

Varying Meanings of Freedom

In developing that reflection, we must confront the varying ways in which freedom has been defined. As subtleties of meaning develop, at least three different connotations of the term arise.[9] In one, the question of whether the will is free becomes the basis of much philosophical discussion. In another, freedom tends to be defined as the opportunity to do as one desires when confronted by such supposedly external obstacles as custom, law, legislation, or the threats of rulers and others. In the third, liberation is seen as emancipation from one's "false self" rather than from external impediments; it is identified with doing what is desirable rather than what is desired. Let us note the relations of these meanings of freedom to the conception of personality we have just sketched.

The notion of freedom of the will has a long history and has attracted the attention of many modern thinkers. Some have seen it as incompatible with the assumptions of science, while others think there is no necessary conflict.[10] The exponent of freedom does not deny that in many situations the will is not free; what he does reject is the idea that it is always unfree. There are points, in other words, during which we are deliberating and utilizing our reason when the will is genuinely undetermined. Once one's decision is made, of course, the person is directed by it. But the decision itself may have been reached by rational considerations alone, and in that sense it is a "free" one — it was not, in other words, simply the inevitable result of a long chain of antecedent events; deliberation about the decision was "real." As C. E. M. Joad points out, when we look at the world "scientifically" or analytically (by breaking it apart), the freedom of the will often seems an outrageous doctrine,[11] as it appears to be, for example, to thinkers like B. F. Skinner.[12] But if we hold that the human personality can act as a whole and is, in fact, not merely the sum total of all its physical and psychological and other parts, then freedom in this sense is a reasonable proposition. While a scientific account of the human being is perfectly legitimate and necessary, it does not exhaust our understanding of the soul, which can be fully known only by direct experience (including introspection) and understood as one would understand a work of art. It is the kind of whole which is more than the sum of its parts; and it has the capacity — shared with God — of bringing things into being out of nothing. It can initiate both thought and action. It can shape and direct its own parts. It is in these senses that the personality can be understood as "free."

Perhaps the idea of freedom of the will can best be understood by looking at the consequences if it does not exist. All decisions would be spurious, even those which we term "rational": We would be going through the motions of decision making, but in reality it would not be "I" or "we" making the decision. Instead, our physiological, psychological, and chemical movements would be dictating to us, and the "I" would be an illusion, reduced to its parts. If human beings are "determined" (in the usual meaning of that term), we could never be persuaded by an argument — an exercise in rationality — but would simply have the conclusion thrust upon us by circumstance. B. F. Skinner could not persuade me that his view was right or true — if eventually I came to accept the words he uttered, it would not really be "I" but rather movements (chemical, psychological, social, etc.) which somehow pushed the illusory "I." In fact, it is difficult to see how under these circumstances one could really speak of an "I."

Here we are obviously denying that freedom, in this sense of freedom of the will, is an illusion. This does not mean that we always decide freely. In fact, in many situations we probably do not. But it does imply that we have the potentiality for so doing.

Freedom in the sense of opportunity to do what one desires is associated particularly with the history of liberalism and with individualist rather than organicist conceptions of society. In one civilization-against-Nature paradigm, it will be remembered, men in Nature were free to do anything they liked to do, and each was the judge of what he liked. Each, moreover, sought to dominate others and to manipulate others for his own benefit. But each also became aware that others, pursuing desires similar to his own, might kill him. To avoid violent death at the hands of his fellow beings, he consented to civilization and the State but did not change his desires. In fact, while civilization presumably reduced the fear of violent death, it did so only to allow greater outlet for fulfillment of desires. In one sense, civilization is a radical departure from Nature; but in another sense, civilization and the State simply provide a better framework for the pursuit of individual desires. This is obviously paradoxical.

While it is not denied that some restrictions on freedom as opportunity to fulfill desires is required, still such restrictions are seen as artifacts, necessary to avoid death but not positively reflecting Nature. Precisely because there is in one sense a very strong antagonism between Nature and civilization, there continues to exist, even in civilization, a very pronounced conflict between individual freedom (defined as the discrete individual's right to pursue his desires) and the commands of the sovereign. Legislation is for the purpose of preventing my neighbor from killing me, so that I can freely pursue my desires. In Freud-like versions, while civilization is supported, personality disorders are in considerable degree traced to the conflict between free expression of primitively natural desires and the necessity for restricting those desires if the tasks of civilization are to be performed.

Although the paradigm which sees Nature as a model for civilization on the whole views man as utilizing his freedom wisely, still it would agree with the civilization-against-Nature view in postulating a somewhat discrete individual who is pursuing "happiness," often in the form of sensual pleasure.

Accent in this view of freedom is on the discrete individual's rights rather than his obligations. In Hobbes's conception, the rights center on freedom from violent death in order to pursue the primitively natural desires associated with "life." In Locke-like views, the rights to be assured more firmly in civilization are those of life, liberty (pursuit of happiness), and estate (material possessions). Freedom is, in fact, "power."

Enslavement, for this view of freedom, tends to consist of absence of power, lack of material goods, and laws or customs which restrict the quest for power or of material goods. In its extreme form, this conception sees the individual as free when he has political power, material possessions, and the opportunity to express his desires. If the state can tell me what I ought to desire, this view suggests, then I am not free.

The role of the state is a negative one and can be expressed in a variety of ways: it should and can make laws to restrict violent death, to suppress robbers (who might seize my material possessions), and to stifle threats I may make against my neighbor's rights to life. But beyond this, it ought not to go. The conception of the "positive" state in civilization is in considerable measure foreign to this perspective on freedom.

We sometimes term this notion of liberty "negative freedom." While this is not necessarily the most appropriate designation, we shall use it here in contradistinction to the third meaning of freedom, which is sometimes termed "positive." Positive freedom, in contrast with negative versions, is usually associated with organicist conceptions of personality, society, and state. In terms of the paradigms of the preceding chapter, it would be closely correlated with certain versions of civilization as preparation and with the classical outlooks.

The accent of positive freedom is not on freedom as emancipation from external constraints and on discrete individual rights but rather on freedom as liberation from illusion and attachment to the finite. One is free when, as a whole person fully conscious of one's organic relation to society, one knows what one ought to do and does it. Power and wealth and freedom from external constraints do not necessarily contribute to positive freedom; instead, they may actually work against it by enslaving the person to lust for glory or possessions or erratic pleasures. One is not free, this view would hold, when one's only purposes are to be found in immediate and shifting desires. One is not free when one lacks insights into how to live. Erratic desires may characterize the beasts, to be sure, but to say that human beings are free when they have the power to express every desire is to deny that they have in some sense escaped Nature and ceased to be mere beasts. "What is it then which makes man his own master and free from hindrance?" asks Epictetus, the ancient slave. "Wealth does not make him so, nor a consulship, nor a province, nor a kingdom; we must find something else. . . . It is knowledge of how to live."[13] Freedom consists in developing the personal integration or moral wholeness (integrity) which will enable one to stand up to tyrants and to despise power and wealth; and even though one is a conventional slave, as was Epictetus, one is still freer than those enslaved by power and possessions.

Hence those who define freedom in this way are dubious about the great value of negative freedom. To be sure, laws can curtail us, and the absence of possessions limit our mobility and the fulfillment of our sensual desires; but these are not important when measured against the achievement of an integrated and rational soul, which will owe little if anything to wealth or political power. As the great neo-Platonist Plotinus once put it,

Men complain of poverty and of the unequal distribution of wealth, in ignorance that the wise man does not desire equality in such things, nor thinks that the rich has any advantage over the poor, or the prince over the subject. He leaves these opinions to the vulgar, and knows that there are two sorts of life, that of virtuous people, who can rise to the highest degree of life, that of the spiritual world; and that of vulgar and earthly persons. . . .[14]

And only those who are truly virtuous and spiritual in this sense are free. Wealth and power and restrictions of law or custom become matters of indifference. Freedom is to be found in self-perfection.

Expressed in a somewhat different way, we obviously have in this notion an expression of the view that the nature of a human being is not to be found primarily in his primitive nature (his "drives" and "passions" and psychological "motions") but rather in the teleological nature from which he is alienated. Freedom consists in doing what is desirable, not what is necessarily desired, and desirable is defined as the encouragement of the perfected, true self. Under positive freedom, one is most free when one has subordinated all desires to the rational self; under negative freedom, erratic desires are not the enemy but rather laws and customs and absence of power. In negative-freedom conceptions, law and legislation are always seen as restraints on freedom, even though defensible under some circumstances; in positive, rational-freedom ideas, law and legislation may not only not be restraints on true freedom but may assist positively in the process of liberation: Insofar as the constraints are on my "lower" (or primitively natural) self, they may be doing me a service by assisting me in discovering and giving expression to my higher and true self.

Although Plato in the *Republic* does not usually speak of freedom in so many words, we may impute to him a doctrine of positive freedom and use the great dialogue to illustrate it. Who are the freest in the *Republic?* Obviously the philosophers. And they are freest not because they have power (in fact, they spurn it and have to be reminded of their responsibility to use it) or wealth (they have no private possessions and seemingly lead rather ascetic lives) but rather because they possess wisdom and subordinate all their acts to its demands. All knowledge tends to constrain, for it excludes illusion, false hopes, and emotions which stand in the way of its pursuit. Our options are frequently reduced as we know more (assuming for the moment that we know when we know), Plato seems to be saying, yet it is only through knowledge and wisdom that we can be free. We become most truly free when we understand the world and how we are related to it. In his seemingly enigmatic way, Hegel appears to concur: "Freedom is Necessity Transfigured."

And thus negative and positive conceptions of freedom are joined in conflict. Negative notions see the enemies of freedom in custom, habit, law, social structures, and organization. Positive freedom analyses, while not necessarily denying that some types of external constraints may be undesirable, would still say that organization, law, and other supposedly external constraints may actually reinforce and undergird the structure of freedom defined as the discovery of the true self, of rationality, and of truth in general. The most onerous restrictions on liberty arise from our in-

86

ability to master our own passions, overcome our own inertia, conquer our own sloth: Once we are liberated from erratic passions, inertia, sloth, and irrationality, political tyrants and tyrannical laws become minor obstacles, since without slavish human beings, no tyranny could flourish. Negative-freedom notions tend to stress nonteleological modes of explanation; positive versions place great emphasis on imputed purpose, seeing an implicit universal goal for human life and society in accordance with which we should evaluate our political experience and define the meaning of liberty. The self-governing fully aware personality is the goal.

Corresponding to the three types of freedom are three kinds of coercion. In the first, the allegedly "free" will is said to be "determined" by antecedent events or "motions." In negative-freedom positions, obstacles to emancipation are forces supposedly external to the human being: restrictive laws, disagreeable options, not enough material goods, rigid customs, inadequate power, and so on. If only these factors could be eliminated so that we could express our desires, we would be free. But in positive-freedom approaches, coercion is applied by the "lower self," material desires, ignorance, lack of awareness, and uncritical attachment to concepts, language, things, power, institutions, other persons, and one's own physical life. We are free when we do what we ought to do, when we "perfect" ourselves, not chiefly when we can do what we desire to do. For negative-freedom conceptions, external constraints on individual desires tend to be regarded as unnatural or artificial. For positive-freedom views, laws, regulations, and other "external" restraints may be seen, on occasion at least, as natural expressions of man's teleological essence.

A Further Distinction in Meanings

Presently we shall comment on the relevance of these three meanings of freedom for the political challenges of civilization. Before doing so, however, we should note another distinction — that between so-called spiritual and intellectual freedom, on the one hand, and freedom of action, on the other. Many philosophies of liberty call attention to this distinction, although they might develop diverse conclusions from it.

Spiritual and intellectual freedom has to do with the realm of religious belief, of speech, of thought, and of literary and artistic expression. This is in the domain of what the ancient philosopher Proclus called "indivisible" goods, "which many may possess at once, and no one is worse off in respect to them because another has them," as William Inge observed in *The Philosophy of Plotinus*. In this area, my expression does not in principle detract from yours and my apreciation of an art object does not deprive you of the same possibility of appreciation, for we are dealing here with the world of unscarce or limitless resources. In some versions, man is seen to be immortal and, at least in some sense, as unlimited by time.

Freedom of action, by contrast, refers to man insofar as he is bound to some extent by limitations of material resources and of time. To quote Proclus again, this is the sphere of "divisible goods, those in which one man's gain is another man's loss." Inevitably, land, time, space, and economic resources must be allocated in some way (unlike truth, beauty, conceptions of God, and ways of worshipping God). Hence one's freedom in this domain can never be limitless, regardless of regime or political philosophy.

The problem arises when we try to relate spiritual and intellectual freedom to freedom of action. In a sense, the issue is an expression of the broader and very ancient question of the relation of soul to body, or the mind-body problem. Existentially, soul and body are closely intertwined, each affecting the other, yet we often seek to define freedom as if they were not. It would seem clear, for instance, that if we assume scarce material goods and time, there will have to be strict limits of some kind on a person's freedom to use them, whether those limits are imposed by law or by some other method. Yet the same person who is restricted in his claim to material goods may assert an unlimited right to freedom in the realm of purely "indivisible" goods. But it is obvious that thought does affect action. and how we regulate freedom in the economic sphere will condition our ability to exercise freedom of thought. Thus, if I am poor, my ability to express my thoughts (through newspapers, travel, and so on) will indubitably be restricted by that fact, whatever the permissiveness of the law; general zoning ordinances confining residential areas to certain sections of the city will prevent aesthetic expression through commercial theaters in those areas; and so on.

If human beings were purely spiritual and intellectual, communicating with one another telepathically, they would no longer be weighted down by the burdens and inevitable limitations of the flesh and of scarce goods. But because they are both spirit and flesh, the spirit's development will be affected and conditioned by the finiteness of the flesh.

The development from the primitive to civilization is obviously characterized by a vast expansion of the possibilities (although not necessarily the actualization) for spiritual freedom, with the growth and expansion of consciousness and awareness. In fact, the notion of civilization itself is closely associated, in terms of its definition, with awareness both of selfhood and of otherhood. The life of the city, with its intellectual stimulation, is an expression of both self-consciousness and social consciousness. Potentialities for multiplication of choices in action, too, are enlarged through the development of technology and the increase in material goods. At the same time, the complexities of civilization — centering particularly on intricacies of the division of labor — and the expansion of possibilities for both freedom and coercion make the development of norms for guidance more enormously trying. What is right and what is wrong, what is the good life and its reverse, are extremely difficult questions to answer, yet the need to answer them becomes more pressing.

Answers to the Freedom-Coercion Question

The paradigmatic responses outlined in the previous chapter tend to give characteristic answers to the freedom-coercion question. Hobbes-like views emphasize negative freedom: While civilization is seen as warring with Nature, in principle its war is for the purpose of enabling discrete individuals to express their desires without fear of violent death.[15] Locke-like versions, too, stress negative freedom, but against the background of a Nature that is relatively more beneficent. In the framework which sees civilization as necessarily and inevitably corrupting, civilization itself is the primary factor in preventing attainment of the true self and therefore the free self; and the true self — contrary to the Platonic and Aristotelean definitions — is identified with a primitively natural self that is innocent, concerned, and loving. Representing this position, Tolstoy seeks negative freedom in the elimination of what he regards as "artificial" civilization, but the purpose is supposedly to restore the positive freedom existing in Nature. In the Marx-like responses, historical civil society seems to be viewed as a coercion essential if man is ultimately to free himself from its external constraints and to internalize the morality which is necessary for positive liberty. However, the Marxian sees positive liberty not in the primitive but rather as the consummation of a civilization which, through its own inner dynamics and particularly its economic growth, leads to a state in which external restraints on desire are wiped out but in which, at the same time, no one chooses the undesirable. Finally, classicism underlines positive freedom, with civilized institutions seen as natural expressions of man's telos to free himself from the erratic passions and material desires which have tended to enslave him. Man is freed, through the achievement of justice, to become himself. But there is nothing inevitable about the process; it entails constant toil, and there is no assurance that its goal will be consummated.

Given the principles of justice espoused in Chapter 2 and the analysis of this chapter, we suggest that both negative and positive freedom must be taken into account as we seek to build the just society. All the paradigms have something valid to say about this, although not always without modification and reinterpretation. Hobbes rightly suggests that there is an egoistic aspect of human beings which makes the tasks of civilization extraordinarily difficult, but he is wrong (as the philosopher David Hume pointed out) when he denies the existence of a natural other-regarding dimension. Locke is more aware of that dimension, and his picture of primitive Nature is therefore legitimately more complex than that of Hobbes. But both are inadequate in grasping the teleological aspect of human nature and the conception of positive freedom which accompanies it. Tolstoy rightly stresses the enslaving aspects of complex civilization but goes too far when he suggests that the elimination of all its constraints would establish freedom in its positive sense. His romantic conception of Nature, while appealing and while an important and partly valid attack on certain versions of Darwinism — "Nature red in tooth and claw" — is difficult to sustain completely in light of what we know about primitive societies. Insofar as it suggests that civilization's conflicts help develop consciousness, the civilization as preparation model obviously has a bearing on the development of freedom. Classicism rightly stresses the teleological dimension of human beings and refuses to define them simply in terms of their origins or primitive conditions; its conception of positive freedom, too, as the liberation brought about by apprehension of truth ("The truth shall make you free") can be confirmed by our experience. But the classical paradigm underemphasizes the importance of spontaneity and seems to suggest that only a few can be free in the full sense of the term. While classicism is certainly aware of the problem of involuntary economic poverty, still it probably gives too little attention to the importance of negative freedom from the galling constraints imposed by too few material resources.

Here we suggest that negative freedom may be an important though not a sufficient gateway to positive liberty. That is, we should be free from tyrannical custom and irrational laws and restrictive involuntary poverty in order to have scope to express and experiment with our desires and to discover the desirable; and this is both an individual and a social process. .The discovery of the desirable, given our unique individualities on the one side and our indispensable social anchorage on the other, is the result of a kind of dialogue between the standards fixed by society and our individual testing of those norms in our experience. Much legislation can reinforce our intent to think or do only the desirable, insofar as legislation is the fruit of this dialogue.[16] Although legislation existentially almost always relies on coercion to some extent, it is usually never sheer coercion; even in despotism, it is always appealing, in however small degree, to standards which are widely if sometimes thoughtlessly accepted.

We have suggested that one aspect of justice is to recognize fully the three dimensions of personhood: the individual as unique, the individual as in some of his dimensions like some other individuals but unlike others, and the individual in yet another aspect as like all others — the universal dimension. A society which provides this threefold recognition would thus, through its laws and institutions, safeguard the eccentricity of the person, the autonomy of the many kinds of groups and associations necessary to express the second thrust of human personality, and, finally, the unity of mankind.

It is partly because modern civilization ignores or gives scant recognition to one or more of these three dimensions — falls far below what justice requires, in other words — that we can speak of civilization and its discontents. Totalitarianism, so ubiquitous in the world of the 20th century, shows contempt for the eccentricity of the individual and the claims to autonomy of groups below the State level. On the other hand, many of the so-called democratic societies often fail to give due recognition to the individual as a social being and to understand that personality itself can develop only in genuine community. The world of international politics is, of course, an excellent example of the ways in which mankind, through its institutions, cuts off that aspiration to universality which is so much a part of the telos of human beings. The threat of universal destruction which hangs over the societies of the 20th century may be thought of as the outward manifestation of the failure to give due recognition to the three dimensions of the soul as conceived in terms of its essential purpose.

Spiritual-Intellectual Freedom Versus Liberty of Action

But, as we have said, a distinction must be made in principle between spiritual-intellectual freedom and liberty of action. This distinction is particularly important in a world where it is assumed we have not yet completely discovered the contents of the good, the true, and the beautiful. That is to say, we do not live in a world where the norms of justice are completely known, where legislation can prescribe or state these norms both in the spiritual-intellectual area and for scarce goods, and where these prescriptions are seen immediately as rational and just and so to be followed without any measure of coercion. We do not live in such a world, but we are in the process of discovering it.

Pending its discovery, the date of which no man can predict, it would seem reasonable to think of the spiritual-intellectual domain as one in which thoughts and beliefs can be expressed without legal inhibitions. This is particularly so since in such a world it is difficult, if not impossible, to discover the ways in which expressions of particular thoughts and beliefs shape particular actions. We do not deny — indeed, we affirm — that thoughts expressed in writing and speech, as well as art work, shape action; but we do suggest that, except in rare instances, we do not know — at least until long after the event — how a given intellectual or spiritual expression will affect what human beings will do. Moreover (unlike the situation in the universe of scarce resources), my admiring a particular picture does not diminish your capacity to admire and criticize it; my worshipping my God does not in principle keep you from worshipping yours; my expressing a thought does not in essence detract from your capacity to do so. For these reasons — and assuming always that discovery of truth, beauty, and goodness is a central value in the justice we seek — legislation ought, in general, to refrain from imposing any restrictions whatsoever on the expression of ideas. Indeed, it should go further and in a positive sense help provide the material base for spiritual and intellectual expression. The very future of mankind depends on this negative freedom in the intellectual-spiritual sphere.

Yet historically, as well as in our day, this principle has been more honored in the breach than in the observance. States use their power over material bodies and goods to restrict the expression of thought. Most of the world today lives under systems of law which check freedom of speech and punish persons for speaking their thoughts. All such regulations are an insult to the dignity of the human person and to his aspirations for freedom in its several dimensions. Yet if the discontents of civilization are to be alleviated, if the tendencies to tyranny in political society are to be checked, this principle of freedom of expression must be implemented.

It is significant that, not only today but in the past as well, one of the first acts of any would-be tyrant is always to suppress freedom of speech or of written communication. This is an enormous tribute to the power of speech and writing, and it reinforces the contention that the word, or the logos, is perhaps the greatest source of power, particularly of political power.

But while unqualified freedom of expression should obtain in the intellectual-spiritual domain, if we are to have justice a similar principle ought not to obtain in the realm of action, the world of scarce or economic resources. Here the problem is not so much *whether* limits on freedom of action should be imposed but rather what or who shall do the limiting. Given scarce resources — water, land, energy, air, particularly in the context of what some see as never-ending demand — the resources will be allocated in some way: by custom, by the market, or by law. No one can possibly have everything he or she may desire, although it could be contended that he or she might eventually have everything desirable. In terms of modern civilization, then, the question is who shall do the allocating and under what principles of distributive justice it shall be done.

Allocation by the market would supposedly impose limits rather impersonally. Legislation would at least presumably reflect an attempt at some kind of rational consensus on precisely how those limitations are to be implemented. To allow accident to impose the limitations would permit irrational factors to govern. Seeking positively, through politics, to state the limitations attempts a rational allocation which can subsequently be criticized and modified if necessary. This frees the individual from his own uncertainties and from mere fortuitous circumstance so he can act with a greater measure of rationality. Nothing can be more disastrous to the development of souls than to find that there are no common expectations binding them to one another; deliberately formulated standards for these expectations both reassure the individual soul and promote the harmony of the whole.

In any event, negative freedom in the economic arena will always have severe limits. The problem is not whether the limits will exist but how they will be defined, and in accordance with what standards. To these problems we shall return in greater detail in Chapter 6, and, to some degree, in Chapter 7.

Freedom, Power, and Authority

Freedom in its several meanings can hardly be understood apart from its relation to the concepts of authority and power. Broadly speaking, authority may be thought of as the *right* to act or not to act, and political authority, of course, implies the right to act in relation to collective affairs. Power, which generally simply means the ability to make or to do, must be sharply distinguished from the notion of authority. We may have authority to act or to do but not have the power to do so; or, contrariwise, we may possess the power but not have the authority. A 200-pound man undoubtedly has the power to mangle or kill a 100-pound girl, but most of us would say he has no moral authority to do so, and the legal systems of the world would confirm that he has no legal authority.

Unlike freedom, power and authority have acquired unfavorable connotations. Authority is frequently thought of as antagonistic to freedom, to the detriment of authority. Concerning political power, it can be said that human beings in civilization have been amazingly ambivalent. On the one hand, when they do not have it, they think of it in a favorable light: Thus, in our day, the respective exponents speak favorably of "woman power" and "black power." On the other hand — and this view seems often to be overriding — we are fearful of power, quoting Lord Acton's famous statement "power tends to corrupt."

Actually, once we enter the civilized state, we cannot avoid freedom, power, and authority. We cannot "abolish power," as Tolstoy once advocated. Just as we cannot fly from freedom very long, so we cannot avoid power relations of some kind. We can say, however, that power without authority is evil and deleterious for mankind. But then the question becomes: What authorizes, or what constitutes the basis for authority?

The Basis for Authority

Perhaps we can illustrate these propositions by assessing anarchist arguments, which, by definition, reject authority or rule. Deliberately arrived-at community standards which are regarded as authoritative do indeed, as anarchists argue, inhibit human freedom in its negative sense. But if the standards are such that they appeal to a common ordering of values and to reason, then legislation arrived at after formal deliberation can hardly be regarded as a substantial restriction of negative freedom, at least for most. And if the standards achieve this level, then they presumably coincide in considerable measure with what the community and its members think of as desirable. To be sure, momentary impulses may be checked, but if the assumptions we stated obtain, they are checked in the name of one's own rational standards. It is true that this is a goal only partially achieved in any politically formulated decision: Most political authority is, in other words, only partially "authoritative," the other part being corrupted by special interests and piratical elements. But then the anarchist must ask himself whether in the absence of these commonly arrived-at standards, coercive though they may be to some degree in application, the human being would not be subject to even greater coercions — of informal pressures, for example, or accident, or immediate impulses which will be later regretted. Is it not true, in other words, that the choice is not between "coercion" and "noncoercion" but rather between "some coercion under publicly established standards" and "possibly erratic and dangerous coercion without publicly established standards"?[17]

Some varieties of anarchism, too, seem to contend that if individuals can develop internalized moral standards, the necessity for common, deliberately arrived-at legislation declines. "Good" men, it is maintained, do not need "government." This is an old argument, of course, although many who espouse it today do not recognize its ancient roots. Historically, it was associated with certain versions of the Fall of Man, notably that which stemmed from St. Augustine. In Nature (or Eden), so it was maintained, there was no State, no property, and no law. But the Fall, breaking the harmony of Paradise, released men from the "natural" restraints of Eden, and God ordained that their wickedness should be checked — through the authority of the State, with coercive powers; through the limitations on acquisition implied by the idea of private property; and through the constraints of positive law rather than merely pure natural

94

law. In this view, it is assumed that both political authority and coercion have arisen out of man's entry into history and civilization. If only men could cease to be wicked as individuals, the argument seems to go, then authority could disappear along with coercion.

The answer to this Augustinian conception of the Fall came, of course, with the version of St. Thomas Aquinas.[18] He argued, quite reasonably, that even if man had not fallen, authority of some kind would have existed, although without coercion. In Nature before the Fall, he maintained, it was "natural" to have a political authority — one which enabled the society to go in one direction for common ends and the common good — even though individual human beings were incapable of wrongdoing. A society has relations among its members which transcend the goodness or badness of its individual constituents, and it is these relations — or, in other terms, the patterns of the whole — which transcend individual parts that need ordering. St. Thomas, in his usual graphic way, points out that the principle of authority is characteristic even of the angels and archangels, who are arranged in hierarchies to enable the society of angels to maintain the common good. In Nature, then, even before historical civilization and hence before man's first sin, the State (or principle of deliberate or conscious social authority) exists. The Fall adds a coercive element which is designed to take account of sin; for God foresaw that man would sin, and ordained as a corrective what, before the Fall, would have itself been a sin, the principle of coercion. After the Fall coercion is added to Edenic authority and is relatively justified in light of the Fall.

The implication of this view is that even if we could "internalize" right conduct or morality in a kind of Edenic way — as anarchists and Marxists (in the ultimate stage of evolution) assume — this would remove only one and perhaps the least important dimension of the political problem. We should still have to make decisions about the good common to all, which no one individual or group of individuals, acting in their individual capacities, and however virtuous as individuals, could determine. Definitions of the common good must arise out of the group experience and be expressed through group authority, just as individual autonomy is expressed by the legitimate authority of the whole rational personality over the elements which in part make it up. Neither in the case of the group nor in that of the person does the existence of the principle of authority mean that the parts are obliterated or absorbed, for authority is designed to order or provide a framework for the relations of the parts to one another and to the whole. And political authority is not designed to supplant the self-government of the person but rather to rule that which is beyond the scope of any person — the good common to all.

Augustinian and non-Augustinian views of the problem of authority and coercion still contest for the field, even after traditional "religious" views of the world have supposedly lost their hold. "Society is created by our wants, government by our wickedness" is Tom Paine's "secularist" reminder of the Augustinian position. A Thomas-like expression will be found in the writings of Thomas Hill Green, who sees true or genuine authority as rooted in a general will that has discovered the rationally derived norms of right and of the common good.[19] When the State is perfected — and this admittedly is far from true in any historical national State — the use of coercion is eliminated. Obviously Green is here defining the State in a quasi-Hegelian way as the rational principle applied to collective affairs. We are to interpret "State," as we are to view human beings in the classical paradigm, not in terms merely of what they are now but also in light of what they are naturally striving and ought to be.

In the existential world, of course (or, using Fall of Man metaphors, in the world of civilization and history), there are sinful men and women, and thus the notion of authority is connected not merely with shaping a society to move in a common direction as a reflection of the individual-transcending common good, but also with correction of the wickedness of man. In the existential world of civilization, in other words, we have always to deal with impure authorities (and to this extent the anarchist is right), just as we have to recognize the existence of fallen men. But in acknowledging the impurity, we should also keep in mind that there may also be, in greater or lesser degree, an element of the morally authoritative. Some regimes may be so unauthoritative as not to deserve obedience, and no regime can be rationally obeyed without serious criticism of its unauthoritative elements.[20]

It is against some such background that we should view the issue of the relation of authority to freedom. Let us now return to freedom.

Politics Related to Freedom

In the preceding section and elsewhere, we made a distinction between spiritual-intellectual freedom and freedom of action. But we should never forget that these two domains are not to be seen in existence as watertight compartments; and the community authority must always keep this in mind. One cannot speak, for instance, unless one has a material platform of some kind from which to speak. Hence the exercise of spiritual freedom depends in considerable measure on how freedom in the nonspiritual realm is ordered. While Maurice Cranston may be right in criticizing Locke for seeming to equate freedom with power,[21] it is surely not exaggerating to say that in certain situations the two are closely linked: Thus the newspaper owner who wishes to express himself is far more likely to be able to do so than nine tenths of the population. The process of deliberate planning and ordering — politics — will always affect both spiritual and nonspiritual domains, just as both domains will condition and shape politics. From one point of view, in fact, politics can be looked upon as mediating between the world of "matter" and the universe of "spirit."

This can be illustrated if we return to the relation between negative and positive freedom. We have seemed to deal with negative liberties as if they were ends in themselves; and sometimes, indeed, modern discussion appears to suggest this. But they should never be seen in a vacuum; they should always be viewed in the context of positive freedom formulations. We should be free from undue restrictions on the use of our material goods not as an end in itself but because some freedom to maneuver with respect to the material world would seem to be essential to develop us as human beings in our spiritual dimensions — our capacity to become autonomous in a community of autonomous human beings, our growth in self-discipline, our training in the arts of management, all of which can be assumed to be desirable ends. Likewise, negative freedom in the spiritual domain — of expression, of religious belief, of the press, of artistic creation, and so on — should exist for the purpose of implementing positive freedom, which again can be assumed to be a good in itself.

Another way of putting this is to say that the person's spiritual freedom should be recognized and implemented by public policy to encourage him to pursue God, truth, aesthetic value, and so on. Whether in freedom of action or of spirit, we are suggesting, the person's purpose is to think desirable thoughts, do desirable deeds, perform desirable actions. But in order to develop a free personality, neither his actions nor his thought ought to be prescribed for him in detail, particularly in the spiritual domain, for by contrast with the beasts and the gods, his essence is to grow to the desirable by always running the risk of thinking or doing and having a certain amount of power to do or think the undesirable. Hence the restrictions and provisions of legislation in the realm of scarce goods should be designed to provide the optimum possible material base for all men and women to exercise negative liberty in order to liberate themselves for positive liberty. They should not be forced to be hungry, let us say, for hungry persons find it difficult voluntarily and rationally to limit their desires and to subordinate material wants to spiritual goals. Although it may be illegitimate or imprudent for positive law to prescribe all aspects of conduct, no person has a moral right to employ negative freedom in such a way as to lessen his own or others' rationality, dignity, or sense of responsibility; and to the degree that this obligation is not recognized, the

97

possibility of freedom in general is undercut. One reason the achievement of democracy seems to be impossible is because, while the "freedom" side of the coin is often demanded, the "obligation" side is ignored.

Throughout, of course, we are taking for granted the normative superiority of spiritual to temporal goods, while at the same time recognizing that the New Testament's "Man does not live by bread alone"[22] means that a certain amount of bread is essential if we are to be free to pursue those spiritual ends which ought to be held desirable in themselves; or, in other words, life must exist before we can lead the good life. An important goal of political institutions should be to assure to every individual enough material resources to carry out his or her social functions and to provide the measure of freedom from involuntary poverty that is essential to pursue his or her spiritual quest.[23] No one should have more than this, on peril of being a parasite; nor should any person possess less, lest he be reduced to the status of a mere tool or chattel slave. Propositions of this kind have an important bearing on the theory of distributive justice, which we shall examine later.

One might, of course, suggest that the purpose of policy in complex civilization should be so to design the structure of things that human beings could do or think *only* what is desirable, or at least so that they would not do or think what is undesirable. Some such conception seems to underlie much of Plato's *Republic*. The *Republic*, however, assumes that the Form of Righteousness, or Justice, has been attained, that supremely wise rulers or coordinators have been discovered, and that the true Form of Education is at hand — all of which conditions are sorely lacking, as Plato himself admits, in existence.

But even if we assume that we virtually know what is desirable in its details, such a policy ought not be be supported; for in the conception of personality suggested here, the very struggle to do the desirable — an always difficult task — is itself an element of the desirable. Even if we assume that it is undesirable for people to see *Deep Throat*, this does not justify the State's suppressing it. Here eloquent 19th-century liberal statements like those of John Stuart Mill have much to teach us.[24] They provide something usually absent from the classical paradigm.

Given the hierarchy of goods supported here and in the preceding chapter, the development of the spiritual and intellectual life of mankind would rank at the top, while material goods would be seen always as a means to the advancement of the spiritual. And among those spiritual goods would be the right of the individual to struggle to achieve his own apprehension of the good, the true, and the beautiful. Allocation of material goods by public policy should be based primarily on the notion that the purpose of politics is the encouragement of free as well as just personalities, in the sense we have suggested. All other ends must be subordinate.

Another way of defining the purpose of politics is to say that it is designed so to order the realm of scarce goods that the potentialities within each human being for becoming a free (positively free) personality will flower. The best way to ensure this flowering is an indirect one: to center any coercion on the allocation and use of material goods and to reduce the direct coercion of individuals. This would seem to be what Marxists mean when they maintain that the government of men should give way to the administration of things. We can put it in a somewhat different way: The government of things, if properly understood and implemented, can and ought gradually to supplant the direct government of men. This is preferable to the Marxist formulation insofar as Marxism, unfortunately, seems to imply the elimination of politics ("administration" has the connotation to many of "noncontroversial"). Our formulation suggests not only the continued presence of politics but its development in terms of subtlety and its transformation in terms of the methods of struggle.

In stating these broad goals, we are not suggesting that history has within it the possibility of eliminating all forms of direct coercion. Indeed, there is a sense in which the development of free personalities, as we have thought of them in these pages, is inseparable from certain forms of coercion, if the word be interpreted as relating to both the spiritual and material domains and as embracing the idea of competition. The clash of ideas and of alternative world-views is never without its coercive elements; and what we call the conflict of "personalities" might in some circumstances actually increase. But while we do not see in human history the elimination of coercion, we do envision the possibility of transmuting violent into nonviolent coercion and, frequently, nonviolent coercion into persuasion. In the following chapter we shall elaborate on this notion and in Chapter 7 seek to dramatize it in terms of the sketch of a utopia.

Such a goal, of course, is conditioned by our idea of both the potentialities and the limits of human beings in civilization. Throughout the discussion, we have constantly emphasized that there *are* limits. Nor is there anything inevitable in the attainment of the goal. It is definitely a contingent potentiality, and it is dependent on modern man's doing certain things and transforming much of his politics during the coming few generations.

But many elements in contemporary society make for a consummation of contrary goals — for an increase in violent coercion of human beings, to take one example, or for a diminution in the development of free personalities. There is the heavy weight of exploitative economic institutions. We should always remind ourselves, too, that today perhaps more of the world is living under despotical or semidespotical regimes than at the beginning of World War II. In fact, both world wars seemed to accentuate the trend toward despotism.

World War I, whatever the slogans of the so-called victors, did not serve to extend in practice the notion of constitutional and democratic rule. The war was a miserable failure, insofar as that was its ostensible purpose. For a time, to be sure, it appeared that the overthrow of Tsarism (if that can be associated in some sense with the war) was a net gain for humanity; but the initial promise turned to dust and ashes with a despotism in the Soviet Union at least as brutal as and probably more efficient than the autocracy of the Tsars. And the conduct of the victorious so-called democracies after World War I played a large role in sowing the seeds of World War II. In the United States, entry into World War I was a large factor in laying the groundwork for a vast expansion of the powers of the Presidency and for acquiescence by the American people in the principles of military conscription and potential despotism or monarchy.[25]

World War II — which in some respects can be looked upon as a continuation of World War I in an age of even more destructive technology — accelerated the trend to a breakdown of the principles of constitutionalism and aspiring democracy at the very time when those notions were allegedly being accepted by the supposed victors. Thus in the United States the monarchical Presidency was enormously encouraged, and while German despotism collapsed, Soviet despotism vastly expanded. By the seventies, torture of prisoners throughout the world was probably more widespread than it was before World War II.[26] More than ever before in modern history, the world was weighted down with armaments that did not protect human life but instead threatened all civilization with death.

Modern civilization, as much as and perhaps more than ancient civilization, seems to support the proposition that with the advance of the division of labor, the expansion of science, the explosion of technology, the development of giant population concentrations, and the proliferation of professions of faith in "the people" and "democracy," there are released destructive forces that rebel against democracy and humaneness and rationality and that escape man's all-too-feeble efforts at conscious and deliberate control of collective destiny.

In light of all this, how can we possibly hope for the development of free personalities and a corresponding decline in violent coercion? The hope would seem to depend in part on a broader and deeper understanding of freedom, power, and coercion and an emancipation from such illusions as the idea that violence can play any role in the expansion of freedom or the development of justice.

Freedom and Coercion in the Light of Equality and Fraternity

The problems of freedom and coercion, moreover, cannot be isolated from the whole texture of modern civilization. Whether freedom be interpreted as emancipation from erratic passions in the name of a wise or true self or as liberation from such external obstacles as involuntary poverty, unauthoritative coercion, or arbitrary custom and law, its achievement is surely affected in some measure by such phenomena as the state of the economy, the division of labor, and the development of the arts. Later on we shall return to these themes.

But before we can deal with them in light of the problems of justice, we must touch on the vexing issue of the relation of freedom to two other explosive concepts, those of equality and fraternity. It is important to do so both because the three concepts are connected with one another by the modern revolutionary tradition and because there has been much controversy about the supposed difficulty of linking the three.[27]

The concept of equality has played an important role in the thought of those who seek to compare a postulated Nature with civilization. In a number of the versions — those of Ovid,[28] many of the Stoics, some Christian conceptions of Eden,[29] Hobbes, and Rousseau — overall equality between and among human beings is assumed in Nature. Quite frequently, equality signifies that differences tend to cancel one another out, so that in relation to his fellows and to the Nature about him, each man is the equal of his neighbors. No man stands above another; each has an equal right to the fruits of Nature; chattel slavery is not known; there is no pattern of super- and subordination.

In certain other versions, however, Nature as defined seems to anticipate civilization. This is true in St. Thomas and Locke, for example. St. Thomas suggests, as we have seen, that in Eden patterns of super- and subordination already existed, although without coercion. In Locke's conception, although a near economic equality was the rule in the most primitive stages of the state of Nature, economic inequalities began to appear and to be justified in its later development — all before the Social Contract.[30]

When equality is seen as present in Nature, civilization tends to be emphasized as a suppressive device and, in some ways of putting it, as an artifact. On the other hand, when some inequalities are viewed as existing in Nature, then civilization often becomes simply a self-conscious working-out and a more sophisticated justification for them.

Whatever our view, it would seem clear that in the civilized state, with its growing ethical and political consciousness, we are forced to justify rationally whatever inequalities we permit.[31] If we accept the first view (equality as existing in Nature), this is necessary because all inequalities were absent in Nature; if we adopt the second, we are compelled to discriminate among types of inequality, since it is postulated that in Nature only some versions existed. If we adopt the Thomist expression of the second view, some inequalities (e.g., property) are justified because they are *added to* but not contrary to Nature, the addition being the result of the utilization of reason, which is itself an expression of teleological human nature. Thus private property is added by reason as a convenience; while it was not present in Nature, to add to Nature is not unnatural. Versions of the first view differ from one another about whether the rise of civilization is in some sense a disaster or not. For Hobbes, it is not, given his postulation about the nature of Nature. For other versions, as, for instance, that of St. Augustine, the inequalities of civilization become a kind of relatively justified punishment for original sin. In the second view, as reflected in Aristotle and St. Thomas, some types of inequality are conceived to be a blessing insofar as they reflect both the condition of primitive Nature and the development of civilization, which is associated with fulfillment of man's implicit and natural purposes.

Here we suggest that some expressions of inequality are justified in terms of legitimate functional differentiations. They do not necessarily mean coercion, nor do they run counter to legitimate claims of freedom. All civilization entails division of labor, cooperation to coordinate the work that has been subdivided, and coordinators to accomplish the coordination. But coordinating roles which involve subordination of others for specific purposes do not necessarily have to be performed by the same persons in all contexts. Thus as a teacher I may be subordinate to you as principal for certain specified purposes, the order of the school; but in the church of which we are both members, I may be a superintendent and you a subordinate choir director in carrying out the purposes of the church. As citizens of the general society, I may be a councilman helping to formulate laws which you obey; but you, with others, may turn me out at election time. Aristotle's conception of citizenship, in fact, was one in which every person took turns in ruling and being ruled. If the purposes are legitimate, we may say, if the means used are morally authoritative (do not involve, for example, the use of violent coercion), then the inequalities could conceivably be justified. But always the burden of proof must be on those who would defend inequality.

Similarly, we might justify inequalities in material goods, providing they are functionally necessary. If, as part of my function in society, I need to travel by air and you do not, then to that extent inequality is legitimate, assuming, of course, that the purpose for which I function is morally authorized. We can quite legitimately raise the question of whether every individual is entitled to material goods simply as a human being, and regardless of his particular function. Here we can lay down the general principle that he is indeed so entitled, providing he recognizes his obligation to use his capacity to serve others in the community of souls. We can rephrase these notions by suggesting that every embodied soul is entitled morally to those material goods necessary (1) to live and (2) to perform his functions as a civilized human being, provided he understands the corresponding obligation to contribute service. Since individuals in fact differ from one another in the food necessary to keep them alive and the material goods and services essential to enable them to perform their legitimate social functions, the net result will be some inequalities in the distribution of material goods. But they are inequalities based on diverse morally authorized needs, not inequalities grounded on accident of birth, or of social status, or of native ability, or of arbitrary decree, or simply of the market.

The application of this principle is, of course, never easy. In our discussion later we shall attempt to spell out some of the difficulties and implications. But it is important to state the principle at the outset, as it bears on the general issue of equality.

Given this notion of equality, what are its implications for freedom, on the one hand, and fraternity, on the other? Obviously, it will exclude some interpretations of what freedom implies. Thus we ought not to be free to act or to use our talents in such a way as to accumulate material goods beyond our need to sustain life and to perform our social and economic functions. Nor ought we to be free to act in such ways as to impair the equality of rights of all. Freedom does not include the right either to exploit others or to pass on substantial wealth to them which will enable them to live without service. It is legitimate for law to restrict our actions in all these respects. When it does, while it is seemingly constraining our negative freedom, it is also removing obstacles in the way of our becoming positively free. Law in itself cannot produce positive freedom, which is the fruit of individual struggle in the context of social or communal dialogue. But law can help remove external roadblocks to the development of positive freedom: Thus it can help shape a distributive system which will reduce or eliminate the possibility that I shall become arrogant or complacent by the possession of unfunctional wealth or power; or, contrariwise, that I shall be tempted by abject, involuntary poverty to place undue value on material goods.

Equality does not mean that all are alike. Instead, it signifies something radically different: that all have equal claims to become fully free, positively, in the kind of community without which this would be impossible. My claim to liberty ought to be equal to yours; but liberty in turn is closely related to the achievement of justice — it does not and cannot flourish in a vacuum. To the degree that I am defined in terms of my social functions — and, of course, I am far more than my social functions, as we have maintained — I am most just and dwell in a just society when I can carry out most fully the function for which I am best equipped by my teleological nature. And your claim to justice in this sense ought to be seen as equal to mine, although your niche and contribution might differ drastically from mine.

In discussing the relation of freedom to equality, we have been assuming that I have a duty to become the true self from which my existential self is somehow separated. But in order to do so, I must recognize duties to others, since my own positive freedom and true selfhood cannot be achieved without others, even though they are not simply the product of others. Again and again we have insisted that my fulfillment is in part conditioned by the degree to which I exist in a human community. Scripture proposes something very similar when it suggests that we ought to love our neighbors as ourselves. Implied in this statement would seem to be the notion that I cannot really love my neighbor unless I have great love or esteem for myself. But the reverse also appears to be true: I cannot really love myself unless I truly love my neighbor.

However we may view the problem of which comes first, love of self or love of neighbor, it is obvious that we have reached the principle of fraternity. How are we to view it, and what are its relations with liberty and equality? And how do we connect the three with the general idea of obligation or duty?

We may suggest initially that, while liberty and equality are often associated with the *rights* of the person, fraternity is above all tinctured with the idea of *obligation*. Claims to liberty and equality must always be seen in the context of obligation, involving as it does the duties which we owe both to ourselves and to others.

Obligation, signifying being bound to a course of action, must always be seen as plural. That is, a particular obligation is always closely related to other obligations. We speak of obligations to oneself, to one's work, and to God. In the first, we can perhaps say that one has an obligation to become the self that one ought to be. But before we can recognize the obligation we must become aware of the gulf which exists between the present or existential self and the true self — in religious language, perhaps, this is partly what we mean by a sense of sin. An obligation does not exist unless separation is acknowledged; but it is also meaningless to speak of obligation without freedom and power to fulfill or not to fulfill it. Thus I can hardly speak of an obligation to become my true self if I am completely shaped by forces outside myself to remain what I am.

In order to become what one ought to be, however, one must also recognize obligations to be a good worker, since labor is one important expression of one's selfhood. Obligation to self and obligation to be a good worker, in other words, are closely related. And again, the notion of obligation is connected with the freedom to fulfill or not to fulfill it.

But obligation to self cannot be sharply divorced from duties to the Author of all Being, including one's own being. One cannot have obligations without corresponding freedoms or freedoms without corresponding obligations, so that one ought to revere God, who, as the creator of humanity, is also, as the hymn puts it, the "author of liberty." When we give reverence to God, we are acknowledging our creaturehood and at the same time our dignity as free human beings, within whom there is "that of God."

These references to interweaving obligations set the stage for the obligations entailed by the idea of fraternity. Both my diverse obligations — to self, for example, to my work, to God — and my freedom and equality are intimately tied to your existence; and I cannot become what I ought to be without recognizing you as contributing to my existence and my potentialities. Likewise it is fatuous for me to speak of obligations to you and to others and the community unless I assume that I have freedom to fulfill or not to fulfill them. The very notion of obligation in this context assumes, too, that at least sometimes there is a gulf (psychic, emotional, intellectual) between me and others which I ought to bridge in order to attain the fraternity which is indispensable to both liberty and equality.

We ought to seek freedom to become our rational selves, and we endeavor to overcome hindrances which might impair that quest. In the process, certain other hindrances might legitimately be imposed. Which external obstacles must be removed and which imposed will depend on the context and probable effects of the removal or imposition. The movement to give the vote to 18-year-olds was animated in part by the belief that removing the restrictions of the 21-year-old ballot law (negative freedom) would, by encouraging the civic activity essential for the development of the rational self, provide a context within which the 18-year-old could advance toward the goal (positive freedom). On the other hand, many states have statutes forbidding the sale of liquor on election day, and such laws could perhaps be justified by Green's reasoning — by drying up the flow of liquor through a legal restriction, we would actually be promoting the freedom of the individual to be his rational self as a voter.[32] But the context for both laws would be the civic community and the obligations of its members to one another. The right to vote carries with it the obligation to vote rationally and after deliberation, and implicit in the arguments for both statutes would be the notion that the individual cannot entirely separate his own fate from that of others. My destiny and yours are always commingled, and neither freedom nor equality can be fully understood, except in the framework of fraternity.

The idea of fraternity has been treated in terms of history,[33] but here we wish simply to characterize its general hallmarks. Broadly speaking, it represents the conception of brotherhood as indispensable both for personal development of rational freedom in civilization and for the community which is so essential to develop deliberate control of collective affairs (politics). I can be free and equal, the idea of fraternity suggests, only in a community; and community, as we have hinted earlier, is built on a sense of oneness or we-ness among human beings.

In terms of the social psychology stemming from thinkers like Hegel,[34] what I am depends in some measure on what you think me to be, and vice versa. Mutual recognition of one another as beings entitled to respect and yearning for love is the condition for any true politics. Without this, violence is ever lurking not far beneath the surface, and violence always undermines and negates the political.

From a somewhat different perspective, the possibility of community may be undergirded and reinforced when we recognize that individual psychic experience may be only one dimension of "mind." Many modern thinkers have suggested, as we noted earlier, that there may be a kind of "group mind" or racial memory which we tap and through which we develop common symbolism, even across cultures.[35] A conception of "mind" as only individualized, if one accepts this view, is very inadequate, for it ignores the realm of the collective unconscious and the very real sense of potential psychic unity. Although all this seems very "mystical" and therefore, according to some modes of thought, irrelevant, it is in fact highly pertinent for the idea of fraternity.

It is often said, and with some justice, that while the American experience has placed great emphasis on negative freedom and equality, it has largely ignored the conception of fraternity. Although there is an element of exaggeration in many such statements, still by and large they have much validity. Freedom, as this distorted view seems to conceive it, means the opportunity to acquire material possessions endlessly, or to expand our individual power over others, or to manipulate or dominate Nature without any sense of obligation. Politics itself, in much American thought, is seen to be simply a struggle between and among possessive individualists and special-interest groups, the results of which can at best be only a kind of compromise and never the discovery of a "good" common to all.[36]

ON JUSTICE: THE IDEA OF LIBERTY, EQUALITY, AND FRATERNITY

Perhaps one reason so many are disillusioned about the American version of politics is because, by stressing freedom and equality almost to the exclusion of fraternity, American culture has opened the way for some of the more depressing aspects of human nature. Liberty and equality, divorced from fraternity, often mean the liberty to exploit and manipulate and equal claims to carry out the exploitation and manipulation.

But the problem of fraternity in modern civilization is more than that of restoring it to its rightful place in the context of liberty and equality. We have also to recognize that even when we accept the conception of fraternity, its interpretations may lead to conflict. In the preceding chapter we suggested that one dimension of justice is full recognition of man's threefold teleological nature — to be an eccentric, to associate with some but not all, and, in yet other respects, to be a universal human being like all others. Each of these ends is essential if man is to be free in a positive sense. Each, moreover, is conditioned by or closely related to the idea of fraternity, man as eccentric arising out of pluralistic and universal dimensions of fraternity. But despite these relations, a problem arises in terms of the intensity of the fraternal bond. Referring to old Stoic conceptualizations, can the *civitas*, with its intimacy and its conflicts with other "cities," be reconciled with the usually less intense bonds tying human beings to humanity as a whole? This becomes particularly acute in modern civilization when intimate communities themselves (extended or nuclear families, small towns, and so on) are broken up by onrushing technological "progress," and rather tenuous *extensive* bonds tend to take the place of *intensive* ones. We shall be returning to this theme, which is celebrated in so much modern literature.

Freedom, equality, fraternity are linked inseparably to one another. Freedom, whether negative or positive, spiritual or related to action, cannot be implemented fully without recognition of the equal claims of human beings to its exercise. But while equality suggests that my claim to freedom is on a parity with yours, it does not signify that we are identical. We have equal claims to the material goods we need to sustain ourselves and to fulfill our particular social and economic functions in life, and any functional differentiation must be strictly interpreted, so that it does not become a cover for domination. But neither freedom nor equality can be fully understood without reference to fraternity and our obligations to others, who are indispensable for our own achievement of rational selfhood. In the long run, it can be said, I cannot be "saved" — cannot free my teleologically natural self — unless you, too, are on the road to salvation.

Although the general principles of liberty, equality, and fraternity may thus be somewhat clarified and their implications drawn out, their

NATURE AND CIVILIZATION

achievement in a complex civilization always tends to be frustrated by certain tendencies in the civilization. These tendencies lead to the despair of civilization and all its works which is characteristic of thinkers supporting the civilization-as-corrupting paradigm. Others see them as challenges to be overcome or prevented, as in the classical outlook, or as factors which somehow will inevitably be transcended, as in some versions of the civilization-as-preparation perspective.

To these frustrating tendencies we turn in the next chapter.

Notes

1 See Plato's *Statesman.*

2 Carl Jung, *Modern Man in Search of a Soul* (London: Kegan Paul, Trench, Truebner, 1933).

3 See, for example, E. V. Walter, *Terror and Resistance* (New York: Oxford University Press, 1969).

4 See Jacques Maritain, *Scholasticism and Politics* (New York: Macmillan Co., 1940).

5 Ayn Rand, *The Fountainhead* (New York: New American Library, 1961) and *Atlas Shrugged* (New York: Random House, 1957).

6 H. G. Wells suggested this very vividly many years ago. See his "The Scepticism of the Instrument," appendix to *A Modern Utopia* (New York: Scribner's, 1905).

7 Sir Alister Hardy, *The Living Stream: Evolution and Man* (London: Collins, 1965).

8 Oliver Sacks, "The Nature of Consciousness," *Harper's,* December 1975, p. 5.

9 Mortimer Adler, in his *The Idea of Freedom,* 2 vols. (Garden City, N.Y.: Doubleday, 1958-61), examines many conceptions and subconceptions of freedom. We are suggesting, however, that the three noted in the text are fundamental.

10 The problem bothered St. Augustine. While he wished to vindicate man's freedom of the will, he yet had to maintain the sovereignty of God. As is well known, he seeks to differentiate God's foreknowledge of what man will do and will choose from any interpretation which would see God as *determining* man's "choices." See St. Augustine, *The City of God,* trans. John Healey (London: J. M. Dent, 1931), Bk. V, ch. 10.

11 C. E. M. Joad, *Guide to the Philosophy of Morals and Politics* (New York: Random House, 1938).

12 B. F. Skinner, *Beyond Freedom and Dignity* (New York: Alfred A. Knopf, 1971).

13 See Epictetus, "Discourses," in Whitney J. Oates, ed., *The Stoic and Epicurean Philosophers* (New York: Random House, 1940).

14 Quoted by W. R. Inge, *The Philosophy of Plotinus,* 2 vols. (London: Longmans, Green, 1948), vol. 2, p. 189.

15   In Hobbes-like views, of course, "desires" tend to be associated with lust for ego inflation and domination.

16   Thus legislation, according to one school of thought, enhances freedom in this sense. This certainly seems to be the position of Thomas Hill Green in *Lectures on the Principles of Political Obligation* (London: Longmans Green, 1895). As is well known, he saw the legal prohibition of liquor as perhaps falling into this category.

17   Part of the anarchist's problem, it would seem, is that he sometimes fails to distinguish between authority and power. Society will be "ruled" in any event — either by standards fixed beforehand and then implemented or by ad hoc actions of various kinds, some of which (e.g., "lynch law") might be very dangerous; and the former kind of "rule" would seem to be more acceptable and less deleterious to human personality than the latter.

18   See Thomas Gilby, *The Political Philosophy of St. Thomas Aquinas* (Chicago: University of Chicago Press, 1958) and *Between Community and Society* (New York: Longmans, Green, 1953).

19   Green, *Principles of Political Obligation,* particularly the section on "Will, Not Force, Is the Basis of the State."

20   See Mulford Q. Sibley, *The Obligation to Disobey: Conscience and the Law* (New York: Council on Religion and International Affairs, 1970).

21   Maurice Cranston, *Freedom: A New Analysis* (London: Longmans, Green, 1953).

22   Or, as the American translation puts it, "The Scripture says, 'Not by bread alone is man to live, but on every word that comes from the mouth of God!' " Matthew, IV:4.

23   A theme treated particularly in R. H. Tawney, *The Acquisitive Society* (New York: Harcourt, Brace, 1920) and *Equality* (London: G. Allen & Unwin, 1931).

24   John Stuart Mill's *On Liberty* (London: J. W. Parker & Son, 1859), despite the many criticisms directed at it in the 20th century, is still a very plausible and persuasive statement insofar as it refers to spiritual as contrasted with economic liberty.

25   It could be argued that it was entry into World War I, more than any other single event, which seemed to provide the occasion and justification for expanded executive prerogatives. The military conscription enacted was without precedent in American history; while it had existed during the Civil War, its enforcement then was sporadic by comparison with the implementation of World War I conscription. In his attitudes, too, President Wilson demonstrated all the tendencies often associated with monarchs of the past — imperiousness, jealousy of status, intolerance of dissent, and self-righteousness. His attitude to Eugene V. Debs, the Socialist leader imprisoned for his opposition to the war, appeared to be rather unforgiving.

26   While it is impossible to document any such comparison, increasing interest in the problem of torture during the sixties and seventies has stimulated efforts to become more exact in its analysis and in the assessment of its extent. See Amnesty

NATURE AND CIVILIZATION

International, *Report on Torture* (New York: Farrar, Straus & Giroux, 1973, 1975).

27 Thus Erik von Kühnelt-Leddihn, in *Liberty and Equality* (Caldwell, Idaho: Caxton Printers, 1952), contends that liberty and equality are in tension and that we should prefer liberty to equality. Some have contended, too, that while American history has stressed both liberty and equality, it has neglected the idea of fraternity. But see Wilson Carey McWilliams, *The Idea of Fraternity in American History* (Berkeley: University of California Press, 1973).

28 In the *Metamorphoses,* Eng. trans. Frank Justus Miller (London: W. Heinemann, 1916).

29 That of St. Augustine, for example.

30 The inequalities before the Contract have arisen in part through the invention of money, which enables human beings to "save" surplus. In "Nature," one is very limited in what one can save without its spoiling, and to allow things to spoil is against the law of Nature.

31 This seems to be the position of John Rawls in his treatise *The Theory of Justice* (Cambridge, Mass.: Harvard University Press, 1971). The "original position" is apparently one of equality, and all inequalities must be justified. We can say that the burden of proof must be on those who would establish inequalities.

32 Green, *Principles of Political Obligation.*

33 See, for example, McWilliams, *Fraternity in American History.*

34 Or like some of those who carry on his tradition, such as George Herbert Mead in his *Mind, Self, and Society* (Chicago: University of Chicago Press, 1934).

35 See, for example, Carl Jung, *The Structure and Dynamics of the Psyche* in *Collected Works* (New York: Pantheon Books, 1953 —), vol. 8, and *Man and His Symbols* (Garden City, N.Y.: Doubleday, 1964).

36 This seems to be a major tendency in American political science itself. Its very proclivity for defining politics as "power" is part of the tendency. Rarely does one find an identification of politics, in "orthodox" literature, with "ideals," to cite only one alternative. Note Bernard Crick, *The American Science of Politics* (Berkeley: University of California Press, 1959).

FOUR

On Justice: Obstacles to Liberty, Equality, and Fraternity

W E HAVE OUTLINED the general idea of justice in civilization and drawn out some of its meanings with respect to the trinity of liberty, equality, and fraternity. Now, in this chapter, we examine some of the factors in civilization that tend to inhibit, restrict, or frustrate achievement of the goal.

Challenges come from a number of sources. Broadly speaking, they develop because, as man moves from Nature to civilization, he becomes puzzled about what to do with the multifarious choices which open before him, and, having a merely human understanding, he finds it difficult to project the consequences of given acts. The greater the complexity beyond a certain point (which may be difficult to define), the more compounded his problem of deliberately controlling events, and man then becomes subject to the coercions of external forces which the development of civilization itself has unleashed. Even assuming that man is clear about his goals and that the language through which he communicates is unambiguous — and neither of these assumptions can be taken for granted — he quarrels about means of implementing objectives, and his very attempts to order the chaotic factors of history lead to the danger that his instrumentalities for ordering will destroy rather than maintain the potentialities for freedom, equality, and fraternity.

But this is a very general statement. Let us become more explicit. Here our interpretation is neither a Tolstoyan one, which emphasizes civilization as enslaving, nor a Marxist-liberal conception, with its tendency to view the development of complex civilization, in the long run, as inevitably liberating. Reserving specific comments on the technological and economic problems for the following two chapters, we center in this chapter on civilizational challenges which include (1) the erosion of the will for freedom, (2) the effects of bureaucracy, (3) the distortions of law, (4) the perils of both over- and undercentralization and integration, (5) the tendency to monarchy and tyranny, (6) the problematics of community and communication, and (7) the danger of violent coercion. All, we contend, become focal points for frustrating the achievement of justice, particularly as it relates to the idea of liberty, equality, and fraternity.

The Erosion of the Will for Freedom

Modern civilization, as we have seen, pulls persons away from one another through division of labor and, in this fragmented state, to some degree it isolates them, making them feel helpless. The traditional community — often small-scale and associated so frequently with slow social change — has been lost, and modern man has not yet discovered the basis for a new one.[1] Under such circumstances, millions of human beings often feel alienated and powerless. While they are thus in principle released by civilization to be free, paradoxically they often find that their will to be free is declining. Where they have the vote, they do not use it, or they use it unreflectively and become simply the voting instruments of leaders whose pronunciamentos they uncritically accept.[2] Where they have the legal right to speak freely, they do not do so; where education is available without payment of individual fees, they barely take advantage of it.

As we look back on ancient politics, we may condemn the masses of Rome who were provided with bread and circuses by their overlords. We note that the ancient proletariat seemed to be satisfied and that the ruling classes profited enormously because of their satisfaction. But modern civilization, too, has its bread and circuses: athletics, which absorb fantastic quantities of energy and time; elaborately organized and State-sponsored recreational schemes that divert the attention of the masses from political issues; and development of the trappings of monarchy, even in supposedly republican countries like the United States.

Sometimes we condemn those who organize these spectacles and who encourage mass participation in them. We say that the media or the ruling classes are manipulating human beings, often for their own ends. This is true, of course. But the other side of the coin is that large numbers of people are often willing to be manipulated and eager to be deceived. Like ancient kings who executed messengers who brought bad tidings, the modern masses frequently dismiss politicians who attempt to speak unpleasant truths. Thus in the financial crises afflicting New York City during the seventies, we saw the fruit of the failure of politicians over decades to be frank.[3] But their obfuscations and too-easy optimism were partly motivated by their fear that if they were indeed honest they might be defeated.

Why are great masses of human beings so gullible and manipulable? This is an ancient question, articulated classically in the comedies of Aristophanes.[4] Answers to it have varied; we can interpret Aristotle as saying that a considerable part of mankind is comprised of "slaves" by nature, meant to be the tools of those who are not slavish. When given political freedom, these people do not make genuine choices but submit themselves to direction by others.

Although exponents of inevitable progress and liberals in general intensely dislike the theory of "natural slavery," we cannot dismiss it out of hand. It must be kept as one kind of possible explanation, in view of the history of the past 150 years. It was frequently contended during the early part of the 19th century that if only the suffrage were extended and men were given greater leisure through expansion of technology, the intensity and extent of civic participation would be magnified, and human beings would respond to the call of positive freedom. It is at least debatable whether this has in fact happened, so that the doctrine of natural slavery must still be retained as a possible hypothesis for the behavior of at least some.

On the other hand, it is doubtful whether it is in itself an adequate hypothesis. Surely one factor is that the sheer scope and heterogeneity of modern political society make most human beings feel even more powerless than they might otherwise have believed themselves to be. Instead of being one ten-thousandth of a small town, each might feel himself wiped out in a would-be community of 40 or 200 million. Feeling so helpless, a kind of fatalism undoubtedly captures him, so that he asks himself, "What's the use?"

As Roberto Michel's classic study *Political Parties* pointed out many years ago, complex organization, by its very nature, seems to encourage "oligarchy,"[5] for the tasks of coordination are those that require vigorous activities of relatively small numbers and not of masses. One does not have to postulate power-hungry men (although they may, of course, exist, and in large numbers) to account for the tendency to oligarchy in complex organization. But whatever the explanation of the tendency to oligarchy, it would seem to be a fact, and its very existence is probably an important factor in accounting for erosion of the will to freedom.

That size and complexity of the organization or society are indeed important variables in accounting for alienation and manipulability would seem to be supported by studies of participation in labor unions. Other things being equal, apparently, the smaller the union, the greater the degree of participation in union meetings and in union affairs generally.[6] While there are always some who can rise above this factor of size and complexity and remain active despite the political alienation of their fellows, there would seem to be little doubt that the absence of a genuine small-community base discourages many human beings from the struggle to be autonomous. As they become passive, for a variety of reasons, they tend to be putty in the hands of those skilled in the arts of manipulation and prevarication.

Under these circumstances, people acquiesce in decisions made by oligarchies, elites, and owners of great wealth, whose power expands in proportion to the decline of the will to freedom. As that will is eroded, one of the most vital elements in the development of power, the impetus to organize for the achievement of objectives, also declines. Thus organized minorities develop an enormous capacity to control unorganized masses, whose mental attitudes are both the root and the fruit of their unwillingness (or apparent inability) to organize.

The factors which tend to erode the will to freedom, then, become the root of despotism and tyranny in modern civilization, as they were in ancient civilization. These factors themselves may be interrelated and complex — sociological, psychological, and spiritual — but their fruits in passivity and the tendency to unreflective and uncritical obedience and acquiescence account for the widespread existence of dictatorship. "There are no tyrants," a French thinker, Anselm Bellegarrigue, is reputed to have said in the 19th century, "only slaves."[7] While views of this kind and those expressed by Erich Fromm[8] may to some degree be exaggerated, there is a large measure of validity in them. The classical paradigm's insistence that the political community must be limited in size and population is in part rooted in this consideration: If, it argues, you wish active citizens with a sense of their own worth and a will to positive freedom, then only a *polis*-type community will make this possible. When Plato unfavorably contrasts the Persian Empire with the idea of the *polis*, this consideration weighs heavily with him.[9] Unfortunately, the modern liberal and Marxist views largely appear to have forgotten this, and conceptions like that of the inevitable-progress outlook seem to assume that the issue is largely irrelevant.

The question of the erosion of the will to freedom is, of course, closely

114

associated with the problem of power. To assert that there are no tyrants but only slaves says much about the nature of power in human relations. It suggests that power is a two-way affair, the line moving not merely from the power holder to the supposed subject of power but also from the subject to the power holder. If the subject is passive or has lost the will to be free, that is the signal to the power holder to expand his manipulations and extend his tyranny. If power in society be the ability of one person or claimed authority to get others to do what he or it wishes them to do, then the successful use of power is not merely a matter of the initiator or leader demanding (on threat of punishment) that others obey him; it also turns on the desires, emotions, attitudes, and beliefs of the persons who are supposed to obey or favorably respond.

The producer of beef, for example, can have little power over the vegetarian (although he will, to be sure, restrict the choices of the vegetarian insofar as he and other beef producers have managed to preempt good land for beef-producing purposes, thus making that land unavailable for production of vegetables). In general, as the notion of positive freedom suggests, the more extensive our desires, the greater will be the power over us of those who can (by reason of personality or social structures) satisfy our desires. Correspondingly, the fewer our desires (for fame, material goods, prestige, and so on), the less likely are others to be able to direct us. An ascetic with no great love for this earthly existence would be much freer in a positive sense than one enamored of wine, women, song, status, and prestige.

Belief systems, desires, fears, and fearlessness are interwoven in the structure of power relations and in the failure of powerholders to gain obedience. No matter how much a Roman official threatened a Christian with death unless the Christian sacrificed to the genius of the emperor, he could not get the Christian to do what he wanted him to do (that is, he was powerless vis-à-vis the Christian) if the Christian believed that sacrificing was a heinous sin and that suffering death was a small price to pay for avoiding the sin.

The power of the Pope during the high Middle Ages basically depended on a widely held belief system, some of the ingredients of which were that only the visible church could authorize holy communion and the other sacraments; that without access to the sacraments, one might suffer the pains of Hell; and that the Pope could impose interdicts and excommunications which would have not only temporal but also eternal consequences. When beliefs in propositions of this kind started to decline, the ability of the Pope to control kings and commoners in their temporal relations — the Pope's power, in other words — began to erode also.

If power holders circumscribe what we think should be our negative freedom, it is in part because we have either negative or positive commitments which allow the power holders to do so. We are in some measure responsible for our own enslavement.

To be sure, the initiator or leader in power relations, or (if we wish) the challenger, can, by appealing to the belief systems of some, often make the responses of others very difficult and their options highly restricted and disagreeable. Thus because Roman soldiers believed that they should obey the emperor in all things, Caesar could compel the Christian to choose between death and sacrifice to his genius. But the basis for his being able to force this painful choice was that thousands of persons — soldiers and officials — believed (for whatever reasons) that they should obey the emperor in whatever he commanded. And other millions believed that they should pay taxes to him. If those soldiers and officials — or even a substantial part of them — should ever have reached the conclusion that they should not obey him, the emperor would have been powerless to force a painful choice on the Christian. Even with thousands of officials and soldiers believing that they should indeed obey him, he was powerless to get the conscientious Christian to sacrifice, given the Christian's attitude to suffering and death. The Christian's response to the challenge of the emperor was a counterchallenge: "You can have no power to get me to do your will, for I simply do not accept your idea that suffering death rather than sacrificing is the supreme evil. Holding these views, I checkmate and frustrate your power."

The Christian's attitude turned on his acceptance of a whole series of commitments not shared by the emperor or his supporters, including his refusal to consider the act of suffering death for a conviction the greatest evil. Given his allegiance to these propositions, and even in the absence of strong political organization on his side, he was able to prevent the emperor and all his cohorts from inducing him to do their will.

What applied to imperial-Christian relations is also relevant to problems of political power and freedom in modern society. Underlying what we call the imbalances and inequities of power relations in the modern world is acceptance of a set of beliefs which makes those relations possible.[10] Thus because most persons either believe or acquiesce in the belief and tradition that large armaments defend human life, we are in an arms race that seems never to end.

Or consider the role of beliefs in the politics of Watergate. We customarily think of it as a kind of conspiracy on the part of some officials to obstruct justice and "abuse" power. The political community, we say, is the victim of this conspiracy, and there is a measure of validity in this diagnosis. But we should never forget that the abuse of power and obstruction of justice would probably never have taken place — or at least would have been much less serious — had it not been for a whole set of beliefs which allowed the Presidency to become essentially a monarchical institution. For years (indeed, since at least the Presidency of Theodore Roosevelt)[11] American beliefs — those of Congress, the President, and the American people generally — had tended increasingly to be built around certain propositions which were rarely if ever questioned, even by scholars. Such beliefs included those that maintained that (1) a "strong" Presidency is essential if we are to have "progressive" legislation (a belief particularly dear to many liberals); (2) some parts of the public business ought to be carried on in secret (this permitted a vast and irresponsible expansion of agencies like the CIA);[12] (3) "national security" matters should be exempt from ordinary regulations about wiretapping; (4) Presidents are not subject to indictment and prosecution while in office; (5) it would be terrible or even unthinkable if a President were to be forced to go to jail; (6) generally speaking, Presidents do not violate the law, although corruption and law violation may be attributed to their agents; (7) Presidents may legitimately lie to the American people where national security and international relations are concerned.[13]

If we combine these and similar beliefs that are held very widely in American culture, we can account for much of the politics of Watergate, including the pardon of ex-President Richard Nixon by President Gerald Ford. Had beliefs of this kind not been very widespread and deeply held, it is entirely possible that the abuse of power and obstruction of justice would or could never have occurred. Here again we find illustrated the notion that beliefs or at least acquiescence in beliefs constitute a very indispensable element in what we call power. And if the beliefs are held uncritically and are not periodically reexamined, it implies that thousands, if not millions, of human beings have in effect enslaved themselves.

Throughout the world and in the history of civilization generally, one of the perennial issues of power relations has been that of landlord and peasant. The latter, we say, has been exploited by the former. Through control of the land and alliances with other elements of the ruling class, the landlord often has power of life and death over those who work on the land, and the "peasant problem" has been the focus of much of historical and contemporary politics.[14] Now all this is true, yet it is not the whole truth. For the power of the landlord rests as much on the attitudes and beliefs of peasants themselves as it does on any independent capacity by the landlord to control them. Peasants often think of themselves as inferior or have not troubled to ask themselves whether or not they ought to be inferior. Frequently, they have thought of the landowner as a kind of god. When they do become aware in some measure that the landlord is gouging them through high interest rates or similar devices, they believe they cannot do anything about it. A change in such beliefs could completely erode the supposed power of the landlord, but this would require first the self-emancipation of the peasant. For example, one belief of the peasant might be that without weapons he cannot oppose the landlord. Once he begins to believe in the power of organization and of the concerted strike, he might come to see that weapons are not only not necessary but are even hindrances in his quest for emancipation from "arbitrary power."

Why has the phenomenon of imperialism been so ubiquitous in the history of civilization? We can analyze it from the viewpoint of the desire of states to expand, a supposed lust for power, the competition for markets and land, the search for security, and so on. But also crucial for understanding imperialism as well as other power phenomena are implicit or explicit belief systems. In the Platonic analysis of imperialism, for instance, its impetus is traced to the tendency for human material desires to become insatiable after a certain stage in the evolution of humanity.[15] Since those desires cannot be fulfilled within the existing territory of the country or with its own natural resources, the state seizes a slice of its neighbor's territory.

If this account has validity, then imperialism arises in some measure out of the belief that we ought to have material goods almost without limit, or we implicitly refuse to check our desires, which tend to be insatiable. If large masses of men were to act on operative belief systems that repudiate limitless desires, presumably the "social forces" making for imperialism — which we sometimes think of as impersonal and beyond control — would be stopped in their tracks. Beliefs play a very vital role, too, in the ability of an imperialist nation to conquer its neighbor: If, for whatever reason, the population is slavish or has easily acquiesced in its previous ruler, the conqueror will probably have little difficulty. If, however, there is a widespread and intense belief that men and women should refuse to cooperate with the conqueror, then the latter will find it virtually impossible to carry out his imperial designs. Freedom of the nation is thus dependent on a strong will to freedom on the part of citizens, and a will to freedom must be closely connected with willingness to challenge and question the orthodox belief systems upon which existing power relations have been built.

The military has power over conscripts and can often treat them as things rather than as persons because thousands of individuals (in the judiciary, police, the army itself, and elsewhere) believe in the necessity of conscription or, if they have doubts, believe in their duty to obey those who do not have doubts. The conscripts themselves contribute to the power because they believe that it is better to be treated as things than to go to jail.

Putting all this in another way, it is always a temptation to blame the inequities involved in distribution of freedom and power on wicked or ambitious men or on evil systems. Without denying that there are indeed wicked men or that evil systems (economic, political, social) have a kind of autonomy of their own which enables them to cast spells on every generation, it remains nevertheless true that wicked men and evil systems continue to have power because millions (for whatever reasons) acquiesce in their wickedness or fear the consequences for themselves if they do not acquiesce.

In some measure, Hobbes is right when he suggests fear as an important factor in accounting for the hierarchies characteristic of civilization. Although his view is far too simplistic in seeking to reduce altruism and love of neighbor to fear for our own lives, he is right in thinking of fear as a significant ingredient in political behavior. In the cities of complex civilization, as studies have shown,[16] we sometimes fear to assist a neighbor who is being robbed because we are fearful of the robber or of the police, who might misinterpret what we have done. Or we may fear for our livelihoods and so refrain from speaking out about corrupt industrial or political systems. The conscript who is morally repelled by war nevertheless will not refuse to enter the armed services because he fears jail or public hostility or possibly death.

Fear is closely associated with the slavishness to which we have referred, and both are foundation stones for tyranny. One of the reasons fearlessness is so stressed in the writings of classical political philosophers is that it is thought of as a pillar of civic virtue. As the Polish philosopher Wincenty Lutoslawski points out in one of his studies based on Platonism, if most of us could overcome fear of suffering and death, no tyranny or despotism could flourish for long.[17] It is fear of death which constitutes at least part of our slavery and often leads us to be silent when tyranny begins and to cooperate with it after it has arisen. And as civilization becomes more complex, fear often seems to be enhanced: Our relations with others are often on an impersonal level, and we have only indirect or vicarious knowledge about so many things that the psychology of fear expands, expressing itself most dramatically in the insecurities and brutality of international relations.

Fear, in turn, is not unconnected with our general belief system. While it is a perfectly normal and "natural" emotion in the face of danger, one of the potentialities of man in civilization is that he can revolt against fear and cease to be subject to its domination. This was certainly true of many of the early Christians who, once they came firmly to believe in the principle of love, even of enemies, became fearless. One of them wrote, as a matter of fact, that "Perfect love casts out fear."[18]

119

One of the attributes which presumably distinguishes the human being from plants or animals is that he does not have to respond automatically and instinctually — in biologically programmed ways — to danger and the threat of death. He can, by taking thought and through the development of character, respond in ways which are unnatural in the primitivist sense of that term but not unnatural in the teleological sense. As T. H. Huxley put it long ago, writing in the context of Social Darwinist conceptions of Nature, man's task is to revolt against Nature in many respects and thus to create a human nature that is distinctive.[19]

Hence a thoroughgoing commitment to the belief that the human soul is immortal might have direct political relevance. It might imply that physical death is a relatively minor evil, and thus the human being might not fear the soldiers of the tyrant even if they were instructed to kill him as a resister. As it is today, while many of us, in words, profess belief in immortality, for the most part we do not mean it. We value the body more than the essence of ourselves as human beings — the substance at the foundation of each of us which, as Socrates and Plato argued, cannot undergo the change which we know as death.

Even without an operative belief in immortality, men and women can, of course, demonstrate courage and fearlessness. Indeed, in a sense and from one point of view, it is more courageous to risk death in opposing tyranny without belief in immortality than it is to do so with such a commitment.

At any rate, courage is a civic and political virtue of enormous importance. Fear, lack of self-respect, and slavish attitudes go hand in hand and lie at the root of despotism, maldistribution of wealth, social injustice, war, and erosion of the will for freedom.

All this has been recognized by persons like Mohandas Gandhi and Martin Luther King, Jr. Gandhi was constantly reiterating that his main problem in the Indian freedom movement was not the British rulers but rather the slavish and fear-dominated Indians. Until and unless slavish attitudes are overcome, the germs of tyranny will always exist. King interpreted the central problem of the civil rights movement in much the same way: While blacks had been formally emancipated a century before, they still maintained attitudes of subservience which prevented their 20th-century emancipation.[20]

But always the issue turns on what leads to attitudes of subservience. Those who think in terms of economic determinism or Marxists who hold that shifts in the mode of production ultimately shape "consciousness" tend to argue that attitudes of subservience will change as capitalism gives way to socialism. And our experience does indeed suggest that the "objective situation" can shake us out of subservience and slavishness. The American civil rights movement did not really become vital in politics until after the relative economic and social situation of blacks had begun to improve; revolutions are often made, as is increasingly recognized, not by those who are at the bottom of the heap economically but rather by those who are on the way up. But even admitting this, we must still ask how long the newly awakened will retain their will for freedom. Political history at this point is not entirely reassuring, for even the ostensibly emancipated seem often to return to attitudes of subservience. The tendency to flee from freedom, with its responsibilities and uncertainties, seems to be ubiquitous. Independent thinkers in politics are astonishingly rare, even when their economic situation gives them the leisure to think. The springtime of the Russian Revolution lasted a few years at best; Mohandas Gandhi's India gave way to Indira Gandhi's; and American blacks, by and large, show every promise of fitting nicely and without much thought into the predominant "bourgeois" culture.

At this point we are reminded again of the tension between negative- and positive-freedom conceptions. Advocates of the former, with some justification, will maintain that removal of such external impediments as inequitable laws, gross disproportions of power, morally outrageous allocations of wealth, and judicial rulings colored by class interest can indeed open the way to freedom. But positive-freedom formulators can, with similar plausibility, maintain that, while elimination of external restraints is no doubt a boon, in itself it is no guarantee that human beings will become free in a positive sense. They may still be enslaved by sloth, fear of freedom, dread of uncertainty, rebellion against their potentially rational selves, and uncritical acceptance of charismatic leaders.

In sum, the problem of the erosion of the will to freedom is many faceted, and no single political philosophy or psychological-social theory is likely to grasp all of its dimensions. We should not reject out of hand Aristotle's hypothesis of natural slavery. At the same time, it would appear that we can do much to understand the psychological and social roots of slavishness and, with that understanding, seek to destroy them. Thus we should fully comprehend that inequitable power relations are always at least a two-way affair, involving both the initiator or power holder and the persons subject to power, who by their attitudes and desires condition and potentially limit the power of the former. We suggest that these attitudes and desires can be affected by the implicit or explicit belief systems to which human beings commit themselves, but these belief systems may in turn be conditioned by the nature of the socioeconomic structure. The objective economic situation may indeed shake human beings out of customary attitudes of subservience, but there is no certainty that they may not fall back into a similar subservience, even if legislative or other change improves their economic status.

The psychology of fear, we have suggested, is at the heart of much tyranny, and a genuine belief, both intellectual and emotional, in immortality could play a role in the elimination of fear. Man does not need to be dominated by his biologically "natural" reactions. Instead, he can create distinctively human ones which escape what is primitively natural; thus instead of reacting to physical attack by physical retaliation, he can deliberately choose the discipline of nonviolent resistance. It may be, too, that the size and scale of social organization play important roles in providing frameworks within which human beings do or do not act the part of slaves; relatively large and complex structures, other things being equal, discourage the will to freedom. And it does seem to be true that the will to freedom can vary considerably from civilization to civilization.[21]

We speculate here that, in addition to size and scale, other social factors which bear on the development of the will to freedom include distribution of income, nature of the class structure, and degree to which individuals are economically independent. Gross disparities in income distribution, class divisions that are rigid and difficult to breach, and income structures subject to such arbitrary and erratic factors as inflation, depression, and political despotism tend to make human beings hopeless and to erode the will to freedom. Always, of course, there is a kind of circularity about issues of this kind: the erosion of the will to freedom leads to despotism but despotism, to the degree that it makes men hopeless, erodes the will to freedom; rigid class systems may lead to personal despair or slavish attitudes, but personal despair and slavish attitudes contribute to the creation of rigid class systems in the first place; inequitable income distribution, if it undermines hope or contributes to fear, may stimulate slavish attitudes on the part of the deprived, but it is equally true that slavish attitudes enable the few to seize disproportionate parts of the income. So long as we recognize such circularities, however, we are justified in at least seeking correlations between social, political, and psychological conditions, on the one hand, and erosion of the will to freedom, on the other.

Justice, Freedom, and Bureaucracy

Bureaucratic coordination would appear to be a well-nigh inevitable accompaniment of complex civilization, with elements of it contributing to the idea of freedom in justice but with other elements running counter to the idea. The term "bureaucracy" itself we are using both in its simple sense as administrative organization arranged in a hierarchy, with professionalism, and, with Max Weber and others,[22] as a scheme emphasizing such values as impersonalism, rationalization, and impartiality.

As the relatively agrarian Roman Republic gave way to imperial civilization, for example, the old largely nonprofessional magistracies were for the most part replaced by bureaucratically arranged professional administrators, the whole structure reaching its greatest development in the reigns of Diocletian and his successors.[23] During the early part of the Middle Ages, when division of labor became less involved, the arts lost much of their sophistication, and cities like Rome became villages frequented by howling wolves, older bureaucratic organization surrendered to slow-changing customary rule and the highly chaotic feudal-manorial system. But as city life began to revive and the universal church emerged victorious over the territorial church conception, characteristically bureaucratic modes of organization made their appearance again. Thus the Inquisition exemplified many of the hallmarks of bureaucracy: major documents to be made out in quadruplicate, a sense of hierarchy, strict lines of responsibility, and a tendency to become autonomous and to make its own self-perpetuation the central end (at times, it even defied papal authority).[24] In the modern large corporation and the national state alike, bureaucracy is a central ingredient, and the larger the labor union, the more bureaucratic (other things being equal) it tends to become.

Although bureaucratic organization begins as an instrument of some larger purpose or goal, it tends to develop ends of its own which may not infrequently find themselves clashing with the original purposes for which it was established. That bureaucracy is rare indeed which, once its original tasks have been fulfilled, gracefully accepts death. There is a tendency in all bureaucracy, moreover, to expand regardless of need. C. Northcote Parkinson and others have dramatized this proclivity, as they have its ability to invent purposes and tasks in order to keep an expanded staff ostensibly busy.[25]

Bureaucracy reflects the character of complex civilization in general. On the one hand, it is indispensable, at least in some measure, if the tasks of civilization are to be accomplished, whether in education, organization of the arts, the structures of business and labor, or those of more general government. On the other hand, without care, constant criticism, and continual revision, it can work to undermine some of the more positive ends of civilized society. In one of its faces it represents a great creative achievement, and at its best it helps establish the conditions for individual creativity of all types, in education, in scientific research, in transportation, and in many other aspects of existence. Yet in another of its guises, it can be an important factor in killing creativity and dulling sensibility. In short, using the imagery of the Fall of Man, it represents both some of the highest achievements of man since he left Nature and, at the same time, certain of his marked tendencies to inertia and repudiation of freedom.

When we remind ourselves of some of the characteristics of justice and the notion of the free personality, the dual tendencies of bureaucracy become apparent. At its best, it can (1) provide a finely tuned administration of law showing no partiality to persons; (2) rationally coordinate the tasks essential to sustain a complex civilization; (3) organize the various forms of expertise so that they can support and sustain one another; (4) so plan the collective life that the chaotic factors released by civilization are kept in check, thus reinforcing both negative and positive freedom; and (5) promote efficient use of goods and services.

Its worst side (in terms of justice and freedom) can be equally noteworthy. In the pursuit of impartiality it can proliferate rules and regulations which strangle the initiative of its members and encourage endless delays. Notoriously, too, it can discourage a sense of responsibility: Inferiors in the structure tend to avoid decisions and to shift them to those higher up in the administrative hierarchy. If the administration does not include a large measure of functional decentralization, it becomes top-heavy and inflexible, showing little capacity for adaptation to peculiar geographical, social, or other circumstances. The "red tape" which is developed to ensure fairness becomes so prolix that it inhibits decisions and therefore halts the process of deliberate rather than accidental controls.

Implicitly if not explicitly, the five great paradigms on the Nature-civilization problem have characteristic answers to the problem of bureaucracy. The civilization-against-Nature view would implicitly see bureaucratic structures as part of the necessarily repressive mechanisms that keep life from returning to the "nasty, brutish, and short" phase of human existence. But the outlook, particularly in its Freud-like expression, would also see the structures as creating a problem for individual personalities restrained against their primitively natural tendencies. The second paradigm, in which the transition from primitive Nature is not nearly so traumatic, would encourage us to believe that market coordination can check bureaucratic coordination, thus limiting the deleterious tendencies of the latter. In the civilization-as-corrupting view, of course, there would be no place for bureaucratic coordination of any kind, for primitive Nature itself is the best coordinator. Or, because of low-level division of labor, little coordination would be necessary. The civilization-as-preparation perspective sees bureaucratic administration as part of the price we pay collectively for the disciplines which will eventually free us altogether from external controls. Finally, the classical position would have a dual thrust: It would see some bureaucratic management as indispensably connected with the presumably desirable growth of civilization, but then it would limit division of labor, technological development, and size of the political community in order to obviate the seamy side of bureaucracy.

Our position is that each outlook has something to tell us but that the classical view, if not taken too literally, possibly comes closest to providing a guide for the development of justice and the free personality. Neither those who see only the bright side of bureaucracy nor those who emphasize only the dark are right. The problem is to provide a social, economic, technological, and political context within which limited bureaucratic organization can remain an effective servant of the common good. But this involves something more than tinkering with the formal organization charts; it entails, in fact, a whole critique of modern civilization.

The Uses and Distortions of Law

The conception of rational freedom in justice is inseparable from the notion of law. Yet here again, while law in its ideal sense is designed to prevent violent coercion and to eliminate the arbitrary in collective and interpersonal concerns, its status in civilization is always an ambivalent one. Thus it tends, in a complex civilization, to be an instrument in the hands of the predominant ruling class. Although it aspires to impartiality, it is not infrequently an instrument for covering up exploitation of the poor by the clever and the designing powerful.

In less complex civilizations, much law is simply custom which is defined as law by the judges. But as complexity develops, the customary element tends to decline and the noncustomary — or legislative — to expand; and what remained rather unorganized and inchoate frequently becomes codified. While all law attempts somehow to reconcile the need for certainty and roots with the fact of social and political change, this appears to be increasingly difficult as civilization becomes more involved: stability seems to disappear, and what used to be regarded as the sure guideposts of the law are destroyed.

In every age, the law tends to stand poised between the pole of coercion and power, on the one hand, and that of righteousness or justice, on the other. The civilization-as-corrupting paradigm would see it as very close to the sheer coercion-power side, with an enormous gulf between it and justice. But others, emphasizing the mixed character of law, would stress its at least potential rationality: Thus Plato sees the law as appealing primarily to man's sense of reason and justice and only incidentally as employing coercion, and then in a very limited sense.[26]

Man's attitudes to law have been ambivalent from the very beginning. On the one hand, he has seen in it a weapon of arbitrary power and even of violence. On the other hand, he has thought of it as the only possible escape from arbitrary power in the civilized state. This ambivalence has justification, as we can see by turning briefly to the two sides.

We might adapt St. Augustine and say that insofar as the positive law falls below the highest standard of justice, it is piratical and indistinguishable from the rules of robber bands.[27] Thus if one of the principles of legal justice be that like cases should be treated alike, then prima facie it would seem that pardon of an ex-President of the United States for Watergate offenses, while two-score associates stood in jeopardy for similar offenses, is unjust. The fact that blacks have been far more likely to be subject to the death penalty than whites surely indicates that "equal justice under law" is still a remote ideal. General Tomoyuki Yamashita, a Japanese commander of World War II days, was killed on order of an international tribunal for the offenses of troops over which he admittedly no longer had control; but those responsible for the illegal and secret bombing of Cambodia during the Vietnam War were not even censured. At times, it would seem that if the offense is great enough and committed on a large enough scale, it is excusable; whereas if an apparently similar offense is small scale, it is condemned and punished as a violation of law. Thus the wholesale bombing and killing of civilians in Dresden, Hiroshima, and Nagasaki were undoubtedly violations of international law, yet they went unpunished; but the man who killed Mrs. Martin Luther King, Sr., was sentenced to be killed by the State for taking the life of only one person. Legal systems supposedly designed to protect life are also responsible for taking it on a large scale, as when they compel thousands of human beings to kill other human beings.

In the United States and elsewhere, laws tend to be applied in such a way as to favor the rich and the powerful and to punish severely the poor and the powerless. Hence while some of the largest corporations of the United States and their executives have been repeatedly convicted of violating the antitrust laws, for the most part they have been assessed only nominal fines or given very light sentences,[28] whereas petty thieves, who are usually poor, are sent to jail for long terms. From the viewpoint of justice, every legal system which allows phenomena like these to occur is undermining its own authority in greater or lesser measure, depending on the extent of the injustice.

Nor is injustice confined to the criminal law. In the civil realm, too, the law and its administration often contribute to anything but justice. The delays involved in litigation, for instance, frequently amount to a denial of justice, if we accept the maxim: Justice delayed is justice denied. While there is some hyperbole in *Jarndyce* v. *Jarndyce*, Dickens's famous fictional controversy in equity,[29] still the endless processes of that case, together with the shameless erosion of the estate by lawyers' fees, constituted gross injustice under cover of law. It may be argued, to be sure, that prolongation of cases of this type is due to the law's insistence on adequate hearings and on fairness. This is true in a measure. But surely when the delays have continued over a generation, they have long ceased to have anything to do with justice as fairness.

Continuing the Augustinian adaptation, while it is true that most existential states and legal systems are to some extent like robber bands, it is also true that pirate-like groups have many of the hallmarks of existential statehood. Gangsters like the Mafia seek an ordering similar to that of the State, develop legislative and executive organs, and have rules for distribution of the spoils which resemble the civil and criminal laws.[30] In films like *The Godfather*, we have become accustomed to the spectacle of combinations of thieves acting in terms of organization very much like states. They even have schemes of "justice," which, granted their premises and purposes, are often as effective in carrying out their established norms as the corresponding systems of states.

Insofar as positive law and its administration always embody elements of exploitation and injustice, they are at war with their presumed status as instruments of freedom and righteous ordering. This is the tendency in law which becomes the object of rightful excoriation by both Marxists and followers of Tolstoy. Although they may be mistaken in thinking of legal systems as always and predominantly merely the reflections of particular interests and in tending to ignore the sense in which many systems are genuinely seeking to undergird the structure of freedom and justice, still it is true that every scheme of law — civil, criminal, public, and private — even at its best, is never far away from at least some piratical elements.

But it is the fact of civilization itself — including the evolution of human consciousness — which creates the problem. In a hypothetical primitive Nature, we may assume, it would not even exist, however that Nature might be conceived.

There is another sense in which law, while supposedly an agent of civilization and hence a promoter of liberated personalities, tends to betray the ideal. By its very nature, as Plato pointed out long ago,[31] law must use categories and classifications, with the hope (as we have said) that those in the same categories will be treated alike. But this is to assume that two or more individuals or situations are so alike that they can be placed in the same classification. This the more radical critics deny, arguing that any classification scheme short of making every individual or situation a category of his or its own is unjust. Every person and situation is unique, it has been urged, and equity demands that we not force him, her, or it into a common mold with others. The very act of doing so creates an injustice.

If one accepts this viewpoint — and it seems to be persuasive in light of our discussion of personality — then to some extent every legal judgment, no matter how carefully shaped, will do injustice to aspiring personality. The radicals thus attack not merely the frequently outrageous applications of law but also the very notion of positive law itself.

How, then, can we accept law at all? It not only frequently leads to injustice in terms of its own inevitable classifications, but the very attempt to classify is inequitable. It always enshrines some elements of piracy and by its very nature must do injustice to the unique. How, then, can it be justified? The answer, of course, has been that while the charges against it may be valid and true, they are not the whole truth. The alternative to legal classifications would be the rule of men, and it is impossible to find men so just that we could entrust them with the task of ruling without law. As Aristotle observes, if there were some men with godlike qualities, then we might dispense with law; but since there are no men with such attributes, we must settle for a system of law, with full recognition that both in its substance and in its administration it may not always be just. In the absence of either godlike men or law, mankind would be subjected to sheer arbitrary power without even a modicum of justice.

If we accept this perspective, every civilization (not least of all the modern one) ought to develop law-governed relations, realizing that in some measure they will be unjust. Human relations governed by law are in one sense ideal but in another a kind of second best. Poised between arbitrary power and violence, on the one hand, and ideal justice, on the other — both of them lawless — law may be said to reflect admirably man's half-way position between the beasts on the one side and the gods on the other.

The good citizen, we may urge with St. Paul,[32] should obey the law not only for "wrath's" but also for "conscience's" sake. Yet in the very act of obedience, the citizen will realize that there are times when he or she ought to disobey for the sake of the same conscience.[33] His obedience will be rooted in the belief that law, generally speaking, is indispensable if we are to avoid the rule of sheer unlimited might; his disobedience will be grounded on the proposition that some laws are so violative of justice that he cannot give them the sanction of obedience, even though he suffer for it. When he obeys, he will be doing so in full recognition that his obedience sanctions some injustice, which, however, does not on the whole reach the point of sheer uncontrolled might. When he disobeys, he will do so only after full deliberation and a weighing of the consequences both for himself and for mankind. The good citizen will be neither slavishly and unreflectively obedient to the laws nor compulsively or self-interestedly disobedient. And he will seek in all the ways he can to narrow the gulf between human law and genuine justice. He will see law as a peculiarly human institution entitled to no unqualified obedience, yet at the same time to be respected as such, even in disobedience.[34]

Given such an outlook, the citizen will become increasingly sensitive to the ways in which human law can liberate and equally sensitive to its possibilities for enslavement. Law, by insisting on performance of certain obligations — for example, those demanding that we act rationally, that we recognize the claims of others, and that we avoid things which undermine the teleological nature of man — can contribute to the evolution of positive rational freedom. At the same time, if it tries to do too much or attempts to regulate minutely all aspects of life, it can help frustrate the quest for positive freedom and constitute an intolerable burden on negative liberty. St. Thomas Aquinas wisely observed long ago that human law should not forbid all acts which the majority of the society may deem morally wrong, for in so doing too great a strain might be placed on the "imperfect," and the problem of implementing law might become so difficult as to lead to violence and to frustrate the purposes of and respect for legal institutions.[35] Where the line should be drawn in each case is, of course, difficult to determine in advance, for much depends on the particular circumstances involved. We have already contended (in Chapter 3) that the whole area of freedom of speech, publication, and religion should be exempt from legal control, in terms of both justice and personality growth. It would also seem wise to wipe out most of the legislation seeking to regulate sex relations, save in cases where violence is used. But legislation involving use of scarce resources may have to be expanded, unless there is a deliberate simplification of life patterns, if negative freedom from want is a desideratum. Here negative freedom from want would have as one of its essential conditions the curtailment of negative freedom from legislation. One negative freedom may have to be gained at the expense of another.

How might we defend such an exchange? Basically, we might contend that if legislation about the economic order can free human beings from the coercion of economic want, it is desirable to do so on two grounds: first, that without satisfaction of fundamental economic needs, life for millions would be impossible, and one must have life before one can have the good life; and second, that it is better in general to be restricted by deliberate and conscious measures (such as legislative acts) than by accident and fortuitous circumstances, which might be reflected in involuntary poverty. This assumes, of course, that we can show that legislation might have this effect.

Always, however, the sensitive citizen will remember that, while general principles are essential if we are to deal with issues of this kind, the drawing of lines in particular situations is never easy and depends in considerable measure on an evaluation of all the circumstances and judgments about likely consequences of alternative actions.

The Perils of Centralization and Decentralization

The first pages of Aristotle's *Politics* are devoted to the sense in which the *polis* is prior to the family and the village. It is surely not chronologically prior but, rather, teleologically so. That is, the establishment of families and villages foreshadows a society in which they can fulfill or complete themselves. The political society idea, we may say, is working within families and villages to bring them together in the teleologically natural political society: The idea of the political is thus present from the very beginning. The primitively natural family, springing from biological division of labor, has as its purpose the association of families for deliberate and conscious control of human destiny. Both the family and the political society are natural, the former in the sense that it springs from sexual differentiation but cannot completely fulfill itself economically, socially, and spiritually, except in the larger whole; the latter because civilization is the teleologically natural expression of humanity.

Aristotle has in mind, of course, the idea of *autarky,* or self-sufficiency, as the goal of chronologically prior entities like the family. The political society is to be autarchic in the sense that it will not be overly dependent on others for its economy and will provide that measure of social interaction necessary to stimulate consciousness and the arts among its citizens. These goals cannot be attained by the nuclear or the extended family nor even by the village. But they can be achieved by the *polis.*

The notion of natural fulfillment in an autarchic city and civilization is thus intimately associated with classical political philosophy. Both Plato and Aristotle doubt that human life can become what it ought to be in either the village, with its tendency to parochialism and its limited intellectual stimulation, or in an empire, like the Persian, where centralized authority and power tend to drain local units of their own life and spontaneity.[36] And had Plato and Aristotle lived in 300 A.D. they would undoubtedly have commented unfavorably on the Roman Empire, in which formerly vigorous municipal life had become desiccated.[37] The picture one gets of the classical ideal is of a political unit very limited in size (5040 households in Plato's *Laws*), with restricted commercial intercourse, and with only very slow change, whether social or technological. For the city to become highly dependent on other civilizations or on some remote monarch would be to destroy its life and to frustrate human nature.

And thus was posed very early the problem of whether life is best fulfilled in large and centralized aggregates or in relatively small and self-sufficient units, connected only loosely, if at all, with other similar units. We have already touched on this issue to some extent in our analysis of the will to freedom. Here we deal with it more generally.

The question was posed dramatically by Brooks Adams,[38] who suggested alternative patterns of characteristics associated with decentralized versus centralized civilizations. In the former (he had in mind the high Middle Ages, before kings began to establish centralized authority in the national state), he urged, artistic creativity is encouraged and moderate-sized towns become the center of highly productive and yet comprehensible and understandable human life. In the latter, illustrated by modern civilization with its high measure of centralization in the national state and the business and finance corporation, artistic creativity dries up, and money values become central. The flexibility and adaptability of a decentralized civilization are lost, poetry declines, and purely utilitarian values reign supreme. The impetus to exercise the human mind and spirit decays with the development of a kind of rigid or pickled structuring of civilization.

Propositions like those of Adams are, of course, rather sweeping, and complete verification for them is almost impossible. There are so many variables involved. The artistic life of the relatively autonomous Italian cities of the Renaissance, for example, has often been favorably compared with the creativity, or lack of it, associated with the modern megalopolis, tied as it is to the large-scale centralized world of commerce and industry. But it is also true that the intense creativity of Florence, for instance, had largely faded away by the 18th century. How would one account for the decline in a period long before the city had been absorbed in a unified Italy?

Nevertheless, certain contentions of the critics can be supported, and others have a certain plausibility. It would appear to be true, for instance, that as modern economic life comes to be administered and controlled from only a few centers, the possibility of genuine local self-government is thereby eroded. The options of city councils and county boards are drastically diminished if the economic structure of the local communities is very much managed from New York or London or Moscow. To be sure, local governing bodies can still decide such issues as the color of policemen's uniforms, the structure of the fire department, and so on. But in such weighty matters as taxation, they are obviously severely limited in what they can in fact do. If tax rates get far out of line with those of other communities, for instance, the cry is raised that the community will lose businesses; if attempts are made to control pollution, they may run the risk of antagonizing giant corporations who may then decide to close down plants in the offending city or county. Local self-government, in other words, at least in its traditional form, fights a losing battle as the economic aspect of modern civilization becomes more and more centralized. And if local self-government of a significant kind declines, the civic spirit so essential for nonautocratic politics tends to deteriorate with it.

Almost every American state and municipality could illustrate these propositions. In Minnesota, for instance, Reserve Mining Company, which produces taconite, or low-grade iron ore materials, has for years been dumping wastes into Lake Superior, with permission of the state. Certain evidence seems to show that these wastes may be cancer producing and that they are ingredients in the water supplies of cities bordering on the lake. The state therefore has asked Reserve to abandon the practice of discharging the wastes into the lake and to dispose of them instead at some point on land. Over the course of several years the issue has been before administrative bodies and the courts. The federal district judge in charge became convinced that Reserve Mining was stalling and became rather blunt in his comments from the bench on the company's tactics. The company thereupon asked the Circuit Court of Appeals to remove the judge from further consideration of the case, and the court granted the request. But the new judge in the case seems to have reached conclusions about the company similar to those of his predecessor. Meanwhile, negotiations between the company and the state over a land disposal site seemed to get nowhere, the company insisting on a site relatively close to the lake, on alleged grounds of economy, and the state — following a hearing officer's recommendation — rejecting this site in favor of a more remote point. If no agreement on a site could be reached, the company, under court order, would presumably have to close down, thus producing considerable unemployment and immediate adverse economic effects in northeastern Minnesota.[39] Later, the State Supreme Court handed down a ruling which in effect mandated selection of the company's site, hence seeming to make the corporation victorious.

Here we have given the barest sketch of the case, whose legal and economic ramifications become very complicated indeed. However we judge the outcome, the controversy illustrates dramatically how tenuous is the exercise of the alleged "sovereignty" of the state government when confronted by the centralized economic power of a private corporation. Reserve Mining is controlled by a gigantic combination of outside economic forces whose wealth enables them to carry on litigation in the courts almost indefinitely.

It was situations of this type which classical political philosophy had in mind when it warned against nonautarchic polities. If political societies allowed commerce with other parts of the world to expand without limit, not only would they run into the dangers of the luxurious state against which Plato warned,[40] but they would be undermining politics itself — the idea of deliberate and conscious ordering of human affairs for the public good. Jeffersonianism, in the early days of the American Republic, issued similar admonitions about the dangers of a highly industrialized and commercialized life. Later professed Jeffersonians have largely ignored these warnings, seeming to believe that, despite the cautions of the master, they could combine economic centralization and complexity with political decentralization. But it would appear that this cannot really be done: while the form of political decentralization may remain, the substance becomes a shadow of its former self.

It can be argued, of course, that the answer is to abandon the idea of decentralized politics and to establish legal and political controls at the national and then the worldwide level. And, indeed, this has been proceeding at the national level throughout economically developed modern civilization. But while this may be in some respects the obvious response to economic centralization, it still does not restore nontrivial local self-government. And if we believe that vigorous local autonomy is essential both to maintain a civic spirit and will to freedom and to develop the human personality, highly centralized politics is no answer. Here the Nature-against-civilization paradigm has something valid to say, even if in rather extreme form.

Some of the broader propositions of writers like Adams, while perhaps not as clear as the relation between economic and political organization, also appear to have at least a limited plausibility. During the Renaissance, it was often the semi-independent centers of power in the city-states which preserved the physical lives and nourished the genius of men like Leonardo da Vinci: When they were out of favor in one state they could flee to another, since in those days there was no Italian national police. Different rulers with somewhat separate power bases, moreover, could provide stimuli for alternative styles in art and literature. During the Middle Ages, the isolated nature of much life and the scarcity of material resources conceivably did provide an atmosphere for the imagination which is lacking in modern times. Since affluence was obviously impossible for most, many men and women accepted their fate and, after the 12th century, turned to noneconomic fields for fulfillment. While bureaucracy on its unfavorable side can certainly exist in autonomous cities (and it did, as evidenced in the life of Leonardo), still alternative bureaucracies would seem to be better than a centralized one covering the territory of a national state or even, perhaps, of the world.

Although we are again treading on difficult and uncertain ground, our experience with historical civilizations would seem to point to the conclusion that the tendency to centralization of administration and control (in politics, economic structure and in general culture) is often pushed far beyond any reasonable need for coordination in life. Centralizing tendencies, beyond a certain point, seem to have a life of their own, very much as bureaucratic proclivities develop purposes apart from those of the general society. In other words, in a complex civilization it would seem that some formal integration is inevitable and desirable; but within the process itself, other things being equal, there is a proclivity for excess or surplus centralization. Thus we have to decide not only whether we wish to pay the price of centralization for complex civilization but also, if we pay the price, how we are to control the tendency to surplus centralization.

In assessing whether to opt for complex civilization or not, we should, of course, not forget to weigh the claims of less developed civilization and its correspondingly greater decentralization. It is one of the assertions of the civilization-as-corrupting paradigm, of course, that centralized controls have no merit and that in Nature, by contrast, we are completely freed from them. In modified versions of the paradigm (perhaps we may count Jefferson's or Lao-Tze's here),[41] small, largely agricultural, and mainly economically self-sufficient communities avoid the perils of centralization, with its subservience of man to man. Political issues are relatively simple, and adjustments and coordination can take place with a minimum of red tape. Since the communities are entangled with other communities in a very limited degree only, they can be genuinely self-governing. Such has been the dream of many "back-to-Nature" advocates, both in our own time and in earlier generations.

But there is a price to be paid for highly decentralized ways of living, as well as for extremely centralized ones. For one thing, decentralized modes do not really recognize in practice one aspect of the teleological nature of man as we defined it in a previous chapter — his universality. They may do justice to his uniqueness and to his quest for intimacy in the smaller group, but they cut him off from the essentially necessary relations with mankind as a whole. It is doubtful, in fact, whether even man's uniqueness can fully flower under these conditions. Then, too, mankind under these circumstances might be more subject to the legislation of accident (the accidents of relatively primitive living) rather than of design; and thus yet another aspect of teleological human nature would be denied. In extreme forms of decentralization, wars and other bickerings, while simpler and less destructive, might be more numerous: Thus the wars between Italian city-states of the Renaissance were almost endless, and in classical Greek history a similar situation obtained. To be sure, if the communities were completely isolated from one another, then occasions for wars would not arise; but so extreme a form of isolation has been rare in history.

We are suggesting, then, that justice entails a kind of balance between centripetal and centrifugal tendencies, and one of the cardinal problems of modern politics is to find where that balance lies in practice. We shall not discover it, however, by taking for granted a particular stage of technological development and then determining how much centralization that stage entails. If we are to be genuinely political, we must ask what man's teleological nature and human justice require and then adjust such factors as technology to those requirements. The answer must be found against the background of our preceding discussion of justice as it relates to freedom, equality, and fraternity.

Our historical experience seems to show that too much authority and power at the center will lead to violence against human personality, just as will too little. In modern civilization, assuming some (although by no means unlimited) acceptance of complex technology, this would appear to entail a kind of *via media* between a centralized world state (or authority of some kind) on the one hand and highly decentralized and parochial communities on the other. This middle way would seem to point to a considerably modified version of the views of such utopists as Robert Owen and Mohandas Gandhi.[42] In the last chapter, which formulates a utopian sketch, we shall attempt to spell out what this might mean.

The Tendency to Monarchy and Tyranny

Although often hindered and obstructed by the bureaucracy which ostensibly serves it, there is a notable tendency in complex civilizations for the executive to become a monarch and in the process to subvert other civic institutions. Societies characterized as democratic or liberal in the beginning will in later developments find their deliberative assemblies surrendering power and authority, at times gladly and sometimes reluctantly; while the executive, which originally was probably looked upon with deep suspicion, will now tend to be magnified and exalted. In the end, the monarch will often become a tyrant and seek to burst the bonds of all law and morality.

What are some of the factors which make for this thrust toward rule by one, or at least attempted rule by one? The very speed of social change is often cited as a significant element, for rapid change frequently seems to demand swift action by political authority and the executive is, it is said, most capable of such action. Another factor is undoubtedly the growth of the military; since the executive directs the armed forces, their expansion implies a corresponding strengthening of executive authority. Then, too, the erosion of the will to freedom and the distortions of law, as we have suggested, will open the way to monarchy and to eventual tyranny. It should also be remembered that from ancient times monarchy has been defended as more efficient than either republicanism or democracy; and given the imperatives of complex civilization, this is often a persuasive rationalization for it. Finally, the search for political messiahs seems to be accentuated as the difficulties and frustrations of widespread citizen participation are encountered; and the quest for the political wonder worker is closely related to the erosion of the will to freedom and the effort to escape responsibility. A kind of magic solution is sought in the savior or charismatic figure, who all too readily is transmuted into a monarch and then into a tyrant.

Obvious examples of these observations are to be found in the histories of ancient Rome and of the modern United States. In the former, the republican institutions (themselves the fruit of an attack on the early monarchy) were gradually undermined, the consequence being the development first of a constitutional monarchy and then of a monarchy moving in the direction of tyranny. Factors involved in this transformation of the Roman state included (1) long periods of war, which led to constant emphasis on the military; (2) the development of the "proletariat," or landless inhabitants of the city, who depended on a few rich men and the government for their livelihoods; (3) the claim that the Senate could not act quickly enough to meet constant foreign crises; (4) the cleverness of the first emperor, Augustus, in manipulating propaganda; (5) the decline of the Senate's will to rule; (6) popular gratitude for the *pax Romana,* which Augustus and his immediate successors supposedly brought to the Roman world; (7) economic polarization and the decline of small farms; and (8) the increasing alienation of the masses from civic responsibility.

In the United States, we rarely think of the Presidency as having become a virtual monarchy (or rule by one), since we associate the word "monarchy" with crowns, hereditary succession, and similar attributes. But it is possible to have an ostensibly elective rule by one, and many monarchs who lack the pomp and circumstance of traditional crowned rulers may have much more power. Certain traditional monarchical attributes were built into the American Presidency from the beginning — the veto power, for example. But for the most part, the presidential monarchical powers, ceremonies, and prerogatives of the 20th century — to which we have already referred in regard to the erosion of the will to freedom — have been built up over the course of years as a result of alleged emergencies, delegation of authority by Congress, expansion of the military, and sheer assertiveness on the part of Presidents like Theodore Roosevelt. Monarchy in the United States, like imperial monarchy in ancient Rome, owes much of its authority and power to economic crises which seemingly call for swift action by the Executive: Thus the New Deal, in the name of liberal economic reform, added notably to the claimed powers and authority of the Presidency.

Gradually, a kind of mystique began to develop around the office of President, as it did around the ancient emperors. This mystique was aided and abetted by attitudes of both Congress and the populace. Congress delegated vast powers, in response to both the assumed necessities of war and the supposed imperatives of economic crisis; and often the legislative body appeared to think that only a single individual could take effective action. As for the populace, over the course of years it came to view the holder of the Presidency as the key to prosperity or calamity, social health or sickness. Not a few, both scholars and nonscholars, hold that while Congress represents many diverse and clashing interests rather than the common good, the President somehow stands above factional conflict and represents the general welfare; and propositions of this kind have been traditionally associated with defense of monarchy. While episodes like the Watergate affair have checked these tendencies in some measure, it is doubtful whether the secular movement toward monarchy has been substantially curtailed.

It is obvious that monarchy in the existential world is difficult if not impossible to reconcile with the general notions of justice, liberty, equality, and fraternity we have outlined. Not only does monarchy usually have within it the seeds of future tyranny, but by overshadowing the political activities of others it dries up the possibilities for personal development, which depend in part on civic activity of many types. The notion of monarchy suggests inequalities of all kinds and the frustration of distributive justice. While many in the past have sought to reconcile the idea of the monarch as a father figure with the notion of fraternity, it is doubtful whether this can be successfully done; for fraternity implies a basic equality of brothers and sisters and a widespread sharing of responsibility. Fraternity should be both the root and the fruit of democracy and cannot coexist with the idea of monarchy.

How, then, can the tendency to monarchy be checked? It is never easy, for the appeal of a single individual supposedly righting wrong or standing for the whole community against special interests is always a powerful one. Mere formal constitutional constraints are powerless in the long run if the bulk of the population have divested themselves of a sense of responsibility or allowed their freedom to erode. The only hope is to develop a much wider consciousness than at present of the basic problem and to check the tendencies to social complexity which often provide so plausible a ground for expansion of executive authority in the direction of monarchy. But limiting complexity is itself a task of enormous difficulty, and it is related to almost all facets of existence we are considering in this book. Thus the problem of monarchy and tyranny is intimately connected with what is done about technology and political economy, as well as with development of consciousness about justice.

Problematics of Community and Communication

Free personalities are dependent (as we have said) on the development of a human community in which seeming conflicts between individuality and sociality are reconciled. This is the sense in which freedom is inseparably bound up with the idea of fraternity. I cannot be the self that I ought to be unless I recognize your indispensability for my existence and your claim to communion with me.

Here again complex civilization tends to be riddled with paradox. According to some views, the developing personality in civilization apparently can look forward to more numerous alternatives and, because of expanding technology, to increasingly extensive and sensitive mechanical and electrical means of communication. While person-to-person relations tend to decline in intensity with civilization, the hope arises that somehow the basis of community will be enlarged through electronics, so that — according to theorists of inevitable progress — every person can eventually communicate effectively with every other person on the globe, thus making possible something like a universal community. (This does not take into consideration the possibilities of telepathic communication, which unaccountably and unreasonably are usually ignored.) To some modern theorists of democracy, this will be community at a higher level than the old community of wont and custom. The dialogue of freely interacting personalities will unite, while at the same time coercion will virtually disappear. Something approaching a genuine consensus can and will arise. Political rule, if it can be said to exist at all, at last reposing on an active confluence of souls and a search for justice, will be less likely to be corrupted by elements of sheer might and thus will approximate more closely an ideal type of pure authority.

Some such vision would appear to be implicit in much liberalism and Marxism. In our discussion, we shall certainly not be discounting the vision, however much we may point out the problematics involved. But we must also face the factors which often undermine any implementation of the conception. The very improved mechanical and electronic communication which lends credence to the goal also works against it. Thus the capital required for modern communications technique is so enormous that systems of communications can be owned only collectively — by the State, or a giant corporation, or trade union, or wealthy church — and the tendency to centralization, together with the thrusts toward highly specialized ruling classes and bureaucracies, would seem to suggest that the communications collectives will tend to be controlled by a very few. And if a few control, they will have not only the power but often also the inclination to control for their own particular interests. This is especially true when we keep in mind (as has already been observed) that while the potentialities for freedom tend to rise with complex civilization, the will to freedom does not seem to develop correspondingly, except perhaps rhetorically. Thus while we may have the possibility of whispering anything whatsoever around the globe, we may not be allowed to do so by those who control the whispering devices.

Then, too, we should remember that in a civilization of vast economic interdependence, the realm which can legitimately be called "public" tends to be expanded at the expense of what hitherto was regarded as purely "private." In some measure, so-called totalitarianism is a kind of distorted recognition of this fact: In essence, it says that the old distinction between the private and public has broken down, leaving everything, in principle, subject to public direction. The tendency is present everywhere and can be defended with powerful arguments. Fifty years ago, for example, most would have regarded as outrageous any attempt by legislation to prohibit us from discriminating on grounds of race in the sale of our homes. Today millions accept such restrictions, if not with equanimity, then with a sigh of resignation. And while American law still makes a valiant effort to distinguish between public utilities — businesses affected with the public interest — and those that supposedly do not have that character, it becomes almost impossible to do so. Can we really say, for example, that the United States Steel Corporation, while not officially a public utility, is any less "affected with the public interest" than, say, the telephone company, which is legally categorized as such an enterprise?

Governments and giant governing corporations appear to have an enormous advantage, moreover, in controlling and manipulating the press, radio, and television. Indeed, throughout most of the world, human beings hear mostly only what governments wish them to hear; and the really open dialogue which modern civilization seems to portend is usually stillborn.[43] Even where a kind of alleged pluralism exists (for example, in the United States) this control is only slightly modified: the government can and does lie and can make its prevarications believable at the time;[44] the airwaves are polluted by commercial claims of doubtful or no validity; and while there is some attempt to present "all points of view" on radio and television, truly radical political positions are almost never stated or discussed at any length. Recent revelations about the FBI and the CIA tend to support the allegation that even in a "free" society, government agencies, particularly those shrouded in secrecy, will not hesitate to flout the law and to show contempt for human beings.

To be sure, governments have lied and censored and curtailed freedom of expression in ages past, and in some respects the modern practices simply carry on this tradition. The point about modern governments, however, is that they have much more powerful technical means at their disposal to deny, through control of material things, claims to spiritual freedom. Their potentialities for manipulation, restriction of dialogue, and deceit are vastly expanded. And when we say "governments" we always intend to include giant business corporations as well — for they are part of the governing structure.

The very universal education we associate with modern civilization has itself vastly enlarged the capacity of ruling groups to stifle discussion. It is a mistake to think of free public education as an unmitigated blessing, for once millions are able to read, the way is opened for yet another medium of propaganda. As Leo Tolstoy used to point out, before the days of relatively widespread literacy ruling elites were limited in the kinds of ways they could endeavor to shape the minds of the masses: the town crier, to be sure, could be used, but his voice did not carry very far, and while the traveling story teller could spread tales tinctured with propaganda, the propaganda was more likely than not to be critical of princes and lords, as in traditional fairy tales. But with literacy of a minimal type — the kind obtaining throughout the world for most persons — the possibilities of official propaganda are enormously expanded. Governments can and do hire intellectuals to ensure that there will be support for war and for government policies of all types.[45] With the coming of radio and television, these possibilities are vastly magnified. Although certain "liberal" societies (and they are very few) seek to guarantee the legal right to talk back, most members of the public lack the economic power to do so.

When countercriticism does eventually affect ruling elites, it is often too late. Thus the full exposure of the way in which the United States entered the Vietnam War came more than a decade after American entry, years after the physical, economic, and spiritual damage had been done.[46] Though it can, of course, be contended that exposure was better late than never, still it was of very limited efficacy.

What, then, is to be done about the frustrations arising out of inability to implement the potential for spiritual freedom in the context of modern communications? The answer would seem to lie in a combination of measures, several of which have already been noted. For example, we must counteract the erosion of the will to freedom, seek to control the rate of technological change, grapple with the issue of centralization, and somehow change the distribution of economic power. So long as income is distributed as it is in most of the world today (a question we shall examine in Chapter 6), it is doubtful whether much progress in the direction of a more just communications system can be made.

One thing seems to be clear: We shall not find the answer simply in still more complex communications technologies. Instead, we shall have to turn to the problem of distribution of power and to the spiritual and intellectual attitudes of human beings.

The Place of Coercion and Violent Coercion

We cannot deny the reality of coercion in our experience, whether in some hypothetical or actual state of Nature or in civilization. The less civilized a state of society, the more man will be coerced by such factors as weather, niggardliness of material resources, and, in certain views, the sheer cruelty of the "struggle for existence." To be sure, in such postulations as Eden or the rule of rigid custom in the sacred society, we are not aware of coercion, since many aspects of individuality have not yet developed. But neither are we free. Once we have left such regimes, the simultaneous evolution of freedom and coercion becomes striking.

In civilization, particularly modern civilization, while some forms of the coercions by Nature tend to fade, civilized coercions take their place. As the individual's own feeling of apartness develops, the substitution of legislative and political controls for custom and wont is perceived as coercive. The sheer magnitude of wars in civilization, with their wholesale threat to all human life; the tendency for formal legislation to be seen as imposed by those who are foreign to one's own personality; and the frequently wide gulf between justice and the contents of legislation — all make for a consciousness of coercion by the individual and tend to give the ruler a kind of specious justification for resorting to yet more coercive techniques. Free personalities in genuine communities based on distributive justice would not perceive themselves as coerced, even when legislative provisions strictly limit their material possessions. But given a system which takes only incidental account of human need, legislation dominated by the interests of the rich, and an international framework built on the threat of mutual annihilation, alienated personalities will view themselves as highly coerced and with their freedom denied.

Short of the perfect congruence of justice, legislation, and the freely developed inner convictions of individuals in a community of constant dialogue, it would seem that coercion of man by man is inevitable and, given the limitations of man in civilization, that some types of it are relatively justifiable under given contingencies. But even justifiable coercion always represents a species of failure, and our aspiration should be to

141

substitute justice, understanding, and inner conviction for even the measure of coercion which at times has a certain contingent defense. Because the development of civilization releases so many chaotic forces and passions, other things being equal, coercion tends to get out of bounds, to become almost unlimited, and therefore to be unjustifiable.

The Persuasion-Coercion Continuum

How can we distinguish between justifiable and nonjustifiable coercion? To answer this question, we can best begin by suggesting a continuum between persuasion or inner conviction on the one end and violent coercion on the other.[47] At the point of persuasion, the individual or group is fully and freely (nonmanipulatively) convinced that a given course of conduct is right and just and that even certain restrictions on what he, she, or it can do are desirable. On the other end of the continuum, violent coercion, irremediable or serious injury of the individual or group, is deliberately threatened or committed.

Genuinely free and open persuasion is always justifiable in pursuit of just ordering, for it reflects man's teleological nature at its highest. By the term "persuasion" we signify, of course, not merely appeals from assumed major premises to minor premises to conclusions, but also free interchange of experiences about the major premises themselves, with the objective of consensus.

Although free and open persuasion is always legitimate, violent coercion — deliberate killing, maiming, or torture of the physical body or the spirit of a human being — is never justifiable, whether by individuals or groups. Violent coercion, besides being morally wrong in principle, negates the purposes of social order — the enhancement of the good life for human beings — and rarely if at all can it be kept subordinate to the values embodied in the concept of justice. Violent coercion by its very nature tends to become an end in itself. While its utilization may appear at the beginning to be essential if we are to preserve civilization or human life, its essence is to destroy and not to preserve, to set up ends of its own, rather than to keep itself strictly under the aegis of nonviolent ends.

In fact, to talk about violence in means as a way to achieve nonviolent ends is like speaking of the necessity for production of hot ice. It is to forget what philosophers like John Dewey have always attempted to teach us — that the nature of the means one uses will shape the ends one attains. This point is stressed, too, in the New Testament and in the teachings of all high religions.[48]

Between the pole of persuasion, on the one hand, and of violent coercion, on the other, are various forms of coercion which may or may not be justified, depending on the contingencies of the particular situation involved. Obviously, we could not justify coercing a child under all circumstances, but under some situations it might be legitimate. Obviously, too, coercing an individual for questionable goals would be ruled out. Restraining a drunk on his voluntary way to a treatment center would have to be deemed out of bounds, while restraining one about to hit another person could probably be justified.

Just where violent coercion tapers off into nonviolent and therefore relatively justifiable coercion will, of course, often be difficult to determine. Lines must always be drawn in the application of general principles to particular situations: This is the nature of the moral quest. Although the general principles might be clear, their interpretation for given cases will sometimes tend to be uncertain and even arbitrary. This is an inevitable accompaniment of man's effort to act justly, when he is guided neither by precivilized Nature (however its characteristics be defined) nor directly by God, who, because he is God, respects man's freedom.

Acts of Violent Coercion

In drawing lines between violent and nonviolent coercion, however, it would seem that some acts clearly fall into the category "violent." Among them are war and capital punishment.

War. All war, particularly in modern times, has for its hallmark the deliberate killing of human beings, and it also means an enormous production of spiritual violence, in the form, for example, of wholesale lying and general denigration of human personality. In terms of practical assessment of the results of war, the burden of proof must always be on those who would advocate it for any cause whatsoever. War has bad consequences of all kinds — including, aside from the killing, social disintegration, a tendency to tyranny, a general undermining of morality, and so on — because it is inseparably bound up with the supreme act of immorality, the destruction of human lives, itself intrinsically wrong.

We sometimes forget how ubiquitous acts of killing are in any war. They take place deliberately, not only in the bombing of cities and on the battlefield but also in the handling of prisoners of war and the survivors of shipwrecks. The spirit of slaughter and disrespect for human life becomes all-pervasive. All acts are justified in the name of winning the war.

In the manuals used for training soldiers, there is often a brutal frankness about these matters. While civilians may be talking of a war against tyranny or for civilization or for democracy, soldiers are often taught to kill even persons who are disarmed or taken prisoner. In a training manual for hand-to-hand fighting widely used by the American Army during World War II, we get a glimpse of war as it is and not as romantic ideologists (and some survive) often talk of it. In this manual, the hand-to-hand fighter is told:

Although the style of fighting which involves kicking a man when he is down, gouging out his eyes, and kicking him in the testicles does not appeal to the average American, we must forget the Marquis of Queensbury rules of sportsmanship when dealing with our present enemies.

Ruthlessness is what we seek to achieve. It is best defined in two words: speed and brutality. . . .

Any hold should be regarded as a means of getting a man into a position where it will be easier to kill him, and not as a means to keep him captive. . . .

After your opponent has been downed, the kill can be made with a kick. This can be done with either the toe of your foot to the temple or by driving the back edge of the heel into the rib section, throat area, or heart area with great force. In either case, it is best to be wearing heavy boots or other heavy footwear.[49]

One of the many war crimes trials at the end of World War II illustrates the centrality of killing and brutality in every war, whatever its proclaimed objective. The case of the *Peleus* concerned a merchant ship being operated by the British Ministry of War Transport which was sunk without warning by a German U-boat under the command of Heinz Eck. The ship sank within two minutes, and many of the survivors clung to the debris in the hope that they would be rescued either by the submarine or by Allied ships. Instead, the commander of the submarine directed a searchlight at the scattered debris and fired, killing all survivors except three. The war crimes tribunal found all the defendants guilty, sentencing three to be shot to death, one to suffer life imprisonment, and the fifth to be imprisoned for 15 years.[50]

The irony in the case of the *Peleus* was that while the Allies were sentencing Captain Eck to death for killing a few survivors of a shipwreck, they were also killing thousands of unarmed Japanese in Hiroshima and Nagasaki. Morally, it would seem to be impossible to distinguish a *Peleus*-type killing from the kind that took place at Hiroshima, unless slaying from the air be somehow regarded as nobler and more defensible. The submarine captain justified his act in terms of "operational necessity," while Hiroshima was defended on the grounds that it shortened the war and was a war necessity.

Most persons would probably agree that war in all its ramifications — in training, on the battlefield, in relation to prisoners, in submarine activities against merchant ships, and so on — entails large-scale killing of human beings, and usually killing is wrong. But most, too, would argue that the killing involved in some wars can be justified, in whatever ways. All

144

deliberate killing is wrong, this view maintains, but some wars are exceptions to the general rule. Here we are fundamentally rejecting this common proposition and asserting that all war, as a type of violent coercion, is morally unjustifiable, whatever its objectives. All wars, however much we may deny it, have certain common characteristics in their means or methods, which tend always to destroy the noble ends for which they may be allegedly waged. The assessor of man in civilization should never ask what the professed ends of a given war might be but should look only to what the war does to human beings. This speaks more loudly than all the rhetoric of glowing goals.

Almost every war begins with claims that it will be short and that, of course, a given nation would not have entered it had not the nation been forced as a last resort to do so by the opposing nation or nations. The enemy is portrayed as less than human; for only by seeing our opponent as not endowed with human dignity and feelings can we tell ourselves that it is right to kill him. On the other hand, we tend to reassure ourselves that we are more than human. Whereas we are a little lower than the angels, as it were, our opponent is an imaginative and diabolically clever beast.

As the war progresses, this sharp dichotomy becomes even greater, since the propaganda mills now grind furiously. In the beginning, we say that we shall restrain our violence and condemn our opponent for not exhibiting self-restraint. In the end, however, there is little to choose from a moral point of view between the two sides: Hitler burned Jews, allegedly as a war measure, and the United States incinerated thousands of Japanese women and children, also as a war measure. The fact that the former acted on the firm earth and the latter from the air does not create a moral difference between the two. When a war finally comes to a conclusion, the often noble ends of the "victors" have been so distorted by the means used and by the alleged necessities of military conflict that even partisans wonder what the war has been about. Sometimes the ends have been completely forgotten, and the results of the war are the direct reverse of what the leaders originally proclaimed as their purposes. Thus Chamberlain entered World War II in 1939 with the avowed objective of "preserving the integrity of Poland"; but by the end of the war, his objective had been completely forgotten, and Poland was as lacking in "integrity" after the war as before it.

The American Civil War, in its net consequences, impeded the struggle for human freedom through the hatred, divisiveness, and sheer destruction it engendered. While its practical alternative — recognition of the Confederacy — would indubitably have created certain difficulties, it would have provided a much better atmosphere for the eventual elimination of chattel slavery and other forms of servitude. Besides wiping out many able future leaders, the war served to help fix many Southerners in their prejudices and did little to eliminate the rampant racism prevalent in the North. Although the North claimed that it was fighting an arrogant Southern aristocracy, in reality it was surrendering to the militaristic biases of that aristocracy by stooping to its own low level of war.

World War I, when we look back upon it now, was (as we suggested earlier) not only immoral but stupid. Its consequences, such as the promotion of social and political instability, the enhancement of the power of the rich (particularly in the United States), and the creation and perpetuation of bitterness, were undesirable, because the war itself was immoral. To be sure, it can be argued that some good was a by-product of the conflict — the deposition of the Hohenzollern dynasty, for instance — but the good was far and away outweighed by the evil it set in motion.

World War II can be looked upon in about the same way. While it destroyed one tyranny, it vastly expanded the power of another. A generation after it was concluded, there was no more "democracy" or political stability in the world than before it was waged; and while the war was not, of course, wholly responsible for this, it is a fair judgment that it did little if anything to help and much, probably, to make worse a bad situation. As many persons lived under tyrannical and torturing regimes 30 years after World War II as before that conflict. The war destroyed a trillion or more dollars worth of precious natural resources, as well as some 30 to 40 million human lives. The claim that American entry into the war somehow helped save "civilization" is utterly spurious, if these judgments have any validity.[51]

As for the Vietnam war, both its immorality and its sheer stupidity became evident, even to nonpacifists, earlier than did the iniquity of other conflicts. Even then, however, the war had gone on some five years (until the Tet offensive of 1968) before a wave of hostile public opinion began to set in. And when the hostility did become widespread, much if not most of it was not based on the sheer immorality and stupidity of the war but rather on the apparent conviction that the United States could not "win" it. When such a slow recognition of its unjustifiability is associated with one of the least defensible wars in all history, the student of civilization might well despair of human beings ever becoming aware that all wars are morally illegitimate.

In every war, large numbers will agree that if the war were to be taken in itself and in terms of short-run consequences, it would not be justified: The killing and destruction are too obvious. Few would support killing and destruction as ends in themselves. But most of mankind still somehow believes that while deliberate destruction of human lives cannot be justified as an end, it can be vindicated as a means to noble ends. In the Vietnam war, for instance, the stated ends of both sides had exalted rings about them: both advocated "self-determination"; both said that human dignity should be respected; both exalted "democracy"; and both placed a high value on "freedom."[52] At many points it was difficult to distinguish the stated aims of the Democratic Republic of Vietnam from those professed by the Americans who opposed Hanoi. Yet while the professed aims were so similar, both sides resorted to indiscriminate killing, prevarication, and contempt for personality. Both justified the war, not in terms of how it was affecting human beings at the time but in terms of what they thought the war would do "in the long run." Somehow out of short-run hate would come long-run love and democracy; out of wholesale bombing of native villages would emerge genuine peace; out of shooting prisoners would come liberation, and so on. And millions of human beings believed such propositions.

What was true of the Vietnam war is true of all war. It is universally repudiated in its short-run consequences. Always we have to vindicate war, if we do so at all, by appealing to its allegedly good long-run consequences which, at the time, can never be seen. In every war, then, we are appealing from the seen to the unseen; from obviously ghastly immediate consequences to long-run consequences which we imagine are there. Curiously enough, any given war is usually defended by the so-called political realists, who spurn the advice of supposedly "unrealistic" pacifists and others. Yet what can require a greater faith in the unseen than what the war defender asks us to believe — that out of killing and hatred will come peace and justice and love? Prima facie, it would appear, the defender of any war is asking us to have a much greater faith than is the opponent of the war, for he is telling us that all the admitted, immediately disastrous attributes of war will help produce their opposites, or will at least, in a negative way, remove the obstacles to their opposites.

Almost every generation will offer new excuses for allegedly new types of war. Thus in our day, while many will oppose war in general, they will make an exception for supposed "wars of liberation." The argument is that there are two types of war, imperialist and liberating, and the latter are designed to eliminate "colonialism" and foreign exploitation. Often associated with the name of Mao Tse-tung, with his curious doctrine that political power grows out of the barrel of a gun, a war of liberation ostensibly eliminates classes who have oppressed peasants and workers, and the latter are then "free." Che Guevara is said to have had a similar notion. Wars of liberation have thrown up their heroes, just as traditional revolutions have produced theirs. During the Vietnam war General Vo Nguyen Giap was said by his admirers to exemplify all the virtues to be found in a war of liberation: he knew how to conduct a successful "guerrilla" war and to hold at bay a mighty imperialist power; he was clever at tactics; and he understood the means of avoiding direct confrontation with the enemy, thus wearing down its power. For these admirers, all this differentiated him from enemies like General William Westmoreland, who stood for "imperialist" war. While both leaders had few compunctions about taking human lives en masse and each side had its own My Lais, somehow the destruction was seen as liberating when presided over by General Giap and as enslaving when directed by General Westmoreland.

Now there is little if any evidence that wars of liberation are any more or less liberating than those designated as imperialist. They are both bloody conflicts showing utter contempt for human beings, for the truth, and for morality. As John Swomley points out, the leaders of wars of liberation have often been rather stupid figures, with very little sense of reality and a tendency to make the violent act an end in itself.[53] Although some will point to China as an example of a nation "liberated" through a war of liberation, the full impact of violence on the Chinese people has not yet been adequately assessed. There seems to be little doubt, to be sure, that economic well-being has considerably improved for the average Chinese, but economic conditions are surely only one test of liberation, and indeed, they may be purchased at the expense of almost every other exemplification of freedom, equality, and fraternity. Certainly there has been little if any political liberation in China, by any definition of that difficult term.

Capital Punishment. Another obvious example of violent coercion is capital punishment. Like war, it deliberately takes human life. Like war, too, it involves depreciating the personality of the one whose life is to be taken: He must be portrayed as the devil or as a sort of nonhuman monster. To be sure, he sometimes becomes a kind of hero to those smarting from the injustices of society, but even in this role his virtues are so exaggerated that he becomes nonhuman in another way. Either to exalt persons to the ranks of godlike creatures or to demean them by denying that they possess any virtues at all shows lack of respect for them as fellow human beings.

As in the case of war, we are often, to be sure, rather ambivalent about capital punishment. Thus we try to conceal its true meaning by euphemistically terming it "execution" rather than using the more blunt term "deliberate killing by the State." Perhaps we do this to hide our own feelings of guilt in supporting the institution at all. As in war, so in capital punishment, the fact that the act is intrinsically wrong is the root of its having long-run undesirable consequences. Its existence makes a mockery of the notion that the State exists to preserve and enhance the value of human life and the good life. There is not even any evidence that capital punishment deters others from crime and, in fact, it may actually do the reverse.[54]

Nonphysical Violent Coercion

But our conception of violent coercion does not stop with the utilization of violent physical force, although that is its most obvious expression. As we noted before, there are forms of spiritual violence against human beings which can be as irremediably injurious as the physical. Thus the utilization of the lie in politics is not only intrinsically wrong; it also tends to lead to consequences which undermine politics as the deliberate direction of collective affairs and entrap the perpetrator in a whole network of situations which destroys him. It is not without reason that Gandhi sees "truth force" as opposed to "violence."[55] When the New Testament avers that "The truth shall make you free"[56] it suggests the notion that freedom and truth are interwoven and that both are opposed to the utilization of violence. The politics of Watergate illustrate in dramatic fashion how, once lies are initiated, there is a tendency for them to multiply, each successive lie seeming necessary in order to cover up its predecessor. Eventually, however, the perpetrator of the lie may be destroyed in the meshes of the untruth he has exalted.

Institutions which build in severe economic exploitation also may be thought of as embodying violence, for they tend to lead to that outrageous injury of human beings which we have associated with the meaning of violence. Although violence is sometimes defined as the illegal use of force, our definition would include under the rubric all those acts, even those under cover of positive law, which either deliberately take human life or build into the structure of society unredressable injury to human life.

Nonviolent Coercion

Between the pole of violence and that of persuasion will lie various types of nonviolent coercion which, depending on circumstances, may conceivably be utilized with legitimacy. Whether or not the act is legitimate or authoritative or justifiable (whichever term one chooses to use) will depend on such factors as motivation and intention, improbability of serious injury to the person involved, possibility of the coercion's being subject to control, timing, and duration of the coercion. All violent coercion, we must repeat, is without authority. Nonviolent coercion may or may not have authority.

When we speak of nonviolent motivation and intention, we mean that what moves us to utilize coercion and to hold the goal we have in mind ought to be the integrity and freedom of the person involved and the good life for the community. The burden of proof must always be on those who utilize the coercion, and such motivations as personal enrichment or power must be ruled out. By definition, the coercion must be such that it is not likely to result in serious injury to the individual and that any injury is incidental, accidental, and remediable. A very important element is the probability of control for the goal we have set up; thus some forms of what appears to be nonviolent coercion might tend more than others to lead, under certain circumstances, to violence. Timing, too, is important: what might be appropriate at one point might not be so at another. If the coercion extends over too long a period, its controllability might be affected and its efficacy impaired.

A forcible act such as pulling a child out of the way of an onrushing automobile is coercive, but it is not violent coercion, for it is directed to a specific, limited, and legitimate object, the saving of a human life, and the coercive means used are such that they can be kept explicitly subordinated to the end. The act, moreover, occurs within the context of love and concern for the child. It is coercion when the child is paddled by the parent, when the drunk is forcibly put by the police in a cell to sober up, when a corporation executive is fined after a hearing for violation of the antitrust laws.

Making the Distinction

But the nonviolent acts described above, although all of them are coercive and probably authoritative, cannot be equated ethically with the bombing of a city or the killing of a person by the State or the torture of a prisoner. The waging of a civil war for the professed end of social justice is certainly an act of coercion, but it is hardly the moral equivalent of the coercion involved in a boycott, or a strike, or mass civil disobedience. (Although boycotts and strikes might, to be sure, under certain circumstances reach the point of violence, as when they lead to starvation.) Here again, the important distinction between violent and nonviolent coercion is illustrated. While we should be frank in avowing coercive elements in some nonviolent resistance (and neither Gandhi nor Martin Luther King fully faced up to this), we should not blot out the important distinction between violence and nonviolence. There will be gray areas, of course, in which the line is difficult to draw, but we should not on this ground fail to make an honest attempt to draw it.[57] Nor can we rely simply on "situational" ethics alone for our judgments — we must attempt to develop certain explicit standards beforehand, even at the risk of what some might pejoratively call "legalism" in ethics.

That the law and the police themselves often attempt, in their rather blundering way, to recognize distinctions of these kinds is illustrated in the development of the criminal law. The refinements in differentiations between types of crimes which characterize the historical evolution of criminal law suggest efforts to draw lines between violent and nonviolent crime. In modern times, the distinction the law tries to make between "deadly" and "nondeadly" force moves in the direction of the line we are seeking to establish between violent and nonviolent coercion. The theory of police action implicit in the organization of the London metropolitan police is itself an example of the point we are making. It is basically a conception of strictly limited coercion within the context of a police system that relies for its effectiveness primarily on widespread respect for the police; and it is significant that the original advice that the London police be unarmed came from a former army officer who had been head of the military police and who had observed that police without arms were far more likely to be respected than those who were armed.[58]

Violence is a heart-thrust at both authority and order, whether the violence be exercised by officials or by ordinary citizens. A police force which turns to the "third degree"; a government which operates in an aura of secrecy; a state which resorts to war under any circumstances — all undermine the possibilities of deliberate ordering of human affairs and in doing so betray the implicit purposes of politics. Moreover, resort to violence, contrary to certain popular notions, does not reflect great power. Rather it indicates that one has lost power. As Charles E. Merriam observes, a rapist is not an example of a man with great sexual power; neither is a government or a revolutionary movement which turns to violence an exemplification of political power.[59]

Despite the fact that utilization of violence reflects the absence of power, it continues to remain one of the sharpest and most poignant challenges to modern civilization. Why? There are, of course, many reasons. One lies in the widespread existence of personality frustration, which has been explored in numerous works.[60] Then, too, sharp and arbitrary class distinctions provoke acts of desperation and inhumanity. We might also mention the deceptive nature of violence; it appears, superficially, to "get things done" quickly: hence revolutionists turn to it, "law and order" advocates defend its use by the police, and governments spend billions of dollars on its instruments. Our image of "revolution" is that it is violent. Hence almost everyone has heard of Lenin but very few have ever known the name of Bishop Nikolai Frederik Grundtvig and his associates, who in the 19th century helped to develop far more basic changes in Danish society than Lenin did in Russia.[61]

How can we reduce the level of violence? The answer to this question is many faceted. Broadly speaking, the creation of a just society, as we have in general defined it, is a necessary condition. More explicitly, all the challenges with which we have been dealing in this chapter are relevant: developing a greater will to freedom, eliminating the distortions of law, seeking ways to make bureaucracy accountable and responsible, endeavoring to discover a balance between centralization and decentralization, and keeping open full and free communication. In the next two chapters, too, we shall suggest the importance of changed attitudes to technology and the attainment of distributive justice in the economic area as significant factors.

In rare situations, it may be that we will be confronted with the choice between committing acts of violence or ourselves suffering violence. (By "we," we mean groups and nations, as well as individuals.) What, then, should we do? If we adhere to the standards suggested here, we shall respond with Socrates' words : "It is better to suffer injustice than to commit it."[62] This is a kind of moral ultimate which one either accepts or rejects. It is an "unnatural" answer, for the natural response would be to say that, unfortunate though it may be, we ought to do violence if the only alternative is to have it done to us. But the unnatural response is teleologically natural, in that it reflects a morality of man as he ought to and might be, rather than as he has been and is. It is the kind of morality pointed to by the great religions, which are endeavoring to state the standards that ought to obtain if man's civility is to reach perfection.

Civilization and Organization: Slavery or Freedom?

A part of what we have been saying in this chapter (and it might have been expanded almost indefinitely) is that civilization entails organization, but the very organization through which we seek justice and freedom tends to become perverted and to result in a kind of slavery and a diminution of possibilities for equality and fraternity. Organization may be reflected in the manipulation of individuals for its own ends, in the tendency to self-seeking oligarchy so carefully noted by writers like Roberto Michels, in the ambivalent character of law, in the curious paradoxes and contradictions of bureaucracy, in the movement toward excessive centralization and integration, in tendencies to rule by one and even tyranny, in the frustration of communication, or in the distortions revealed in political violence. In any case, organization, on one of its sides, does indeed entail a kind of servitude, as Nicolai Berdyaev and others have argued.[63]

How, then, do we wrest from organization anything resembling liberty, equality, and fraternity in justice? Broadly speaking, we have suggested two ways. One involves the deliberate effort to check tendencies to complexity in civilization, after the manner of the classical model. This entails some hostages to the Tolstoyan point of view and, as we shall see in the next chapter, involves serious criticisms of technological development. It means that by questioning the idea that progress is primarily a matter of material accumulation, we may be able, through social, political, economic, and legal reorganization including structures encouraging accountability, to check centralization, oligarchy, irresponsible bureaucracy, tendencies to monarchy and tyranny, frustration of free communications, and proliferation of political violence. The second way entails development of a much more sensitive political consciousness on the part of individuals. This would mean that their will to freedom would develop and that increasing numbers would, for example, be ready to disobey illegitimately claimed authority.[64] It suggests, too, that a much more acute consciousness of power as a two-way affair would flourish and that principles of nonviolence would be held by millions rather than thousands. Perhaps we can say that the first approach deals with the issue from an external point of view, while the second concentrates on internal consciousness. Actually, of course, the two approaches supplement and sustain each other; external constraints and limitations on complex civilization provide a context within which a new political consciousness can arise, but the new political consciousness and broadened awareness are essential if external constraints and limitations are to be effective.

Both external and internal avenues are involved in one of the most vital issues of the Nature-civilization problem — that of technology. Both, too, are deeply connected with the political issues posed by the economy. And neither the technological nor the economic problem can be divorced from the questions we have been considering in this chapter.

In the following two chapters, then, we turn to the politics of technology and economy, seeking to relate it to the issues of this chapter and to the general problem of achieving justice.

Notes

1   Cf. Robert MacIver, *Community* (London: Macmillan, 1917) and *Society* (New York: R. Long and R. R. Smith, 1931), and Robert Nisbet, *The Quest for Community* (New York: Oxford University Press, 1953).

2   Attempts to explain "apathy" in modern politics are, of course, varied. Voting studies, such as the early one by Charles Merriam and Harold Gosnell, *Non-Voting: Causes and Methods of Control* (Chicago: University of Chicago Press, 1924), attempt to get at one dimension. Many factors appear to be involved and, in the end, one often continues to remain mystified. Psychological, sociological, economic, and other factors are supposed to be at work, but in any given situation it is difficult to say which are primarily responsible. It may be that we should turn the question around and, instead of asking why human beings are politically apathetic, inquire why a few are not. Perhaps we can say that the tasks of politics are relatively so recent in the evolution of mankind that it would be surprising if the majority were nonapathetic. See, for example, S. M. Lipset, *Political Man* (Garden City, N.Y.: Doubleday Anchor Books, 1960).

Stein Rokkan, in "Mass Suffrage, Secret Voting, and Political Participation," in Lewis A. Coser, ed., *Political Sociology: Selected Essays* (New York: Harper Torchbooks, 1967), pp. 101-31, suggests that the very success of movements for broader participation by way of the suffrage may lead to less intense political activity, on the whole. Ronald V. Sampson, in *The Psychology of Power* (New York: Random House, Vintage Books, 1968) attempts to analyze, along with the psychology of domination, the psychology of submission or subordination. Unfortunately, far too many political scientists seem to think of voting as the decisive act of political participation, whereas discussion, organizational work, and similar commitments would seem to be far more basic and significant.

Both normatively and empirically, Carole Pateman, *Participation in Democratic Theory* (Cambridge: University Press, 1970) is important. On political alienation, see Robert Lamb et al., *Political Alienation* (New York: St. Martin's Press, 1975).

Curiously enough, some writers seem to think that a certain amount of apathy is desirable. Thus Gabriel Almond and Sidney Verba in *The Civic Culture* (Boston: Little Brown, 1965), p. 343, appear to believe that apathetic or indifferent citizens provide a cushion for desirable sociopolitical change. If many of them were active, they might, being conservative, tend to inhibit change.

3   Whatever their party label, successive mayors of New York City sought to hide the fact of budgetary imbalances by such devices as using borrowed money for current expenditures rather than for the capital expenditures for which it was intended. But the leaders of New York City were not unique in this respect.

4   See particularly the *Knights,* whose plot turns on the apparent subservience of leaders like Cleon to the spoiled Demos. But Demos is not aware of the ways in which his ostensible subordinate is actually manipulating him.

5   See Roberto Michels, *Political Parties,* trans. E. and C. Paul, rev. ed. (Glencoe, Ill.: Free Press, 1949).

6   On union democracy, see Martin Lipset, M. Trow, J. S. Coleman, *Union Democracy* (Glencoe, Ill.: Free Press, 1956). On democracy and size, note R. A. Dahl and E. R. Tufte, *Size and Democracy* (Stanford: Univ. Press, 1973).

7   Quoted in Bart. De Ligt, *The Conquest of Violence,* trans. Honor Tracy, (New York: E. P. Dutton, 1938), p. 109.

8   See Fromm's *Escape from Freedom* (New York: Farrar & Rinehart, 1941), *The Sane Society* (New York: Rinehart, 1955), and similar works.

9   *Laws,* Bk. III.

10   See, for example, Charles E. Merriam, *Political Power* (New York: McGraw-Hill Book Co., 1934), particularly ch. 4, "The Credenda and Miranda of Power."

11   The importance of Roosevelt's Presidency in shaping American conceptions can be grasped by studying such critical biographies as H. F. Pringle, *Theodore Roosevelt* (New York: Harcourt, 1931). Volumes of this kind demonstrate Roosevelt's conception of the "strong" or, as it is often called today, the "imperial" Presidency.

12   On the CIA, see particularly Victor Marchetti and John D. Marks, *The CIA and the Cult of Intelligence* (New York: Alfred A. Knopf, 1974); Patrick J. McGarvey, *CIA: The Myth and the Madness* (New York: Saturday Review Press, 1972); and H. Paul Jeffers, *CIA: A Close Look at the Central Intelligence Agency* (New York: Lion, 1971).

13   During the Kennedy administration, Arthur Sylvester, Assistant Secretary of Defense, publicly stated that he believed it was legitimate under certain circumstances for the President to prevaricate in statements to the people. Thomas A. Bailey, in his study of the control of foreign policy, *The Man in the Street* (New York: Macmillan Co., 1948) seems to take a similar position when he justifies what he calls the repeated deceptions of Franklin Roosevelt before American entry into World War II. See pp. 11-14.

14   Speaking of peasant exploitation and revolts immediately calls to mind such episodes as the Circumcellion rebellions of St. Augustine's day and the peasants' insurrections of the 16th century. The literature on agrarianism, exploitation of the peasant, and agrarian insurrections is, of course, enormous. See W. B. Bizzell, *The Green Rising* (New York: Macmillan Co., 1926, reprinted 1973), which is a historical survey of agrarianism, with particular reference to the United States. The 16-century peasant insurrection was treated by Friedrich Engels in *The Peasant War in Germany* (New York: International Publishers, 1926). Much of the theory of economic development in modern times turns on the impact of Western industrialist civilization on peasant cultures, with the "terms of trade" usually in favor of the former.

15   *Republic,* Bk. II. St. Augustine takes a similar position.

16   On the tendency for "community" to break down in large cities, see, for example, Jane Jacobs, *Death and Life of Great American Cities* (New York: Random House, 1961). See also Robert Park, *Human Communities* (Glencoe, Ill.: Free Press, 1952).

17   Wincenty Lutoslawski, *The World of Souls* (London: G. Allen & Unwin, 1924), p. 161.

18   I John, IV:18.

19   Thomas Henry Huxley, *Evolution and Ethics* (New York: D. Appleton, 1896).

20   See Martin Luther King, *Stride toward Freedom* (New York: Harper, 1958) and *Why We Can't Wait* (New York: Harper & Row, 1964).

21   This seems to be in part the teaching of Arnold J. Toynbee in *The Study of History*, 12 vols. (New York: Oxford University Press, 1934–1954), one of whose major themes is that civilizations disintegrate not primarily because of external attack but rather by reason of internal "decay." Part of the problem of decay may be the erosion of the will to freedom.

22   See Max Weber, *Theory of Social and Economic Organization* (New York: Oxford University Press, 1947) and H. H. Gerth and C. Wright Mills, trans. and ed., *From Max Weber: Essays in Sociology* (New York: Oxford University Press, 1946). Gaetano Mosca, in *The Ruling Class* (New York: McGraw-Hill Book Co., 1939) provides a semiclassic statement of the tendency to elite rule in civilization. Robert K. Merton and others, eds., offer essays in the sociology of bureaucracy in *Reader in Bureaucracy* (Glencoe, Ill.: Free Press, 1951). George Santayana, in *Dominations and Powers* (New York: Scribner's, 1951), sees the possibilities for freedom as remote in a civilization characterized by "dominations and powers," including bureaucracy. See also Thomas Bottomore, *Elites and Society* (Baltimore, Penguin Books, 1969); W. Boyer, *Bureaucracy on Trial* (Indianapolis: Bobbs-Merrill Co., 1964); Charles Hyneman, *Bureaucracy in a Democracy* (New York: Harper, 1950); and C. Jacobs, *Policy and Bureaucracy* (Princeton, N.J.: D. Van Nostrand Co., 1966).

23   Diocletian's attempt to develop a feeling of awe in attitudes of the people to bureaucracy is well known and was treated classically in Edward Gibbon's *Decline and Fall of the Roman Empire*, ed. H. N. Milman (New York: Ward, Lock & Co., n.d.), vol. I, pp. 252–55. Gradation of titles was one method of promoting awe; the Emperor apparently believed, perhaps with some justification, that ordinary men and women would be overwhelmed by such titles as "most excellent."

24   On the Inquisition, see particularly H. C. Lea, *A History of the Inquisition of the Middle Ages*, 3 vols. (New York: Russell & Russell, 1958). One is impressed in reading Lea by the extent to which the Inquisition reflected the characteristics so often associated with what we think of as "bureaucracy."

25   C. Northcote Parkinson, *Parkinson's Law* (Boston: Houghton Mifflin Co., 1957), and *Mrs. Parkinson's Law* (Boston: Houghton Mifflin Co., 1968).

26   Plato, *Laws*, Bk. IV, where he stresses the importance of the "Preface" to a law. In the preface, the purpose of the law is to be stated at length, thus appealing to man's sense of rationality and hopefully leading to his voluntary compliance.

27   St. Augustine, *The City of God*, Bk. IV, ch. 4.

28   See Ferdinand Lundberg, *The Rich and the Super-Rich* (New York: Lyle Stuart, 1968).

29   Charles Dickens, *Bleak House* (New York: Dodd, Mead, 1951).

30   See President's Commission on Law Enforcement and Administration of Justice, *The Challenge of Crime in a Free Society* (Washington, D.C.: Government Printing Office, 1967), particularly pp. 192–96. A chart of organization of an "organized crime family" is provided at p. 194.

31   Plato's *Statesman* and *Laws*.

32   St. Paul, Romans XIII.

33   See Mulford Q. Sibley, *The Obligation to Disobey: Conscience and the Law* (New York: Council on Religion and International Affairs, 1970).

34   Of course, there is always a problem of defining the term "law." To be law, according to some views, there must be adherence to certain basic principles. The fact that a decree may be issued by a ruler does not necessarily make it law. The quasi Natural Law views of such writers as Lon Fuller bear on this issue. See Lon Fuller, *The Law in Quest of Itself* (Chicago: Foundation Press, 1940).

35   Aquinas, *Summa Theologica*, I-II, Question 96, Art. 2, "Whether It Belongs to Human Law to Repress All Vices."

36   Both Plato's *Laws* and Aristotle's *Politics* emphasize this point.

37   By the time of Trajan, early in the second century, observes Samuel Dill, and certainly by the time of the Antonines, late in that century, signs of the doom of free city life were to be seen. Despite much civic spirit, Dill goes on,

> there broods a shadow. It is not merely the doom of free civic life, which is so clearly written on the walls of every curial hall of assembly . . . , to be ful-filled in the long-drawn tragedy of the fourth and fifth centuries. . . . It is the feeling of Dion, when he watched the Alexandrians palpitating with excite-ment over a race in the circus, or the cities of Bithynia convulsed by some question of shadowy precedence or the claim to a line of sandhills. . . . It is the burden of all religious philosophy from Seneca to Epictetus, which was one long warning against the perils of a materialized civilization.

Samuel Dill, *Roman Society from Nero to Marcus Aurelius* (London: Macmillan, 1905), Bk. II, ch. 2, "Municipal Life," pp. 249-50.

38   See Brooks Adams, *The Law of Civilization and Decay* (New York: Macmillan, 1895).

39   A situation like that of Reserve Mining illustrates many facets of the rela-tion between the modern State and the business corporation. While the former's laws allow the latter to exist, the latter is able, through its economic power, to threaten its legal creator.

40   *Republic*, Bk. II.

41   While Thomas Jefferson and the sixth-century B.C. Lao-tze should not be equated in their political philosophies, both were at least dubious about the value of complex civilization. Both seemed to see as one of its perils the apparently in-evitable development of political centralization. And Jefferson's well known "That government is best which governs least" is matched by Lao-tze's "That government is best which governs not at all."

42   Both Owen and Gandhi envisioned a world of relatively small, only semi-industrialized communities rather loosely confederated with one another. On Owen's views, see J. O. Hertzler, *History of Utopian Thought* (New York: Mac-millan, 1926), pp. 213-221. Gandhi's outlook developed over the course of a lifetime, as he observed the effects of large-scale technology on Indian life and reflected on the advantages of small-community existence.

43   On mass communications and government control, see, for example, Mor-

ris L. Ernst and Alan N. Schwartz, *Censorship* (New York: Macmillan Co., 1964); Zechariah Chafee, Jr., *Government and Mass Communications: A Report from the Commission on Freedom of the Press,* 2 vols. in 1 (Hamden, Conn.: Shoe String Press, 1965); and William E. Hocking, *Freedom of the Press: A Framework of Principle* (New York: Da Capo Press, 1972).

44   See Bailey, *The Man in the Street.* While government lying has perhaps been most noteworthy in the field of foreign relations, it has also been present in matters involving domestic policy.

45   The attempt on the part of the Committee on Public Information to manipulate opinion during World War I is well known. And, as Walter Lippmann points out in *Public Opinion* (New York: Harcourt, Brace, 1922), much if not most of the information gained by individuals in a complex civilization is obtained indirectly or vicariously. This naturally makes it easier for remote agencies, including the government, to shape the kind of world that ordinary citizens "see."

46   And we still do not know all the details, but see the *Pentagon Papers* (Boston: Beacon Press, 1971) and David Halberstam, *The Best and the Brightest* (New York: Random House, 1972). One of the many depressing aspects of American involvement in the war in Vietnam was the way in which brilliant minds were employed to obfuscate issues and to suppress information.

47   Compare with C. J. Cadoux, *Christian Pacifism Re-Examined* (New York: Garland Library of War and Peace, 1972), pp. 14–45, where Cadoux suggests his own continuum.

48   The organic connection between ends and means is stressed throughout Dewey's works on ethics and politics. See, for example, John Dewey, *The Public and Its Problems* (New York: Henry Holt, 1927) and *Human Nature and Conduct* (New York: Henry Holt, 1922). Dewey's emphasis on "process" is closely related to the notion that means shape ends. The general emphasis of the New Testament, too, is in the same direction. A classic statement drawing heavily on the great religions is Aldous Huxley, *Ends and Means* (New York: Harper, 1937).

49   Rex Applegate, *Kill or Get Killed* (Harrisburg, Pa.: Military Service Publishing Co., 1943), pp. 4,5,23.

50   For details, see John Cameron, ed., *The Peleus Trial* (London: Wm. Hodge, 1948).

51   For discussions of American entry into World War II, see Charles A. Beard, *President Roosevelt and the Coming of the War: A Study in Appearances and Realities* (New Haven: Yale University Press, 1948) and Charles Tansill, *Back Road to War* (Chicago: Henry Regnery Co., 1952). A recent "revisionist" view which maintains that it would not have injured the cause of "democracy" had the United States not entered the war is expressed in Bruce M. Russett, *No Clear and Present Danger* (New York: Harper Torchbooks, 1972). Russett's volume is subtitled *A Skeptical View of the United States Entry into World War II.* The main weakness of analyses like Russett's is that they do not go far enough. They still suggest that war can be used for constructive ends, whereas it would seem clear to me that it can never be employed for such purposes.

52   For discussions of the war aims of the North Vietnamese, South Vietnamese, and the United States, see Marcus G. Raskin and B. B. Fall, ed., *The Vietnam Reader* (New York: Random House, 1968); Lyndon B. Johnson, "Remarks at Johns Hopkins University, April 7, 1965," *The New York Times,* April 8, 1965, p. 16; and the policy declaration of Premier Pham Van Dong, reprinted in *The New York Times,* April 14, 1965, p. 13.

53   See John Swomley, *The Ethics of Liberation* (New York: Macmillan Co., 1972).

54   For documents dealing with the problem of capital punishment, see, for example, Hugo Bedau, ed., *The Death Penalty in America: An Anthology* (Garden City, N.Y.: Anchor Books, 1964); Johan T. Sellin, ed., *Capital Punishment* (New York: Harper & Row, 1967); Arthur Koestler, *Reflections on Hanging* (New York: Macmillan, 1958); James A. Joyce, *Capital Punishment: A World View* (New York: Nelson, 1962); and John L. Pritchard, *A History of Capital Punishment* (New York: Citadel Press, 1960).

55   See Gandhi's autobiography, *An Autobiography: The Story of My Experiments with Truth* (London: Phoenix Press, 1949). See also his *Satyagraha in South Africa* (Stanford, Cal.: Academic Reprints, 1954).

56   John, VIII:32: "If you abide by what I teach, you are really disciples of mine, and you will know the truth and the truth will set you free." (Goodspeed)

57   See Cadoux, *Christian Pacifism Re-Examined.*

58   On the London metropolitan police, see, for example, *Royal Commission upon the Duties of the Metropolitan Police,* 3 vols. (reprint of 1908 ed.) (New York: Arno Press, 1971) and Charles Reith, *A New Study of Police History* (Edinburgh: Oliver Boyd, 1956). Of the views of Sir Charles Rowan, first Commissioner of the London Metropolitan Police, Reith observes: "Rowan's conception of police law-enforcement machinery was, and is, something new and unique in history. The theory that crime and other forms of breach of law can be controlled more effectively by benevolent prevention than by repression," while it did not originate with Rowan, was given "infinitely wider scope" by him. "Prevention" of crime was seen as being "if used practically and scientifically, superior in effectiveness not only to repression but also to detection" (p. 35).

59   See Merriam, *Political Power.* Note also Hannah Arendt, *On Violence* (New York: Harcourt, Brace, 1970) and Paul Tillich, *Love, Power, and Justice* (New York: Oxford University Press, 1954).

60   The literature on aggression and frustration, directly and indirectly, is many faceted and abundant, but conceptions vary. Alternative psychological theories are treated, to take one example, in Calvin S. Hall and Gardner Lindzey, *Theories of Personality* (New York: John Wiley & Sons, 1957). Hans Selye, in *The Stress of Life* (New York: McGraw-Hill Book Co., 1956), deals with the physiological responses of human organisms to the pressures of existence. T. W. Adorno, Else Frenkel-Brunswik, Daniel J. Levinson, and R. Nevitt Sanford, in a very well-known earlier study, *The Authoritarian Personality* (New York: Harper, 1950) seek in their analysis to probe such factors as frustration and aggression in

the shaping of personality and presumably culture. H. G. Wells, in one of his more imaginative nonfictional works, *The Anatomy of Frustration* (New York: Macmillan, 1936), explores in a nontechnical way some of the issues.

61 On the activities of Bishop Grundtvig and the folk school movement in 19th-century Denmark, see Johannes Knudsen, *Danish Rebel: A Study of N.F.S. Grundtvig* (Philadelphia: Muhlenberg Press, 1955), and Paul G. Lindhardt, *Grundtvig: An Introduction* (London: S. C. M. Press, 1951).

62 *Gorgias,* in *The Dialogues of Plato,* trans. Benjamin Jowett, 2 vols. (New York: Random House, 1937), vol. 1, p. 528.

63 Nicolai Berdyaev, *Slavery and Freedom* (London: BLES, 1943) and similar works.

64 See Etienne de la Boétie, *Voluntary Servitude,* trans. Harry Kurtz, reprinted as *The Politics of Obedience: The Discourse of Voluntary Servitude* (New York: Free Life Editions, 1975).

FIVE

Civilization, Politics, and Technology

WE HAVE SUGGESTED, in the three preceding chapters, some of the elements of justice, particularly as they relate to the conceptions of freedom, equality, and fraternity. We have seen these issues against the background of five responses to, or ways of looking at, the general problem of Nature and civilization. In the preceding chapters our concern has been to show how civilization, and particularly modern civilization, creates dilemmas or exacerbates contradictions in the very process of its quest for liberation of the personality.

ʹ From time to time in this discussion we have noted the importance of man's tool-making capacity in the definition of civilization and have suggested its impact on the political quest for justice. Technology, we have hinted, plays an important role in creating the political challenges and may conceivably be an instrument in their solution.

But thus far our references to technology have been incidental. It has not occupied the center of the stage, so to speak. In this chapter we make technology the focus and seek to assess its relation to the Nature-civilization paradigms, the political challenges, the quest for justice, and the goal of freedom, equality, and fraternity. In the process, we inevitably touch on the problem of energy in the development of civilization, the relation of technology to vegetable and animal nature, and what has come to be called ecology.

161

We first consider the enormous impact of technological change on the development of civilization and the human consciousness. We then turn to an analysis of the ambivalences of the human consciousness about it, particularly but not exclusively in modern times. Finally, we take a position about technology, in light of alternative views of Nature and civilization and of the issues of justice and politics.

Man as a Tool-Making Animal

While man has often been described as a political animal, sometimes as a laughing animal, and at other points as a rational animal, one especially important way of identifying him would be to say that he is a tool-making animal. This can be understood in two senses: He makes physical tools and devices which extend his powers over Nature, and he invents social tools or institutions. Here we shall be concerned primarily with the former, although obviously it is inevitable that the two will influence and shape each other. Thus the techniques worked out by law for human relations will both influence and be influenced by physical technology. And both forms of technology will be the fruit of nonmaterial factors — imagination, intelligence, foresight — which we particularly associate with the term "humanity" as civilization evolves.

Technē, art or skill, is present in the human species from the very beginning; and while other animals, to be sure, have this capacity to some extent and perhaps to a greater degree than was formerly thought,[1] the difference between animals and the human species in this respect is a difference of kind rather than merely of degree. Within the human species, moreover, as civilization supplants primitive human nature, consciously and deliberately contrived techniques in the social realm become highly significant, thus setting the human species apart even more emphatically from the other aspects of creation, whether beasts or angels.

As we move from Nature to primitive human nature to civilization, the evolution of technique plays a key role; the development of politics itself is in no small degree the result of shifting techniques in man's relation to Nature. The emergence of civilized man from hunting and fishing and pastoral-nomadic stages is profoundly associated with the refinements of his tool-making proclivities. The characteristic tools of each age deeply affect the nature of personal, cultural, and political life. We have already suggested that as the tools become more complex, the primitively natural recedes in significance, and man often tends to believe that he has completely transcended Nature.

Many traces of technological development and evaluation in ancient times are to be found in the Bible. Tubal-Cain, a descendant of Cain, is the first worker in brass.[2] The superior technology of the Egyptians is apparently admired by the Hebrews through many generations. Other nations, too, are recognized for their outstanding skills in some areas: Solomon calls on the Sidonians to help him construct the temple, since they are known for their techniques as builders.[3]

Biblical accounts pay particular attention to the technology of war. Just as distinctively political leadership often emerges first in the context of military conflict (as after the period of the Judges, who may be looked upon as ad hoc leaders raised up for particular situations but not for long-run political leadership), so men's skills in the mechanical area are intimately bound up with the evolution of warfare. Biblical writers are both frightened and fascinated by the development of the Egyptian war chariot, seeming to see in it a kind of symbol of civilization: It is an expression of civilized ingenuity and simultaneously a devilish instrument for destruction.

Outside of the Biblical tradition, too, the ancient world stood in awe of technological achievement. The enumeration of the Seven Wonders of the World gives us a clue as to the kinds of techniques the ancients admired: the pyramids were seen as exhibits of engineering skill; the Hanging Gardens of Babylon as reflections of man's capacity for creating his own world of the beautiful, beyond Nature; the statue of Zeus by Phidias as the utilization of technology for a noble religious purpose; the Colossus of Rhodes as a kind of gigantic representation of man himself; the temple of Artemis at Ephesus as a combination of the aesthetically and religiously valuable; the Mausoleum at Halicarnassus as an example of astounding architectural skill; and the remarkable lighthouse at Alexandria as a kind of technological symbol of all that commerce stood for in the life of man.

But despite the fact that ancient civilization was at one point on the verge of developing steam, and with it a vast expansion of available energy, it never took that step. And medieval civilization witnessed at first a decline in skills and only much later some revival — although such devices as the plow apparently underwent an almost continuous and remarkable evolution.

The significant fact about modern civilization is that its leap in terms of technology was so great as to constitute something comparable to the transformation that must have been wrought in the remote past by the invention of the wheel. Emerging from a 16th- and 17th-century world characterized by growing empiricism and nominalism, science insisted on studying Nature itself (or at least what it thought was Nature), rather than Aristotelean or other doctrines *about* Nature. The galaxy of scientific speculators from Bacon to the Cartesians laid the groundwork for the mechanistic view of the universe that characterized so much of 18th- and 19th-century thought. And this conception was in turn closely connected with its practical application — the explosion of technology.

Here it is impossible to indicate adequately the enormous significance of that explosion. Its immediate and remote implications have been traced out in the economic histories of modern times, in sociological analyses, and in works seeking to discover its meaning for politics and policy.[4] But it is well at least to remind ourselves sketchily of some of the more startling hallmarks and developments associated with complex technology. There has been an astounding release and consumption of energy — so fantastic, in fact, that it is scarcely imaginable: steam, electricity, internal combustion, atomic fission, and, in the future, possibly nuclear fusion and direct utilization of solar energy.

To illustrate the explosion, we can take the United States. Although throughout the 19th century per capita utilization of energy increased at a fairly rapid rate, making earlier civilizations pale into insignificance, the truly enormous consumption began toward the end of the century. By 1970, energy consumption was a startling 10 times as much as it had been in 1890. To be sure, the population during the same period tripled. But this still meant that per capita use was more than three times what it had been in 1890. In recent years, the utilization of some energy sources has been doubling every decade. While these estimates are for the United States, the rate of growth in some parts of the world is now even greater than in this country.[5]

It is small wonder that a sensitive thinker like Henry Adams, writing in 1907, should stand in utter awe at the energy developments of his day. He tried to relate man's techniques for the release of energy to cosmic developments. Although the atom had not yet been split, and he based his awe in part on the doubling of coal output every ten years from 1840 to 1900, his words are applicable to all periods of modern civilization. He saw man in relation to the forces of Nature and technology as a kind of catspaw of evolution in the release of power:

> Since 1800 scores of new forces had been discovered; old forces had been raised to higher powers, as could be measured in the navy-gun; great regions of chemistry had been opened up, and connected with other regions of physics . . . . Complexity had extended itself on immense horizons, and arithmetical ratios were useless for any attempt at accuracy. The force evolved seemed more like explosion than gravitation.[6]

And speaking of the "progress" of modern times in releasing the forces of Nature, he went on:

Power leaped from every atom, and enough of it to supply the stellar universe showed itself running to waste at every pore of matter. Man could no longer hold it off. Forces grasped his wrists and flung him about as though he had hold of a live wire or a runaway automobile . . . .[7]

As Adams looked about him, he concluded that John Stuart Mill's old dream of a "steady state" earth in which accelerated release of energy might stop would never come to pass. Man seemed to be in the grip of powers which would actually increase their stranglehold.

Flowing from the release of hitherto undreamed-of energy has been a vast increase in capacity for production of material goods. The land, which in previous history had surrendered its substance reluctantly and only after great toil, was now forced by the application of agricultural techniques to give up its treasures, seemingly without protest. The potentiality of relatively cheap food for all seemed to be at hand, particularly following the so-called Green Revolution of the 20th century's sixties.[8]

Other things being equal, too, the technological age meant that the proportion of those engaged directly in agriculture would drastically decline, almost to the vanishing point. Thus civilization, which even in its most urbanized expressions in the past was still built on the labor of a huge preponderance of agricultural workers, free and enslaved, for the first time in human experience found itself relying primarily on men and women living in centers of high population density. While previous civilizations, moreover, depended in considerable measure on the labor of chattel slaves or of serfs attached to the land, modern civilization has everywhere tended to substitute some mechanical contrivance for the often brutalizing labor of the slave. All this would have vast ramifications for the nature of politics.

With the expansion of complex technology, Nature itself retreated, or in the process was so transformed as to be scarcely recognized as Nature. Complex technology, in extending man's power so vastly, also made it possible for him to gut the earth very rapidly, to push wild animal life aside, to exploit the underground for its fossil fuels, and, far more than in previous ages, to counteract the effects of hot or cold weather or even, potentially, to change the weather itself. Nature, something previously often thought of as fixed or immutable, seemed now to be a factor that could be completely manipulated by man.

Likewise human nature, regarded by perhaps most political philosophers as basically unchanging, now appeared to be opened to all types of alteration through the development of biological sciences and technology.[9] By the 20th century, men were speaking about the possibilities of affecting the germ plasm directly, producing children out-

165

side the body of the mother, modifying behavior through surgical treatments, and prolonging human life to an average of 100 or 200 years (a prospect which had been envisioned long ago, of course, by certain utopian theorists).[10] If the basic character of human nature could be drastically changed, the technological age appeared to be wiping out the distinction, so ubiquitous in both psychology and political philosophy, between Nature and nurture.

After the beginning of the age of complex technology, some had envisioned the possibility of the human creature leaving the earth itself. Man's horizons would be so enlarged and his technology so perfected that he would be able to go to the moon or Mars or even some of the stars. By the middle of the 20th century these judgments about the possibilities of technology were more than dreams, and the earth seemed, even more than it had begun to appear at the outset of the modern age, merely a tiny speck in a universe which probably embraced countless forms of intelligent life.

By the seventies of the 20th century, space colonies between the earth and the moon were being seriously discussed. As envisioned by such physicists as Gerald O'Neill of Princeton and considered further by the National Aeronautics and Space Administration, the possibilities developed that colonies might provide living spaces for 10,000 former earth dwellers, generate electricity from sunlight and send it to the earth by microwave relay, and manufacture products from moon materials. One such colony could supposedly supply enough energy to satisfy New York City's needs, and 40 to 50 of them could fulfill the demands of the entire United States. While a single colony might cost as much as $100 billion, this would represent only a fraction of the value of the energy that might be produced. Proposals for such colonies were defended not only on economic grounds but also because they could satisfy man's apparently incurable desire for adventure and living on the frontier.[11]

Space explorations dramatized what astronomers had long known — the vastness of the world "out there," with its seemingly endless galaxies. At the same time, there was the usual dual implication: the very technology which helped confirm the vastness of the universe and made man seem a pigmy was itself the product of human ingenuity.

In another respect, too, there was a kind of paradox about the development of modern technology: on the one hand, it could be looked upon as an expression of human nature teleologically conceived; on the other hand, the more this telos was demonstrated, the less there seemed to be anything so fixed as human nature. In the closing days of the 20th century, for example, biological technology seemed on the verge of being able literally to transform the germ plasm, thus raising both the promise and the peril of all-too-frail human beings tampering directly with the course of biological evolution. Depending on how one viewed the psyche-body relationship, this might mean, if one were a "materialist," that manipulating the genetic nature of man could literally change his soul, or, if one were a nonmaterialist, that new ways of expressing man's soul through so-called matter would be provided. To use an analogy, a materialist interpretation might say that a newly designed radio — analogous to the newly transformed human body — would change the radio waves — analogous to the human soul — it received; a non-materialist could argue that the alteration of the physical instrument would simply make it either more or less sensitive to the radio waves. In either interpretation, genetic engineering of this type would constitute something of a revolution.

Technology and the Ambivalences of the Human Consciousness

As we proceed to analyze the responses of human thought to technology, we find a curious but understandable ambivalence to be one of its outstanding characteristics. The issue is, of course, an old one in political thought. We have already referred to Plato's discussion of it in Book II of the *Republic* and in the *Laws*. Here we attempt to spell out a little more explicitly some of the main lines of the debate, with particular reference to the modern consciousness.

The Historical Debate

The historical debate on the issue of man and technology took place in an environment not yet characterized by the ubiquity of complex technology, and dramatic illustrations of the impact of technology on man were therefore fewer than in the modern world. It is nevertheless instructive to recall the past discussion, since so much of it has more than echoes in the modern world.

An old tradition reflected in the Bible suggests that man was placed on earth to subdue it and to become master of the "fish in the sea" and the "fowl in the air."[12] He was to carry out this mission not because he had superior strength — which he did not — but by virtue of his capacity to know and to invent. Raw Nature was to be subordinated to human nature, first in a kind of spontaneous way — before the Fall of Man — and then later on within the context of his knowledge of good and evil. Man's technical capacity apparently was one of the hallmarks which made him a "little lower than the angels."[13] He was endowed with capacities for sharply differentiating himself from the lesser breeds of God's creation. When the children of Israel entered the Promised Land, Scripture tells us, they found the indigenous inhabitants worshipping Nature and natural objects.[14] But to revere stones and the moon and the stars, Yahweh taught, was to reverse the order of things: men would be denying their God-ordained role of subduing Nature through their skills and would be worshipping fellow creatures rather than the Creator. The ancient Hebrews were entitled to Palestine in part because they recognized this — because they were aware that beasts and trees and birds and fishes were made for man's use and were not designed to be exalted. The theological implications of this view are obviously far-reaching.

In the non-Hebraic ancient tradition, too, there is an awareness of man's technical prowess and of its implications for his place in the universe. The myths built around Prometheus are a recognition of this fact. The arts of shipbuilding and navigation among the ancient Phoenicians were widely seen as one of the most significant achievements of antique man. And we have already referred to the exaltation of the Seven Wonders of the World, which surely reflects the same tendency.

The ancients, too, were quite keenly aware of the close interrelation between the development of mechanical, commercial, and primitive industrial skills, on the one hand, and the nature of sociopolitical organization, on the other. Urban centers were a necessary condition for growth of the complex practical arts, even though more primitive technology might flourish in communities where cities were less developed. With the introduction of more intricate mechanical devices, human beings were compelled to devise more involved social technology.

In Greek thinking, as we suggested earlier, the very notion of "humanity" tends to be associated with at least a minimum development of technology. The practical arts, the growth of sociopolitical structures, and the development of human nature from its primitive form to its implicit goal go hand in hand.

Despite this general encomium on technology, however, there was an important element of doubt and fear which is reflected in many ways. The myth of the Fall of Man surely means in part that while man after the Fall becomes fully aware of the possibilities of knowledge, both pure and applied, he also has a nature which tends to make him use his techniques for destructive ends. He can improve his lot materially, as with the cultivation of the vine and the fig tree and many other improvements on Nature, but he pays an enormous price; for as he separates himself from primitive Nature and develops human nature, he tends to take pride in his achievements and to disregard the limits imposed by God on his actions. Because he can both know and apply his knowledge, he forgets his kinship to the beasts, on the one hand, and his subordination to his Creator, on the other. He believes he can, through his skill, create a completely new world, independent of vegetable and animal nature at one end and of God at the other. Too late, he is shocked into awareness, but only after great destruction, turmoil, and death. Periodically, God punishes him for his arrogance in forgetting that he is a creature who "cometh forth like a flower, and is cut down,"[15] a being who cannot really be a god.

Much of Genesis can be interpreted along these lines. Cain, who symbolizes the agricultural stage of development, offers the fruits of his primitive technology to God, who finds them less pleasing than the offerings of the pastoral Abel.[16] In anger, Cain kills Abel, thus becoming the first murderer.[17] Cain is "cursed" for his deed, but in him there remains the urge to improve the world technologically. Hence he becomes the founder of the first city, which carries him even farther from Nature than he had been before. Interestingly enough, he also becomes, according to some versions (that of Josephus, for example) the instigator of private property. Thus murderous impulses are associated with the development of the city, the growth of complex technology, and the institution of private property.

After the Flood, it will be remembered, man seeks through his technology to construct a tower which will reach to heaven. All the skills of ancient technicians are devoted to it, and it is well on its way to becoming one of the wonders of the world. But God is displeased by this challenge to him, and he punishes humans by confusing their tongues and dividing the world, up to now of one language, into many speeches and dialects.[18]

In sum, scientific and technological creativity after the Fall almost always leads to death and to social and cultural disintegration — at least to one side of the human consciousness. Much of the prophetic movement in ancient Israel sees the story of the Hebrews in this light, even though it does not accept the much later (and unorthodox, from the viewpoint of predominant Hebrew thought) interpretation of original sin. The development from tribalism to political society and from political society to centralized monarchy is in part the fruit of more involved technology, particularly the technique of war, and it is associated with bureaucratic social structures which supposedly distort man's true nature. Men forget their primitive simplicity, and their political structures become virtually uncontrollable. They worship their own creatures, instead of bowing before the raw Nature for which the original native inhabitants of Palestine were chastised; and this expression of the sin of idolatry, like the worship of Nature, is condemned as a central offense against the Lord.

In much of the prophetic movement, there is a nostalgic longing for an imagined early primitive community, where technical capacities are only partly developed and where money is virtually nonexistent. The ancient Hebrew consciousness sees Egypt and Assyria as symbols of technological development in its worst guise, and Egyptian war chariots become representative of the ever-present tendency in man to exhibit his enormously destructive proclivities, as commerce and technology expand.

In the non-Hebraic tradition also, man's technical capacity, while greatly admired, is also seen, after a certain stage, as showing a momentum of its own which offends the gods, who in anger then cause destruction to descend on the human race. The figure of the semihuman, semidivine Prometheus, although symbolizing humankind's vast scientific and technical potentialities, also reflects in his suffering the fact that the gods impose severe limits on what human beings can do without incurring the divine displeasure. Technical progress means social change, and there are strict bounds on man's ability to control social change through acts of deliberation. All this is very much reflected in Plato's Book II, which can be taken to stand for the notion that man's true teleological nature is not attained either in the primitive state, with technology at a bare minimum, or in a state where technology becomes too intricate or is allowed to develop too much momentum of its own.

Leo Strauss thus correctly characterizes the attitudes of both Plato and Aristotle to technology:

> The classics were for almost all practical purposes what now are called conservatives. In contradistinction to many present day conservatives, however, they knew that one cannot be distrustful of political or social change without being distrustful of technological change. Therefore they did not favour the encouragement of inventions . . . . They demanded the strict moral-political supervision of inventions; the good and wise city will determine which inventions are to be made use of and which are to be suppressed.[19]

The general position of classical political philosophy (and of the corresponding Hebrew view) may be said to have obtained down to the end of the Middle Ages (it is still reflected, to some extent, for instance, in the *Utopia* of Sir Thomas More), when it began to be supplanted by outlooks which do not have the dubiety expressed in the classics. Although the classical view continued to be held, to be sure, it was much less central than it was before the 17th century, though some might argue that it becomes more important again in the sixties and seventies of the 20th century.

Diverse Frameworks

The frameworks within which the problems of technology and politics have been viewed are closely related to the paradigms on the Nature-civilization problem which we noted in Chapter 2. There are at least three of these frameworks: (1) wholehearted acceptance of complex technology, without limits, as a key to the good life; (2) radical distrust of technological development; and (3) the adoption of some forms of technology and the rejection of others.

Wholehearted Acceptance. In the first framework for viewing technology and politics, complex technology is accepted rather wholeheartedly and without substantial limits on commitments to it. Characteristic of this view would be Hobbes-like paradigms and at least one version of notions akin to those of Locke. In the civilization-against-Nature paradigm, technology would be an important factor in the suppression of Nature, for it demands disciplines which either repress or sublimate raw natural energies, whether they be conceived as the overwhelming quest for domination or the direct expression of the Freudian id. To be sure, in all such paradigms the repressions of raw nature are purchased at an enormous price, but nevertheless they are necessary. Although Hobbes is by no means consistent, in general he seems to be saying that the more we repress direct expression of the desire to dominate by adopting the expediencies of the "laws of nature," the more we can indirectly express our egos under the artificialities of civilization. The development of technology is part of that process.

In Locke-like paradigms, technology antedates the dawn of the civil state, which came after the invention of such devices as money. By inference, then, the civil state is designed to protect the development of man's ingenuity which was already being expressed in the state of Nature. To be sure, some Locke-like thinkers (such as Thomas Jefferson) are wary of pushing technology too far beyond the limits of primitive Nature, lest its economic, social, and spiritual concomitants subordinate most men to the arbitrary power of other men rather than to the relatively benign laws of primitive Nature. Other Locke-like thinkers, however (and here we might mention the somewhat ambiguous William Godwin explicitly), seem to think that the economic, social, and political imperatives presumably set up by technology can be overcome or transcended, if necessary by further ingenious technology. Thus somehow, even elaborate technology can be made reconcilable with relatively simple and decentralized social and political organization. Godwin envisions one-man orchestras and similar devices which would not entail complex social organization.[20]

Some of those who wholeheartedly accept the supposed wonders of modern technology appear to ignore its seeming social and political imperatives. Francis Bacon,[21] one of the more naive thinkers in this respect, seems to think only of the supposed benefits and has little comprehension of the possible revolution in politics and social organization that might be entailed. Bacon, too, appears to suggest one of the more characteristic fruits of the modern technological spirit — that those who are proficient in science and the applied arts ought, ipso facto, to have a very weighty voice in political rule.

The Baconian outlook and some versions of the Lockean view became a basis for many philosophies of laissez-faire, which, beginning with the assumption that man's extension of powers through the machine could only amount to a net benefit for mankind, proceeded to argue that technological innovation is simply a private affair and of no concern to the politician. Privately introduced innovations in the technical sphere, it was said, would somewhat automatically redound to the public weal. In this view, whether or not the machine is introduced should depend on an individual's judgment about his own welfare, and in the long run there will be no conflict between thousands of judgments as to individual welfare on the one hand and the true public good on the other. The sole basis for one's judgment about whether to introduce a new machine will turn on one's estimate of whether or not it will benefit one economically. Naturally, if one gains by introducing a new mechanical device, one's competitors must emulate one to stay in business. The result is that the complex machine comes to be universally used. And, on the whole, the judgment of exponents of this view is that what profits individual entrepreneurs in their quest for economic gain will, without deliberate public planning, benefit the public. As in the 18th-century Bernard Mandeville classic,[22] "private" vices (seeking riches as a central aim in life) become "public" benefits, and the difficulties of political judgments can be avoided.

It should be emphasized, of course, that while political views such as laissez-faire have been historically associated with the wholehearted-acceptance framework, there is no necessary logical connection. One can have enormous faith in the power of technique to cure all evil and at the same time reject laissez-faire.

As a matter of fact, the paradigm which sees civilization as preparation for justice, as reflected in Marxism, does just that. Generally speaking, it holds that complex technology must be wholeheartedly accepted because, in the long run, it will emancipate man from the repressions of historical civilization. While the initial impact of modern technological development will create great dislocations in social life and enable capitalists to intensify their exploitation, this is simply a preparation for the time in which both negative and positive freedom will triumph. The Marxists hold that as technological innovation becomes more and more sophisticated, the "unprogressive" peasant will be largely liquidated[23] — and Marxism for the most part rejoices in this. The very processes, including intensification of technology, which enable the capitalist to exploit the worker will liquidate the capitalist. Of course, the State will have vastly expanded its powers in the "socialist" phase of evolution, but this, too, is part of the repression which leads ultimately to emancipation. Technological development, moreover, will produce the "objective situation" that will stimulate enlarged class consciousness, without which the revolution cannot take place.

Most socialists, moreover, whether Marxists or not, have tended to view technological development in this favorable light: It is assumed that regardless of short-run social evils attributable to technological innovation (unemployment, pollution, intensified exploitation, and so on), technological growth means progress in all areas of existence. Thus in the index to G. D. H. Cole's many-volumed *A History of Socialist Thought*, for example, "technology" plays an astonishingly small role. Most socialists since Marx seem simply to assume its "progressive" character and then go on to discuss political tactics which will presumably release its powers for the benefit of mankind.

To be sure, some early utopists — men like P. J. Proudhon and Charles Fourier,[24] for example — were less than enthusiastic. But most later utopian writers — like Edward Bellamy and H. G. Wells — seem largely to have cast these doubts aside. While Bellamy and Wells recognized that basic acceptance of long-term technological development would entail fundamental changes in the social and political structure, both seemed to be willing to pay the price.[25] The price included, in the case of Bellamy, a highly centralized and integrated political system in which citizens did not participate in politics until the age of 45. Bellamy understood the impact of complex technology, with its requirement of enormous pools of capital, on corporate and political structure. But he preferred to adjust the political structure to the needs of technology rather than use only those types of technology compatible with a decentralized political system. Wells sketched out a highly disciplined World State which presumably puts the most advanced technology at the service of mankind; and he regards his governing class, the samurai, as absolutely essential if the intricacies introduced by wholehearted adoption of modern technology are to be regulated, leisure is to be increased, and an abundance of material goods is to be made available for the masses.

Running through the wholehearted-acceptance framework is the notion that technology will improve the material lot of human beings, and with this improvement will somehow come all other goods. Although previous writers in the classical tradition (such as Sir Thomas More) had deliberately sought to keep human wants simple and limited, exponents of wholehearted acceptance appeared to see nothing dubious about the multiplication of human desires and their supply by an ever-expanding and less simple technology. The Baconian world of multifarious technical wonders appeared to them to be a universe wherein technological and material progress went hand in hand and in which material development almost automatically assured the good life in the social, aesthetic, and spiritual life of man as well.

A late 20th-century version of this confidence, at least in part, was to be found in those who criticized what they regarded as alarmist views about the exhaustion of energy sources. By the seventies it had become obvious to many that existing sources of energy (particularly petroleum) were very finite and that even total potential energy sources were not unlimited. The Club of Rome's *Limits to Growth* stressed this thesis, and other studies seemed to move in the same direction.[26] But the response of the critics was essentially that the alarmists or pessimists had not taken into account the ingenuity of human beings and their capacity through developing technology to make use of energy sources about which few had yet dreamed. The British economist Wilfred Beckerman[27] was one of the optimists. Basically, thinkers like Beckerman maintained that technology is the fruit of the human mind, and that mind has few if any limits on what it might do. Many pointed to the fact that there had often been "energy crises" before in human history and that the technical prowess of humankind had transcended them. Human ingenuity would and could do so in the future. Some pointed to the possibilities of utilizing other planets or even other galaxies. From this perspective, the natural resources supposedly depleted by one form of technology would be more than replenished by another. This was part of a whole attitude which seemed to suggest that the problems created by technology (pollution, waste, and many others) would be solved by it.

The Radical Criticism. Reacting sharply against the formulations which wholeheartedly accepted modern technology as a key to the good life were those who expressed a radical distrust of technological development. Rooted mainly in the civilization-as-corrupting paradigm (although present also in some Locke-like and Rousseau-like frameworks as well), the radical critique grounds its outlook on a number of propositions.

Perhaps one of the most fundamental of these propositions is that beyond a relatively primitive level, men become so dependent on machines that the machines in effect take over, direct, and sometimes destroy their creators. Subconsciously, perhaps, the Luddite movement of the early 19th century had this in mind, although the immediate occasion for the machine smashing was the fear of worklessness.[28] Mary Shelley's novel *Frankenstein* (1818), with its manmade mechanical monster who walks like a human being, certainly embodies the theme, even though the monster in the story does eventually develop a conscience.

Although, in the abstract, human beings can still control the machine, they are paralyzed in attempting to do so due to their utter and apparently irreversible dependence on it and to the sheer religious awe with which they come to view it. The machine literally becomes their idol. And some writers in the tradition of Darwinian evolutionary views suggest that just as the human creature evolved from beasthood into a conscious being, so are the machines developing from clocklike products of human artisanship into entities having an independence and consciousness of their own.

In his inimitable satire *Erewhon*, Samuel Butler, through "The Book of the Machines," expresses this viewpoint well:

There is no security against the ultimate development of mechanical consciousness, in the fact of machines possessing little consciousness now. A molusc has not much consciousness. Reflect upon the extraordinary advance which machines have made during the last few hundred years, and note how slowly the animal and vegetable kingdoms are advancing. The more highly organized machines are creatures not so much of yesterday, as of the last five minutes, so to speak, in comparison with past time. Assume for the sake of argument that conscious beings have existed for some twenty million years: see what strides machines have made in the last thousand! . . . . Is it not safer to nip the mischief in the bud and to forbid them further progress?[29]

And Butler goes on to suggest that men become increasingly helpless as they expand their machinery. Machines become extensions of human bodies. Thus the human being turns to a railroad to move him, an umbrella to take the place of his "natural" equipment, and factories to multiply the power of his natural body almost indefinitely. But in the process, this "progress" reduces the original body of the man to a piece of flabby muscle and his mind to a mechanism serving the superior mechanisms and wills developed by the machine.

If complex technology could be isolated from life as a whole and did not seemingly carry with it so many imperatives for all areas of existence, many argue, it would not be so nefarious. As it is, however, for every benefit the machine produces — at least beyond a relatively primitive stage of evolution — there are several effects which, in the judgment of the critics, are deleterious. Men and women spend a large part of their time tending the machine, adjusting their labor schedules to its needs, and mechanizing their own lives in order that they might serve it better. Because complex technology, to function, demands certain uniformities in the environment, all life tends to take on a uniformitarian character. As Jacques Ellul has emphasized, complex technology affects the nature of politics, of culture, and even of man's supposedly personal activities.[30] George Grant has observed:

As for pluralism, differences in the technological state are able to exist only in private activities: how we eat; how we mate; how we practice ceremonies. Some like pizza; some like steaks; some like girls, some like boys; some like synagogue, some like the mass. But we all do it in churches, motels, restaurants indistinguishable from the Atlantic to the Pacific.[31]

Associated with technological progress, too, the radical critic maintains, is a very strong tendency to identify progress in general with technological progress, and people become so fascinated by their creations that they literally worship them. The creature eliminates the will of the creator to resist what he has created. The machines deprive men of significant labor and consume natural resources at a fantastic rate. Yet they never have enough. They make a mockery of the decision-making process developed by human beings: since the multiplication and use of machines is the decisive factor in social change, politics itself becomes a secondary activity designed to serve the machine. Men are hypnotized not only by the machine but also by the things which the machine brings about. Thus, for example, speed becomes an end in itself and not merely a means to an end. As the human creature's separation from Nature becomes more extreme, he forgets that in the absence of constant communion with subhuman Nature he may destroy himself spiritually.[32]

These are some of the themes which run through the antitechnology literature. In one of the greatest antitechnology utopias (A. T. Wright's *Islandia*),[33] Lord Dorn, who is defending the traditional agrarian life of his country, engages in a colloquy with John Lang, an American who is urging technological progress. The discussion centers on transport, which in Dorn's country is by foot or by horse. Dorn asks:

"Would it be pleasanter if we had come by train from the City? It is only ninety miles or so — say three hours. A railroad route has been surveyed, you know. and the line would come looping up the grazing land . . ."
[Lang replies]: "It would save time."
"Yes, in one sense. I like to travel at a horse's gait."
"If you were used to another?"
"I'm not. Why should I change?"
"Progress!" I said.
"Speed, is that progress? Anyway, why progress? Why not enjoy what one has? Men have never exhausted present pleasures . . . ."
"With us, progress means giving pleasures to those who haven't got them."
"But doesn't progress create the very situation it seeks to cure — always changing the social adjustment so that someone is squeezed out? Decide on an indispensable minimum. See that everyone gets that, and until everyone has it, don't let anyone have any more. Don't let anyone ever have any more until they have cultivated fully what they have."[34]

Attitudes to social change are crucial to politics, and the problem of social change is intimately tied in the modern world to technology. In Lord Dorn's country, there is great skepticism about social change. And thus Dorn argues before the council against the "opening" of his country to "progress":

. . . The way of life of the foreigner has changed completely in the last few hundred years, and changes daily at what seems an accelerating rate. Who dares tell us that a thing so new and so unfixed is good for us? With them the son and the father are of different civilizations and are strangers to each other. They move too fast to see more than the surface glitter of a life too swift to be real . . . . The rush of life past them they call progress, though it is too rapid for them to move with it . . . . Men may live many sorts of lives, and this they call "opportunity," and believe opportunity good without even examining any one of these lives to know whether it is good. We have fewer ways of life and most of us never know but one. It is a rich way and its richness we have not yet exhausted.[35]

In Dorn's country, the politics of nondevelopment eventually wins, and technology is frozen at relatively primitive levels.

The views which Dorn-like critics attack can be illustrated by turning to a popular writer like Alvin Toffler. According to Toffler, at least as he expresses himself in some contexts, social change is inevitable, and technology is the most important factor in it. Man's duty — if it can be called that — is seemingly to adjust gracefully and without undue rebellion to the inevitable social change produced by a technology whose general course he apparently cannot control, even though he has created it. As Toffler puts it: "For education the lesson is clear, its prime objective must be to increase the individual's 'cope-ability' — the speed and economy with which he can adapt to continual change."[36] The education must be a "super-industrial" one; and in order to create it, we must "generate successive, alternative images of the future — assumptions about . . . the kind of technology that will surround us and the organizational structures with which we must mesh."[37] The language of Toffler is significant: "Assumptions about . . . the kind of technology which *will* surround us" (not that which we would like to surround us); and "organizational structures" with which we "must mesh" (not the kinds of organizational structures that we might find desirable). To be sure, Toffler does not say that any one form or type of technology is inevitable: he clearly suggests that several types of future existence are to be projected. But the emphasis tends to be on intricate technology and the seeming inevitability of rapid social change. As in many projections, it appears to be the human being who must adjust to the technology and structure, not the technology and structure which must adjust to systems of values that the human being has deliberately chosen.

177

According to some writers — and Toffler, in at least some of his statements, would seem to be among them — the alternatives are apparently confined to diverse systems of increased technological complexity and accelerated social change. There is little or no provision for options of low-level complexity and decelerated social change. Man's task and mission, some "futurists" seem to suggest, must be viewed always as one of intelligent adjustment, and constant change must be seen not as necessarily desirable but rather as a factor about which we can do little if anything, whatever its effect on the human psyche.

The proliferation of dystopian literature since World War I is an indication of growing dubiety about all complex technology; central to many of the dystopian works is a kind of despair about men controlling their creations for good. A few illustrations will point up this type of analysis.

The most extreme example of a dystopia of deliberation in which technological development plays a central role is Eugene Zamiatin's We.[38] Here men and women have so succumbed to the alleged technological imperative that they have almost become machines themselves and in their machinehood have discovered a security which in historical experience they lacked. Although Zamiatin is ambiguous as to whether they can ever leave this state — for in the very triumph of machine-man, the "natural" man apparently begins to undermine the foundations of the security — still he appears to think that the state itself is already reflected in existential orders. In the society of We, the constant change postulated by Toffler has been transmuted into a social model where change is always in the direction of making human beings still more machinelike: they have the bodies connected historically with the expression "human," but their souls have been purged of much that was of the very essence of humanity.

All this can be suggested more concretely if we turn to some of the details of the novel. In the United State, primitive Nature has receded so far that human beings live in a society physically separated from Nature by a gigantic glass wall. Beyond the wall, shapes of animals and primitive men can be seen; but the citizens of the United State can legally have no communication with them. The hallmark of the good citizen is to be as far removed from Nature as possible. Thus the growth of hair on the male body is regarded with disfavor because it reminds one of one's origins in beasthood. Weather control is perfect, and there is a vast development in biological technology, which is used quite often to keep citizens tame and in conformity to their rulers. The State itself is directed by the semimythical Well-Doer, who is the center of the governing structure.

Mathematical precision is the keynote of the society in We, because, it is said, in mathematics we can achieve a certainty which should be the hallmark of all conduct. Thus the erratic and the unpredictable are almost eliminated, only a few rebels lingering to challenge the supremacy of the principle that all aspects of life must be regulated and directed in minute fashion. According to the mythology of the United State, our first parents were given the choice between Freedom and Happiness and foolishly chose Freedom, with all its miseries of choice; but now the United State has deliberately reversed this decision and chosen Happiness (that is, security and certainty) rather than Freedom. Freedom and Happiness cannot co-exist, and thus in the interests of Happiness, Freedom in the United State has been suppressed. We may say that mankind has moved from relatively slow social change in the era prior to complex technology, to almost constant change during the age of complex technology, to a period in which social stability has once more arisen, but only at the expense of destroying all of the hallmarks traditionally associated with the concept of humanity.

In *We,* human beings no longer have names but are only numbers, and thus they simply carry out the logic of the contemporary technological society in which we are increasingly reduced to mere numberhood in the interests of the machine — Social Security, telephone, postal zone, credit card, checkbook, employee, identification, and other numberhoods. Even sexual intercourse is strictly regulated and confined to a few "private hours" during the week. Men and women eat in the same way, exercise at the same time, and engage in recreation according to identical formulae. The object of the United State is to eliminate emotion and passion; here, the pump cylinder is a model: It does not smile and has no restlessness.

Obviously, Zamiatin is suggesting that in revolting against freedom and its uncertainties, the dystopian mind has been shaped by the seeming logic of technology. Involved technology entails a situation under which human beings fit into neat grooves, like their machines. The society portrayed in *We* is the obverse of freedom, whether it be interpreted in its negative or its positive aspect. "Freedom" becomes a dirty word; and "right" — if it can be called that — has been completely defined in detail by the Well-Doer, who makes certain that citizens are programmed to adhere to it.

In reading an account like that of Zamiatin, one is strongly reminded of civilization-against-Nature portrayals. If Hobbes's Nature is one of supposed freedom and a short life, with the ever-present danger of violent death, his notion of civilization is one of a state in which the certainties decreed by the sovereign eliminate the anxieties of the natural state. The sovereign potentially defines everything, including the meaning of words and the content of religion. While Hobbes does not suggest that the sovereign will actually use all these powers, there is no question about his having the authority to do so (under the Contract which supposedly ends Nature). In Zamiatin's model, the sovereign has actually utilized these powers and has confirmed the gulf between Nature and civilization in the

179

most emphatic way. It is, of course, a model which Zamiatin thoroughly disapproves; but in seeking to show us what he believes to be the end result of an uncritical, wholehearted acceptance of technology and phenomena associated with it, he has provided one of the most thorough attacks on that formulation.

One aspect of technology is, of course, that the machine tends to supplant human labor, first at the unskilled level and then at the skilled. This takes us far away from the primitively natural state in which men and animals are the major sources of energy. But it may also contribute to feelings of alienation, of being unwanted by one's fellow human beings. No matter how much believers in the idea of progress tell the technologically unemployed that "in the long run" the machines will somehow provide more employment, they are naturally skeptical, since certainly in the short run this is simply not true; and in the long run, as Keynes quipped, we are all dead. Labor of a significant kind appears to be indispensable if man is to become his rational self and hence free; yet the tendency of a civilization characterized by complex technology is constantly to work against this, even while its devotees preach the ideal of rationality. It is natural, too, in a teleological sense for human beings to lack fulfillment if they seem not to be needed by their fellows; the idea of fraternity seems to be denied. Yet a technological society is constantly leading to a situation in which human beings are regarded as "redundant." Kenneth Boulding rightly comments that

the greatest human tragedy is to feel useless and not wanted, and with the rise in the intelligence of machines, we may face a period in which the human race divides into two parts, those who feel themselves to be more intelligent than machines and those who feel themselves to be less.[39]

Both the more intelligent and the less come to be alienated.

One of the most bitter of those who attack the displacement of man by the machine is Kurt Vonnegut, Jr. In his *Player Piano*, the central emphasis is on this theme.[40] Muscle labor is the first to go, and those who see the machine pushing them aside feel inferior to it and deprived of their rights. Next to be displaced are those engaged in routine mental work. As the story develops, the world is on the verge of having the complex and creative labor of the intellect taken over by technology. Advanced computerlike devices reign supreme. Most humans feel utterly useless, and life has become meaningless. Although material goods are abundant, all people are economically secure, and the gross national product continues to increase, there is an inner void in the lives of most men and women, including many of the scientist-engineer-rulers who supposedly still have creative work to do.

It is within this context that a revolt takes place in *Player Piano* against the domination of an increasingly automated world. The rebellion is led by several of the engineer-rulers and receives widespread support from members of the Reconstruction and Reclamation Corps (the "Reeks" and the "Wrecks"), who are weary of being assigned what is essentially "made" and meaningless work. In his manifesto announcing the projected revolution, the key figure asserts:

I deny that there is any natural or divine law requiring that machines, efficiency, and organization should forever increase in scope, power, and complexity, in peace as in war. I see the growth of these now, rather, as the result of a dangerous lack of law.

. . .

Without regard for the wishes of men, any machines or techniques or forms of organization that can economically replace men do replace men . . .[41]

In the end, the proposed revolution is not successful, and its leaders surrender to the triumphant and arrogant machine-dominated order. The clear implication is that mankind in the 20th century is already so much in the grip of technological imperatives that to attempt any reversal of the momentum is hopeless.

Out of all this, according to some radicals, can only come a kind of helpless human being who will tend to lose even the mental capabilities he has acquired. As Lewis Mumford puts it: "If automation begins by establishing infantile dependence it ends, to the extent that its regimen is successfully imposed upon the whole community, by producing senile alienation and deterioration, marked by the lapse of such faculties and functions as have developed."[42]

The momentum of technology is already so great, others seem to suggest, that the technology of destruction can and probably will emerge supreme over the supposedly beneficial aspect of the machine. Nevil Shute's *On the Beach* (1957), a story of the last survivors of a horrible nuclear war, was followed by Mordecai Roshwald's *Level Seven* (1959), in which the utter stupidity of "defense" through mutual terror is demonstrated when in a nuclear conflict even the ruling classes await destruction in their supposedly safe shelter at the lowest level beneath the surface of the earth.[43]

In Walter M. Miller's *A Canticle for Leibowitz*,[44] the ancient cyclical view of politics is vividly restated: The war technology of a supposedly sophisticated age results in the utter disintegration of complex civilization, but after hundreds of years of primitive life, men are on the verge of rediscovering the electric light and with it a new civilization which will

181

presumably lead to a new destruction. *A Canticle* describes the myths and legends about the destruction of the technological society which developed in the ages of Simplification:

It was said that God, in order to test mankind which had become swelled with pride as in the time of Noah, had commanded the wise men of that age . . . to devise great engines of war such as had never before been upon the earth, weapons of such might that they contained the very fires of Hell, and that God had suffered these magi to place the weapons in the hands of princes, and to say to each prince: "Only because the enemies have such a thing have we devised this for thee, in order that they may know that thou hast it also, and fear to strike. See to it, m'Lord, that thou fearest them as much as they shall now fear thee, that none may unleash this dread thing which we have wrought."

But the princes, putting the words of their wise men to naught, thought each to himself: If I but strike quickly enough, and in secret, I shall destroy those others in their sleep, and there will be none to fight back; the earth shall be mine.

Such was the folly of princes, and there followed the Flame Deluge.

Within weeks — some said days — it was ended, after the first unleashing of the hell-fire. Cities had become puddles of glass, surrounded by vast acreages of broken stone. . . . Nations had vanished from the earth, the lands littered with bodies, both men and cattle. . . . There were great deserts where once life was. . . .[45]

The spirit of the radical antitechnological argument has become accentuated, too, because of the growing consciousness that the so-called ecological crisis, which threatens the whole earth, is created in considerable measure by man's utilization of his complex technology to exploit Nature intensively. Thus, though India is often condemned for its supposed "overpopulation," the per capita exploitation of natural resources through technology is at least 30 times greater in the Unites States than in India. The formulation which wholeheartedly accepts complex technology, radical critics have urged, is hardly aware of all this, or, if it is, seems not to give it great importance. Nature, which Bacon-like perspectives had come to view as something to be dominated, is revolting and exhibiting greater and greater reluctance in yielding up its fruits. Therefore some radical antitechnology views foresee a day when, in the absence of new sources of energy, first civilization and then physical man will be destroyed.

Radical models of detechnologized societies have, however, been difficult to envision, in part because once the era of complex technology is entered, our consciousness tends to become dominated to so large a degree by patterns to which we have become accustomed. In Tolstoy's model — perhaps the sharpest of the civilization-as-corrupting paradigm — the stripping away of civilization leaves a kind of Russian peasant culture, with very simple plows and other utensils. The *mir*, or village community, would represent its organizational form. Since to Tolstoy primitive natural men lived in harmony together, the coercions of civilization would disappear. In Wright's *Islandia* the picture is of a civilization going no further than the wheel, the simple plow, the horse, and a bit of primitive crop rotation. Family ties and tribelike sentiments would be far more significant than the State.

In William Morris's *News from Nowhere*,[46] one of the most notable 19th-century radical attacks on complex technology, money has been completely wiped out; men exchange goods and services on the basis of mutual needs; walking often takes the place of complex modes of transport; and spiritual as well as physical closeness to the land is a highly characteristic note of the life-style.

No radical antitechnologist would eliminate all developments of *technē*, but generally speaking, the argument would propose the suppression of all extremely complex technology. Although the question is rarely discussed, the thoroughgoing critic would presumably include in the forbidden forms even advanced medical techniques.

Almost all visions of the antitechnological society would project a diminution of the role of the State and, quite logically, of "politics." For as one strips away complex technology from the fabric of civilization, all of its accompaniments, including the imperative of deliberate and conscious social controls, would presumably go with it. The level of economic interdependence would decline, social change would be much more nearly glacial in nature, and most cities would disappear. Habit and custom would come once more to be central. There would be a depreciation of the value of formal learning, which, according to the radical critics, produces a kind of extreme sophistication in utter conflict with "natural" man. In sum, when one talks of an antitechnological framework, one is speaking not merely of an undermining of technological complexity but inevitably as well of an erosion of all those features of a society which tend to be woven into the general structure of a civilization.

Selective Technology. Serious criticisms of technology need not lead to models in which all complex technology is rejected. It is possible to project a society in which deliberate or political control has as one of its primary objectives the adoption of some forms of available technology and the spurning of others. This framework we call selective technology.

Selective technology takes its point of departure historically from the classical view of the Nature-civilization problem but may also be said to be reflected to some degree in versions of Locke-like paradigms (that of Jefferson, for instance). Some of the early 19th-century utopian socialists also suggest it, at least in some measure. But it is contrary to the civilization-against-Nature and civilization-as-corrupting paradigms and some versions of the one which sees civilization as preparation for sophisticated harmony. Neither Marxism nor traditional liberalism would have much sympathy with its spirit.

In this framework, the problem of Nature and civilization is seen in terms of a kind of *via media,* and the technological issue is viewed as the center of the question. In its classical formulation, man cannot attain his teleologically natural end without considerable technological and accompanying development. At the same time, because technology has enormous social, economic, and political implications, the introduction of new techniques must be essentially a political decision. Thus Plato's Nocturnal Council is charged with the task of carefully examining proposed innovations and rejecting those that entail too much social instability or in other respects undermine essentials of the social order.[47]

A modern version of the selective-technology framework will be found in Aldous Huxley's *Island.*[48] In it, decisions about new technology are the result of public deliberation and are made with the guidance of certain general or "constitutional" norms. Thus a distinction is made between biological and medical technology, which is on the whole, approved, and the kind of technology useful mainly for the mere accumulation of material goods beyond those required for strictly limited needs.

The selective-technology position furthermore assumes that it is feasible psychologically, sociologically, and ethically to discriminate in the introduction of new contrivances. It is possible to do so even when the result of the discrimination is likely to be an immediate economic disadvantage. Quite typically, in modern civilization it has been assumed that technological development is a whole and that, while men may for a time hold up new techniques, in the long run, if they promise to increase the sum total of material goods or to economize in terms of time, they will inevitably be adopted. In fact, C. P. (now Lord) Snow has asserted that all available new technology has eventually been introduced, even if of dubious economic or other value;

There is no known example in which technology has been stopped being pushed to the limit. Technology has its own inner dynamic. When it was possible that technology could bring off a moon landing, then it was certain that sooner or later, the landing would be brought off. However much it cost in human lives, dollars, rubles, and social effort.[49]

Obviously, the selective-technology conception maintains that the situation described by Snow would and could be reversed. But if Snow is right, this reversal would be virtually without precedent in the history of modern times.

Another proposition of this formulation is that in judging what innovations to accept and what to reject, decision makers would be guided by overall evaluations of a syndrome of ends and not merely by short-run economic cost-benefit analysis. The ends would include political, social, and aesthetic objectives, as well as economic. If, for instance, the adoption of a new complex device gave promise of leading to unusual and largely uncontrollable pressures for severely dislocating social change, it might be rejected, even if it promised to increase the gross national product by 25 percent. In a community of selective technology, one might even imagine a situation in which a technique that seemed to make possible a lengthening of the human life span could be turned down: It might conceivably be concluded that the dangers of senility were a greater threat than the disadvantages of a shorter life span. One might also imagine that innovations could be rejected if they threatened existing work habits, the value of traditional labor patterns being regarded as greater than the admitted assets of the proposed machines. Above all, the central value of the human soul would be stressed: The proposed innovations would always be judged primarily in terms of their probable effects on the development of the rational soul, all other considerations being secondary.

Unlike the wholehearted-acceptance framework, the selective-technology outlook would contend that political or public policy limits must be placed on expansion of the division of labor. Beyond a certain point, division of labor runs counter to human integrity or wholeness. Although the individual ought not to seek an autarchy which would deny the conception of a free personality grounded on fraternity and a certain essential interdependence, neither should he allow himself to be reduced simply to his function or functions in organized society. The danger of uncontrolled, uncritical, and unselective technological development is that it will not only impede free personality but will also stimulate those elements in the social and political structure that have a tendency (as we saw in the preceding chapter) to distort and impede the achievement of justice.

Unlike the antitechnology viewpoint, that of selective technology would see both principled and practical objections to the back-to-Nature ideal type. In principle, it would argue, the effort to restore a simply primitive technology would frustrate man's attempt to carry out or implement his natural end, that of becoming civilized and hence extending his powers considerably through the development of tools. Just as human beings can attain their true nature only under the conditions of intellectual stimulation characteristic of the city at its best, and just as they cannot become fully rational without the development of political experience, so the development of technology beyond the merely primitive is essential. In fact, it cannot be sharply divorced from the growth of the city and the acquisition of political experience.

Practically speaking, too, a hypothetical selective-technology advocate would argue, the utter destruction of complex technology would create untold suffering, unless it was carefully planned to extend over several generations. Population has grown in the expectation that technological complexity would continue at some level. Although the wholesale attack on technological intricacy has merit in the sense that it points out the enormous degree to which human beings have become utterly dependent on their contrivances — and hence, in a sense, are at the mercy of their creations — insofar as the attack appears to suggest a complete reversal of civilization, it is mistaken.

Thus the selective-technology framework, in repudiating both the wholehearted-acceptance view and the antitechnology position, carves out for itself a very difficult task: that of providing the values, decision-making structure, and will to distinguish between and among kinds of technology, rejecting some types and accepting others. Selective technology suggests a faith in the possibility of the political process sorting out and differentiating between and among tools, encouraging some and discouraging or forbidding the rest.

Strengths and Weaknesses of the Frameworks. The wise political speculator will recognize a certain validity in each of the three frameworks for viewing technology and politics: Each in its own way gets at something of the human condition. The wholehearted-acceptance view rightly stresses, if too uncritically, the enormous constructive possibilities which technology, rightly used, can bring to human history. The antitechnology stand correctly emphasizes both the possibility and the probability that men will use their tools to destroy Nature and man himself. The selective-technology position understandably seeks a *via media* between the two extremes — a position which will do justice both to man's teleological need for close ties to primitive Nature and his equally great requirement for a modicum of technological development to fulfill himself in rational freedom and justice.

But equally, the philosopher will see a characteristic weakness in each view. In the first position, there is too much confidence that human beings, through more technology, can correct the problems created by technology in the first place. Moreover, the tendency of complex technology to set up ends of its own and to become autonomous is inadequately recognized. In the second perspective, a too romantic glow is cast over Nature and primitive human nature, which tend to be seen as always harmonious in the absence of the technological and accompanying structures of civilization. But nonhuman Nature, like human civilization, is often wasteful and sometimes — though this can be exaggerated — "red in tooth and claw." Although Marxism may be wrong in gloating over the doom of a peasant culture scheduled to be liquidated by an onrushing technological civilization, for indeed many admirable qualities are lost, Tolstoyans and their supporters underemphasize the narrowness, lack of intellectual stimulus, and spirit-distorting drudgery historically associated with primitive life on the land. As for the third outlook, while it is the one which would seemingly most nearly reconcile and harmonize the claims of Nature with those of teleological human nature, it is still in its infancy with respect to suggesting how it can implement its conception of selective technological development.

A Desirable Politics for the Technological Future

What, then, is a desirable politics for the future technological problem, in light of our preceding discussion of freedom, personality development, and justice? We need, it would seem, a clear recognition that technological development should be subject to the general political process; a will and the skill necessary to create the institutions which would serve this purpose; and, finally, a reminder that the values of premodern classical political philosophy as related to the selective-technology outlook may have a high degree of relevance.

Throughout a large part of the world today — notably, of course, in the capitalist United States — it is assumed that the introduction of new contrivances is primarily a matter for the private sector. As we have pointed out earlier, there is still a kind of sublime faith in the notion that if only we allow decisions about technology to be made in reaction to the pressures for short-run profit, somehow the public interest will be served. We must submit ourselves to the dictates of technological evolution, wherever it may lead. The initiating forces for social change, it has been held, should come from those in the corporate business structure who have the power to introduce new technology. Once they have made their determinations, in response to the motivation of immediate economic gain, the tasks of the remainder of the community are to "adjust" to those decisions.

We are told, for instance, that in the declining years of the 20th century, certain inevitable rapid changes are coming in medical technology, in genetic techniques, in the rapid expansion of computer or computerlike devices, and in speedier modes of transport. We are then asked as human beings to make our thought patterns, our way of life, our education, our sex lives, and our politics conform to these inevitable technological changes. If we have an occupation that is wiped out by technological in-

187

novations, we must, it is said, be ready to retrain ourselves so that we can manipulate the new technology. To seek this retraining, even if we live in a community which we like and in which our half-grown children have made friends, we must nevertheless give up the community and move to towns where there may be centers for retraining.

Nor are other adjustments ignored. When and if new agricultural techniques are available, we must, an official report says, adapt ourselves to them by further depopulating the countryside in the interests of economic efficiency.[50] If the needs of the new technology demand that we alter our social structures, the only thing we can do is to obey. We are unprogressive and romantic if we do not do so.

Officially, in other words, our ideology is in effect one of "first understand what technological forces are producing and then serve those forces by adjusting all other aspects of your life to them. The machines must be served, regardless of what it costs in terms of personality growth, social values, or spiritual life."

This underlying attitude was nicely reflected in my personal experience when, a few years ago, I was very tardy in submitting my grades. We have a 72-hour deadline on grades, and mine are almost always late. We also record grades through the use of very elaborate mechanical equipment. But on this occasion I found it impossible to an even greater degree than usual to meet the deadline. Someone then complained about my tardiness. The complaint finally reached the dean's office and the dean, as is often the case, referred the problem to his secretary. The secretary called me and in a very sweet voice asked me when my grades would be submitted. "When I finish my papers," I replied, "and I can't tell when that will be, as it depends on students' handwriting and many other factors." "But," she responded, "can't you give us an approximate date?" "I don't think so," I parried. "Well," she pleaded earnestly, "just try." "Well," I said, trying to be obliging, "perhaps by next Tuesday they will be available." To this she replied very solemnly indeed: "Well, I certainly hope they will be in next Tuesday. *The machines are waiting!*"

Amusing as I found this incident personally, it also symbolized for me the ways in which Western civilization, by and large, has organized and thought about the problem of introducing new techniques. It has assumed that their development is a kind of given which should not be tampered with, and has then taken for granted that human beings must accommodate themselves to the imperatives of the machine. The secretary's attitude typified the implicit viewpoint of millions of human beings throughout the course of the past two centuries. I, who was told that I must get my grades in on time, was also informed that I must not keep the machines waiting, for that would waste the time of the machine. At the same time, I, a human being, had never been consulted about whether I wished to adopt the machine in the first place. I was to adjust my schedule, my standards of performance, and my relations with students to the demands of a mechanical device.

This individual experience has been essentially duplicated millions of times during the past 200 years. Whenever small farmers find that they can no longer make a living without new machinery which is too expensive for them to buy, a similar but infinitely more grievous situation exists. Whenever thousands of employees are told that they have been made "redundant" (a terrible word when applied to human beings and their work) by a machine, they are put in the same spot. The most striking aspect is not that technological "progress" has occurred but that those most deeply affected have not been consulted in the process. There has been little or no public debate about decisions which will uproot them from the land or force them to give up the skills of a lifetime.

If we continue as we have in the past, the technological upheavals of the future will subject human beings to still more painful and sometimes soul-distorting experiences — all without debate or collective deliberation. Just how far-reaching these traumata are likely to be may be indicated by turning to the writings of the "futurists" who, projecting tendencies already present today, suggest the kind of world to which these tendencies, unchecked, may point. Thus Herman Kahn tells us, as did Kurt Vonnegut in fiction, that "By the year 2,000, computers are likely to match . . . . or surpass some of man's most 'human like' intellectual abilities, including perhaps some of his aesthetic and creative capacities, in addition to having some new kinds of capabilities that human beings do not have."[51] And he goes on to list a few of the likely inventions: new pervasive techniques for surveillance, monitoring, and control of individuals; astounding, reliable educational and propaganda techniques for affecting human behavior, public and private; chemical methods for improving memory and learning; new techniques for rapid language teaching; and home education by way of videotaped, computerized, and programmed learning.[52]

To be sure, as the wholehearted-acceptance viewpoint has always tended to see it, there are still those who seem to contend that technological development in itself will somehow eliminate the undesirable and, in the long run, and apparently without much deliberation, will lead to the emergence of the desirable. Thus Arthur C. Clarke, a science fiction writer, maintains that satellite relay technology will "make available vast new bands of the radio spectrum, providing 'ether space' for at least a million simultaneous TV channels, or a *billion* radio circuits!"[53] But to him this would obviously lead predominantly to desirable results: "Think what this will mean. . . . Any form of censorship, political or otherwise, would be impossible."[54] Gone would be the provincialism which for so long made narrow the outlooks of mankind. And he discusses a "mechanical education which could impress upon the brain, in a matter of a few minutes, knowledge and skills which might otherwise take a lifetime to acquire."[55]

The difficulty about such visions is, of course, that while they may be accurate forecasts up to a point, they are not the whole truth. As the antitechnology outlook stresses constantly, all our experience with technological development would seem to suggest that every desirable result must be paid for, sometimes at enormous cost, by undesirable outcomes, whether social, technological, or political. Events do not occur in isolation. Improvements in technique almost always cut both ways; and while we may decide in the end that certain available technology should be introduced, we should be under no illusion about the price to be paid.

Clarke's seeming faith in the long-run beneficence of historical evolution has been the essence of the wholehearted-acceptance view. We are questioning it on the basis of our actual historical experience with technology. At some points, the questioning can validly be as pointed and extreme as that of the antitechnology outlook. If, for example, our ancestors had forbidden the development of the gun, would not modern civilization have been infinitely better off? By almost any standard, it would seem, weapons of this type have worked against man's natural end of rationality and freedom. To be sure, many contend that anything can be a weapon. The gun is only one instrument of destruction out of many. This is true. But it surely does not follow that because we can use many things as killing devices, we should therefore allow one of the most destructive to be manufactured.

The selective-technology paradigm is essentially right in condemning both the wholehearted-acceptance outlook and the antitechnology perspective. The former is too uncritical and has a misplaced confidence (like laissez-faire economic views) in the automatic working out of "social forces" for the benefit of mankind. The latter, which exalts a kind of primitive technology, is somewhat naive in its portrayal of primitive human nature and does not see that a measured and controlled development of technology is necessary to fulfill that nature teleologically.

But what are the implications of the selective-technology idea in political affairs if we accept the general view of justice and freedom expressed in this book and if we also assume the notion of democracy? The implications would seem to be two.

First, we should take the analysis and values of the antitechnology paradigm seriously, while at the same time admitting the value of some technological growth. Perhaps we can best state this position by maintaining that the burden of proof must be on those who would introduce still more complicated techniques. This would basically reverse the outlook now present almost universally, whether in "capitalist" or "communist" societies, whether in "developing" or "developed" economies. Earlier we cited C. P. Snow as saying that the tendency has been to introduce all types of technology, once they exist. To place the burden of proof on those who demand innovation would itself be one of the greatest revolutions of modern times. It would mean, for instance, that the advocates of new complicated tools would have to show that their adoption in the economy would be positively beneficial, in terms of the conceptions of justice and freedom presented here. They would have to demonstrate that the invention is not only economically desirable but that its probable effects on human lives, and particularly on justice, the idea of freedom, and the subordination of material to spiritual values, would not be deleterious. They would have to provide, in other terms, an "environmental impact statement" which is vastly enlarged in contents.

Second, no complicated innovations could be introduced without public discussion and approval by an appropriate, democratically controlled assembly. It is a curious fact in the history of modern Western civilization that while there has been so much talk of democracy, many of the most important issues have not been subjected to democratic decisions. The medievalists had an excellent maxim which well reflects at least one dimension of the conception of democracy: *Quod omnes tangit ab omnibus approbetur*, "Whatever touches all should be approved by all." Now nothing touches all more directly than the introduction of new technology, which shakes up millions of lives, dissolves families, pollutes cities, promotes chaotic social change, and affects standards of well-being.

Yet in a society supposedly governed by the norms of democracy, this most important factor affecting, touching, and concerning all is, with only a few exceptions, not subject to public deliberation and approval. For the most part, in other words, we allow many of the most significant decisions about collective life to be made, in Plato's words, through the legislation of accident. Americans will often insist on submitting relatively trivial issues to public referendum: for example, whether or not to authorize $2 million worth of bonds for construction of a new schoolhouse. Meanwhile, the most revolutionary changes of all, those involving technological innovation, are made in secret by corporate managers or boards of directors in response to the demand for immediate economic gain and with little or no consideration for the possible social impact or how they will affect the lives of future generations. At the very time when so-called democratic slogans are most ubiquitous, what is perhaps the central matter "touching all" is not subject to the determination of all. Our public decisions, under present practice, must be confined to those involving adjustment to the technological changes about which we have not been consulted.

These two selective-technology proposals will obviously be attacked vigorously on various grounds. Would they not discourage technological development? Would not self-interested workers who might be deprived of employment by proposed adoptions of new machines check mechanical progress? Would we not be inhibiting scientific progress?

The proposals would indeed make possible a limitation on technological progress, and self-interested workers certainly might consider only their own immediate concerns in making decisions. We can go further and say that the proposals assume that this would often be true: If it were not, the scheme itself would be pointless. But scientific progress would not necessarily be impeded, nor even technological progress, in one sense of that term. Scientific progress is supposedly the development of an understanding of the universe and need not involve practical applications in the economy. We could still encourage science while yet establishing public direction and control of technological development. To be sure, much scientific progress depends on the encouragement of a technology useful in experimental laboratory work. Here the rule could be interpreted in such a way as to permit the use of machines for scientific experimentation, even if those same machines were not to be introduced for general use. If technological progress be interpreted as including the testing of new available techniques, this, too, could take place, even if the new technology were to be vetoed for public introduction.

Even Herman Kahn, who himself seems at times to gloat about future technological progress, is aware of the very mixed character of all technological development. He sees, moreover, that there is something seriously wrong about the wholehearted-acceptance viewpoint, and he notes that the attempt to dominate and exploit Nature, so characteristic a feature of the past three centuries, must have its limits. Thus he advises that we should "try in general to moderate Faustian impulses to overpower the environment, and to try to decrease both the centralization and the willingness to use accumulating political, economic, and technological power. . . ."[56]

But if we do wish to "moderate Faustian impulses," the basic decisions must be public, since technology itself is a social product and affects the lives of billions. Moreover, the values and analysis we bring to such collective decisions must be substantially different from those that have dominated in the past.

A more nearly valid objection to our suggested scheme would be that our institutional structures and our ways of thinking are very poorly equipped to formulate and implement public policies of this kind. So used are we to making decisions about merely "adjusting" to the fact of technological development that we are not organized and patterned to decide about the fundamentals. Thus today it is very firmly engrained in us that new technology will be introduced, unless there is a (very rare) public decision to the contrary. To reverse this ordering would be an accomplishment of no trivial nature.

Moreover, political discussion and the structures of electoral campaigns are today frequently focused on relatively minor issues, and our whole body of implicit premises assumes that debate about such matters as social security, the construction of new schoolhouses, or the building of a new civic center are and ought to be the limit of political controversy. While there are exceptions to this general view — as in the debate about the supersonic transport plane — the generalization's thrust is still sound.

Even where exceptions do exist, the discussion usually occurs within a relatively narrow context. Thus in the fifties Congress debated the issue of an interstate highway system; but despite the fact that the eventual planning of this system would have profound effects on transportation as a whole and on such issues as energy consumption, family life, and social costs, these larger questions remained in the background, when they were referred to at all. Only a few farsighted critics such as Lewis Mumford were prescient enough to point out the probable effects of the proposals on such matters as urban sprawl, enhancement of the ungovernability of cities, waste of resources, and undermining of public transportation. Transportation itself has but rarely been debated as a whole. At best, it has been discussed only segmentally — highways, railroads, subsidies for airports, and so on. Yet every particular dimension of transportation technology will affect all other aspects.

Once we accept the overall principle that technological change ought to be subject to the political process, we have the task of developing institutions and practices which could adequately carry on the task. Here we are very poorly equipped to do what the proposal requires — to work out a social technology and set of standards adequate for the control and direction of physical technology. What kinds of legal norms should be established, and how can such a clumsy instrument as the law take into account such subtleties as aesthetics as well as more measurable things? Should the decisions be made, in at least some instances, by referendum, or should all of them be determined by legislative or administrative bodies? What should be the unit of decision making? How should one relate expertise about technology to the decisions themselves which, while taking into account expert opinion, would necessarily have to go beyond it and pass judgment in terms of the values of the community itself (and, under our hypothesis, these values would have changed in many fundamental respects)? These are some of the questions which would have to be answered. It is not surprising that in view of their difficulty and complexity, many might despair of developing a civilization of publicly controlled selective technology and might turn instead to Tolstoy-like paradigms about Nature and civilization.

It is at this point that we are reminded again of the normative principles of classical political philosophy and their relevance for the issues which mankind confronts in the 20th century. They are cognizant that it is man's teleological nature both to move away from Nature and to impose deliberately contrived or political limits on that movement. If technological innovation is taken simply as a kind of inevitable constant and not as a factor to be controlled and circumscribed by deliberation, it will destroy humanity, just as the attempt to return to Nature would undermine it.

In the selective-technology viewpoint, which is built on the classical paradigm, the problem of the values one brings to the decision-making process is crucial. We might well agree that the introduction of technology should be subject to the direction of public policy, and we might devise institutions which could carry on the deliberations effectively and rationally. But if our outlook remains one which sees technological progress as always good, then with every decision in favor of innovation there might be set in motion forces very similar to those that have beset Western civilization during the past 200 years. The ecological problem might become worse, for example. Thus in the Soviet Union, where the principle of planned introduction of technology is ostensibly accepted, the technologizers and industrialists almost always win out, according to the Russian physicist Andrei Sakharov. Even when the irreplaceable natural resources of Lake Baikal are threatened, he appears to say, it does not seem to be possible psychologically or ideologically for the public decision makers to resist industrialization.[57] The mystique of technological and industrial progress appears to be widely accepted in the Soviet Union (as one would expect, given Marxist ideology), just as it is in the United States. The classical view that innovation and, beyond a point, accumulation of material possessions are suspect is rejected in practice.

One can, of course, ask *why* the first-order values of classical political philosophy ought to be accepted. It can be argued that their modern practical repudiation, even though it does lead to waste of natural resources and harmful disturbance of ecological relations, nevertheless is an option that every human being ought to have, and that the option may have been the right one to select. The waste, destruction, and primacy of the material which seem to be characteristic of industrial and now "post-industrial" civilization — whether so-called capitalist or socialist — cannot be shown to be wrong except in relation to other ends, which themselves must ultimately be accepted on faith. This is true. Such fundamental values as the primacy of the spiritual and intellectual over the material, the intrinsic superiority of love over hate, the suspicion of complexity, and so on, are principles which are intuited or revealed. This does not mean, of course, that they are simply a matter of emotion; for an intuition, while it may have emotive elements, is a kind of direct perception of value reality, just as physical sight of material objects is that direct perception of physical appearance which must precede any scientific or indirect inquiry.

If one does indeed accept the principle that the spiritual development of human beings should be regarded as the first-order value, then the necessity for deliberate collective control of technology in light of that end becomes central. The task of the defender of the selective-technology viewpoint, then, becomes to show the ways in which uncritical acceptance of technological development frustrates the attainment of the primary end.

Adequate deliberation about and control of collective affairs entails a recognition of man's many-sided nature. Thus a fully rational decision implies a weighing of economic, social, and political goods in terms of the fundamental norm of the centrality of intellectual and spiritual development in the context of freedom, equality, and fraternity. But a recognition of man's many-sided nature would seem to imply also a ranking of his qualities — some are more valuable intrinsically than others; some are good as ends, others primarily as means to ends. Thus in moments of sober reflection on life as a whole, we understand that we ought to eat to live rather than to live to eat.

We can summarize the important conclusions about the politics of technology in terms of four propositions:

1. The introduction of technology ought to be subject to general public policy direction. And the decisions ought to be carried out democratically.
2. We need to develop the will and the skill essential to establish institutions through which public direction can be attained.
3. Our goal ought to be a society in which we seek neither to "return to Nature" nor to allow an indefinite development of division of labor and complex technology, since both these positions undermine the teleological nature of humanity.
4. In utilizing the institutions we build for the ordering of technology, we should keep clearly in mind the centrality of spiritual develop-

ment and the merely instrumental character of material goods, which, while necessary in strictly limited degree for the good life, are not at all sufficient for it and, indeed, if allowed to become central, are utterly destructive of it.

But the problem of technological development in any civilization is inextricably bound up with the nature, ideal ends, and organization of the economy. Both descriptively and prescriptively, the two are interwoven. In the next chapter, therefore, we turn to the politics of the economy and its relationship to the problems of Nature and civilization.

Notes

1   Nest building among the birds and primitive tools among the great apes are often cited. Yet within most species the largely instinctual nature of technology appears to be infinitely greater than among men. The element of social transmittal grows immeasurably in the human species, and consciousness of technology arises very early in the evolution of mankind. After all, men develop history, which is not true of ants, or birds, or even the anthropoid apes. Pioneer studies on the anthropoid apes include those of the late Ernest A. Hooton, for example, *Why Men Behave Like Apes and Vice Versa* (Princeton, N.J.: Princeton University Press, 1940).

2   Genesis, IV:22. The verse speaks of Tubal-Cain as an "instructor of every artificer in brass and iron."

3   I Kings, V:6.

4   A number of years ago Paul Meadows critically appraised modern industrial culture in *The Culture of Industrial Man* (Lincoln: University of Nebraska Press, 1950). More recently, from a very critical point of view, Jacques Ellul has appraised the impact of technology in *The Technological Society* (New York: Vintage Books, 1967); while Victor Ferkiss has attempted to present a rather balanced view in *Technological Man* (New York: George Braziller, 1969).

5   From an unpublished mimeographed statement of Paul Kramer, technical adviser to Northern States Power Co., June 27, 1974, pp. 3-4.

6   Henry Adams, *The Education of Henry Adams* (New York: Modern Library, 1931), pp. 490, 491.

7   Ibid., p. 494.

8   On the Green Revolution, which provided new and remarkably productive strains of rice and wheat, see Stanley Johnson, *The Green Revolution* (New York: Harper & Row, 1972) and Lester R. Brown, *Seeds of Change: The Green Revolution and Development in the 1970's* (New York: Frederick A. Praeger, 1970). A brief critical appraisal of the Green Revolution is offered by James P. Sterba, "The Green Revolution Hasn't Ended Hunger," *The New York Times*, Sunday, April 15, 1973, p. 23.

9   On the possibilities of genetic engineering for the future, see, for example, D. S. Halacy, Jr., *Genetic Revolution: Shaping Life for Tomorrow* (New York: Harper & Row, 1974).

10   Tommaso Campanella in *The City of the Sun*, in Frederic R. White, ed., *Famous Utopias of the Renaissance* (New York: Henrichs House, 1955), published first during the early part of the 17th century, foresaw the development of biological and medical science to a point where life would be vastly prolonged. And of course Aldous Huxley, in his dystopian novel *Brave New World* (Garden City, N.Y.: Doubleday Doran, 1932) anticipated "test tube" babies and other reflections of biological engineering which by the seventies of the 20th century seemed on the verge of realization.

11   Sandra Blakeslee, "Space Colony Urged as New Energy Frontier," New York Times Service, *Minneapolis Tribune*, August 23, 1975, p. 1.

12   Genesis, I:28.

13   Psalms, VIII:5.

14   Exodus, XX:25. See also Deuteronomy, VI:15-28, the commandments against idolatry.

15   Job, XIV:2.

16   Genesis, IV:2-5.

17   Genesis, IV:8.

18   Genesis, XI:1-9.

19   Leo Strauss, *Thoughts on Machiavelli* (Glencoe, Ill.: Free Press, 1959), p. 298.

20   William Godwin, *Enquiry into Political Justice* (1793).

21   Francis Bacon in the *New Atlantis*, in White, ed., *Famous Utopias of the Renaissance*.

22   Bernard Mandeville, *The Fable of the Bees* (London: Printed for E. Parker, 1723).

23   See David Mitrany, *Marx against the Peasant* (New York: Collier Books, 1961). Marx and his disciples, Mitrany observes, "paid attention to the peasants only because they looked upon them with dislike in which the townsman's contempt for all things rural and the economist's disapproval of small-scale production mingled with the bitterness of the revolutionary collectivist against the stubbornly individualistic tiller of the soil" (p. 35).

24   Proudhon idealized the countryman with a small farm and suggested only a limited industrialism, and Fourier, while open to a certain amount of industrialization; was by no means enthusiastic about the indefinite development of technology. See, for example, Marie-Louise Berneri, *Journey through Utopia* (London: Routledge and Paul, 1950).

25   Edward Bellamy, *Looking Backward* (Boston: Tichnor, 1888); H. G. Wells, *A Modern Utopia* (New York: Scribner's, 1905).

26   *The Limits to Growth*, a report for the Club of Rome's Project on the Predicament of Mankind by Donella H. Meadows and others (New York: Universe Books, 1972). See also the Club of Rome's sequel, Mihajlo D. Mesarovik and Eduard Pestel, *Mankind at the Turning Point: The Second Report to the Club of Rome* (New York: E. P. Dutton & Co., 1974).

27   See Wilfred Beckerman, *In Defense of Economic Growth* (London: Jonathan Cape, 1973).

28   While the modern consciousness has generally condemned the Luddites (they were "unprogressive"), when looked at in the light of subsequent developments in the history of the technological civilization, they may not appear so obviously wrong.

29   Samuel Butler, *Erewhon and Erewhon Revisited,* Modern Library ed. (New York: Random House, 1927), pp. 223-24.

30   Ellul, *The Technological Society.*

31   George Grant, *Technology and Empire* (Toronto: House of Anansi, 1969), p. 26.

32   This seems to be in part the theme of such biting dystopias as Eugene Zamiatin's *We* (New York: E. P. Dutton & Co., 1952), a novel in which most humans have been completely cut off from primitive Nature, which is regarded as dirty, chaotic, and hostile to the mechanistic and bureaucratic United State.

33   A. T. Wright, *Islandia* (New York: Rinehart, 1958).

34   Ibid., p. 76.

35   Ibid., p. 490.

36   Alvin Toffler, *Future Shock* (New York: Random House, 1970), p. 403.

37   Ibid., p. 403

38   Zamiatin, *We.*

39   Kenneth Boulding, *Beyond Economics* (Ann Arbor: University of Michigan Press, 1968), p. 175.

40   Kurt Vonnegut, Jr., *Player Piano* (New York: Avon Library, 1967).

41   Ibid., p. 285.

42   Lewis Mumford, *The Myth of the Machine: The Pentagon of Power* (New York: Harcourt Brace Jovanovich, 1970), p. 341.

43   Nevil Shute, *On the Beach* (New York: New American Library, 1958); Mordecai Roshwald, *Level Seven* (London: Heinemann, 1959).

44   Walter M. Miller, Jr., *A Canticle for Leibowitz* (New York: Bantam Books, 1959).

45   Ibid., pp. 51, 52.

46   William Morris, *News from Nowhere* (New York: Longmans Green, 1901). For a recent sharp criticism of the impact of technology on modern civilization, see Theodore Rozak, *Where the Wasteland Ends* (Garden City, N.Y.: Doubleday & Co., 1972).

47   Functions of the Nocturnal Council are discussed in Book XII of the *Laws.* There is no doubt that Plato is distrustful of innovation; this distrust extends even to innovations in children's games. Yet there is also another side to his thought. One ought not, he contends, to exclude the city from awareness of possible innovations, for simply clinging to the old or the customary without challenge will tend to make us lose sight of the valuable in what we already have. As A. E. Taylor (*The Laws of Plato,* London: J. M. Dent, 1934) translates this passage in Book XII, "A State unacquainted with mankind, bad and good, will never in its isolation attain an adequate level of civilization and maturity, nor will it succeed in preserving its own laws permanently, so long as its grasp of them depends on mere habituation without comprehension." To make sure that the society will become aware of in-

novations, whether social or mechanical, Plato provides for sending observers to other lands who, under supervision of the Nocturnal Council, are to assess possibilities for change. Innovation, under thoughtful collective auspices, and to a limited degree, just may be desirable.

48   Aldous Huxley, *Island* (New York: Harper & Row, 1962, and Bantam Books, 1968).

49   C. P. Snow, "The Moon Landing," *Look,* August 26, 1969, p. 70.

50   Bernie Shellum, "Butz Gets Report Urging End of Farm Supports," *Minneapolis Tribune,* June 17, 1972, p. 5-A. As quoted by the press, the report says:

> National policy should not be directed at assuring any particular level of income from farming for the nation's farmers. Income from farming should be of concern only to the extent that it affects the industry's ability to produce efficiently adequate supplies of food and fiber. National policy should be directed toward maintaining agriculture as a viable industry, and not as a way of life.

The "parity" policy is described as a "welfare measure." Acknowledging that its recommendations would reduce farm income by $6 billion a year in the short run, the report admits that

> . . . a reduced income earned per acre would result in the need for larger farm units to provide adequate farm income for the farm family. This would tend to accelerate the reduction in number of farms, a fact which would not disturb the committee, assuming adequate nonfarm jobs can be found in the rural communities and a sufficient number of producing units remain to ensure that the industry remains competitive.

51   Herman Kahn, *The Year 2000: A Framework for Speculation on the Next 33 Years* (New York: Macmillan Co., 1967), p. 89.

52   Ibid., pp. 51–55.

53   Arthur C. Clarke, *Profiles of the Future* (New York: Harper & Row, 1962), p. 188.

54   Ibid., p. 189.

55   Ibid., p. 199.

56   Kahn, *The Year 2000,* p. 413.

57   Andrei Sakharov, *Progress, Co-Existence and Intellectual Freedom* (New York: W. W. Norton, 1968), particularly p. 49 and the note by Harrison Salisbury, pp. 107–9.

SIX

Nature, Civilization, and Political Economy

IN THE PRECEDING CHAPTER, we explored some of the political implications arising out of man's technological development from Nature to complex civilization. We now turn to the closely connected question of the movement economically from preindustrial to industrial and then, according to some, to "postindustrial" society. Although we concentrate on economic questions in this chapter, it should always be remembered that the politics of economy will affect all aspects of life. Thus the distribution of wealth and income will have an important impact on personal views of existence and the beliefs by which men live. However, although economic questions are very central to any political philosophy, we are not contending that they are the only basic issues; nor are we arguing for an interpretation which would suggest something like economic determinism. Despite the efforts of Hobbes-like paradigms to reduce man to "matter in motion" and of Marx-like endeavors to interpret his history as determined by modes of production, we do not believe that such attempts do justice to man's many-faceted nature. In a sense, this is unfortunate; for if we could only find the key to politics in some kind of reductionism — whether genetic, physical, psychological, or economic — many of our difficulties in giving an account of Nature, human nature, and civilization would disappear.

We first contrast economies in preindustrial and modern complex societies. Then we turn to the problem of the degree to which modern economic phenomena can be made subordinate to the goals and norms suggested in the three preceding chapters.

Preindustrial versus Industrial Economy and Society — and Beyond

Broadly speaking, we have suggested that as man moves from a preindustrial, precommercial society to an industrial society, he departs from Nature in certain vital respects. The greater the distance becomes, the more startling are the challenges of politics. As he travels from the preindustrial to the industrial, the division of labor becomes more minute and, other things being equal, economic forces in themselves tend to become ever more blind. Under these circumstances, the tasks of subordinating the economy to the whole person and of attaining the goals set forth in preceding chapters are enormously involved.

More explicitly, we can note certain sharp contrasts that constitute the background for politics in modern civilization. These turn on (1) density of population, (2) prolongation of life, (3) urbanization, (4) the degree of personalism, (5) the per capita amount of material goods, (6) economic instability, and (7) ethical-political perspectives and implications.

Population Density

Density of population tends to increase substantially in modern civilization. Some have estimated that when the human race was "born" as a species, it consisted of only about 750,000 individuals living in scattered bands throughout the earth. Division of labor was at a low level, except for sexual specialization. With the movement from Nature to preindustrialization, population increased, but very slowly indeed; the total population of the world did not reach 1 billion souls until 1830, about two generations after the birth of the industrial era. It took another century for the human species to increase to 2 billion. But in only 30 years — from 1930 to 1960 — the figure became 3 billion; and by now we have reached approximately 4 billion, a billion having been added in only 17 years. Something like a near geometric progression seems to be at work; and even where the technological age has in many respects just begun, sanitation and similar measures have enabled larger and larger numbers to live to adulthood. To be sure, after the first stages of industrialization there frequently appears to be a leveling off. But even so, the contrasts are startling — England in the days of Elizabeth I had perhaps 4 million souls, and after about two centuries of industrialism there are upwards of 50 million. It is obvious that the economic implications of this startling multiplication are far-reaching, and the political significance would seem to be equally great.[1]

Prolongation of Life

Along with sheer increase of population came a prolongation of human life and a correspondingly greater challenge to politics. Whereas at birth the average life expectancy in a preindustrial civilization may be in the neighborhood of 20 to 30 years, industrial civilization — through its superior technology, its more abundant food, sanitation measures, and other factors — prolongs this expectancy to 60, 70, or more. Politically, this will have important results, for never before in the human experience will the older citizens have constituted so large a proportion of the population. Then, too, while mere prolongation of life is sometimes looked upon as ipso facto a good (apparently without regard to the quality of life), it should be remembered that a central stream in political philosophy is always saying that the purpose of politics is not only life but the *good* life. Life measured simply quantitatively and economically is never enough — or ought never to be enough. At best it can merely provide a longer opportunity for developing a deeper and broader consciousness of the meaning of the good life.

Urbanization

The increase in population takes place in such a way that the tendency is to concentrate people more and more in cities which have only a relatively slight resemblance to the cities of antiquity or even to the cities of early modern times. As Lewis Mumford and others have suggested, the transformation of the city in modern civilization is a central theme of political and cultural history.[2] We call both ancient Athens and modern Los Angeles "cities," but in a sense this is like comparing tomatoes with squash. Ancient Athens at its height had perhaps half a million souls, most of whom were slaves; and the city itself (as contrasted with the surrounding agricultural belt) was confined to a relatively small area of land. Los Angeles, by contrast, with its sprawling millions, has relatively little sense of unity and is more a kind of mixture than the compound that Athens strove to be, at least for its citizens.

The social change so characteristic of modern life — closely connected, as we have seen, with almost unlimited confidence in technology — is constantly transforming the city, and the continuity associated with tradition is often attenuated if not destroyed. The modern large city becomes, at best, a kind of loose confederation of neighborhoods, some of which may themselves have the characteristics of what we might call communities; but the city itself increasingly finds its integration undermined as the suburbs mushroom in a chaotic way. Although the modern city remains the center of art and literature, many of its preindustrial attributes, such as establishing the framework within which citizens are trained for their obligations, have been eroded. One of the strongest elements of attack on "advanced" civilization legitimately centers on the inadequacy of the modern urban complex, at least in many parts of the world.

Impersonalism

Classically, the idea of the city was bound up with the conception of civility,[3] though we should not assume that any given city ever fully realized the norm. Civility embraced a whole syndrome of characteristics: friendship among the citizens, so that all felt bound to one another by ties that extended beyond mere economic utility; politeness in manners; social polish; a sense of civic or public responsibility; political consciousness; stimulating conversation leading to enlarged and deepened insights. These hallmarks were frequently contrasted with those said to characterize existence outside the city: a kind of herdlike existence; crudeness and boorishness in manners; social ineptitude; provincialism; low-level political consciousness; and conversation primarily at the level of personal gossip.

Now the modern so-called city of the megalopolitan type tends to be so lacking in integration that its jumble, sprawl, and constant and often purposeless change tend to pull it away far more radically from the conception of civility than the ancient existential city. In the megalopolis, citizens do not know one another, since their relations are often merely economic and their mobility so great that they do not establish roots; their politeness is often superficial, hiding deep anxieties and insecurities; their social polish is only a kind of thin veneer; their sense of civic responsibility at a very low level; their political consciousness is produced by a second-hand experience through the newspapers and TV; and their conversations more frequently than not are concerned only with getting and spending.

While the movement from the "primitive" to modern civilization frees the individual in one sense — he is no longer, for example, subjected to the rigidities of custom, or, as in the Adamic myth, to the direct control of God — in another sense it tends to work against his developing personality. As we have suggested earlier, he must be freed from the merely primitive in order to become a human being, but no sooner does he enter complex society than he finds that personal relations tend to be eroded, and he is frequently treated simply as an impersonal unit in a contrived organization — a union, a business organization, a reform movement.

There is a powerful tendency, as we have maintained, for the individual to become merely a number for the convenience of the machine he has created. He often interacts with other human beings not in relation to his soul as a whole but in terms of his several *personas* or roles — as a producer, consumer, politician, reformer, and so on; and the bureaucratic structures which he creates to coordinate his divided labors have impersonalism as their hallmark. This is in some respects an advantage, of course, for the individual is now less at the mercy of personal and family favoritism than before; but at the same time, the impersonalism and impartiality which must characterize bureaucracy subtract something valuable which existed in relations closer to the primitive. In a feudal or semifeudal society, one could often identify one's "enemy," for good or for ill; in modern society, one is increasingly victimized by impersonal social forces or "faceless" bureaucrats. Thus the Joads in John Steinbeck's novel of the Great Depression of the thirties were forced off their land and, while they endeavored to identify their enemy as the banks that held the mortgage, they were really hard pressed to divorce the banking system from other elements of the economic and social structure with which it was inextricably connected.[4]

Per Capita Worth in Material Goods

One of the most striking hallmarks of an industrial civilization is the vast growth in average per capita material goods: the fruits of labor constitute in volume a difference in degree which has in effect become a difference in kind, as compared with earlier civilizations. Through the application of complex technology to Nature, men for the first time in history seem to have it within their grasp to get beyond merely economic concerns — and this is, indeed, a proposition of one version of the civilization as preparation paradigm. The solution of the central economic problem — that of providing enough material things to enable men and women to transcend concern for the next meal and to pursue noneconomic goods — seems to be at hand. Later we shall maintain that, like most of the fruits of complex civilization, this has by no means been an unmixed blessing. But the existence of the apparent possibility cannot be controverted, and it constitutes one of the most striking contrasts between industrialized-postindustrial societies and those that preceded them.

Economic Instability and Planning

With the great increase in per capita material goods has come the phenomenon of economic instability. To be sure, earlier civilizations had their own forms of economic instability — when weather failed, or trade routes were cut off, or locusts multiplied, or great plagues drastically reduced the supply of labor — and they often tried to guard against them through such devices as the establishment of reserve granaries and irrigation projects. But industrialization, as usual, magnifies the phenomenon and makes it less easy to account for. Economic instability in the modern age is more closely, dramatically, and clearly related to the impersonal forces released by complex economic interdependence — forces which are reflected in the ebb and flow of the market.

The market and bureaucracy vie with each other in their degree of impersonalism. To the ideologists of the "free market," the decisions of the market are, on the whole, just: It distributes its rewards to those who labor most diligently and penalizes those who malinger; and its coordinations and judgments are the best safeguards against the alleged evils of its great rival, bureaucratic coordination, according to apologists like Ludwig Von Mises.[5] To the defenders of bureaucratic or deliberate coordination, the market is erratic and may or may not achieve economic justice; they believe its efforts at coordinating men's divided labors need to be at least supplemented and at most supplanted by deliberate planning. Defenders of the market, like Von Mises and Friedrich Von Hayek,[6] often seem to imply a rough equality in economic power of individuals, and they appear to suggest that men and women are actually governed in their conduct chiefly by economic considerations. Defenders of deliberate coordination, like Barbara Wooton, Herman Finer, and Oskar Lange, suggest that in the existential world economic bargaining power has never been equal and that human beings do not in fact act in accordance with purely economic considerations. Moreover, they suggest, collective and bureaucratic management is more likely than the market is to provide the conditions essential for economic justice.[7]

Much of the political struggle of modern times has turned on this conflict between market- and nonmarket-bureaucratic coordination. When the heavily customary regulations and practices of the Middle Ages began to be eroded, mankind was dramatically confronted with the issue, and as the complexity of division of labor was magnified the political question became more acute: It could not be evaded. Actual experience with market competition tended to show that the units in the market never were roughly equal and that some tended to absorb others as a result of the market forces themselves, thus enhancing the inequality.[8]

The joint stock corporation, that great device for collective ownership of capital, was an important factor in the erosion of true economic individualism, and impetus for its development was due in no small degree to the fact that capitalists in their individual capacities could no longer supply the resources necessary for the purchase of increasingly complex technology. As corporate ownership of capital increased, the competing units became collectivities rather than individuals; and the strong corporations, like the strong individuals before them, began to absorb the weak, thus reducing the degree of competition. Capital was at first collectivized not primarily by governments but rather by so-called private combinations which developed in the course of supposedly free market competition.

Once the process had been launched, it became ever more obvious that economic questions could not be seen in isolation from social and political issues. The growth of corporate enterprise, as it moved to what some call oligopoly,[9] tended through such devices as price leadership to restrict the degree of purely market factors.[10] The deliberate planning involved in direction of the large corporation was itself a political act, and the bureaucratic coordination entailed in the management of the corporation raised issues similar to those engendered in State bureaucracy.

It was even more important that the problem of justice could no longer be simply a matter of free market forces, unless through deliberate action of the State the development of corporate enterprise could be reversed and a larger measure of market determination could be restored. Even at the height of laissez-faire ideology, in fact, people had shied away from its full implications: Thus they did not allow the mentally unbalanced to be obliterated by pure competition, as would have happened had market forces been allowed to predominate; justice for children was not only a matter of market determination; and while nonmarket measures for care of the poor and those defeated by the process were almost always inadequate, yet there was widespread recognition that somehow limits must be imposed on the degree to which the market could be allowed to reign supreme.

The quasi-oligopolistic economies of the 20th century seemed to demand more than ever an overall political or deliberate direction, as it became evident that market factors must be kept subordinate to deliberately arrived-at norms of social justice. One could not rely simply on the market to distribute goods and services equitably. Although general planning increasingly became an imperative, this did not mean that market coordination needed to be eliminated completely; indeed, in any planning scheme, it would probably play some role. However, the market could no longer be seen as autonomous; its mission must be performed within the larger whole which was deliberately governed by standards embracing not only economic but also social and political values.

By the 20th century, then, the question increasingly was not whether overall planning of some kind was essential but rather what values planning should implement and by what scheme of distributive justice it should be guided. Although some looked back, indeed, to a destruction of the modern complex economic order, the civilization-as-corrupting paradigm had serious problems in this respect, being based on rather oversimplified views of what precivilized Nature might be. Similarly, those who thought that it might be possible to return to a regime of pure market coordination (assuming for the moment that it had ever existed) were hard pressed to show how this could come about. If both Tolstoyan and pure market answers were rejected, it was necessary to face the central issue of planning relatively complex economies according to some deliberately arrived-at standards.[11]

Ethical-Political Attitudes

Finally, we can contrast preindustrial with industrial civilization in terms of their characteristic attitudes to economics and related questions. In preindustrial civilization, with its extreme scarcity of material goods, expectations of great wealth for the many are largely absent, and the tendency is to teach people that they should be satisfied with their stations in life. Although the notion of rising from a low to a high economic status is certainly not entirely absent, it plays a much smaller role in preindustrial than in industrial and "postindustrial" civilizations. It is assumed that poverty is to be the lot of the vast majority, and ideology attempts to reinforce this position by limiting the expectations of most. Either through custom or legislative decree, attempts are frequently made to assure that the scanty resources which are available will be equitably distributed. The devices used include the just price and wage or the prohibition of advertising in the Middle Ages and, in the Inca Empire, regular redistribution of land and publicly defined priorities as to how income is to be alloted.[12] At the level of formal political philosophy, as in the theories of Plato and Aristotle, a minimal standard of material well-being is recognized as essential for effective citizenship, but there is also deep suspicion about fever-heat economic growth. It is held that development of this type tends to set up a momentum of its own which overcomes the coordination provided by custom and makes it well-nigh impossible for human beings to subordinate the economy politically to the polity. In classical preindustrial political treatises like that of St. Sir Thomas More, the leisure essential for the good life is to be gained primarily by reducing material wants, making long-lasting houses and clothing, having both sexes directly engage in the productive process, and deliberately providing equitable distribution.

In contrast with outlooks of this type, those of modern civilization stress the supposed economy of abundance and the faith that with economic development all good things will follow. The notion of an economy of abundance foresees a constant and increasingly progressive production of material goods and services. Where this has not yet taken place, it is anticipated; and if it is not forthcoming, political crises of various kinds can be predicted. Thus what we call the revolution of rising expectations arises (whether in developed or developing areas), and the notion that there are limits on the material goods we can or ought to gain recedes. Leisure is seen primarily as the product of advancing technology rather than of deliberately restricted wants and an equitable division of the scarce goods available, as in nonmodern civilization.

At the level of high political philosophy, the preindustrial thinker defines leisure (as do Plato and Aristotle) as time which is available for doing those things that are valuable in themselves; and the things that are valuable in themselves center in study, reflection, and contemplation of Nature, man, and the universe. Freedom is liberation from doing those things that are only instrumental so one can do those distinctively human things one ought to do. In industrial culture, by contrast, leisure tends to be transformed at the popular level into time available for idleness and mere consumption of material goods. Even among scholars, it often comes to mean time and opportunity to do what one desires rather than what is desirable; in fact, in some philosophies of freedom, the distinction between what is desired and what is desirable is blurred, if not blotted out.[13] In preindustrial civilization, there is very little faith that economic development in itself will ensure such goals as moral and political progress; in the modern era, by contrast, many political philosophies (Marxism would appear to be an example) seem to suggest that if only we can attain an era of material abundance, all else will follow.[14]

The preindustrial outlook is perhaps typically reflected in those views that are very ambivalent about man's potentialities and see him as being forever torn between the prehuman Nature to which he is akin and a too complex civilization which could destroy his distinctive humanity. The modern world — again speaking very broadly and recognizing many exceptions — tends to see the problem of scarce or economic goods as historically accounting for many aspects of human nature which have been traditionally called evil. Once man is released from the thralldom of economic necessity, the modern spirit (whether in the various varieties of liberalism, of Marxism, of non-Marxian socialism, or of anarchism),[15] argues that he will be expelled, as it were, into the domain of freedom and will use that freedom as he ought to use it.

Yet despite this general optimism which has characterized the modern mind, severe critics of industrial or postindustrial civilization call attention to several factors which seem to cast doubt on part or all of the optimists' contentions. Many of the criticisms, indeed, come from those who, in terms of the long run, seem to be most complacent. Others proceed from those who are most akin in spirit to some of the economic outlooks of the preindustrial ages. To those criticisms and possible responses we now turn.

Subordinating the Economy to Justice

Throughout the previous discussion we have stressed the view that, while civilization brings with it many things which are widely accepted as benefits, it does so at an enormous price — at a cost which in some respects and in some areas appears to be greater than the benefits. This has been widely recognized by many modern political philosophies, whose problem is to suggest the conditions under which the benefits that can be obtained will be fully realized, while at the same time the price is reduced. This is the task of politics, as we have defined it. Some views (as we have seen) deny that this is possible, while others would support the possibility. The view we shall maintain aligns itself with the second position but contends that the possibility depends on our ability to fulfill conditions which will not be easy to establish. With particular reference to industrial society and the economy, we shall argue, in general, that the possibility depends on our willingness and ability to limit the pace of social change deliberately and to accept principles for the control of technology such as were suggested in the preceding chapter. It also depends on our capacity to transcend the national State politically.

Assuming the ends of liberty, equality, and fraternity outlined in Chapters 3 and 4, let us recall the proposition that while civilization opens up great potentialities for the development of rational freedom, it also tends, without extensive deliberation on collective affairs, to reduce would-be whole, free human beings to partial men — economic, sexual, and so on. Those who appeal for a return to Nature, of course, are quite aware of these difficulties and indeed despair of overcoming them, with much reason.

Here we consider seven eruption points of criticism concerning highly developed societies and economies — or what we might call distinctively modern civilization: (1) technological determinism, (2) the phenomena connected with alienation, (3) the issue of employment opportunities, (4) tendencies to centralization and destruction of the small community, (5) man's relation to Nature, (6) economic instability, and (7) disparities of wealth and power.

Technological Determinism

Since we dealt with this question extensively in Chapter 5, only a few words will be necessary here. We are not contending that complex technology will always shape men for its own ends; rather we say that this is often the tendency, considering the low level of political consciousness, the myths about technology which are characteristic of modern society, and the whole context of social structures which arise in a technological age. To some degree, however, technology, once on its way, does indeed impose its imperatives, regardless of the level of consciousness or the nature of the belief system. A culture in which advanced technology is central will tend to be one in which men and women themselves act and think like machines.

In the final section of the preceding chapter we contended that the tendency to technological determinism could be checked, although not completely reversed, and a desirable politics for the technological future could be devised only under three conditions:

1. The introduction of any new technology must be subject, in principle, to the political process.
2. A critical examination of existing political institutions must be conducted with a view to their fundamental modification for purposes of technological control.
3. Most difficult of all, we must break the idol and destroy the traditional myths of technological progress.

We argued that a distinction in principle could be made between scientific speculation, which, in general, should be free, as an aspect of spiritual liberty, and the introduction of new complex technology, which would be subject to public deliberation and control. This does not imply a rejection of all new technology but rather suggests that the burden of proof should be on those who would adopt it. For example, the case for a new technology in the deliberate and planned cultivation of seafood — the development of "farming" in fisheries — might be so clear and evident that the new methods would be adopted after very little opposition. On the other hand, given the notions of the good life and of justice suggested earlier — strictly limited material desires, emphasis on the problem of equitable distribution, and a value system which does not stress the desirability of mobility, constant change, and speed — we should be less than candid if we did not envision the outright rejection of much available technology.

Alienation

The problem of alienation is a many-faceted one, and the word itself has been used in a wide variety of contexts.[16] It is closely related to many of the issues touched on in this book, particularly to those examined in the preceding chapter and in this one. As the critics of a runaway technological society might employ the term, the broad signification of alienation is that modern civilization breaks up the traditional community and makes it more difficult for human beings to know one another on a personal level. Civilization also forces men to become part of a work process which, by minutely subdividing tasks, erodes the interest of the worker in his work; and it promotes social instability through constant change, thus possibly leading to mental illness. The tendency is often, as in the United States, to manipulate human beings through advertising to consume material goods, almost as an end in itself, and, by encouraging huge concentrations of population and the centralization of industrial control, to make the individual feel less and less significant, thus promoting apathy and lack of interest in the political process. The rise of impersonalism we have noted elsewhere in this chapter.

The ramifications of these propositions are immense. Here we can only hint at the lines along which alienation, to the extent that it exists (and there have been those, of course, who have argued that it is a figment of the minds of "intellectuals"), might be overcome. In part, it would seem, men tend to become alienated from themselves, their work, and other men because of the sheer rapidity of technological change and its social consequences. To subject the process of technological change to public decision making, including the decision making of the workers most directly affected, would have a tendency to slow the pace of change and hence to limit the alienation related to it. The very fact that the worker would be consulted about technological innovation, both as worker and as citizen (through his representative bodies), would add to his self-esteem as a human being. By contrast with the situation today, where he is consulted (through elections) about issues that are often rather trivial, he would be called upon to make basic decisions about fundamental matters underlying all social change. Because of this, his apathy might be diminished, since there is validity in the aphorism that if one wishes an individual to become responsible one must thrust responsibility upon him. Then, too, as we shall argue a little later in greater detail, while certain fundamental economic decisions would have to be made centrally, there is room for considerable political and functional decentralization, and this should assist human beings to identify with the decision-making process.

One facet of the problem of alienation is the old complaint that under industrial capitalism labor is regarded as a "commodity." Attempts have been made in legislation (the Clayton Act, for example) to declare that this should not be. Nevertheless, we are bought and sold on the labor market, whether we are professional people, manual workers, or clerical laborers. We fetch a certain price, just as does a bale of cotton. With all the politics of unionism, which attempts to collectivize wage slavery, the commodity dimension of workers persists. And, indeed, the notion of "free labor" — in which workers are free to seek alternative employment and employers to offer it — would seem to imply a commodity dimension: workers "sell" themselves for wages, hours, and other inducements and employers "buy" the workers.

The problem is whether we can create conditions in which, as workers, we shall not be *simply* or *primarily* commodities. Such policies as the notion of the economic minimum, the expansion of "free" goods and services, and equalization of incomes would seem to move in this direction. To the extent that a worker shares in the product of collective toil as a human being or a citizen, rather than strictly as a worker, he would be regarded as more than a commodity.

There are ways that should be considered as methods for overcoming alienation in general: collective control of technological change, extension of the principles of due process to the production unit, workers' self-management, possible decentralization, and vast expansion of education, particularly adult education. Expansion of education could, by bringing people together for nonvocational concerns transcending the workplace, help to develop common vocabularies and to break down separation attributable to specialization. In the United States, for example, we are grossly deficient in continuing political education. Political consciousness is intimately tied to the kind of formal and informal educational schemes obtaining in any given civilization.

Employment Opportunities

Work opportunities are enormously significant — psychologically, socially, and politically, as well as economically. The issue can be broken down into two parts — the question of unemployment in general and, of equal importance, the problem of satisfaction in work. The first phenomenon is a familiar characteristic of industrial civilization which has been analyzed many times in terms of its impact, both on the worker and on the society as a whole.[17] But work satisfaction, though equally significant, is sometimes slighted.

When men are close to Nature, they almost always have work, difficult and narrowing as it may often be; when they move into complex civilization, they may frequently be workless and thus feel spurned and rejected by fellow human beings who, despite goodwill, often regard them as useless and therefore as worthless. The image we have of our neighbor depends in considerable degree on whether we regard him as "productive" or not. When he has no regular work — whatever the reason may be — we think of him as not contributing to the community; he loses merit in our eyes and becomes something less than a human being.

It is, of course, not civilization in itself which leads to worklessness but rather our failure to respond adequately in a political sense to the phenomena that give rise to worklessness. Thus in ancient Roman civilization, the small peasant was uprooted from his land through the machinations of conquerors enriched with the booty and the slaves produced by war, as well as by the economies of large-scale production. Thousands of peasants were forced into the burgeoning cities, where they often lived in idleness and became the "proletariat," those good for nothing except reproduction. But the existence of the proletariat was not inevitable. Had the Romans possessed sufficient political imagination — had they, in other words, demonstrated as much ingenuity in planning for peace as in planning for war — the proletariat need not have existed. But both the imagination and the will to use it were absent, and thus the proletariat continued to exist as a kind of festering sore which became one of the factors leading to the disintegration of the empire.

Similarly, in modern complex civilization, millions of unemployed are created by technological innovation and other factors, and the modern proletariat are expanded in numbers. Again, this need not be, if modern man possessed the political imagination and will essential to bring people and resources together to create new employment. In economies like that of the United States, relatively extensive unemployment is taken for granted. Thus in this country there has never really been full employment in modern times, except during periods of war or of large-scale preparations for war.[18]

While worklessness presumably does not exist in such states as the Soviet Union, its absence appears to be purchased at a tremendous cost: much of the economy is highly inflexible, cost of production in many sectors is enormously great, and agricultural production particularly is not what it might and ought to be. Unpublicized inefficiencies often conceal wasteful use of both men and resources. Moreover, personal liberties are held in contempt.[19]

The problem of satisfaction in human work is equally significant. It has been the theme of much social criticism during the past century and has recently been treated at some length in an elaborate report of the Department of Health, Education, and Welfare entitled *Work in America*.[20] The report reminds us of the familiar charge that blue-collar workers tend to be alienated and bored, seeking refuge at the end of the day in alcohol, spectator sports, or mindless TV, but it also suggests that the alienation and boredom are expanding to white-collar workers. There is serious job dissatisfaction or even "despair" at all "occupational levels," not excluding that of managers.

Furthermore, the report goes on, work-related dissatisfaction is leading to a decline in physical and mental health, to family instability, and to greater irrationality in politics. "Growing unhappiness with work is also producing increased drug abuse, alcohol addiction, aggression and delinquency in the work place and in the society at large, the report finds."[21]

Similar refrains are to be found in the writings of many modern social critics. The late Paul Goodman suggested that the young person confronting the world of employment today faces the probability of having to accept a job which will be boring, psychologically unrewarding, and soul destroying.[22] And Goodman, too, included not merely blue-collar work but also white-collar employment. The politics of worklessness in an age of severe economic depression turns on the issue of getting any type of work. In an epoch of relative prosperity, the political issue becomes not merely one of maintaining work opportunities in general but also of multiplying the kind of work possibilities which will be significant and spiritually rewarding.

At no point is the teleological nature of man better illustrated. Contrary to some views which see man as wishing to *avoid* the expenditure of his energies, in this view man not only finds it desirable to employ them but also hopes to use them in ways which help the community and challenge his own powers.[23] All too often in complex civilization, this facet of the human condition is ignored; and while the mechanical contrivance is characteristically given tender loving care, the frameworks essential for making human labor rewarding not infrequently receive little attention.

Nor is dissatisfaction about the work situation confined to so-called capitalist segments of modern civilization. The notoriously high rate of drunkenness in the Soviet Union, for example, probably reflects in part, at least, underlying dissatisfaction about the structuring of work.

The issue of worklessness is closely bound up with that of economic instability, which we treat a little later. But basically, it raises the question of whether industrial and postindustrial civilization can politically and therefore deliberately transcend what Plato called the legislation of accident and subject so-called economic forces to the political will of man. It is also intimately connected, of course, with the problem of the relative rapidity of social change, which is in turn closely related to the technological challenge discussed in the previous chapter. Broadly speaking, we are contending that the issue of worklessness can be resolved without impairing a large measure of freedom of choice in occupations and commodities, but that this result can be brought about only by a type of public planning not yet present — or present only partially — in any part of the world. And the planning must be associated closely with the limits on technological and social change which we have reiterated. The implications of this kind of planning will be drawn out more fully elsewhere.

As for the question of work satisfaction, some of the suggestions of the HEW study are well worth considering, even before adequate planning is established. In general, *Work in America* maintains that we should substitute for the notion of "industrial efficiency" that of "social efficiency." We might interpret the latter term as meaning that the values we ought to implement should take into consideration not merely immediate dollars-and-cents desiderata but also such standards as human dignity, aesthetic appeal, and "happiness" conceived in more than economic terms. If we apply Aristotle's "by-product" theory of happiness, *eudaimonia* would be a kind of side effect of the worker's responding to an employment situation so structured that he is challenged to put forth his best efforts.

Work in America also suggests what it calls a fundamental redesign of jobs, to attempt to make labor more challenging. The worker would be given more responsibility, would be less subjected to detailed control by a supervisor, and would share in the surplus. All these proposals are, of course, very old, many of them having been suggested by traditional socialists; but that they should have been offered by a far from radical administrative agency may be hopeful in our prognosis for modern civilization.

One of the central problems in contemporary work life is that large numbers of manual, clerical, and professional workers feel "trapped" into positions from which they cannot escape, even though they would like to do so. They may have made a wrong decision early in their lives and find that, with family responsibilities, they cannot afford to train for an alternative occupation. Or they may have liked their employment at one time but now seek other kinds of challenges. Whatever the reason, a feeling of being trapped is somewhat like being placed in prison for a life term: Both the industrial prison and the jail for "criminals" tend to demoralize one and to encourage sloth and evasion of responsibility.

The HEW study suggests ways for transcending the consciousness of entrapment. It maintains that there should be large-scale programs for worker retraining and "self-renewal." Any worker (and again by worker we mean not only industrial laborer but also service employee or professional man) could enter such programs, either to enhance his opportunities for labor mobility or to change careers entirely. And one of the suggestions of the study is particularly noteworthy — that a sabbatical year (somewhat like the sabbatical now offered to many academics) be established.

Work in America goes on to develop the idea of total employment, rather than merely full employment. By this it means that creative employment would be provided not only to those unemployed in the existing work force but also to those outside the presently defined labor pool who wish to work — young people, housewives, the retired, and so on. This suggests what many socialists have long advocated — that there should always be more challenging work opportunities than there are persons seeking them. But again we stress that this is unlikely to be brought about simply by accident. It requires conscious public deliberation, that is, politics.

Some of the proposals of the HEW study have already been partially implemented by certain corporations. At the American Telephone and Telegraph Company, the work force was broken down into small teams, each of which was assigned the task of producing complete telephone books. Evidence indicates that mistakes declined and morale rose.[24] Unfortunately, however — and this again dramatizes the mystique of technology in the modern world — often no sooner is restructuring of work organization adopted than a machine will be introduced which has the effect of undermining the new work situation. This happened in the case of AT&T when a machine displaced the telephone-book teams. As we have maintained again and again, modern American society seems to be characterized by a kind of fatalistic acceptance of technological innovation, whatever its consequences for human beings.

Work in America emphasizes throughout that the overwhelming mass of human beings seek creative work through which to self-actualize themselves. Significant work makes life meaningful. Work dominated by routine or lack of social importance or tending to destruction (such as cutting off the ear of a hog on the assembly line eight hours a day — an actual case — or making ammunition to kill human beings, or parroting advertising slogans that are misleading or downright fraudulent) tends to show contempt for the human being and to destroy his vast potentialities for a life of quality. Even if an economic minimum were guaranteed, human beings would still seek to work for social as well as personal creative objectives. The study makes this explicit when it observes: "It is illusory to believe that if people were given sufficient funds, most of them would stop work and become useless idlers."[25]

We cite at some length the study's proposed remedies, not because its authors are infallible but because the answers they suggest ought to be considered very seriously if we seek to make modern civilization genuinely human or humane in a teleological sense. The study is also a reminder that many of the prevalent clichés about human beings and their work are probably wrong — dogmas such as that men and women must be goaded to work by threat of starvation, that most persons on welfare are inherently lazy (do not wish to use their energy for some purpose), that purely economic answers to work dissatisfaction are adequate, or that most workers are not capable of much greater autonomy or self-rule in the work process.

In general, the broad thrust of the study ought to be approved, even though we may legitimately argue that it does not provide a final answer. Without the virtual revolution in attitudes and practices suggested by such enquiries, we face in modern civilization increasing tensions, demoralization, and all forms of alienation — even if the gross national product continues to rise. And we deny many of the elements of justice we have sketched out in this book.

It should be remembered, too, that we are not confining our proposed revolution in employment opportunities to the United States. Throughout technological society, whether on this side of the Iron Curtain or on the other, the problems of creating challenging work opportunities are increasing. The dogma that mere nationalization of economic enterprise would be a kind of magic solution for the problem of order and freedom in industry was met legitimately with the response of many workers in British nationalized industries: "There's still the bloody boss!" In the Soviet Union, as we have already said, disquietudes similar to those in the United States are also present.

In the whole area of employment, worklessness, and work dissatisfaction, all modern political tendencies need to be self-critical. Democratic socialism, for example, must broaden and deepen its understanding of the nature of human beings. Too often in the past it, along with liberalism, accepted rather uncritically the mystique of technology. Socialism also sometimes seemed to say that nationalization of economic enterprise would in itself provide an answer.

Then, too, socialism in the past was frequently and rather naively antagonistic to the civilization-as-corrupting paradigm as represented by Tolstoy. It seemed never to doubt that man could fulfill himself within the

217

framework of increasingly complex division of labor. There is a very plausible argument for the position that no matter what the form of economic and social reorganization, unless we deliberately attempt to control the rate of social change and the tendency to specialization, dissatisfaction about work will continue. What seems to be required is not merely reexamination of the work process and the development of some scheme of workers' control but also, in areas of great technological complexity, an actual reversal of the tendency to greater and greater specialization. But this would involve movement in the direction of Tolstoy-like perspectives, even though we halt long before the point to which he bids us return. At some locus between Tolstoyan agrarianism on the one hand and the pace and structure of modern civilization on the other, we are most likely to find the condition in which relative stability in fruitful and significant employment will flourish.

But before we can discover that point, we must turn to the problem of controls in economic life.

Centralization and Controls in Economic Life

In general, modern civilization, on its economic side, tends to put a premium on large aggregations of capital and to create huge organizational structures (corporations and governments) to manage them. Thus is posed in a particular context what we referred to in Chapter 4 as the perils of centralization versus those of decentralization.

In neocapitalist nations like the United States, the politics of the giant economic enterprise are at least as significant as what passes for formal government. Indeed, the American people are in some respects more profoundly governed through corporate politics (which are frequently secret and concerned with the advancement of special interests) than they are by means of such institutions as Congress.[26] Particularly in a semi-monopolistic economy, the managers of large aggregations of capital are in certain ways clothed with far greater coercive potentialities and power to build up and destroy than are governors of states; and the bureaucracies these managers direct take on the characteristics of most other bureaucracies. Americans believe that their governing process is open, by contrast with that of the so-called "totalitarian" nations, just as they believe that it is democratic. But both these beliefs rest on shaky grounds. Not only is ostensibly public life often clouded in secrecy, as the Watergate affair illustrated, but large segments of Americans' lives are directed and manipulated by the governors of the business corporate structure. And if democracy means that that which touches all shall be approved by all, then we have already seen that the most important factor affecting all — technological innovation — is largely immune to anything resembling a public democratic determination.

In the process of building up these huge, highly centralized structures, whether in oligopolistic capitalistic states like the United States or in State-capitalist states like the Soviet Union, effective local control is eroded. Even where the form of local control exists, the limitations imposed on it by the State, the corporation, and, indeed, industrialization itself gradually destroy its substance. Public central legislative bodies themselves are undermined and doctrines which exalt the executive branch as the only agency capable of dealing with complexity and so-called national security are propounded.

Now all this tends to make the individual human being feel insignificant. To be sure, he may have considerable economic security — particularly in the so-called totalitarian states — but he obtains it at an enormous price. And in both private oligopolistic and State-capitalist nations, his livelihood may be wiped out by decisions of remote executives, whether industrial or nonindustrial, whom he cannot effectively control.

The problem which emerges for the student of politics is whether all this is an inevitable concomitant of the technological society — as the extreme antitechnology view would argue — or whether there are ways of combining a measure of industrial technology with a decline in centralization, a restoration of representative legislative authority, and a reinvigorated local community of some kind. This is one of the central questions of modern civilization, and we are by no means on the road to an answer.

In states like the United States, analysis of the issue seems to indicate that part of the problem is the hodgepodge and internally inconsistent nature of the system: Lines of responsibility and accountability are often blurred, and the possibilities for evasion of responsibility are thus enhanced. We have a kind of irrational combination of nonmarket coordination by corporations and government, on the one hand, and limited market coordination, on the other. We are neither fish nor fowl. Some prices are competitive; others are managed through devices like price leadership. The system defies both the theory of automatic adjustments implied in a pure "free enterprise" scheme and notions of rational democratic planning and control. Contrary to the picture presented by classical economic theory, inflation and high unemployment often accompany each other. In the quasi-oligopolistic, quasi-market economy, we have neither the supposed advantages of perfect competition nor the presumed desirable features of rational and accountable planning for the public interest.

Instead, we have planning of giant corporations for their own economic interests, administered and often rigid prices, and increasing tendencies to the consolidation of economic power. Private holding corporations affecting millions of human beings control many ostensibly separate companies; and private decisions made in a few board rooms in New York and Chicago make millions of workers the pawns of industrial and financial manipulations. The most costly crime today is white collar in nature — the result of the peculations of the captains of industry and finance — and not the relatively petty offenses for which low-income "criminals" are sent to prison.[27] By the standards of many state statutes, as Ferdinand Lundberg has pointed out, a sizable proportion of our major corporations are habitual criminals, having been convicted several times of offenses against the law.

Now the answer to a political economy controlled in this way is surely not that of the Soviet Union, with its dogmatic centralism, its lack of flexibility, its even more extensive secrecy, and its equally great devotion to the mystique of technology. Neither the American nor the Soviet economy is a model to which we can point with any confidence. In terms of production, in the former a large percent of plant capacity is frequently idle; while in the latter agricultural production often is particularly deficient. Neither economy is "democratic," and neither conforms to the norms of justice outlined earlier.

It would seem that the lines along which we might find an answer would include three principles. First, we should not endeavor to return to an extremely primitive economy. While, to be sure, the stripping away of extensive commerce and industry might tend to erode central controls and to restore the possibilities of local self-rule, unless it were brought about very gradually it would also entail the destruction of millions of human beings. Moreover, if we follow the classical paradigm and consider teleological human nature as a whole, we would not only destroy many men physically but would stunt the possibilities of their spiritual self-fulfillment. A certain level of economic development is a necessary although not a sufficient condition for man to become a human person.

Second, if our previous contentions have validity, at the same time we should place limits on economic growth and on the development of division of labor, as well as on the complex technology. While this would not eliminate the need for formal and planned coordination, it would make that coordination — always difficult at best — more manageable. If a deliberate effort is made to combine public coordination with a strictly limited market mechanism, production, distribution, and capital formation should be facilitated, as compared with the "command" economy of the Soviet Union or the oligopolistic scheme of the United States.

Third, with an economy of this kind, in the context of a strictly limited technological society and slower social change, it should be possible to carry out a rational decentralization of many decisions. Sometimes, however, this might be done within frameworks which have no congruence with traditional local communities. Generally speaking, it would seem that, given the values we stated in earlier chapters, a limited industrialism and highly selective technology would entail some public planning decisions at the world level, with much policy and administration reserved to regional groupings. Assuming a slower rate of social change implied by highly selective and deliberately introduced technology, it might be possible to expand fruitful, significant units of local governance. But such units would not be merely territorial in nature — they would also embrace decision-making groupings in factories, schools, and the professions. There is no reason, for example, why the principle of workers' selection of foremen should not be introduced, as well as general self-government for every productive unit, within broad limits to be prescribed by general rules. Already, in fact, experiments of this type exist in certain parts of the world.

When we discuss the issue of economic instability below, we shall enlarge on the possibilities of this kind of structure as they bear on that theme. Here we simply reiterate that the process as we envision it would entail a simultaneous centralizing and decentralizing movement, with the former pointing to world controls of several types and the latter involving a devolution in many respects more extreme than anything known in modern civilization.

Man and the Natural World

We have pointed out that primitive man often deified Nature. As humanity moves into complex civilization and particularly into modern civilization, however, it tends to deify its technologies and to run roughshod over primitive Nature. As civilization encroaches on the wilderness, it destroys the habitat of nonhuman creatures. The beasts, wild-eyed and fearful and hungry, flee and die in huge numbers. Natural resources are consumed at ever-mounting rates and without much regard for future generations. Even in the ancient Middle East with relatively low technological development, the supposedly high level of civilization was attained at the expense of virtually wiping out the forests, just as in modern times species after species has become extinct.

As nonhuman Nature retreats, vastly increasing human populations press finite resources to the limit. Rivers and the air become polluted, and the powerless particularly are subjected to the whims of industrial contamination, as they are to the demands of technology. In later stages of industrialism, man becomes aware that in exploiting Nature at so ferocious a

221

pace and in idolizing the machine which makes this possible, he runs the risk of destroying himself — for ultimately he remains dependent on the Nature he has appeared to hold in such contempt. By the time he once more realizes his dependence, however, he may wonder whether it is too late. Crowded into cities and fatalistically dependent on complex tools and seemingly declining energy sources, man appears to be awaiting either the destruction produced by irrational politics or the obliteration engendered by exhaustion of natural resources. The ecological crisis, as some have called it, is upon him.[28]

To be sure, this type of analysis is not without its critics. Wilfred Beckerman contends that the problem of exhausted resources is not likely to trouble mankind for about 100 million years. For all practical purposes, he maintains, resources are not really finite.[29] Many arguments of this kind turn on our definition of what we mean by a "resource." It can be pointed out that this term must be seen in relation to the cultural and technological level of a given civilization. For the ancients, uranium would not have been a resource because they had not yet discovered atomic fission; whereas for modern technological civilization it is very much of a resource. Whether the land is adequate depends on how we use it: Parts of North America were crowded in pre-Columbian days because many native Americans were still in the hunting and gathering stage and had not yet begun to lead an agricultural mode of existence. The exhaustion of wood in Britain during the 17th and 18th centuries appeared to produce a resources crisis until accessibility of coal became greater.

In other words, we have notoriously failed at times to take account of man's potential ingenuity when brought to bear on Nature. Even at our present stage of evolution and with such widespread reliance on fossil fuels, we are probably grossly underestimating reserves of fossil energy (for with respect to other resources, this has often been true in the past). Some point to development of solar energy as a way of supplying vast quantities of the wherewithal for agriculture, industry, transportation, and domestic life. Others look forward to the advent of the "breeder reactor" which will ostensibly provide an inexhaustible source of energy.

But even if we take a relatively optimistic view about possibilities for tapping new sources of energy during the coming century — a prospect by no means certain — other problems arise in the process. For example, some have contended that if the world continues to accelerate its consumption of energy at its present rate, within a relatively brief time (possibly 100 to 150 years hence), the "thermal pollution" problem would become unbearable. The world would become so hot that the polar ice caps might melt, flooding large parts of the globe. Changes in general climate are part of the scene. We point all this out to suggest again what the "progress" of

civilization already seems to demonstrate: that with every step in supposedly desirable developments, there is the possibility of equally undesirable consequences.

We might point out, moreover, that even if difficulties of this kind could
be overcome in the long run, human beings must also live in the short run.
(We have noted Lord Keynes's quip, "In the long run we are all dead.") To
say that in the long run we might overcome the pressure of population on
recognized resources and somehow avoid the apparent threat of thermal
pollution says nothing about short-run (two-generation or so) consequences. There has often been a lag between our perception of an issue of
this kind and the "solution" which presumably was eventually reached. In
the meantime, thousands of human beings suffered and died. Time considerations are important, and we cannot simply hope that crises perceived
now will somehow be resolved in the long run.[30]

Given this perspective, how can we respond? We can, of course, do
nothing — in other words, evade what is essentially a political challenge.
But this policy of no policy is likely, within the relatively near future, to
result in the random and horrible deaths of millions of human beings as we
try to adjust, too late, to the fact of culturally perceived limited sources of
energy. As a matter of fact, crises of starvation and malnutrition have been
with us for years, due to a multitude of factors, including present income
distribution, failure of political will (for example, in planning on a world
scale for adequate food reserves), always stupid wars, and refusal to utilize
technological resources already available. Some estimates have it that at
least one third of the human race is either malnourished or starving. In
part, crises of this kind are due to the fact that we have allowed the legislation of accident to rule supreme. In one way or another, a pessimistic view
of the issue would suggest, "growth" indubitably will be halted, if we
assume that we live in a finite world.

But the issue is not merely a narrowly "economic" one. Population and
economic growth, if pushed indefinitely and erratically, threaten not only
the physical existence of man on the globe but also his psychological and
spiritual fulfillment. That is, even if we could support economically a
population of 10 to 12 billion human beings at a "high" material standard
of living (and economists like Colin Clark have argued that many more
than this might be supported at a reasonably high standard of living), we
can raise the question as to whether this is desirable. Already large parts of
the inhabitable globe have ceased to be raw Nature, and animal and plant
life to be "wild" in any sense. Burgeoning populations inevitably entail the
extension of "farming" methods far beyond their present scope. Thus fish
farming has already begun, and in order to preserve wild animals in many
parts of the world, we have to herd them into reservations, where in-

evitably their raw natural character is drastically changed. In the very effort to sustain larger populations economically, we have to destroy much of what remains of primitive Nature. The world is turned into one vast technologized, highly concentrated, human population which, in order to preserve the very existence of lions and tigers and mountain goats, has to destroy their wildness and turn them into something like domesticated cattle.

Now it can be and has been plausibly maintained that man himself is frustrated in his teleological nature if he exists in a world where the notion of wildness and primitive Nature is only a memory, and his only reminder of the stuff out of which he has emerged is a zoo or a man-made garden which, by definition, have lost much of their character as primitive. Where wilderness is no longer available, where the only plants and animals are those that are carefully cultivated by man, where even the possibility of returning to the primitive, however briefly, has disappeared — man's own spiritual nature is diminished. Yet paradoxically, the only way we can assure that this undesirable consequence does not come about is to prevent it politically, through deliberate controls on population and economic growth.

Through civilization and politics, we must limit the erratic development of civilization, lest it wipe out the image and fact of the primitive, which civilized man requires to sustain his spiritual nature. The Bible says "I will lift up mine eyes to the hills, from whence cometh my help":[31] we can interpret this as saying that while human beings cannot be human except by departing from Nature, still if Nature is simply an object to be plowed or transformed, without simultaneous respect for its primitive state, then man's stature itself is depreciated. The grandeur of unoccupied hills and deserts and unspoiled forests reminds human beings from whence they came; it says to them that they, too, are mere creatures, ultimately dependent on Nature and on the Being who created both it and them, and that awe and mystery remain at the heart of things, despite the development of the arts and sciences and of civilized nature.

To be sure, deliberate rather than accidental legislation cannot, and ought not to, simply return us to Nature. We cannot flee entirely from the coercions and the freedoms of a civilization into which we all were born. But we can, through selective technology and deliberate control of the rate of growth, seek to conserve and replenish energy and to distribute it more equitably. We can counteract the effects of legislation by accident through legislation by design.

If we are to respond to the ecological issue by positive actions rather than by a kind of less-than-sublime faith in the virtues of doing nothing, and if we further assume that technical "solutions," while important, are not in themselves sufficient, three courses seem to be required: (1) halting population growth, (2) sharing resources and developing new ones, and (3) changing values.

Halting Population Growth. The rate of population growth must be drastically halted both by public decisions and the development of individual consciousness about the issue. Classical political philosophy was always keenly aware of the population issue, whether reflected in Plato, Aristotle, or St. Sir Thomas More. Where other paradigms (the Locke-like ones, for instance, and the Marxist and Tolstoyan views) were aware of the question at all, they considered it relatively unimportant, or thought the evolution of civilization would somehow throw up an answer, or believed a rather drastic regress in the direction of primitive Nature and individual asceticism would provide an adequate response.

We have already suggested that the argument for population control must be grounded not only on economic but also on social and political considerations. In classical political thought, the economics of population control entailed limiting the population of the city, controlling the size of families, exposing defective infants, and encouraging emigration to unsettled areas. If this could be done, Plato seems to suggest in the *Laws,* and if economic growth could be carefully and politically controlled, there would be economic sufficiency for all. In modern civilization, of course, the economic aspect of population control has become worldwide in nature, and at least some of the decisions will have to be at the ecumenical level.

We have also adverted to the ecological question and to its bearing on economic growth; here we specifically refer to the social and political implications of uncontrolled population. The idea of freedom, whether conceived in negative or in positive terms, would seem to entail limitations on population density. Highly dense populations, under modern civilization, inevitably require more regulations and engender greater personal frustrations because of the regulations. Other things being equal, moreover, there seems to be some evidence for the notion that beyond a certain point in density (and what that point is for human beings we do not know) general frustration is so different in degree that it becomes a difference in kind; and at this point, irrational behavior of all kinds is more likely to ensue. Freedom to become rational and autonomous beings thus tends to be counteracted by the magnified tendency to irrationality.

To be sure, one has to be very careful in making statements of this kind. Human beings are not rats and are very ingenious in circumventing many of the effects that high density would otherwise create, as is indicated by the relatively high degree of rationality obtaining in many of the crowded cities of Europe.[32] Despite this, however, we can still plausibly maintain that the general tendency to irrationality exists in densely populated areas, and it may be increasingly difficult in the future to counteract it deliberately.

Even if we can retain our rationality in areas of high population density, moreover, it may be very unappealing aesthetically and physically to live in such close proximity to one another. If the physical height of men and women continues to increase — as it has during the past 100 years in industrial civilization — each person would seem to require greater elbow room. There must be an aesthetic limit, moreover, to piling human beings one on top of the other in high rises.

We are not maintaining, of course, that there are not equally great perils in a density which is too low. Normally speaking, it would seem, man's teleological nature requires the possibility of a close commingling with other human beings. An individual forever living in the wilderness apart from others would cease to be a human being. If he were placed there as infant, he might not even appear to be a human being physically, let alone psychologically and spiritually.

The task of the political philosopher is to discover, with the aid of as much research as possible, the optimum density of population, taking into consideration not merely man's primitive nature — that from which he has sprung and to which he must return periodically for refreshment — but also the many-sided teleological nature which seeks fulfillment. Obviously, this is no easy task, and it cannot be reduced to a simple formula.

The problem can perhaps be viewed in terms of our religious experience. The great religious seers have seemed to require *both* the crowd *and* the solitary retreat for the full development of their natures. Had Christ not retired into the mountains and the desert, he probably could not have become the spiritual figure he did; but close relations with groups of human beings also seemed to be a prerequisite for the evolution of his spiritual dimension. So it is for most human beings; and any system of political thought which does not recognize both facets of the human personality is inadequate.

Can overall population control and reduction, whether for economic or for sociopolitical reasons, ever be brought about deliberately? This is one of the most basic challenges with which modern politics is confronted. Certainly reduction is unlikely without much greater development of political consciousness than is apparent today. Throughout most of the world, the desiderata for family size seem to be based primarily on such considerations as general philoprogenitiveness, short-run capacity to support the child, desire for many children to help in old age, and similar criteria. And for hundreds of millions, there is little thought of any kind when bringing children into the world. It is important to develop an awareness that one's decisions about the size of one's family are in effect political as well as personal choices; that is, the choices have direct political relevance. The effect of producing large families on the population issue for mankind as a whole must be weighed in making personal decisions.

But formal collective or political decisions are also required. If our analysis has validity, public policy might well seek to reward those who have families of only one or two or no children, provide for free population planning clinics, establish tax preferences to encourage personal awareness and relevant action, and undertake similar measures. If reverence for human life be a first-order value, however (as we have suggested earlier), public policy should not encourage abortion or infanticide, the line between the two being a very thin one indeed. To be sure, it will be argued that taking the life of the embryo may, by preventing unwanted children and reducing the chances of poverty, show reverence for life in the long run or as a whole. But such reasoning is specious. We do not encourage long-run reverence for life by taking it in the short run: Here again, as in war, the means shape the ends. To the degree that we encourage abortion for ends of population control, we are likely to provide a basis for supporting other forms of deliberate killing — mandatory destruction of the old and decrepit, for instance. After all, the usual way of distinguishing a fetus from an infant is to say that the former is biologically dependent on the body of the mother, whereas the latter is only socially, economically, and psychologically dependent. But at the other end of the life span, many an older person is almost in the position of the fetus — not technically in the biological womb, to be sure, but more dependent in other respects than an infant who is moving rapidly away from dependence.

Although we might hope that public policy would encourage methods of birth control short of abortion (there is a basic ethical difference between preventing the union of sperm and egg and killing a fetus which is the result of that union), far too much emphasis in the past has been placed on mere techniques of birth control or family planning. Conceivably, foolproof techniques could be available and yet the population would continue to increase. The basic issue is whether human beings can be motivated to curtail the generation of children in fact as well as in words, and this motivation turns on many interrelated social, political, and psychological factors which go far beyond mere availability of mechanical techniques. For example, there seems to be a close positive relation between a relatively high level of economic well-being and motivations to have small families.[33] Or again, carelessness in using birth control devices appears often to be associated with a lack of self-respect, and this in turn may be connected with the failure of others to show reverence for the individual. Admittedly, we know very little about such matters, but at a minimum we do seem to have firm ground for saying that the politics of population control goes far beyond the existence or nonexistence of mechanical or chemical contraceptive instruments.

To plan deliberately for population control and ultimately reduction is itself a revolutionary conception. While utopian thinkers from Plato to H. G. Wells have dreamed of it, and occasionally there have been erratic and unsustained attempts to effect it, for the most part mankind has proliferated and been wiped out through legislation of accident. As victims of the plague, or economic forces, or always-stupid wars, human beings have hitherto been treated as objects by a historical process to which they have been subjected. The politics of population control is an effort to reverse this pattern. It seeks deliberation, collectively as well as individually, before men and women reproduce themselves, and in so doing it pays the greatest possible tribute to man's teleological nature. No longer merely the victim of impersonal forces, man would demonstrate that aspect of his nature which makes him akin to the gods.

Sharing and Developing Resources. The second response to the ecological issue calls for a sharing of technical and natural resources and a publicly directed exploration for new sources of energy. The sharing ought to take place if we recognize man's finitude and limits to growth, and the exploration for new sources of energy would be a tribute to that aspect of human nature which stresses that man is not wholly at the mercy of primitive Nature. By sharing man recognizes that he is not a god, that he exists in time and in space. By exploration he shows his awareness that, despite his finitude, he is also a little lower than the angels.

The rapidity with which we are exploiting natural resources is enormously greater in some parts of the world than in others, and population figures must always be seen in relation to this rate of exploitation and consumption. Thus if we assume, as we did in Chapter 5, that the average American's consumption rate is about 30 times that of the average citizen of India (which is probably an understatement), then the population of the United States, in terms of Indian consumption rates, is about 6 billion souls; and given the modern situation, the gulf between India and the United States in this respect continues to become greater. The so-called developed nations as a whole have found themselves growing relatively richer, while the developing nations have become relatively poorer. Although India has developed technologically since World War II, it has barely been able to keep up with its population growth; and the unbelievably crowded conditions of Calcutta, with thousands living and dying in the streets, reflect the general state of possibly a third to a half of mankind. Although the "energy crisis" of the early seventies seemed to promise some redress in favor of the underdeveloped petroleum-producing countries, much of the gain, given the sociopolitical structures involved, would probably benefit primarily the rich, thus accentuating the gulf between the underdeveloped poor and their wealthy fellow countrymen.

It is doubtful whether the disparity between developed and developing nations can be substantially narrowed by setting as a standard for all the American consumption and exploitation rates, for there are definite limits, certainly in the short run, to what education and technology can do. Moreover, even if we assume that key natural resources are much more abundant than the pessimists will allow, their accessibility remains a problem. And there is always a distinction between the long run and short run: Even if we assume that in the long run (several generations, let us say) the gulf can be narrowed, the crises of the short run remain with us.

Our sights for the next several generations, if we keep these considerations in mind, should be focused on a combination of publicly controlled technological development and encouragement of willingness on the part of the developed parts of mankind to lower their consumption rates, so that any surplus could be contributed to a world capital and education fund which would be at the disposal of the developing countries. This reduction of rates of consumption would entail a substantial limitation on desire for material goods which would be reflected in legislation as well as in a radically altered private operative ethic. Although the search for new sources of energy holds out considerable promise, in itself it is not sufficient: plainly, we require not only new sources of energy, but also a population curve going downward and a redistribution of resources, both domestically and on a world basis, according to some consciously developed standard of distributive justice.

It is doubtful whether this can be accomplished without acceptance of such principles as public ownership of land and natural resources, regulation of migration on a world scale, the establishment of world-administered food reserves, and fundamental changes of consumer habits within the developed nations. There is enormous waste in such oligopolistic capitalist nations as the United States; some estimates are that Americans waste approximately one third to one half of all the energy they consume. In the United States, 200 billion tons of garbage are generated each year, most of which is not recycled into reusable materials. The automobile is notoriously inefficient, about 80 percent of the heat it generates being dissipated. We are not criticizing merely the capitalist portions of the industrial world, however; tremendous waste is also built into such inflexible systems as that of the Soviet Union, particularly in agriculture. Both oligopolistic capitalism and Soviet State collectivism have much to answer for when we assess the politics of natural resource use for the future.

Changing Individual Values. Underlying the kind of revolution we are envisioning would be drastic changes in the way industrial civilization has perceived the ordering of values during the past two centuries. Without a transformation of individual values, the context for desirable political change would not be present. Simultaneously with a dramatic heightening of political consciousness, therefore, would be the third course — a decline among the industrialized populations in what we perceive we "need." Such a phenomenon as meat eating — so widely associated by millions with the law of nature itself — would have to be sharply reduced, for if there is any supremely inefficient way to supply needed proteins it is through the eating of grain-fed cattle. The artful manipulation of human desires, so central to the cultures of the Western world, would have to disappear. There would have to be a widespread reversal of the expectation, so characteristic of the past five or six generations, that material goods will continue to multiply indefinitely.

How a consciousness of this kind can develop is, of course, not entirely clear. It must be part of the evolution of a broad new political awareness quite different from that of traditional Marxist, liberal, or conservative outlooks. Nor is there anything inevitable about its growth: It must be envisioned clearly, defended rationally, and then labored for. It should be evident that most contemporary political leaders have no such vision, or, if they do, they conceal it effectively. Instead, they engage in the politics of soothing rhetoric and repeat hollow clichés about progress. With only a few exceptions, they are like the naked Emperor receiving the plaudits of his bamboozled subjects for his nonexistent beautiful clothes. They remind one of Plato's Athenian leaders, all of whom — whatever their faction might be — were rhetoricians rather than statesmen.[34]

By contrast with most contemporary outlooks, the new world-view must take seriously the criticisms of even the most extreme Tolstoy-type or Gandhi-like critics. At the same time it must recognize that the goal ought not to be an extreme return to the primitive; rather, the new objective would be a very difficult attempt to restrain blind industrialization and to provide the institutions within the confines of which the basic technology of the world will be subject to introduction according to our assumed change in operative values.

Among specific implications of such a world outlook might be the reservation of a very substantial part of the globe for perpetual wilderness, a drastic reduction of the average size of cities, and the collective establishment of those priorities that would free men and women to pursue intellectual, aesthetic, and spiritual development. Although changes in political institutions could themselves encourage alterations in beliefs, it is also true that without fundamental revision in the mythologies of industrialism deliberate institutional changes would be impossible. The revolutionist must work at both levels simultaneously, endeavoring to develop more adequate institutions and at the same moment seeking to criticize contemporary operative values.

Economic Instability

As Nature gives way to simple and then to complex civilization, our very interdependence, other things being equal, tends to magnify economic instabilities and to make them turn not merely on such natural factors as the weather but also, and more importantly, on an impersonal, erratic market or unpredictable, tyrannical men. Millions of American farmers during the 1930s were brought to the verge of economic liquidation, and thousands were actually liquidated, by a combination of impersonal market forces and the humanly created dogmatism of laissez-faire political philosophy. At about the same time, millions of Russian farmers were economically or physically wiped out through a combination of Marxist dogmatism and political tyranny. The seeming whims of Nature are partially supplanted by those of uncaring social forces and of men.

Just as human beings become subject to a kind of technological determinism, so are they thrown about as bits of flotsam by markets and rulers, at times prospering and at other times deprived of the little they possess. Just as in a "primitive" stage of human history they may worship the Nature which frequently treats them so meanly, hoping by their propitiatory sacrifices to appease the wrath of the gods who govern Nature, so in a market economy, they hold the market to be a kind of divinity, however cruelly they may be manipulated by it. Thus political leaders of the United States in 1974 and 1975 largely stood idly by while millions were thrown out of work, and they seemed to contend that they could do nothing to avert still greater unemployment: Market forces, they said, would eventually work out a solution to the problem.

In oligopolistic capitalist societies, the business system becomes a sacred object, and even intelligent men prostrate themselves before it. In so-called totalitarian command economies such as that of the Soviet Union, the rulers insist on their own near infallibility, even though their irrational decisions may deprive human beings of bread.

Are there ways and institutions which could make men less subject in their economic lives to the irrational, the fortuitous, or the tyrannical? Or is it utterly impossible to avoid or mitigate the instabilities of either Nature or civilization?

It is difficult to envision an economy in which some instabilities do not occur, given the nature of Nature and the goal of genuinely free human personalities. Even if we could control the weather, no doubt the controls would be imperfect and subject to the administration of human beings, who themselves would often be prone to error. Although positive-freedom conceptions imply that as one becomes freer one is bound by universal rationality, it is also true, as we have suggested earlier, that existential man has a well-known tendency to rebel against his own rationally derived conclusions. The rebellion, to be sure, is not uncorrelated at times with particular types of social and psychological environment and thus can be greater or less; but even at best it is always present, in however small a degree.

But while we recognize the probability of instabilities and uncertainties of various types, we should not accept the proposition that the instabilities and irrationalities of modern economic systems need to be as extreme or as heartless as they are today. If we assume the evolution of consciously established limits on technological development and economic growth, it should be possible to mitigate drastically any undesirable severe changes in overall employment, prices, and economic conditions generally. Just as an imagined rigid stability might be deleterious to free human development, so do drastic instabilities greatly impair it.

A world such as we are suggesting would attempt to combine a publicly accountable nonmarket coordination with the market. Within overall priorities set by public planning through a democratic assembly, and with a system of "free" goods and services in kind, supply and demand would operate through a pricing mechanism. A scheme of this kind would attempt to take account of men's common material needs (through "free" goods and services), while at the same time offering them options through the market. Within a context of a more equitable distribution of income, supply and demand would be more nearly equatable with what most human beings genuinely need; by contrast, radical monetary income inequality such as obtains among much of humanity today tends to distort demand in the direction of producing goods and services which the purchasing power of the relatively few well-to-do can buy.

By quickly adjusting prices and supplies to demand and supply indicators in a society of near economic equality, the planning board would be able to avoid in considerable degree the phenomenon of "sticky" prices which is associated with oligopolistic economies. Thus prices and employment would probably fluctuate within a very narrow range as compared with today. General priorities in use of resources might be fixed for a period of one to two years, after public debate in a political assembly; and within that period, in planning time units of, let us say, three months, adjustment of supply to demand and demand to supply would be regulated by quickly responding pricing mechanisms. In such an economy, it might be possible to avoid both the autocratic planning characteristic of such states as China and the Soviet Union and the pricing rigidities and economic instabilities which have become so much a hallmark of systems like that of the United States, where much of the pricing is not competitive but rather is administered by publicly unaccountable and profit-motivated corporations.

A system of this kind has been termed "market socialism." It seeks to combine the principle of overall democratically controlled planning and coordination with that of a carefully limited market. But the market would be strictly subordinate to values publicly and consciously proclaimed by a body representative of the whole community. A generation ago, there was widespread debate about how such a combination would work in terms of the calculations which any economic system must provide; and this debate is still worth very careful study by those concerned with constructing a socialized economic order.[35]

If the proponents of market socialism are right, the values of considerable freedom of choice in economic matters would be combined with those of relative economic stability. The bureaucratic structures inevitably entailed in deliberate planning would be kept in check by the political decisions of a democratically elected body, on the one hand, and the guidance of a chastened and less erratic market, on the other.

Criticisms of socialism originally centered on the supposed impossibility of deliberately making the enormous number of calculations presumably essential for administration of the pricing system. It would not be possible, the critics said, to retain the rational determinations guaranteed by a "free" market scheme. But economists like Fred Taylor and Oskar Lange provided models of a market socialism in which, within established limits of deliberate planning, the calculations could still be made by the market.

It might be urged, to be sure, as it has indeed been maintained, that even apart from the calculations problem, socialism is undesirable on the ground that it subordinates man to the State. After World War II, this "political" argument against socialism — or, indeed, against any public planning — tended to become central among critics, who, following Von Hayek, argued that any public planning tended to lead to "serfdom."[36] The argument appeared to contend that once one embarked on public planning in the economic realm, even of the limited market socialist type, planning and direction in the spiritual realm would inevitably follow. If the State planned the heights of the economy, it would also have to begin to control thought and expression of opinion.

Arguments of this kind were rather effectively answered by defenders of economic planning.[37] They maintained that it was fallacious to contend that merely because society sought to plan one aspect of life, other dimensions must follow. Some of the defenders of planning pointed to actual experience with societies in which public planning, while not yet socialist, did not seem to generate restrictions on spiritual freedom. Nations like Great Britain and the Scandinavian countries, it was maintained, which had well-established traditions of civil liberties, did not need to fear the development of socialist planning. "Conventions" of the constitution and long-standing allegiance to freedom of speech and the press would check any tendency for economic planning to "spill over" into the intellectual area.

The debate about the relation of economic to spiritual freedom echoes our earlier discussion of freedom in general. Man lives in two worlds — one of scarce resources of time, space, and material goods, and another, the spiritual dimension, of unlimited resources. There can be no doubt that the two realms inevitably affect each other, since our power to express ourselves depends on our being alive and having access to material resources; and our use of those resources is determined by our ideas (the spiritual realm). But it does not follow from this that public planning of the market socialist type will be any more deleterious to spiritual freedom than the oligopolistic kind of planning characteristic of so-called capitalist societies. Indeed, it would seem that the opportunity to safeguard spiritual freedom would be enhanced, since the planning machinery would in principle be subject to public control, and business life would be conducted in the open rather than in secret. To be sure, if the public consensus does not value intellectual and spiritual freedom, then public planning of the economic order could degenerate into control of the spiritual order as well. The central problem is one of providing the conditions, educational and otherwise, under which an active public will for freedom can be maintained.

The issue illustrates again the central question of this analysis: As the political challenge is greatly magnified with the development of complex civilization, how can we collectively, deliberately control the complexity and consciously direct the evolution? If we assume that mankind is altogether incapable of this, then, of course, we can reach conclusions only of despair. Our position, to reiterate, is that larger numbers of humanity can indeed become much more conscious of the issues of political economy, but that the burden should not be allowed to become unbearable. Therefore, the answer must lie in some version of market socialism combined with conscious, collective efforts to limit the rapidity of technological change and perceived material need. Public and social ownership of land, natural resources, and major productive mechanisms, to facilitate planning and equity, must be combined with circumscriptions on tendencies to complexity.

Disparities of Wealth and Power: The Problem of Distributive Justice

Disparities of wealth, power, and income have constituted a central theme in the history of civilization and a vital question in the great political philosophies. At no time have they been more significant than in the modern era.

It is hardly necessary to document the fact of vast disparities in wealth and income in the world of the 20th century.[38] Although it is difficult to measure precise purchasing power across different economic systems and cultures, annual income differentiations range from $50 or $100 in certain nations to $6,000 to $7,000 in parts of the highly industrialized world. Robert McNamara, president of the World Bank, has said that "Some 900 million people are now subsisting on incomes of less than $75 a year. They are the absolute poor, living in situations so deprived as to be below any rational definition of human decency."[39]

In an ostensibly free enterprise state like the United States, disparities have actually been growing since World War II, contrary to some impressions. Writers like Gabriel Kolko have made us familiar with the broad outlines of distribution,[40] and a recent study by Letitia Upton and Nancy Lyons of the Cambridge Institute supports his conclusions.[41] This study found that the highest 20 percent of American families (in terms of income) have had incomes which totaled more than all the income received by the bottom 60 percent. In 1972, the 10,400,000 families in the poorest 20 percent received less than 6 percent of the total national money income, or an average of $3,054 per family. The 10,400,000 in the upper 20 percent, by contrast, received more than 40 percent of the income, or an average for each family of $23,100.

And the rich have become both relatively and absolutely richer. In terms of 1970 dollars, the lowest 20 percent of families gained income from $1,956 in 1958 to $3,085 in 1968. The highest 20 percent, by contrast, went from $15,685 in 1958 to $21,973 in 1968. Hence the gap between rich and poor *increased* (in constant dollars) from $13,729 to $18,888, within a period of ten years. The study goes on to point out that "transfer payments" to the blind, aged, welfare mothers, and so on account for only 7 to 8 percent of all personal income. Thus so-called government subsidy has little if any impact on income distribution, especially when we remember that over half of the transfer payments go to social security recipients, who are not only taxed for their benefits (through regressive social security taxes) but who are found at all income levels, not only in poverty-stricken groups.

Summarizing the Upton-Lyons study, an able journalist, Tom Wicker, says: "In other words, the rich are staying rich and the poor are staying poor, despite rare and highly publicized exceptions. Moreover, the poor are paying relatively more in taxes, while the effective tax rate on the affluent has been declining since World War II."[42]

The problem for the political philosopher, of course, has usually been not the fact that gross economic inequality and seeming egregious injustice exist but rather what positive principles we should follow in distributing wealth and income. Most historic civilizations have exhibited vast inequalities. Throughout the history of China, the poor peasant has been exploited by the rich landlord and the government which protects the landlord.[43] The early church fathers descanted on the perils of possessing great wealth. Protests like those of John Ball in the 13th century centered in considerable measure on the growing gulf between rich and poor and its social consequences. St. Sir Thomas More in the 16th century commented bitterly on the idle rich, noting that the poor and unemployed are forced in desperation to turn to theft.[44] While there have been societies, to be sure, which have sought deliberately to make certain that no person lacked a minimal standard of life (one thinks of pre-Columbian Peru, for instance),[45] still, by and large civilizations have continued to be characterized almost perennially by gross disparities, which have been central factors in their discontents. Thus the facts are relatively clear. What has been wanting has been agreement as to principles which should govern distribution. In general, history reflects in practice the principle of no principle, or at least that of conflicting principles.

But the search for principles of guidance has not ceased. In our day, it continues to reflect many of the varied systems of thought so familiar in the past. They may be summarized as the principles of (1) indifference, (2) an inverse relation between the extent of one's noetic qualities and the material goods one receives, (3) fortune, (4) merit or deed, (5) equality, and (6) need. We shall comment briefly on each and then suggest the principles that should guide any commonwealth, based on the notions of justice we have suggested.

Indifference. One of the characteristics of most civilizations is that they give birth to philosophers who regard distribution of income and wealth as a matter of relative indifference. Thus Plotinus, the great neo-Platonist, thought that it was rather absurd to be concerned about such matters. Since the material world was a lower-level reality and weighted down the soul, why should the true philosopher worry if certain persons received less than others?[46] Some interpretations of Christianity would seem to take the same position, thus opening them up to the charge of critics that religion reinforces and supports gross injustices in the distribution of wealth and power.

236

Noetic Qualities and Material Goods. Plato, in the *Republic,* seems to suggest an inverse relation between noetic qualities and one's claim on material goods: those who are most nearly true philosophers — and hence true rulers — will not ask for more than a relative pittance; material goods will be spurned by those who center their attention on intellectual and spiritual matters. On the other hand, for less noetic persons the soul's nature must be satisfied by many creature comforts. This principle would be almost the reverse of that obtaining in most historical polities, where possession of great wealth and income seems to lead to vast political power, and vice versa.[47]

Fortune. Some have seemed, in their attitudes, to defend fortune as a kind of principle. Those who justify inheritance appear to take this position: Because one is lucky enough to have been born into a wealthy family, one ought to be allowed to inherit the wealth of that family, regardless of one's contributions. Or again, those who justify what one is able to get through a free market economy would seem to be emphasizing fortune; for while many might argue that one's "success" in the market reflected one's "merit" and hence was not mere "fortune," still one might well ask whether a considerable part of one's supposed merit was not grounded on one's native capacity for which one was hardly responsible.

Merit or Deed. That merit should be a central principle seems obvious to many, but when one asks for a definition of merit, there are varying answers. Some will say that it is measured by one's success in the marketplace: Everyone who succeeds in getting goods from the market must ipso facto be entitled to them, because he is meritorious. Others interpret merit in terms of what one contributes to the society, so that he who contributes most would receive most, and he who contributes nothing would presumably receive nothing.

The problem with merit interpreted as "contribution" is that it is extremely difficult in a highly technological and labor-subdivided civilization to determine the exact contribution of every individual. Because technology is a social creation, moreover, to which millions have contributed over the course of generations, and because its existence is the chief basis for producing massive quantities of material goods, Edward Bellamy argues, the importance of individual differences drastically declines as technological civilization advances.[48] Overall increases in productivity, which can, of course, be measured, will, if one accepts this analysis, be primarily attributable to technology.

To the degree that merit (however defined) is based on heredity, moreover, one might ask why a person should be rewarded for what he did not create. Or again, he may have been fortunate in being born into a family of culture and high educational achievement, which would in itself, and aside from heredity, give him an unmerited advantage.

Equality. Some, including Edward Bellamy and certain of the utopian socialists, have suggested the principle of monetary or credit equality. Since, in a highly technological society, by far the largest factors in productivity are complex machines and social organization, whatever may be the differences in productivity between and among individuals are utterly dwarfed by the *social* factors — technology and cooperation — which go beyond any individual efforts and which are the products of generations of workers and of social structures which have grown up over time. Thus, the argument concludes, individuals might as well be given equal monetary credit, since differences in individual productivity, relative to the social elements in production, would not be worth bothering about.[49] Everyone would be expected to work up to his or her capacity, of course.

But Bellamy's basic defense of credit equality goes beyond such considerations and reposes on the notion that since human beings ought to be equal in rights and in claims to fraternity, the only way to express this equality-fraternity in the realm of scarce goods is through giving to every person the same claims on the socially produced material stock. Equality in credit follows from the basic right to equality in general.

As is true of most distributive principles, that of equality can be legitimately questioned. It does not, for example, take account of variations in need as between and among individuals. I may legitimately need more food than you, since I have a hyperactive thyroid or am six feet five inches tall as against your five feet four. But you may need more than I in other respects because your occupation requires that you travel, whereas mine does not. To be sure, credit equality does correctly imply that most defenses of economic inequality today are rather specious, and it sees that in fundamentals my needs are probably not all that greater than yours: There is a limit to what both of us can eat, for example, and that limit is reached rather soon. Nevertheless, monetary or credit equality does not seem to acknowledge sufficiently the principle of need.

Need. Enunciated many times from early civilizations to the present day, the principle of need was the distributive ideal of the first-century church at Jerusalem[50] and became central both to many utopian socialists and to Marxists. The idea of "From each according to his capacity, to each according to his need" is one of those propositions which seems to be almost self-evidently true, particularly when seen in the context of the concept of fraternity. That we ought to contribute what we can to the community cannot be refuted, and that we should get from the community everything we need seems equally persuasive.

The principle allows for individual differences between and among personalities as well as for the social dimension of individual experience. It assumes that contributions may vary, whether widely or not, but does not make distribution turn on contribution.

It is subject, of course, to variation in interpretation. What, for example, is "need"? One interpretation, sometimes called the functional theory of property, is that everyone should be alloted what is necessary for him to perform his function in society. Often this conception has been associated in modern times with the name of R. H. Tawney,[51] but it is really a very old one, having been present in some medieval theory and particularly in the notions of St. Thomas Aquinas. If one adopts a functionalist view, then, one's station in life, as well as one's personal needs for food, shelter, and clothing, would be considered. Thus if one's occupational tasks could not be carried out without considerable traveling, then one would receive more than someone whose occupation did not entail traveling. The functional theory obviously gives rise to many questions which are not easy to answer.

Another issue growing out of distribution according to need is that of who determines the need, the individual or some agency of the community. The goal of many who adopt the need principle is a situation in which each person defines his own need, having developed principles of self-restraint and being able to distinguish between needs and wants, the desirable and the desired. Short of this, various combinations of individual and community might define need. In many instances, no doubt, relative need would be so evident as to be beyond dispute. Today, for example, public school services are distributed in accordance with the principle of need, and there are relatively few problems about application of the idea: Thus a family of five normal children, it will be agreed, should have the right to use school services five times as much as a family of one child, even though the latter might conceivably contribute five times as much as the former in school taxes.

Determining the Ideal of Distributive Justice. Discussion of distributive principles cannot be divorced, of course, from the problem of incentives for production. In defense of the principle of merit, for instance, it is often said that unless individuals are rewarded according to deed, they will cease to be highly productive, and laziness will be encouraged. The assumption of this criticism is that the most important factor (or at least one of the most significant) in motivating individuals to work is economic reward. The question is, of course, a very complicated one, involving psychological, social, and cultural considerations. Thus it might be plausible to argue that economic incentives could be extremely significant in one culture but, because of drastically different social values, of almost no importance in another. The individual cannot be divorced from the cultural expectations. In the Platonic system of the *Republic,* the problem of incentive was solved by fitting the square pegs in square holes and the round ones in round holes. Thus the noetic, by their teleological natures, speculated as an end in itself, and for them material rewards were irrelevant in evoking needed contributions to the polis; but the appetitive, again by their teleological natures, fulfilled themselves primarily through acquisition and material enjoyments, and in the process contributed most to the whole.

What principle, then, should we adopt? When asking this question, we assume human beings as they are or as they might conceivably become during the next generation or so. We have already suggested, in Chapter 2, the lines along which we should respond to the question of distributive justice. We said, it will be remembered, that the answer lay, in the long run, in the principle of need, assuming contributions according to ability. In the shorter run, a combination of need and approximate equality might be suggested, given the types of human beings and the social heritage which must inevitably have an effect on the transition to a just commonwealth.

The principle of contribution according to ability and distribution according to need would seem to be the ideal of distributive justice. It takes account of the real diversities between and among human beings and at the same time recognizes the idea of fraternity. It is compatible with the notion of personality we outlined earlier. It embraces within one principle those who cannot labor and those who have rare talents. It could accommodate both Plato's appetitive man and his noetic personality. Given the technological constraints and the value system emphasized in this and the preceding chapter, even the needs of the appetitive would be strictly limited, although less so than those of the noetic.

Moreover, most political economies already distribute many goods (albeit somewhat roughly) according to this desideratum. Parks, schools, playgrounds, and police services are good examples. This list might well be extended until it ultimately embraces all goods and services — somewhat as in William Morris's great utopian work,[52] in which if one wishes a pipe one goes to a pipe-maker and he makes one, without any immediate exchange payment of money, goods, or services. Later on, of course, the pipe-maker may go to his patron for the extraction of a tooth, again without any immediate monetary or other payment.

It may be objected, of course, that we are very, very far away from such a state. This is true. But we shall never attain it if we do not try to draw out the meaning of the principle and then ask ourselves how we can implement it.

240

For the immediate future — the next several generations — we undoubtedly would have to limit our application of the principle, given human beings as they have been molded in past civilizations, particularly in the capitalist culture. But there is no reason why we should not extend the principle of free or communist goods and services beyond the situation obtaining today. In many parts of the industrial world, for example, medical services are provided according to the principle of medical need. This ought to be applied everywhere, particularly in the United States. And if medical services, why not legal services and, let us say, transportation within the urban complex? Two generations ago Bertrand Russell was arguing for the feasibility and desirability of free distribution of bread.[53] Perhaps we might modify this and make it free distribution of bread and of the ingredients for bread (thus allowing for home baking).

Obviously which particular goods and services can or should be distributed free will depend in some measure on our experience. In the beginning, possibly, we shall have to compromise with the idea of individual judgment of need, at least in some instances. If, for example, experience tends to show unusual waste in distribution of bread, then some upper limit for a given time period might be fixed. But it is unlikely that this would be necessary in the case of urban transport, education, parks, and legal and medical services.

The general notion of free goods and services is meant to be an implementation of the idea that the individual, in order to become a free personality, should be less subject to the whims either of Nature or of Man than he is today or than he has been in most historic civilizations. In a world of potential sufficiency, at least in essentials, his dependence on an erratic money system, or administrators, or employment should be reduced to a minimum. He should in an emergency be able to fall back on a modicum of free goods and services, somewhat like the preindustrial farmer who, when the "putting out" system failed to provide the raw materials for him to work up, was able to fall back on his garden, his cow, and his helpful, personally known neighbors. As Aristotle suggested long ago, an overreliance on money and money payments often obscures what an economy should be all about — the nurturing and development of human life.[54]

By-products of the expansion of free goods and services might include an encouragement of independence on the part of the individual; a reduction in the necessity for most types of welfare payments, with their accompanying bureaucratic manifestations and invidious class distinctions; and furtherance of the idea that the human being is entitled, simply because he is a human being, to certain basic goods and services.

It is recognized, of course, that even a limited extension of this kind depends on certain corollaries. A moderate level of technological civilization would have to be maintained, for example; self-restraint and a sense of responsibility would have to be widespread; and the vast majority of the population would have to be employed at gainful labor. We have been maintaining throughout that while technological innovation would be publicly controlled, we would not be making the civilization-as-corrupting paradigm our primary or only guide. As for restraint and a sense of responsibility, in some measure, no doubt, these characteristics would have to develop beyond their existing levels. But in recognizing this, we should also remember the enormous waste in our present distributive system, given today's predominant values — a waste much greater than that which would obtain in the new order. With respect to the vast majority being engaged in gainful labor, this basically would be rooted in a strong motivation to work, due to the fact that most individuals would now be in occupations which suited their talents. It would be assumed that if one is exerting one's energies in the way one intrinsically enjoys, one has the very highest motivation for labor.

The provision of "free" goods and services, then, would be the first charge on the social budget, along with replenishment and, possibly, expansion of capital. According to what principles would remaining production be allocated? Merit? Contribution? Equality? If we accept the view that the primary incentive for production is to place the square peg in the square hole, then the central issue of distribution beyond the "free" sector would seem to turn on whether or not we should accept Bellamy's notion of credit equality or, alternatively, a vastly reduced disparity between low and high incomes. There is much validity in Bellamy's argument about civilization reducing relative differentiations in individual contributions. It strains credulity to think that a General Motors executive is 60 or 70 times more "productive" than the average worker. To be sure, it is often maintained that the talents of the executive are very rare and that this "naturally" makes him more "valuable" in a monetary sense. But if all incomes were strictly limited by public decision, surely the person of supposedly "rare" talents (assuming that they are indeed scarce) would rather work in an occupation where he could exercise them, entirely apart from monetary considerations, than in one where they could not be used. On the other hand, it may be that, until certain mythologies in favor of irrational income disparities begin to fade, some differentiation may be justified as a kind of concession to the weaknesses of historical human nature. Given the existence of an expanded distribution according to need, one should be willing — at least for a time and until all square pegs have been fitted into square holes — to allow limited discrepancies in the name of individual "merit" or of "contribution." The remote goal would, of course, be distribution of everything according to need.

Taking all these factors into consideration, we suggest a maximum annual disparity ratio of 1.2 to 1 or 1-1/5 to 1 as plausible and sufficiently flexible to accommodate our desiderata. To introduce this principle would be revolutionary in most of the world today, whether industrialized or nonindustrialized.

The critic may ask why distribution through money is permitted at all. We have argued, it may be urged, that money values often obscure and distort what is taking place in the lives of human beings; and calculation of the gross national product in monetary terms does not tell us *what* is being produced — whether poisons, missiles, or useful things. To be sure, money facilitates a certain kind of freedom of choice; and it is supposed to be a store of economic values. But while it may under some circumstances enlarge freedom of choice, its fluctuations in value may also erode that freedom. Our modest defense of money here would be that, in the context stated or implied — of expanded free goods and services, relative economic stability through market socialism, social ownership of natural resources and the major instruments of production and exchange, and publicly controlled technology — it would be less likely to show its deleterious side and more likely to provide a measure of freedom and flexibility. Under the circumstances suggested, it could become a servant rather than a master.

It almost goes without saying that within such a distributive framework, inheritance of all except those minor goods which might be regarded as an extension of the personality would be eliminated. Then, too, since land and natural resources would be owned and administered publicly, no individual could gain from land speculation — an important source of some of the greatest fortunes in the modern world and therefore a significant basis for oligarchical political power.

In Sum: The Call for a New Utopia

The import of all we have said in this chapter is the call for a market socialist, collectivist order which will be closely related to the norms of justice and the conception of human personality outlined in previous chapters.

In fact, the question is not whether we should have collectivism rather than individualism in the economic order: Complex technological civilization everywhere entails collectivism, whether through the giant corporation or trust or through some form of avowed public administration. The question is rather what kind of collectivism we shall develop and how we can establish institutions to make it accountable. Shall it be the politics of the private corporation, the combine, or the trust; or shall it be the politics of some variety of democratic socialism?

More than a hundred years ago, Orestes Brownson, that great critic of early American industrialism, remarked that modern civilized man had been freed from "medieval superstition" only to gain the "Gospel of the cotton mill, laissez-faire, save who can, and the devil take the hindmost, and we can do what we please with our own."[55] But, he argued, the fact that he was a severe critic of modern civilization did not mean that he shared the lament of Edmund Burke that "the age of chivalry is gone." "Chivalry is gone," remarked Brownson, "and thank God for it." Those who yearned for peasants in thatched huts, he went on, were apt to forget that most peasants lived on scraps in hovels.[56]

Brownson was right. The alternatives for the politicist in modern civilization are not simply the "thatched hut," on the one hand, or runaway industrialism and technology, on the other. Rather, we must, while acquiring a new respect for the primitively natural and collectively controlling and limiting the pace of technological change, seek to construct a political economy that, although no longer enamored of the inevitability or desirability of economic growth, will seek to treat human beings as ends in themselves rather than simply as statistics in ever-mounting gross national products. To construct such a political economy, however, will entail rather drastic changes in the values which actually operate in our lives and the destruction of such idols as free enterprise, the inevitable triumph of the proletariat, the notion that genuine revolution can take place through violence, and the desirability of accumulating ever-increasing amounts of material goods.

We have suggested at numerous points that the general values of the community and its mythologies heavily condition the framework within which such issues as those of coercion and freedom, technology, and political economy develop, and from time to time we have referred to the political beliefs and institutions within the framework of which the vast social changes engendered by technological innovation have taken place. The challenges of politics in modern times are so interrelated that their full implications, as they bear on justice and the norms of political life, require the portrayal of the kind of world within which those challenges can conceivably be more nearly met. In sum, we need an adumbration of political goals for the coming few generations, which, while it will take into account what we have said during the previous chapters, will attempt, too, to go beyond it by presenting more concretely a sketch of the kind of world which is desirable and, conceivably, possible. This is another way of suggesting that we need a new utopia which will seek to apply the principles we have been developing and which will avoid both the pitfalls of a supposed return to Nature and the equally great hazards of a world in which largely uncontrolled technological and economic forces are allowed to dominate man.

It will be the object of the final chapter in this book to present such a sketch.

Notes

1   Richard M. Fagley deals with the population issue from the viewpoint of moral and religious obligations in *The Population Explosion and Christian Responsibility* (New York: Oxford, University Press, 1960). More recent discussions include Paul Ehrlich, *Population Bomb* (San Francisco: Sierra Club Books, 1969) and Paul Ehrlich and Anne H. Ehrlich, *Population, Resources, Environment: Issues in Human Ecology* (San Francisco: W. H. Freeman & Co., 1970). Sometimes the economic implications of population growth are emphasized to the exclusion of the political. But the latter — inasmuch as they are connected with the dense and sometimes rootless populations of cities, the problems of governing complex and populous urban areas, and the difficulties of public planning for large numbers in general — would seem to be at least equally important.

2   Lewis Mumford, *The Culture of Cities* (New York: Harcourt, 1938), *The City in History* (New York: Harcourt Brace, 1961), and similar works.

3   See Ernest Barker, *Traditions of Civility: Eight Essays* (Hamden, Conn.: Shoe String Press, 1967).

4   John Steinbeck, *The Grapes of Wrath* (New York: Viking Press, 1939).

5   Ludwig Von Mises, *Omnipotent Government* (New Haven, Conn.: Yale University Press, 1944).

6   Friedrich A. Von Hayek, *The Road to Serfdom* (Chicago: University of Chicago Press, 1944).

7   See Barbara Wooton, *Freedom under Planning* (Chapel Hill: University of North Carolina Press, 1945); Herman Finer, *The Road to Reaction* (Boston: Little, Brown & Co., 1946); and Oskar Lange, *Essays on Economic Planning*, 2nd ed. (New York: Asia Publishing House, 1968).

8   Classic studies such as Ida Tarbell's *History of the Standard Oil Company* (New York: McClure, Philips & Co., 1904) tended to stress this. See also the Monographs of the Temporary National Economic Committee, which inquired into the subject from 1937-1939, 43 vols. (Washington, D.C.: Government Printing Office, 1940-41). Other studies of quasi-monopolistic or oligopolistic tendencies include such volumes as William Fellner, *Competition among the Few: Oligopoly and Similar Market Structures* (New York: Alfred A. Knopf, 1949) and G. Warren Nutter, *The Extent of Enterprise Monopoly in the United States, 1899-1939* (Chicago: University of Chicago Press, 1951). For more recent studies, see, for in-

stance, Paul Baran and Paul Sweezy, *Monopoly Capital: An Essay in the American Economic and Social Order* (New York: Monthly Review Press, 1968); Mark Green et al., *The Monopoly Makers: The Report on Regulation and Competition,* Ralph Nader's Study Group Reports (New York: Grossman Publishers, 1973); Estes Kefauver, *In a Few Hands: Monopoly Power in America* (New York: Pantheon Books, 1965); and an expansion of Nutter's earlier volume, G. Warren Nutter and Henry Einhorn, *Enterprise Monopoly in the United States, 1899-1958* (New York: Columbia University Press, 1969). The economic aspects of oligopoly are explored by Joan Robinson in *Economics of Imperfect Competition* (New York: St. Martin's Press, 1969).

9   Theoretical and other problems of oligopoly have been treated in such works as Gardiner C. Means, *The Corporate Revolution in America: Economic Reality vs. Economic Theory* (New York: Crowell-Collier, 1962), and Edward H. Chamberlin, *Theory of Monopolistic Competition: A Re-Orientation of the Theory of Value,* 8th ed. (Cambridge, Mass.: Harvard University Press, 1962).

10   For specific cases of price fixing in the American economy, particularly in the electrical industry, see, for example, John Herling, *The Great Price Conspiracy* (Washington: Robert B. Luce, 1962). The extent of price fixing and price leadership in the American economy has been much debated.

11   But Milton Friedman in the sixties of the 20th century was still apparently insisting that a market economy of the old type was both possible and desirable. See, for example, Milton Friedman, *Capitalism and Freedom* (Chicago: University of Chicago Press, 1962). He deals with his "monetarist" theories in *Dollars and Deficits: Inflation, Monetary Policy, and the Balance of Payments* (New York: Prentice-Hall, 1968).

12   For a hostile view of the Inca Empire as showing the incompatibility of a planned economy with "liberty," see Louis Baudin, *A Socialist Empire,* trans. Katherine Woods, ed. Arthur Goddard (Princeton, N.J.: D. Van Nostrand Co., 1961). Baudin tends to view the "planned" society of the ancient Incas as "static" and as tending to destroy initiative and spiritual freedom. The Incas, he avers, were a "nation of grown-up children."

13   See Mortimer Adler, *The Idea of Freedom,* 2 vols. (Garden City, New York: Doubleday, 1958, 1961).

14   While some may view this interpretation of Marxism as a distortion, it seems to me that it is essentially correct. One sees it not only in the writings of Marx and Engels themselves but also in the studies of quasi Marxists like Herbert Marcuse, who, in such works as *Eros and Civilization* (Boston: Beacon Press, 1955), seems to see abundance as releasing men from the repressions of civilization and as freeing them for spontaneous play activity. To be sure, in *One Dimensional Man* (Boston: Beacon Press, 1964), Marcuse appears to see the technology on which abundance depends as having a life of its own that may transcend given social systems. But in his later writings, he seems to return to at least a quasi-Marxist position.

15   G. D. H. Cole's *History of Socialist Thought,* 5 vols. (London: Macmillan & Co., 1954 to 1960), which touches on all strands of socialist, quasi-socialist, and

anarchist thought, seems to me to document this proposition with respect to the "radicals." With some exceptions, they tend to think of the development of complex technology as, on the whole, "progressive," at least in the long run.

16   See, for example, Robert Blauner, *Alienation and Freedom: The Factory Worker and His Industry* (Chicago: University of Chicago Press, 1964); Franz Pappenheim, *The Alienation of Modern Man* (New York: Monthly Review Press, 1959); Bertell Ollman, *Alienation: Marx's Conception of Man in Capitalist Society* (Cambridge: Oxford University Press, 1971); Kenneth Keniston, *The Uncommitted: Alienated Youth in American Society* (New York: Dell Publishing Co., 1965); Erich Fromm, *The Sane Society* (Greenwich, Conn.: Fawcett, 1955); and Norman Birnbaum, *Toward a Critical Sociology* (New York: Oxford University Press, 1971). Many facets of the general notion of alienation are, of course, associated with the history of religious thought. Thus man was alienated from God and from his fellow men, and he tended to worship both Nature and the works of his hands, rather than his Creator.

17   On unemployment and its effects on the worker and society, see E. W. Bakke, *Citizens without Work* (New York: Yale University Press, 1940); Mirra Komarovsky, *The Unemployed Man and His Family* (New York: Dryden Press, 1940); and The Pilgrim Trust, *Men without Work* (Cambridge: Cambridge University Press, 1938). Much of the best literature on the psychology and spiritual effects of worklessness was, of course, stimulated by the Great Depression of the thirties.

18   For statistics on unemployment, see particularly the *Monthly Labor Review* of the Department of Labor, Bureau of Labor Statistics, and the *Statistical Abstract of the United States* of the Bureau of the Census.

19   On earlier problems of the Soviet economy, see particularly Boris Brutzkus, *Economic Planning in Soviet Russia,* trans. Gilbert Gardner (London: Routledge, 1935). For more recent discussions, see M. Ellman, *Soviet Planning Today, Proposals for an Optimally Functioning Economic System* (Cambridge: Cambridge University Press, 1971). Technical problems of planning are also discussed in M. Ellman, *Planning Problems in the USSR: The Contribution of Mathematical Economics to Their Solution,* 1960-71 (Cambridge: Cambridge University Press, 1973). See also George R. Feunel, *The Soviet Quest for Economic Efficiency,* enlarged ed. (N.Y.: Frederick A. Praeger, 1972).

20   Report of a Special Task Force to the Secretary of Health, Education, and Welfare, prepared under the auspices of the W. E. Upjohn Institute for Employment Research, *Work in America* (Cambridge, Mass.: M.I.T. Press, 1973). See the summary in *The New York Times,* December 22, 1972, by Philip Shabecoff, "H.E.W. Study Finds Job Discontent Is Hurting Nation," pp. 1 and 14. Analyses of this type are, of course, very old in the history of thought about industrialism and are frequently central in socialist literature. For an older study, see Daniel Bell, *Work and Its Discontents* (Boston: Beacon Press, 1956).

21   Shabecoff, "Job Discontent Is Hurting Nation," p. 1.

22   See Paul Goodman, *Growing Up Absurd* (New York: Random House, 1960).

23   This is the general thesis of the HEW study *Work in America*.

24   See the discussion summarized by Agis Salpukas, "Conflicting Theories on Efficient Work: Repetition vs. Satisfaction," *The New York Times*, December 22, 1974, p. 14.

25   *Work in America*, p. 8. The writers cite a survey by James N. Morgan.

26   Long ago, Thurman Arnold in *The Folklore of Capitalism* (New Haven, Conn.: Yale University Press, 1937) and *The Symbols of Government* (New Haven, Conn.: Yale University Press, 1935) provided an analysis of the curious way in which human beings concentrate their consciousness on what is formally labeled "government" and ignore the many profound ways in which they are governed through organizations which are formally labeled "economic," although economic structures and practices may in fact more profoundly direct the lines of human beings than the formally labeled "political" structures. C. Wright Mills in *The Power Elite* (New York: Oxford University Press, 1959) suggests the same point, as does Ferdinand Lundberg in *The Rich and the Super-Rich* (New York: Lyle Stuart, 1968). See also Graham Bannock, *The Juggernauts: The Age of the Big Corporations* (Indianapolis: Bobbs-Merrill Co., 1971); and James O'Connor, *The Corporations and the State: Essays in the Theory of Capitalism and Imperialism* (New York: Harper & Row, Colophon Books, 1974).

27   The classic work on white-collar crime is E. H. Sutherland, *White Collar Crime* (New York: Holt, Rinehart & Winston, 1961; first ed., 1949). The ubiquity of white-collar crime is emphasized by Lundberg, *The Rich and the Super-Rich*, particularly pp. 107-23.

28   See, for example, Barry Commoner, *The Closing Circle: Nature, Man, and Technology* (New York: Bantam Books, 1972). Note also Barry Weisberg, *Beyond Repair: The Ecology of Capitalism* (Boston: Beacon Press, 1971). On the problem of economic growth in relation to ecological issues and the fate of the human race, see, for example, E. J. Mishan, *Technology and Growth: The Price We Pay* (New York: Frederick A. Praeger, 1970), and, of course, Donella H. Meadows, Dennis L. Meadows, Jørgen Randers, and William W. Behrens, III, *The Limits to Growth*, report for the Club of Rome's Project on the Predicament of Mankind (New York: Universe Books, 1972). Mishan criticizes our "remarkable faith in the ultimate beneficence" of industrial progress, noting its cost in terms of depletion of natural resources and human frustration and violence. The Club of Rome study has become a frequently cited source for those who stress the finiteness of natural resources and therefore the need to limit our wants and population. For an earlier study of the "energy" problem in relation to economic growth and change in general, see Fred Cottrell, *Energy and Society: The Relation Between Energy, Social Change, and Economic Development* (New York: McGraw-Hill Book Co., 1955).

29   Wilfred Beckerman, *In Defense of Economic Growth* (London: Jonathan Cape, 1973).

30   The sacrifice of one generation for the benefit of others is treated in an older work by Winwood Reade, *The Martyrdom of Man* (London: A. K. Butts, 1874).

31   Psalms CXXI:1. But the Psalm goes on to say, of course, that "my help cometh from the Lord, which made heaven and earth," suggesting that the hills themselves and Nature in general are the handiwork of God, to whom the soul needing help must ultimately appeal.

32   Thus cities like Antwerp are enormously "crowded" in terms of persons living within a given square mile, yet are amazingly orderly. Such comments could also be made about Amsterdam, Rotterdam, and Stockholm. Many variables are involved in the conditions making for "order" or "disorder." Population per square mile is only one of them, and it must be seen in the context of other factors, such as the nature of city planning, and the education of the population.

33   On relations between level of economic well-being and family size, see, for example, Thomas J. Espenshade, *The Cost of Children in Urban United States* (Berkeley: University of California Press, 1973). See also Wilson Yates, *Family Planning on a Crowded Planet* (Minneapolis: Augsburg Publishing House, 1971).

34   See Plato's dialogue the *Gorgias,* one of the bitterest diatribes against all existential polities ever written. The philosopher condemns all the eminent political leaders of Athens from the "democrats" to the "aristocrats."

35   See T. J. B. Hoff, *Economic Calculation in the Socialist Society,* trans. M. A. Michael (London: W. Hodge, 1949). A critic of socialist-type planning has been Ludwig von Mises, in such works as *Planning for Freedom* (South Holland, Ill.: Libertarian Press, 1952). Benjamin E. Lippincott has edited the writings of Fred Taylor and Oskar Lange, which contend that a socialist society through planning can indeed carry out rationally the necessary economic calculations. See Lippincott's *On the Economic Theory of Socialism* (Minneapolis, Minn.: University of Minnesota Press, 1948). On the same subject, and reflecting the same confidence, is the discussion in Henry D. Dickinson, *The Economics of Socialism* (London: Oxford University Press, 1939).

36   Friedrich A. Von Hayek, *The Road to Serfdom.* See also Ludwig von Mises, *Socialism: An Economic and Sociological Analysis,* trans. J. Kahane (London: Jonathan Cape, 1936).

37   See, for example, Herman Finer, *The Road to Reaction* (Boston: Little Brown & Co., 1946) and Eugene Rostow, *Planning for Freedom* (New Haven, Conn.: Yale University Press, 1959).

38   On income statistics for the world as a whole, see *United Nations Statistical Yearbook* (New York: United Nations, 1975).

39   Quoted by James Reston, New York Times Service, in *Minneapolis Tribune,* September 14, 1975, p. 20-a.

40   Gabriel Kolko, *Wealth and Power in America: An Analysis of Social Class and Income Distribution* (New York: Frederick A. Praeger, 1962).

41   Letitia Upton and Nancy Lyons, *Basic Facts: Distribution of Personal Income and Wealth in the United States* (Cambridge, Mass.: Cambridge Institute, 1972).

42   Tom Wicker, New York Times Service, in *Minneapolis Tribune,* July 3, 1972, p. 6-A.

43   A ninth-century A.D. poet and sometime government official, Po Chü-i,

recognized this exploitation and his own privileged position in a poem written about 806 A.D. Entitled "Watching the Reapers," it speaks of

> The strong reapers toiling on the southern hill,
> Whose feet are burned by the hot earth they tread,
> Whose backs are scorched by flames of the shining sky.
> Tired they toil . . .
> A poor woman follows at the reapers' side
> With an infant child carried close at her breast.
> With her right hand she gleans the fallen grain; . . .
> And I to-day . . . by virtue of what right
> Have I never once tended field or tree?
> My government-pay is three hundred tons;
> At the year's end I have still grain in hand.
> Thinking of this, secretly I grew ashamed;
> And all day the thought lingered in my head.

Arthur Waley, *Translations from the Chinese* (New York: Alfred A. Knopf, 1941), p. 142.

44 *Utopia,* trans. Paul Turner (Baltimore: Penguin Books, 1970).

45 Baudin, *Socialist Empire.*

46 See W. R. Inge, *The Philosophy of Plotinus,* 2 vols. (London: Longmans, Green, 1948), vol. 2, p. 189.

47 One reason Plato condemns all historical polities lies precisely here. In all of them possession of material goods tends to lead to political power or political power to acquisition of material goods. Certainly Americans should not have to be reminded of this fact, particularly in light of the politics of the post-World War II period.

48 See Edward Bellamy, *Equality* (New York: D. Appleton, 1897), pp. 88-89.

49 Ibid.

50 Acts, IV:34, 35, trans. by Goodspeed as: "No one among them was in any want, for any who owned lands or houses would sell them and bring the proceeds of the sale and put them at the disposal of the apostles; they were shared with everyone in proportion to his need."

51 R. H. Tawney, *The Acquisitive Society* (New York: Harcourt, Brace, 1920) and *Equality* (London: G. Allen & Unwin, 1931).

52 William Morris, *News from Nowhere* (London: T. Nelson & Sons, 1911).

53 Bertrand Russell, *Proposed Roads to Freedom* (New York: H. Holt, 1919).

54 *Politics,* Bk. I.

55 Orestes Brownson, "The Present State of Society," *Democratic Review,* July 1843; *Works,* 20 vols. (Detroit: T. Nourse, 1882-1907), vol. IV, pp. 438-42.

56 Orestes Brownson, "The Laboring Classes and the Age of Chivalry," *Boston Quarterly Review,* April 1841, p. 183.

SEVEN

Nature, Civilization, and the Problem of Utopia

Utopias — portrayals, whether experimental or literary, of what the world ought to be — have not been fashionable for the two generations that have elapsed since World War I. They have been attacked on the ground that they assume the desirability of "wholesale" social engineering,[1] which, according to this view, must be rejected in the name of what some call incrementalism. Others have criticized literary utopias because most of them seem to advocate very highly organized societies, in which, in the critics' judgment, citizens are unfree and lack spontaneity.[2] In some of the critical literature, it seems to be assumed that if one projects a utopian scheme, one must be willing to impose it on the world by force — although why this should be so is not always clear.

In Dispraise and Praise of Utopia

The dubiety about utopia has been reflected in the enormous proliferation of dystopias, which are either extremely pessimistic about the future of the world or, in their portrayal of "bad" states (dys = bad), seem to be attacking the possibility of formulating and carrying out a utopia. Not infrequently, as we pointed out in Chapter 5, dystopias assume the triumph of technology and associate with it the dehumanization of man.

The criticism of utopianization has been associated with a number of factors. World War I perhaps initiated a mood in which the "idea of progress," while still largely prevalent, particularly in the United States, began to be increasingly questioned;[3] and since many associated the idea of a utopia with the conception of inevitable progress, the two tended to be undermined together. The days of the pre-1914 universe seemed to be gone forever.

Allied with the increasing criticism of the notion of progress was the rise of a neoorthodox theology. Rooted in the ideas of Karl Barth,[4] one of the most influential theological minds during the early part of the 20th century, and expressed, though in considerably modified form, in the writings of such thinkers as Emil Brunner[5] and Reinhold Niebuhr,[6] neoorthodoxy represented above all a revival of the idea of original sin as a key factor in human nature. Man's predicament was seen not merely as the fruit of inadequate social and political institutions or sheer ignorance (as much liberalism and Marxism appeared to say), but as due to a radical fault in the species as such.

Thus Niebuhr attacked the very notion of utopianization, seeing in it a kind of pretentiousness which fails to recognize the inevitability of sin, whatever our knowledge or institutions. Niebuhr attempted to distinguish between the "hard" utopians, supposedly associated with fascism and fascist-like thinkers, and the "soft" utopians, represented by such allegedly naive perspectives as those of the liberals, Quakers, and many others. The "hard" utopians thought that sheer force could discipline the human race and subordinate individual recalcitrance to the ideal of a hierarchically organized society. "Soft" utopians, by contrast, tended to reject force altogether and thought that the recalcitrancies of human nature could be overcome by good will and moral suasion alone. But both the hard and the soft utopians, Niebuhr maintained, were wrong, the former because they underemphasized man's potentiality for good, the latter because they seemed to deny the reality of evil.

Socially and politically speaking, the central theme of neoorthodoxy was that human nature permitted only a relatively narrow scope for reform. To expect too much of it was to run the risk of not accomplishing what, given a more modest view of human nature, might actually be within the limits of attainment.

For some, the very word "utopia" became an epithet of opprobrium. There were relatively few who defended what critics called "impossible ideals,"[7] though some of the critics might, it is true, be rather sympathetic to "middle-range" (and therefore seemingly attainable) utopias as contrasted with "long-range" projections.

The fact that fascist and National Socialist politicians appeared to come so close to attaining their goals perhaps led nonfascists to reject the formulation of comprehensive ideals altogether. So-called democracy increasingly became identified with a kind of muddling and blundering through ideology, and "incrementalism" became its watchword. Even when planning was widely discussed, it was frequently the kind of planning that seemed to call for a sort of day-to-day coordination, without much of a holistic vision.

Insofar as the critics were reiterating the enormously great difficulty of bringing collective affairs under the conscious control of rational human beings, they were, of course, rendering a service. Throughout these pages, we have stressed the same point. But we have also repeated that if we opt for some measure of civilization, we must also, if we are to be rational, accept the challenges of politics, with all their difficulties. And among those challenges is that of utopianization, or something very much like it.

Most literary utopias are not designed to forecast what will come about inevitably (although some utopists do indeed conceive their task to be this)[8] but rather to present alternative visions of what the future might or ought to be. And even if none of these paradigms is ever attained completely, some may be partially achieved precisely because the whole vision — "impossible" as it may have been — was at one point presented. Just as we need to formulate alternative frameworks within which we might attempt to understand past and present (every historical analysis must assume a framework of some kind), so is it indispensable, if we are to become fully rational and free, to formulate frameworks of what the future might or ought to be. Or again, as Plato suggests in Book IX of the *Republic,* even if a city is "laid up in heaven," so to speak, our vision of it can help guide us both personally and politically in the existential world and provide a point of departure for criticizing established institutions.

The vision of a utopia can maintain the tension which ought always to exist between patterns of life in existence, on the one hand, and the ideal, on the other. All of us tend to become weary with well-doing and reform and are frequently tempted — particularly those of us who fancy ourselves "intellectuals" — to identify utopia with a given existential national state or condition of affairs. Thus the utopia of a "democracy" is sometimes identified with Great Britain or the United States, in both of which the antidemocratic features are notorious and deep-seated. During the thirties, many persons who should have known better were blind to the tyrannies of the Soviet Union and stubbornly insisted that somehow Stalin's Russia was getting closer to the ideal socialist or communist society.[9] They did not renew their vision and failed to remember that no polity on earth has ever even approximated the ideal justice or the ideal commonwealth about which the greatest utopists have dreamed.

When Plato condemned all the existing and past politicians of Athens, whatever their faction,[10] he was criticizing them because they seemed to have no vision of what true justice would be. Or, if they had a vision — which was doubtful — they too quickly forgot it and tended to identify justice merely with the triumph of the factions to which they belonged.

Utopia building is eminently practical. It helps save us from the illusions which both revolutionary leaders and defenders of the status quo constantly tend to propagate. By keeping before us a relatively remote goal, it prevents us from uncritically embracing any short-run panaceas. It helps us see civilization in perspective and to realize dramatically the enormous distance between what is and what ought to be.

It may be highly relevant, too, for the development of individual souls. There is a parallelism between the problems of the polity and those that every soul confronts. The personality which emerges from childhood, with its dependence on father and mother, seeks autonomous action and a goal around which it can integrate its life. If the person is to be rational, that goal must take on a highly self-conscious and explicit character — a kind of personal utopia. But the more an individual soul is self-aware, the greater is its consciousness of its intimate ties to other souls and to the would-be community of souls. It sees, if it is wise, that its personal utopia is related to, if not wholly dependent on, the utopias which are proposed for the community. The greater the activity in utopia building for the community, the greater will be the stimulus provided for constructing personal visions; and the more articulate the personal vision, the more likely it will be that souls developing in the community will move toward the rational in conduct. Even if it is assumed, with St. Paul, that we often rebel against what we know to be right,[11] still it is better to formulate conceptions of what we deem to be right for soul and community, and then rebel against them, than not to have had the visions in the first place.

In terms of the Nature-civilization tension, utopia building may be thought of as central to man's teleological nature. Whatever our precise formulation of primitive Nature (whether Hobbes-like, or Augustinian, or Locke-like, or Tolstoyan), man closely tied to it is dominated by the immediacies of nonhuman Nature. Yet there is within him from the very beginning an implicit albeit a ragged vision of how and why human nature should transform the nonhuman world. But no sooner do human beings become aware of that vision than they become conscious, too, of the intricate ties which must continue to bind them to primitive Nature.

At this point, human beings are confronted by three basic choices as they seek to formulate their social and political utopias. They can sketch out an ideal society close to what they deem primitive Nature to be; or, on the other extreme, they can seek to eliminate the last vestiges of primitive

Nature, as in effect Eugene Zamiatin's dystopians try to do.[12] Finally, they can seek some kind of synthesis, difficult as that may be, between their version of Nature and a hypothetical situation in which they imagine human beings have completely eliminated their dependence on Nature.

In choosing between these three alternatives, the utopist is soon confronted by one of his central problems — how is he to define a human being? If he rejects a definition in terms simply of physical description (an animal-like creature, let us say, who walks upright on two legs and ranges from four feet ten inches to six feet five inches in height), he is forced to ask such questions as: If we assume that "man" as we know him is not a perfect man, what would perfect him? What would be the role of emotion in human life? How can we reconcile the factor of spontaneity with that of order and predictability? The utopist presumably would discover or rediscover that what is essential about human beings is not at all physical but psychical, emotional, intellectual, and spiritual. The problems of building utopia are those of discovering the right relations of primarily spiritual beings, and "right" in this context means those standards that are most likely to make souls "truly human."

Utopists who tend to identify human fulfillment with closeness to primitive Nature would of course have to define what they mean by primitive Nature; but negatively, at least, they would agree in somehow spurning such obvious characteristics of historical civilizations as cities, most technology, and conscious planning. Those who would define teleological man as sharply contrasted with Nature would presumably stress what the Nature utopists would repudiate. And, as we have emphasized at several points, this would move them very close to what we have hitherto defined as divinity. The first kind of utopist would tend to say: Strip away all the accretions which have been added to Nature by man, and you will find the true human being who has been stifled by civilization. The second, by contrast, would have to maintain: Accentuate all those factors that man has added to Nature and all those that tend to separate him from Nature, and you will find the true human being who is stifled by his many ties to primitive Nature.

Throughout the preceding chapters we have contended, in varying contexts, that one is likely to discover the true human being in neither of these directions. Somehow there must be a point between the utopia of Nature and that of sharp differentiation from Nature where the essence of humanity is most likely to be discovered. But, the critic may say, at what point? Surely, he may go on, it cannot be defined mathematically as, let us say, half way between the two extremes! Of course not. But neither can its contours be fully understood merely by developing the kinds of rather abstract principles which have characterized the preceding chapters. We need, in addition to, but building on, the abstract principles, a portrayal which is more concrete and which seeks to relate means to ends, institutions to goals.

Such a utopia would be somewhat like the blueprint so indispensable to the architect. The further we move from primitive Nature and thus find ourselves increasingly being challenged politically, the more significant do utopias become. If politics is the art of deliberately creating order and directing human collective affairs, then the formulation of utopias is at least as important as scientific research. An adequate utopia would, indeed, draw heavily on the humanities, philosophy, historical experience, and scientific research in formulating its conception both of the ends toward which we ought to be moving and the means or strategies which might take us there.

Building on the discussions of the previous chapters, but at the same time providing a somewhat broader base, we seek to specify some of the features of a possible utopia which will take account of our assumptions and propositions about primitive Nature, teleological human nature, and civilization. This is a sketch only, and we shall not be able to defend fully every feature and to show the reasoning and empirical basis of the conclusions. But if the previous chapters are kept in mind, the proposals will not seem to be without foundation.

The Telos of Person-Community

Before we begin the actual sketch, let us attempt to restate, in a somewhat different way, the value presuppositions and ends which have been outlined at greater length elsewhere.

Both individual personality and community, as we have seen, are in some sense *real*. Neither can be reduced to the other. The person is potentially *not merely* a group "product" — he or she is creative, bringing into existence (like God in Genesis) many worlds out of nothing. On the other hand, the social is not *merely* the sum total of discrete individuals. Instead, it is more like a jigsaw puzzle whose parts are properly fitted together rather than scattered around the floor at random. Each part is indispensable to the whole. But each part is also unique: it is not duplicated by any part now in existence nor by any part formerly in existence, and it will probably never be exactly duplicated in the future.

In the ideal society created by utopian politics, the person would not fit into the whole by virtue of either negative or positive reinforcements — either punishments or rewards. Instead, the framework of the polity would be such that both rewards and punishments would be superfluous. The

256

person would work, love, associate, and strive to fulfill his or her true ends or true self because the structure of the community would recognize fully both the individual's teleologically natural sociopolitical dimension *and* his being as an immortal soul with legitimate ends of his own. The person would work vigorously because he would have a social, economic, and intellectual function that is spiritually rewarding in itself. He would love actively, as others love him, and because the structure recognizes his personhood and individuality; express his individuality and eccentricities without impairing like expressions of others (that is, be "free" within "order"); and understand the close relation between his own fulfillment and that of his fellows.

Such an ideal is, of course, very difficult even to conceive in concrete terms, let alone to implement. As Henry Adams once put it in discussing the problem of unity and multiplicity:

Army, Church, State, each is an organic whole, complex beyond all possible addition of units, and not a concept at all, but rather an animal that thinks, creates, devours, and destroys. The attempt to bridge the chasm between multiplicity and unity is the oldest problem of philosophy, religion, and science, but the flimsiest bridge of all is the human concept, unless somewhere, within or beyond it, an energy not individual is hidden; and in that case the old question instantly reappears: What is that energy?[13]

Yet the utopist, beginning with our premises and recognizing both the one and the many, unity and multiplicity, must undertake this task. A formula destroying the one in favor of the many is dystopia, as is a framework which would obliterate the many in favor of the one.

Yet we are always tempted to move in the dystopian direction, for it is much easier and simpler to do so than to seek due recognition and a certain autonomy for both the whole and the parts. Obviously the more complex task is riddled with difficulties: those of conceptualization, of developing relevant means, of communicating the vision. Every utopian statement is, therefore, always a partial failure and requires constant revision in light of new insights, information, and understandings. Every generation, to be fully human, must write its own utopias, just as it must rewrite its story of the past, or history.

Of one thing we become more and more certain, however, as we engage in the utopian quest, and that is that the formulation of schemes for ideal societies demands as much in terms of logic and empirical generalization as any science does. Although ultimate or first-order value propositions, to be sure, rest on faith — or perhaps we might say on intuition or revelation — once one accepts a certain logical system or mode of reasoning and a few fundamental value assumptions, the construction of a utopia depends on the same kinds of references to supposed facts and reasons as those found in so-called behavioral science. Contrariwise, the supposed certainties of behavioral science — including its intersubjectively testable propositions — all depend (as do ethical principles) on acts of faith and intuitions. An "emotivist" account of ethics, in attempting to reduce all ethical judgments simply to "hurrah" words or feeling statements, goes much too far in the reductionist direction. On the other hand, some behavioral scientists do not seem to realize the degree to which their scientific work depends on acts of faith — as the Bible puts it, "the substance of things hoped for, the evidence of things not seen."[14] The world of the ought is both as easy and as difficult to understand as the world of the is.[15]

Let us turn now to some of the details of our utopian construction.

The General Framework

In Chapter 2 we suggested that as man leaves Nature and enters complex civilization, the direct coercions of Nature tend to be supplanted in part by those of men. At the same time, the possibilities of spiritual or rational freedom are enhanced. We also distinguished between things of the body — the material realm — and those of the mind and soul. In the former, limitations of some kind would seem to be inevitable, given limited resources, although they may conceivably become somewhat less pressing with civilization, particularly as men and women come voluntarily to accept them as essential. But in principle, spiritual freedom can and ought to be legally without limits, even though, in the process of developing free personalities, the spirit will utilize its freedom in order to be bound by an objective order of truth, aesthetics, and moral value (freedom in reason, or positive freedom). To be sure, the possibility of utilizing spiritual freedom is strongly conditioned by the fact that the spiritual and the material are closely interwoven in this life, which means that essential restrictions in the latter realm will inevitably affect expression in the former. But this interweaving of the two spheres should not lead us to forget their separation in principle.

The evolution of free personalities is heavily dependent on both the development of community and — as far as possible — a liberation of the individual from excessive concern about the material realm. In our examination of technology and the economy, we maintained that mankind must guard against the illusion that it can or should "return" to primitive Nature — whatever its securities, for some, are supposed to be — but it should also prepare itself for consciously and deliberately contrived limitations on the blind growth of technology and economy. A society concerned about the complete fulfillment of that which is desirable in human beings will thus always have to stand somewhat precariously poised between the primitive, on the one hand, and chaotic, sightless economic, technological, and social development, on the other.

In other terms, society will have to recognize that while civilization is in some measure a necessary *suppression* of the primitive, as the Freudians suggest, it is also an effort to *express* that which is teleologically natural and desirable, as classical thinkers stress. Civilization cannot be reduced merely to artful sublimation of primitive drives or to a struggle between a primitively "natural" Eros and Thanatos. In other terms, oakness is not merely a "conquest" of the acorn, in which negative suppression triumphs over primitive expression; rather it is also an *expression* of what the acorn is naturally attempting to become. Because man is endowed with freedom he is, of course, uncertain as to how his teleological nature can best be expressed in concrete terms; but in his role as utopist he is seeking to reduce that uncertainty by using his powers of reason, analysis, and imagination. The justice for which he searches would presumably be a state of affairs in which both soul and community would be what they ought to become and in which both the primitively natural and the teleologically natural could be recognized in a kind of synthesis. Of course, justice is never achieved, and there is always a conflict between existential and ideal civilization. But this does not excuse us, as human beings, from striving for the ideal; indeed, this is one of the characteristics which differentiates the human from the nonhuman.

In its general framework, then, utopia must give due recognition to these many aspects of what we call "humanity." Although we shall be able to touch only lightly on most of these facets, we propose here, drawing on the principles we have suggested in other chapters, to sketch out a few of the characteristics of a utopia for our time. Using the present tense throughout to indicate both the reality and the urgency of the utopian dream, we shall note (1) its ecumenical character, (2) its general cultural and language characteristics, (3) its treatment of population, (4) its primary groups, (5) the relation of its city-country regions to civilization, (6) its technological and economic orders, (7) the polity or political order, and (8) the strategies and tactics through which it is attained.

Ecumenical Character

Our utopia is necessarily a world order; for, particularly in our day, Dante's argument that Reason can be most fully developed only in the context of a universal polity[16] has deep poignancy and relevance. At the same time, we should not confuse unity with uniformity: The utopia must embody great cultural and other forms of diversity within unity. To establish this principle in existence is never easy, of course, for it involves the task of giving simultaneous recognition to the fact that although all men and women are like all other men and women in some respects, they are also like only some men and women in other ways and like no other human beings in yet other very significant attributes.

The sense in which we are all alike is the basis for the ecumenical nature of the new order. Cultural and other forms of group diversity reflect the ways in which we can find fulfillment — or bridge the gulf between our existential selves and what we ought to be — through closer association with only some rather than with all human beings. Finally, the fact that, as Emerson said, every human being is "an unique" is mirrored in utopian provisions for privacy, retreat, idiosyncrasy, and eccentricity. There is a sense in which each of us must transcend all the groups which have been so important in making us what we are. Each of us, from this point of view, is a kind of irreplaceable artistic whole which is more than the sum total of all its social, psychological, biological, chemical, physical, and other parts.

Culture and Language

We might term the three attributes of human beings we have described above universality, diversity, and uniqueness. Human beings are bound together ecumenically by their universal qualities, are diverse from one another in terms of groups built around particularistic objectives and attributes, and, in their uniqueness, set themselves off from all groups.

This trinity of characteristics is reflected in all aspects of utopian life, beginning with culture and language. There is a single universal language which every person on earth learns as a matter of course. The utopians look back with no regret on those times when no common language was spoken throughout the globe. The universal language has been constructed by combining features of nine of the languages of preutopian days, but it is much simpler than any one of those tongues. Naturally, there was much wrangling before the new language evolved, for it was politically contrived in the days before contemporary utopian political institutions existed.

At the same time, each major region of the world has its own language, and there is a rather complex diversity of cultures. In fact, with the decline of the nationalism of preutopian days, many of the language tendencies partially suppressed by the old national states have begun to flourish. All children learn one of the regional languages, and some of them will also become proficient in a subregional tongue.

The utopians take considerable pride, too, in the fact that they have discovered the conditions under which human beings can communicate telepathically with one another. Both the sender and the receiver participate, the former by transmitting the message, the latter by either receiving it or refusing to do so (since it is held offensive for one to intrude on the privacy of another's thoughts without permission).[17] Telepathic communication thus exists as a system parallel to ordinary language, being more effective in some respects than sensory modes but perhaps less appropriate in others. It is regarded as particularly useful for those who are intimately related to one another, such as lovers. In group marriages, telepathic communication is probably predominant, although the utopians so dread uniformity in all except essentials that many of them deliberately employ ordinary language in situations where they might otherwise use telepathy, for fear that the latter might completely supplant the former under those conditions.

Telepathic communication usually involves direct transmission of images rather than of the words that symbolize those images. Many find this aesthetically appealing, even if for other reasons they might use ordinary language communication.

In some communities, telepathic communication has become so embedded that one can walk down the streets or visit homes and parks and never hear a word spoken. The city, in the preutopian days noisy with the sounds of industry and talk, now often resembles a Trappist monastery. In other communities, telepathy is almost never utilized. Utopian scholars are engaged in developing hypotheses about this phenomenon, seeking to compare cultural forms, politics, and life-styles of telepathic communities with those in which telepathy is rarely employed. To some degree, there is a correlation of telepathy use with education; for, like deep meditation, telepathic communication takes years to master, and many never attempt it. On the other hand, not a few communities in which substantially large groups have learned the art almost never use it. So the researches continue.

No one in utopia is regarded as "queer" if he or she decides at times not to communicate or receive communications, whether through language or by telepathy. Eccentricity here, as in other realms, is highly valued.

Population

The population of utopia is in the neighborhood of 1 billion souls, and if plans do not go awry it should remain at that figure permanently, given slight deviations either way. The reduction from a previous high of over 3 billion took place through growth in understanding of the "man-land" problem and awareness of the fact that decisions made in the bedroom have important political implications. There was also a rise in the average standard of living — and particularly an increase in per capita consumption of proteins — which was associated with the development of interests outside the family, so that reproduction became only one out of many ways of fulfilling oneself. Of course, the technique of birth control has also improved. But the utopians, unlike some of those in preutopian days, recognize that mere technique is not enough — there must also be a will and a strong motivation to use the new methods.

As the idea of utopia gradually began to take root, there was a vigorous discussion of the ethics and politics of abortion. Eventually, a widespread consensus arose that most abortions would be excluded, the exceptions being very few in number. Thus abortions for saving the life of the mother are permitted, but both law and opinion condemn the notion of abortion "on demand." To the utopians, abortion involves disrespect for human life, which they hold dear,' as well as being aesthetically unappealing. Just as they repudiate the ancient notion of infanticide, so do they reject abortion.[18]

No birth is regarded as illegitimate, but adoption is encouraged in those instances where the natural mother feels she does not desire the child. Where the father is known, he, too, must be consulted about the matter. But haphazard and unplanned births are relatively rare under utopian conditions.

If families accidentally become too large, according to their own judgment, the community encourages them to make arrangements with childless families to adopt their about to be or newly born children. This is by no means regarded as an outrage but rather as justice for the child and for both families.

One of the most important functions of the world authority is to keep abreast of population trends; for while the population has become virtually stable in numbers, some migration continues to take place, despite a great decline in mobility. The utopians think that the relation of people to the land and resources, to other people, and to the whole commonwealth is one of the most important factors to be taken into consideration in constructing and perpetuating the commonwealth.

Primary Groups

Given the emphasis on diversity in unity and on the unique aspects of each human being, it is not surprising to find a wide variety of primary groups in utopian society. Full legal recognition is given to many types of what in the old days would have been called "families": monogamous; polygynous; polyandrous; group marriage; homosexual. Although most marriages continue to be of the monogamous, heterosexual type, there is a considerable number of polygynous and polyandrous unions. Celibacy, too, has grown as a way of life, for the utopians hold that while for most human beings the achievement of a free personality can be enhanced through sexual relations, still they are so impressed by the unique aspects of human personality that they do not think of the celibate as peculiar. As a matter of fact, a great many celibates live together in communes of various types, some of the communes being composed of both sexes, while others are unisexual.

Some might ask whether "free love" relationships exist and to what extent they are tolerated. Here there can be no doubt about the position of the utopians. They consider it atrocious for their ancestors to have punished human beings for loving each other; many criminal statutes in those days actually made "fornication" an offense at law. In utopia, love is "free" in the sense that sexual relations as such depend on the consent of the individuals involved and on no one else. No license is required to sanctify love.

On the other hand, there is a very widespread belief in utopia that, for most human beings, living together in a relatively small, intimate group over a long period of time is the condition under which human personality generally develops best. Their philosophers also teach that a formal public commitment about intent to live together may actually strengthen the will to do so and carry those involved through difficult times, for their long-run benefit. The sexologists of utopia, moreover, hold that a long-term relationship has the potentiality for deepening both sexual and nonsexual love.

Love in Utopia

The problem of the primary family grouping, whatever its specific form, takes us into the question of the relation between sexual and supposedly nonsexual love. All forms of love — whether of neighbor for neighbor, man for woman, man for man, an individual for his enemy, mother for daughter, or father for son — have in common the elements of outreach, concern, and active goodwill. Sexual love itself is obviously far more than the simple "lust" for another body; the occasion for it may be another body, to be sure, but the implicit natural end (natural in the teleological sense) is communion and communication, as well as, in some instance, reproduction. Like all love, it suggests the basic loneliness of the human being when he is cut off from intimate relations with other human beings. For most persons, the overcoming of loneliness entails sexual relations with others. And for most, the "others" will be persons of the opposite sex. Sexual love, narrowly defined, is the gateway through which we begin to understand the full implications of community.

But love in general has many aspects and ramifications which are interrelated and which sometimes seem to lead to the opposite of love. We often hate most bitterly those whom we have previously loved. The utopians have read Freud and the post-Freudians and are quite aware that civilization inevitably demands some restrictions on the direct expression of sexual love. They are not unaware either that there may be a primitively natural element in human beings which seeks destruction and which is at war with the community-building and, on the whole, constructive dimension reflected in sexual love. Nor are they ignorant of the inevitability of some sublimation — or the utilization for nonsexual ends of energies which would in a primitively "Natural" sense be used for directly sexual purposes. There is validity in the contention that the city is in some measure built upon a diversion of sexual drives into the tasks of building construction, parks planning, symphony orchestra development, and all the other multifarious activities which we have associated with the historical city.

At the same time, the philosophers of utopia do not believe that such an account is complete. Civilization is not merely suppression. In one of its aspects, it is as natural an expression of man as the direct reflection of the sexual urge. Art, literature, music, and the dozens of other attributes of civilization are not simply the fruits of sublimation but are as teleologically natural as sexual intercourse. To be sure, the utopians hold, we may reach a point in the development of civilization when the tendency to "rationalize" everything is pushed so far that sexual relations can take place only with permission or when an effort is made virtually to abolish them, as in the great novels by Zamiatin and George Orwell.[19] But short of this point the constructive tasks of civilization are accomplished by a complicated blend of sublimation and of teleologically natural activity, for which the sublimation may be said to be one means.

The utopians are far less pessimistic than Freud and some of his followers about the future of civilization, holding as they do that it is possible to provide innocent and even constructive outlets for the supposed "death instinct" and that sublimation itself, up to a point, is teleologically natural. With William James, they would argue that hostility need not be reflected in killing nor aggression in war.[20] But they would strongly contend that these reconciliations in civilization will not come about automatically but only through deliberation and counsel about collective affairs — that is, by politics.

Love between and among human beings, moreover, cannot be sharply divorced from love (or at least a very similar emotion) for place and for Nature. The being who is striving to be human, the utopians maintain, will naturally require roots of some kind, not only for himself but for the descendants who are so closely bound to him. Moreover, his quest for the naturally human in civilization entails a certain reverence for his ancestors. Respect both for descendants and ancestors — what we might call a kind of vertical love, as contrasted with the horizontal love in the contemporary generation — is intimately bound up with attachment to place; and for most human beings, that place must be something less than the whole globe. In other words, the utopians believe society must be so organized that its citizens can strongly identify with a particular locus. Their mobility must not be so great that they have no sense of "belonging" to some portion of the geographic earth.

In addition to identification with a particular place, utopian philosophers believe, the idea of humanity entails some rather close relations with nonhuman Nature. In the early days of civilization, when most human beings were herdsmen or farmers or hunters, this might come about more or less spontaneously. But as civilization becomes more complex, conscious political effort must be expended in perpetuating this association. The possibility of communion with rocks and flowers and birds is as essential as the potentiality for identification with place. Nor is vicarious communion — through books or films, for instance — sufficient, any more than vicarious communion with other human beings would be adequate.

The love relationship is even broader than this, however. In addition to various degrees of communion with other human beings, with place, and with Nature, human natural fulfillment involves communion with higher spirits and with what some call God. In some measure, to be sure, the utopians hold, we can commune with the source of life and existence through other human beings and through Nature. But this is never enough. As for communion with other spirits, the utopians maintain a highly active belief that human beings are simply part of a vast hierarchy of beings. They think it absurd to hold that there are no other beings between man and God — or, for that matter, between man and the pole (whatever we call it) opposite to God.

Thus love in utopia is a many-faceted phenomenon. The human being, to become fully himself and to be free, must reach out through love to others, to place, to Nature, to nonhuman spirits, and to God. He or she is part of this wider community. Only as the aspiring human seeks this many-dimensioned communion can he become his true self. And in civilization, politics must establish the framework within which this is possible, even though it cannot specify directly how it shall be sought. But since political activity itself is both rooted in the possibility of community and the fruit in some measure of the attainment of community, communion through love must somehow be at the heart of the political and therefore the human search.

Arrangements for Living: The Neighborhood

It is with these considerations in mind that the utopians have provided the structure within which most inhabitants — and there are not a few exceptions, as we shall see — carry on their lives. Most families live in what can best be described as a neighborhood, a grouping of 250 to 400 souls. The neighborhood is a kind of extended family in which the multiple marriage system finds its partial completion. Consisting of all members of families, from infants to older persons, it thus defies the preutopian tendency to isolate the "retired" from others. The neighborhood, to use another expression of the utopian theorists, is the second of the concentric circles, beginning with the family and ending with the whole human race, out of which human personality grows and to which it relates itself.

In its physical arrangements, the neighborhood is built around a central plaza or park (rectangular, oval, circular, triangular, or hexagonal in shape), the houses being arranged around the plaza. Since the central theme of utopia is diversity in unity, it is not surprising to find the houses — whether single or multiple dwellings — reflecting great individuality yet at the same time exhibiting a kind of harmony of the whole. Thus there is considerable variation in color without a clashing of colors. One of the important functions of the neighborhood assembly, as a matter of fact, is the regulation of buildings. Instead of this task being performed by some remote building inspector, as it was in preutopian days, it is carried out by those most familiar with the neighborhood — the inhabitants themselves.

The neighborhood is, of course, much more than a set of physical arrangements. The physical aspects express an idea of society, of which the neighborhood is a fundamental unit. Part of that idea turns on the notion that human beings, to become fully human, must participate actively in a small community. The participation, moreover, must involve the performance of concrete tasks for and by persons known to one another. Only thus can the conditions be satisfied for the development of a consensus whose attainment is the basis of utopian political life. The relatively limited numbers of inhabitants in a neighborhood, together with their common performance of certain specific functions, the utopians believe, will be the best assurance that a common will can emerge.

What, then, are some of the tasks which members of the neighborhood perform? One of the most ubiquitous is care of the children. All of the adults participate in this care on a rotating basis, thus permitting most men and women to pursue their vocations. Every neighborhood, moreover, has attached to it a kindergarten and nursery school, supervision of which is entrusted to a committee chosen by the whole neighborhood. Any relatively minor altercations, too, are settled at the neighborhood level by a body of lay judges, under the general utopian law. There is also a restaurant which needs supervision and requires at any given time the attention of numbers of citizens. The assembly hall must be swept and kept clean, and this work likewise is carried out on a rotating basis. In some of the tasks children, from a very early age, are expected to be of assistance — for example, in plucking dandelions from the lawn of the plaza. Teen-agers help with the mowing on a regular basis. Much of the repair work of houses is done by residents of the neighborhood, again according to a scheme of rotation. Older persons — those who in preutopian days might have been called the "retired" — are often the storytellers; on a good day they can be seen on the plaza regaling the children with reminiscences or with anecdotes made out of whole cloth.

The neighborhood assembly is composed of all members of the neighborhood over the age of 17. Attendance at assembly sessions, which are held regularly once a month, is expected, except in case of illness. The assembly is the general governing body of the neighborhood and is, indeed, the basis for all utopian political life. In general, it strives after consensus in all its decisions: discussion continues until no one strongly objects to a given proposal. While this is a time-consuming process, utopian thinkers believe that it is fully justified: majority rule, which was so emphasized as "democratic" in preutopian days, is at best only an unhappy expedient and often leaves seriously disaffected minorities. Genuine consensus represents the transcendence of individual policy positions and the attainment of a group view which is probably better than any individual view or combination of individual views which may have been brought into the meeting. True consensus reconciles liberty with authority. It emphasizes creative discussion and meditation, not voting. In emergencies, to be sure, majority rule is permitted; but most assemblies are jealous of the consensus principle and strive mightily to achieve a genuine rather than merely a spurious consensus. The political philosophers of utopia believe that consensus is facilitated because of the habit of direct and ongoing cooperation among neighborhood members, ease of communication, the close connection between many of the issues involved and the personal experience of the members, and widespread acceptance of the practice of mutual criticism.

It is out of neighborhood assemblies that other authorities emerge. Thus delegates from the neighborhood assembly are selected, by consensus if possible, for service in the divisional assembly, from which some are later sent to the city assembly. From the city, the process moves to province, region, national culture, and world. These authorities represent the general consensus-gathering structure of utopia. Of course, there is a similar structure for workers in the several branches of industry, in the professions, in transportation, and so on. General assemblies are concerned with matters of common interest to all persons as citizens, economic assemblies concern themselves with human beings as producers, and consuming groups have a similar (although not necessarily identical) series of groups.

But while there is a very public side to the neighborhood, it would be a mistake to think that utopians think of human beings as simply social. They are also private, "subjective," and unique, and provision is made for this dimension of their personalities. Thus under the plazas of every neighborhood are retiring rooms suitable for retreat and meditation and study, and individuals may go into these rooms either alone or with others to escape the larger group. They can lock the doors from the inside and be by themselves, without anyone asking the reason. Retiring rooms are sometimes used for courting, since with the virtual demise of the automobile, preutopian places for such activities were reduced in number.

Provisions for Eccentricity

The utopians recognize, however, that some personality types may be unsuitable for life in the neighborhood, however fully it recognizes claims to privacy. In extreme instances, these persons (known as voluntary exiles) can retreat to live in the wilderness, to exist away from the many constraints necessarily associated with civilization. Approximately one half of the surface of the earth is reserved for wilderness areas. While relatively few choose this option, still the number is not insignificant, varying from about 75,000 to 200,000. The voluntary exiles can, if they wish, come to the edge of civilization for free medical and certain other services, but since they have themselves opted to live alone, sometimes they do not even take advantage of these opportunities.

And between the wilderness and the neighborhood, there are less onerous forms of isolated living, either for the long term or for short periods of time. Some choose to live in caves or in isolated man-created cells under the surface of the earth, working in regular occupations during the day but reserving their other hours for the solitary existence. Those who decide to live over a long period of time either in the wilderness or in other semi-isolated places usually do not elect to share in the political decision-making process in any way. Theirs is a rejection of civilization in varying degress, and civilization itself gives full recognition to their idiosyncrasies. At times, strange-appearing voluntary exiles will return temporarily to civilization, where they become objects of curiosity, particularly for children, who enjoy their stories but on occasion fear them because of their often uncouth appearance.

Dress

The utopians dress in a wide variety of ways, from nothing to rather elaborate costuming. In warmer climates, they more frequently than not spurn any clothing, and even in more temperate zones they sometimes shed it. The human body is not regarded as an object of shame, and nudity is considered an expression of the simplicity which is one of the leading utopian values. Furthermore, many suggest that nudity encourages proper physical care of oneself: instead of concealing one's defects behind drapery, there is a stimulus to remove the defects.

Simplicity in All Things

The value of simplicity is exalted, too, in other areas of existence. "Civilized simplicity" is the term often used. Generally speaking the utopians have relatively few personal possessions, and they look back upon the industrial capitalist, acquisitive societies of the old days with horror. Their attitudes to past State-capitalist societies such as the Soviet Union are similar.

Pleasures and Contemplation

Their pleasures, too, reflect a similar emphasis. They do not believe that they have to be constantly moving about physically to attain spiritual, intellectual, and aesthetic fulfillment. With the ancient Epicureans, they hold that stimulating conversation among friends is the highest pleasure. Many of them agree with the spirit of Wordsworth's lines: "To me the meanest flower that blows can give / Thoughts that do often lie too deep for tears."[21] Quiet contemplation of the Nature at one's doorstep in the neighborhood, of the human nature reflected in themselves and their friends, of the starry heavens on a clear night, of the children growing in their midst, of the gardens many of them plant, of the ultimate mystery at the heart of religious experience — these are the kinds of activities which renew and recreate them.

City-Country Regions and Civilization

The utopians recognize that without civilization man cannot become fully free and rational in the several meanings of those terms, and that the development of civilization is closely associated with those concentrations of population which are called cities. At the same time, however, they are wary of allowing the concentrations to become too great or their populations too numerous. They look back with repugnance on the sprawling, noisome, and often unappealing megalopolitan areas which in the 20th century went by the name of cities. At the same time, they do not idealize the manure heap or the kind of image Thomas Jefferson developed in the figure of the "yeoman" farmer.

City and Country

Most cities can best be described as city-country regions. There is the city proper, consisting of the neighborhoods and cultural institutions of varying types, as well as of industry. But around each city is a wide belt which, depending on geographical location, consists of farming land or orchards or combinations of the two. There are several neighborhoods in this area. Around the agricultural or orchard zone is yet another wide circle of largely unoccupied land which contains forests, desert, or mountains. Precisely what will be grown in the first zone and the specific contents of the second zone will depend not only on geographical potentialities but also, in some measure, on the decisions of the cities themselves. Usually there will be some latitude for choice.

The utopians believe that each city (with its surrounding countryside) should strive to have within its borders enough resources of skilled workers, industry, and agriculture to enable it to survive for a long period on its own. Thus diversification is a keynote; while this in some cases may be "uneconomic" in a strict sense, still the utopians believe that if genuine self-government is to be a reality, every substantial part of humanity should be as self-reliant as possible. Obviously, this in no way implies that the some 3,000 or more cities of utopia do not exchange products — they do, and many of the tasks of planning beyond the level of the city turn on the problem of equitable distribution of goods. But the high degree of specialization characteristic of life in preutopian days has been considerably modified. Even from a purely economic point of view, these arrangements may have their advantages; thus transportation costs are lowered to the degree that each city, province, region, and national culture seeks, insofar as possible, to stress collective self-reliance.

No city (with its surrounding countryside) can have more than 450,000 souls. Many have fewer than this, being in the range of 250,000 to 350,000. These figures are not arrived at arbitrarily; they represent what utopian theorists have concluded is the optimum range in size of city-country regions. On the one hand, the city must be populous enough to provide a sound economic base and to sustain cultural activities. On the other hand, the citizens must not become so numerous that they develop a feeling of anonymity and a sense of individual powerlessness. Most cities (embracing within the term both city proper and the surrounding belts) consist of 1,000 to 2,000 neighborhoods, which in turn are grouped into divisions (some cities call them wards) numbering 30 to 50 neighborhoods each. As we suggested earlier, each division is governed by the divisional assembly and the city by the city assembly; and both assemblies arise out of the consensuses gathered in the respective neighborhoods.[22]

Institutions and Values

Reserving further comments on the economic and political orders for later discussion, we now point to certain other general features of the structure, institutions, and values of utopia.

Of all their institutions, the utopians value education most. But their conception of it embraces both the informal and the formal. The child, they hold, cannot become a rational and self-governing human being without the intimacy of some family life and the emotional reassurance which this provides. But since the family system is represented by several types, the kinds of intimacy will vary. Thus in a polyandrous household, the existence of two or three fathers and of a single mother is likely to have a somewhat different emotional impact than a monogamous household could have. But the utopians do not believe that the one is necessarily "worse" than the other, so long as both show concern and love for the child. In group marriage situations, there are usually the same number of men as women (most frequently two or three of each sex) and thus the variation, as compared with other households, turns mainly on sheer numbers of individuals involved. Theoretically, of course, the group marriage could involve large numbers; but the utopians discovered very early that more than six persons in the relationship inhibited the free flow of emotion both for the individuals involved and for the children.

But while the utopians believe that the small family unit must be the underlying basis for informal education and for the budding human personality, they also hold that the somewhat wider circle of the neighborhood is indispensable. For one thing, in the atmosphere of responsible parenthood prevalent throughout the utopian world, the numbers of children in any one family are very few. In most families, there will be no more children than the numbers of marriage partners. But the existence of the neighborhood provides all the advantages of a large family, with children rather closely related to one another and to the adult world. In one neighborhood there may be about 100 children; and while they will not get to know one another as well as they know their siblings, still the degree of intimacy will be considerable. Although the adults will not consider themselves to be fathers and mothers of all the children, as in some utopias, still their relation will necessarily be rather close, since they will share in caring for all the children and help plan the nursery school and kindergarten. Moreover, many alternative adult role models will be dramatized for the younger members of the community — a vital factor in the development of personality.

Every child will thus have the advantages of both the intense emotional life of the nuclear family and the less intense but highly significant relations of the extended family. Any tendencies for the former to become ingrown may be checked by the activities of the latter.

Of course, education in utopia is also formal. The utopians hold that while informal schooling is vital and that direct experience of life is also important, still there is no substitute for disciplined formal learning. "Learning by doing" as the only version of the educational process would mean that most persons would never become educated. There is simply too much to know. We cannot come to comprehend the vast storehouse of the past without careful organization, planning, and discipline.

At the neighborhood level, the nursery school and kindergarten are managed by lay committees, with the assistance of a few professional personnel. The relation between all the parents of the neighborhood and this first step in the educational system is a very close one. Degree of formality is low. Nevertheless, utopian educational philosophers believe that this very beginning of formal education is crucial as a foundation upon which subsequent steps will be built.

At the divisional level in a city, there is what preutopians called elementary education. The city as a whole is in charge of the equivalent of secondary and collegiate education, but cities combine in the province for highly technical and graduate education. At every level, one of the most important functions of the assembly is the general overseeing of the educational process.

To some degree the utopians say, education means government and true rule implies education in its broadest sense. To govern, whether at the level of the individual soul or at that of the collectivity, is to educate; and to educate is to govern. But in both cases government means self-government, rather than government of passive souls by an active elite of some kind. In their allocation of resources, the utopians give highest priority to education in all of its ramifications.

Just as they seek to avoid economic overspecialization within the city, province, and region, so in the cultural, entertainment, and educational fields they strive for as much variation and local administration as possible. The utopians believe that active participation by many is better for the development of free personalities than mere spectator culture, entertainment, and education. They endeavor to secure active copartnership between and among specialists and laymen, as in the management of the kindergarten and nursery school in each neighborhood.

Long before the establishment of utopian institutions, the operative value system had begun to change, and with the actual initiation of the new society, the system was altered even more. The new scheme of governance and economy is both the fruit and the root of the shift in priorities which actually guide mankind.

Thus dietary habits have been substantially altered: some 99.2 percent of all the utopians, the statisticians estimate, have become vegetarians. The shift to vegetarianism was not sudden and was the result of many considerations. In the old days, the highly industrialized parts of the world consumed vast quantities of meat, and some indeed asserted that meat was essential for an adequate "civilized" diet. To be sure, a considerable segment of mankind even then was comprised of near vegetarians, out of economic necessity. The utopian consciousness about diet was built on several principles. Ethically, increasing numbers were repelled by the idea of eating animals, like cattle and pigs, which in many respects are physiologically so close to man. Then, too, repugnance to killing in general had grown, affecting not only attitudes to meat eating but also to hunting and war. Aesthetically, the notion of eating what many thinkers came to call "corpses" was viewed with revulsion. Finally, it became fully recognized that the main dietary contribution of meat, protein, could be obtained far more economically in other ways. Preutopian students had estimated that an acre of forage and grain fed to cattle produced 43 pounds of edible protein as beef and 77 pounds as milk, but planted to soybeans, the same acre would produce 450 pounds of edible protein. Soybeans had 34.1 percent protein and lean ground beef only 20.7 percent. Planted to alfalfa, an acre yielded some 600 pounds of extracted alfalfa protein. Some preutopian thinkers, moreover, held that a vegetarian diet, properly balanced, was actually healthier for human beings than one in which meat played a large part. Whether or not this was true, the utopians are certainly healthier than their ancestors were.

The change in operative values can also be illustrated by considering the role of fashions in clothing. Through both public policy and individually expressed preferences, the culture now insists that clothing be made to last a long time. The utopians look back to the old days and deprecate them for what is called their "tyranny of fashion," under which perfectly good clothing used to be discarded simply because of the whim of some fashion designer in New York or Paris. The absence of fashion tyranny in utopia means, as we have seen, that there is wide variation in style of dress, or undress, at any given time.

Another change of great significance is that the mobility of persons has greatly declined. Men and women change their habitations less often than they did in the old days, when workers for the large corporations were constantly being transferred and a kind of perpetual restlessness pervaded industrial and so-called postindustrial cultures. The decline in mobility has come about partly as a result of changes in the economic system and in part through a growing realization that the greatest satisfactions in life do not lie in frantically rushing about or in constant travel to see the sights but rather in the contemplation of things close at hand: natural objects, fellow human beings, and one's own self. The cities are so arranged that walking is deliberately encouraged; and in the forest or desert lands lying beyond the agricultural zones surrounding the cities, walking paths facilitate the contemplation of Nature.

Intellectual and Cultural Expression

According to law, every governing unit must provide both halls and open spaces where people can publicly express themselves about anything. Organizations can obtain the halls virtually rent free. In the old days, utopians point out, while there were often formal guarantees of freedom of expression, the actual ability to utilize that freedom was not infrequently impaired by difficulties in obtaining facilities (rentals of buildings, police permits, and so on). In utopia, there is no legal restriction on what one can say or how one can say it; and from neighborhood to ecumenical levels, public debates and discussions are almost continuous. The incentives for such discussions are much greater than in the old days, since public decision making settles so many more issues than in the 20th century, and experiences of public life are more direct and less vicarious than in days past. One is trained in the neighborhood from the beginning, although rather informally, to speak and express oneself publicly.

Just as the practice of widespread public oral discussion is encouraged (at times, speakers will even advocate the overthrow of the whole system) so is written expression greatly valued. As in every aspect of utopian life, variety is the rule. By pooling resources, a number of neighborhoods may combine to establish a newspaper; or individuals from many neighborhoods may decide to do the same. Sometimes a city has its own paper, or individuals across provincial or regional lines initiate a publishing venture. All papers, of course, are nonprofit in nature, with editors and staffs paid for by the combined credit contributions of individuals, cities, or other organizations, as the case might be. Such advertising as does exist (of course it has drastically declined since preutopian days) is purely informational in nature.

Cultural expressions in utopia are many and varied. Insofar as music, art, and other exemplifications of the aesthetic are professionalized, they are underwritten financially in very much the same ways as the press. But the startling phenomenon here is that amateur performances have proliferated, as compared with the old days. Although the utopians greatly admire the professional, they hold that actual participation by the individual here, as in politics, is to be valued as an end in itself. Thus almost every utopian is involved in amateur aesthetic activities of many kinds: drama, music, painting. On occasion, various voluntary exiles from the wilderness will appear in a city and give their own rather unorthodox performances.

Utopian doctrine at this point holds that artistic expression is of value not only as an end in itself but also as therapy. It affords an outlet for pent-up emotions and provides constructive avenues for energies which might otherwise be utilized for destruction. It is also closely related to direct sexual expressions, reinforcing their spiritual dimensions and strengthening them by providing the communication that is so central to sexual life. In the process of constantly renewing a sense of community, which is so essential if the politics of utopia are to attain their true end and to be nonviolent, this widespread participation in artistic activities plays a vital role. The utopians agree with Plato when he adumbrates the close relationship between musical and political developments.[23]

These, then, are some of the crucial general features of utopian life.

Technological and Economic Orders

At various points we have referred to the utopian economic order as well as its connection with attitudes to technology. Here let us become somewhat more explicit.

Introduction of Technology

Among those issues settled by public discussion in utopia is, of course, the introduction of new complex technology. The utopians value technology, but beyond a relatively simple level (which is defined by the ecumenical assembly), they think that its introduction is so fraught with the public interest that only public decisions should pass on its adoption. Although new types of basket weaving, new devices for opening cans, or similar relatively unintricate techniques might be introduced without formal public decisions, the acceptance, for instance, of complex medical technology, computers, and methods for constructing houses cannot take place without the positive decision of an assembly. In other words, the burden of proof is on those who propose the innovation.

Within limits imposed by the world or ecumenical assembly — which is charged with providing that basic technological development essential for mankind's minimal standard of life — every assembly above that of the division is charged with the task of technological inspection. Thus the national-culture assembly passes on the acceptance or rejection of technological innovation for the national culture. But if that assembly permits a certain device, regional, provincial, or city assemblies can deny the device to their areas. Although this permits considerable variation in technological development throughout the world, the utopians believe that this is the price they must pay if they are to combine some uniformity with considerable diversity in the technological and economic orders. There is a kind of basic standard for mankind as a whole, but at the same time considerable latitude for national, regional, provincial, and city idiosyncrasies.

Decisions are made only after careful discussion. To each relevant assembly is attached a committee of experts representing as many aspects of technical proficiency as possible. Before any decision can be reached, the assembly also sets up a committee of laymen reflecting alternative points of view. The committee of experts is permanent, the committee of laymen is chosen ad hoc for any given decision. Prior to action by the assembly, the two committees discuss the matter; the laymen inform themselves of the technical ramifications, and the technical experts learn the judgments of the laymen about values and social and aesthetic concerns. Eventually, the committee of laymen debates the issue before the assembly, assisted and supplemented by the committee of experts.

In general, several different kinds of statements on technological proposals must be provided for consideration by the assembly. Separate statements deal with the possible impact of the innovation on employment, its effects on the general economy, how its use will affect standards of beauty, its effects on the environment as a whole, and its relation to social stability. The ultimate decision, of course, must be made by the assembly whose own values and judgments will necessarily shape its conclusions.

Those values and judgments are profoundly influenced, however, by a widespread consensus in utopia on the relation of technology and economic growth to such issues as ecology and the optimum conditions essential for development of human personality. The utopian consensus is shaped by such preutopian evaluations as this:

Actions taken in the pursuit of material progress must have a profound, if subtle, effect. Our psychosphere is impoverished by the progressive degradation of our environment. Every day, all of us are assaulted, directly or subliminally, by the spectacle of decaying cities, garbage-strewn countrysides, tasteless strip developments, streams and lakes laden with filth . . . and by a callous disregard for other organisms that share our planet.

More subtle are other costs of sustained economic and technologic growth. All of us feel a rising anxiety because we live close to the brink of obsolescence and because ever-growing technology needs to create disaffection with present conditions to promote ever greater consumption. The dignity of labor has declined because two centuries of technological innovation, in the name of efficiency, have reduced artisans, craftsmen, and clerks to machine minders. This is because labor is considered a disutility, while all output is considered a utility and hosts of efficiency experts work at reducing the ratio of labor to output without the slightest regard for social consequences. Further, things that tend to get done in modern industrial society are those particularly conducive to economic growth. This is almost the sole consideration determining the crops we sow, the style of our houses, the shape of our cities and landscapes. . . . In sum, the technologic conditions of industrial, business, and agricultural production evolve in response to output efficiency and are not chosen to enhance man's experience of life. The predominant influences bearing on man's welfare are thus generated accidentally, simply a by-product of technologic advance. This is not to deny the benefits in goods and services that man receives from technologic advance, but rather to underline the fact that other pervasive influences on his welfare arise from so-called technologic advances. These affect him directly as a worker who responds passively to evolving machinery. Technology also affects him directly, and critically, by its ultimate determination of the matrix of society, by its effect on the natural, institutional, and psychological environment.[24]

It is against a preutopian situation of this kind that the utopians have reacted so sharply. By the standards of preutopian industrialized civilization, they would be regarded as technological "reactionaries," to be classified with William Morris and Mohandas Gandhi.

In fact, the utopians are very fond of quoting certain passages from Gandhi. For example:

> Replying to a question whether he was against *all* machinery, Gandhiji said "How can I be when I know that even this body is a most delicate piece of machinery? The spinning wheel is a machine; a little toothpick is a machine. What I object to is the craze for machinery, not machinery as such. . . . The supreme consideration is man. I would make intelligent exceptions. Take the case of the Singer's sewing machine. It is one of the few useful things ever invented. . . ."
>
> "But," said the questioner, "If you make an exception of the Singer's sewing machine and your spindle, where would these exceptions end?"
>
> "Just where they cease to help the individual and encroach upon his individuality. The machine should not be allowed to cripple the limbs of man."[25]

Or again: "I do want growth, I do want self-determination, I do want freedom, but I want all these for the soul. I doubt if the steel age is an advance upon the flint age. I am indifferent. It is the evolution of the soul to which the intellect and all our faculties have to be devoted. . . ."[26]

There are many instances in utopia of proposed devices being denied licenses — sometimes in the face of obvious demonstrations that they will greatly increase material wealth. Naturally, very vigorous verbal battles are often waged about technological innovation, both in the public forum and in the assemblies. Political lines are frequently drawn more tightly on this issue than on any other; for while there is widespread agreement on repudiating many of the operative values of the old order, the exact implications of the new operative values for particular situations are often far from clear. And the weights given to one value consideration as against another vary considerably from individual to individual or city to city. Even some versions of new medical technology have been turned down by particular segments of mankind, in face of evidence that they might prolong very old persons' lives by a few years. The arguments of the opponents apparently turned on the quantity v. quality issue, the critics contending that four additional years of senility were not qualitatively desirable. Devices which would have brought into being the development of embryos outside mothers' wombs were also rejected in utopia. A vigorous campaign was conducted against the devices by mothers' organizations, which said that it was the birthright of women to have the joy of womb-developed children; they feared that the mystique of the new devices might become so overwhelming that many mothers might succumb and have children against their rational judgments. We are not saying that decisions of this kind were necessarily right, but we are pointing out the vast significance of the fact that the decisions were made publicly, after often conflicting testimony of experts as to possible impacts in a number of areas.

The philosophers of utopia recognize, of course, that judgments about the effects of technology are often very difficult to make. Nevertheless, they hold that explicit, deliberate public judgments — however shaky they might be — are to be vastly preferred to allowing the decisions of accident to rule.

The utopians make a careful distinction between the *introduction* of new complex devices, on the one hand, and discoveries about their feasibility, on the other. In the utopian research institutes and universities, pure scientific inquiry is going on constantly, and applied scientific investigation is also very energetically pursued. Science, so to speak, is "free," at least within the limits of the resources assigned to it and the availability of personnel. But general adoption of new techniques having any great magnitude of complexity is always subject to the process we have described.

It is within this cultural and technological context that the economy operates.

The Economy

In principle, all the land and natural resources of the whole world belong to the human race. But subject to varying conditions and limitations, the world assembly grants long-term leases to the various divisions of mankind, which are obliged, of course, to submit to periodic inspection and to make public reports. In acting, the assembly tries to keep in mind two considerations: that land and resources were given by God to humanity as a whole; and that while they should not be fundamentally alienated from the human race, it is also desirable to decentralize administration to promote a large degree of flexibility, variety, and adaptation to local or peculiar circumstances, as well as to avoid the perils of centralized bureaucracy. Thus a typical arrangement is for the ecumene, or world, to lease land and natural resources to a given national-culture area for, let us say, 100 years. The lease is subject to a report and inspection every ten years and to observance by the national-culture area of the general principles of land use promulgated by the world assembly (these regulations are general in character, detailed implementation being a function of the entity which is leasing the land). The national-culture assembly leases its land to regions, provinces, and cities for periods of, for example, 33 years. Individuals lease it for 20 to 40 years, although there is considerable variation.

The utopians believe that a scheme similar to this is not only right morally, in that it adopts the trustee principle for land ownership and management, but that it eliminates some of the worst features of the old order, which tended to promote economic inequality and to inhibit rational social planning. In utopia there is no private appropriation of the publicly generated economic rent of land. Although the philosophers of utopia do not believe that Henry George's conceptions were in themselves adequate to account for the poverty and inequality of the old days, still they think that his theories were partially correct.[27]

Aside from the common ownership and administration of land and natural resources, it is difficult to describe the economic system of utopia. This is because there are innumerable variations. In general, the "system" is many systems, held together by a few common principles and by a certain degree of world planning. Among these principles are the ideas that the ecumenical assembly should be responsible for the wilderness area of the earth (which, as we have seen, constitutes about one half of the land surface), should establish standards for the use of the high seas, and should lay down the general framework for economic enterprise and technological innovation. The assembly also sets up a scheme of world food reserves.

In carrying out these functions, the assembly has determined that almost all business shall be nonprofit in character, the exceptions being mainly small proprietor-operated businesses and handicrafts. This means that for the most part business enterprise takes the form of cooperatives or direct management by the cities. The assembly also establishes a minimal standard for the extent of "free" distribution of goods and services: thus all parts of the world must use this principle to distribute medical and legal services and to provide much of the education. When distribution is according to money differentials, the yearly differential (hours worked may vary) shall not be more than 1-1/5 to 1. The assembly has the right so to regulate capital flows between and among parts of utopia that the possible basic material standard of life does not vary too markedly from region to region.

These uniformities — and others of similar character — of course constitute a substantial integrating factor in the economic life of the world. They in effect imply a minimal planning at the world level. But within these limits, national-culture areas, regions, provinces, and cities have a wide latitude as to how, in specific terms, they are to regulate their economic life and their technological innovation. For example, a few national-culture areas have become completely "communist" in distribution — that is, all goods and services are distributed "free," and thus the wages system has been abolished. Other areas observe only the world minimum with respect to free goods. Most regions of utopia commingle market with nonmarket coordination: in other words, they observe the principles of market socialism. Certain regions, provinces, and neighborhoods have in effect become ascetic; that is, they have reduced their material wants so much that they are able to survive on far less than the minimum officially decreed by the ecumene. Of course, this asceticism is purely voluntary, for the utopians emphasize the sharp distinction between involuntary and voluntary poverty. In general, as we noted earlier, the average of perceived economic need has fallen far below what it appeared to be in the industrialized nations before the establishment of utopia. Between this average, however, and the needs of the extreme ascetics, there is a considerable gulf.

But while the diversities in the utopian economy are significant, it is possible to detect certain broad tendencies which exist everywhere. Thus it is widely believed that most people have diverse possibilities as producers, and the economic structure in most parts is so arranged that during the course of a lifetime a person may have several vocations. Since it is assumed that education continues throughout life, in any event, part of that education consists of retraining persons for new vocations, even in their middle years. Thus there are not a few who begin their careers in one field and end them in another. Within very broad limits, this is an option open to every person; and while it might involve moving from one city to another — and mobility, as we have seen, has greatly declined both as a value and as a fact — still many think that moving is worthwhile.

We might pause at this juncture to reflect on how profound the changes in value judgments have been. During the old days, in highly industrialized countries, human beings often preferred costly consumers' goods — elaborate housing, highly refined food, expensive entertainment — to variety in occupations. The result was that they had neither time nor money to retrain and reeducate themselves for a diversity of occupations, even though they were frequently very unhappy in the work they were doing. In utopia, however, this situation has on the whole been transformed. Most utopians prefer variety in occupations, and the education and training this entails, to conspicuous consumption of material goods or such obviously harmful and expensive things as tobacco and hard liquor. To the utopians, adventure often consists of experiencing a multitude of life tasks, rather than of futile attempts to escape from a life of boredom and frustration through material consumption.[28]

Within each work unit, where supervision is needed, the immediate supervisor is chosen by members of the unit involved, and the supervisor is the spokesman for the unit in relations with other administrators. In industry as a whole, as is true of the general society, a few basic decisions are made at higher levels, but there has been a vast devolution of decision making on lower units.

Throughout most parts of utopia — although the practices vary considerably — there is no fixed retirement age. Instead, many continue working, at least part time, into their eighties. The principle of gradual retirement is also widespread, with a progressive tapering off of work — a process which is usually not completed except in cases of illness. Even when they do "retire," older utopians are kept very busy in the tasks of the neighborhood, as we have seen. And their incomes remain the same.

In industry and the production system generally, principles of due process of law (in the old days confined to a relatively limited sphere) are established. This means that an effort is made to eliminate arbitrary action at all levels and to ensure that in the work process, just as in the general rule of society, the individual is respected as a human being.

The principle of the sabbatical year (in preutopian days confined largely to educational institutions and sometimes not present even in them) is extended to work generally. Some utilize the year for acquiring new skills, whether vocationally or in sports, some simply for getting better acquainted with their neighbors, while yet others may go off to the wilderness for meditation and roughing it. Since the automobile has virtually disappeared, the latter get to the edge of the wilderness mainly through public transportation, although not a few hardy souls walk, even hundreds of miles.

Restraint in Development

Transportation can be used as an example of the peculiar mixture of economic and technological development, on the one hand, and restraint and retrogression in such development, on the other. In attempting to take account of both primitive Nature and of civilization and to keep in mind that the human telos demands a restricted measure of both, the utopians have deliberately rejected further development of the airplane and general use of the automobile and have instead done an enormous amount of research on intracity as well as intercity fixed-roadway and other forms of transport. The result is that it is possible to move from neighborhood to neighborhood in the cities fairly swiftly, noiselessly, and cleanly. The utopian simply walks to the edge of the neighborhood, waits five to ten minutes for the car, enters it, and, without any payment, rides it to his destination. Since cities are restricted in population concentration and area, this means that almost any part of the city can be reached within about 20 minutes at most.

Intercity transportation, too, has been vastly improved in convenience and safety and even in speed, usually averaging 175 to 225 miles per hour. In portions of utopia, of course, citizens have decided to *reduce* the availability of public transportation, arguing that some provinces and regions tend to stimulate too much mobility. Technically, it is possible to build ground-transport vehicles that can attain 400 miles an hour; but the utopians (with a very few exceptions) have rejected these possibilities, contending (rather stubbornly, according to some of the critics) that an average of 225 miles an hour is enough.

We can also illustrate the combination of economic-technical development and restraints on other kinds of technology by reference to utilization of sewage, garbage, and human and animal wastes. In most cities, a very high percentage can be reclaimed for agricultural purposes; the waste materials, after treatment, will be conveyed directly to the surrounding agricultural zone, thus avoiding enormous transport charges, which in the preutopian days greatly increased the cost of fertilizer and hence of food. Waste is also reclaimed for other ends; some is transformed into perfume, while other portions are turned into fuel.

We must constantly be aware, of course, that developments of this kind take place within the context, already described, of a people who are mostly vegetarian; whose material wants have been reduced, on the average, below the per capita consumption of the old industrialized nations; and whose frantic mobility has abated.

In terms of agriculture, this context is also important. Thus the production of beans of various types, which had greatly increased even before establishment of the utopian order, continued to accelerate as the demand for nonanimal proteins grew and the industrial uses of the bean became more apparent. Fruit orchards, too, expanded greatly: in preutopian days, while nutritionists were constantly advocating the use of fruits in the diet, for millions of human beings most types of fruit were too expensive; and in California and elsewhere, many orchards had been destroyed to be replaced by missile sites. The agricultural zones around certain utopian cities, where conditions are favorable, might emphasize fruits as against other types of produce, just as the zones of other cities might stress wheat, rye, or oats. To be sure, the goal insofar as possible is to provide a diversity of crops for each city; but this does not mean that some zones will not be compelled by the nature of the climate and soil to give disproportionate attention to particular types of production rather than others.

Implicit in this analysis of the utopian economy is the considerable decline of trade, as compared with preutopian days. To be sure, world and other assemblies make provisions for periodic exchange of commodities on an orderly basis. But the chaotic and often frantic trade of the old days is gone. This has been brought about by a number of factors: the effort to promote a considerable degree of diversity and self-sufficiency within each city and the surrounding belts; the decline in material desires, as compared with preutopian "developed" regions; full utilization of locally produced wastes; reduction in desire for mobility; and public control and direction of technological development. Because hit or miss and uncontrolled trade tends to promote a kind of uniformity, there is actually greater variety in utopian life, taken as a whole, than in the old days. Although cities, provinces, and regions are not isolated from one another, still their development is less subject to the uniformitarian tendencies promoted by the rampant trade and rather chaotic industrialism of the old days.

The Polity

We have necessarily indicated many of the features of the polity during our discussion of the general culture, the technology and the economy of utopia. Here, assuming the structure of the assemblies already outlined and the neighborhood as the basis of political life, we draw out more explicitly the utopian rationale for its polity.

The Public and Publicity

The utopians assume, of course, that all things which deeply and broadly affect the public should be controlled and directed publicly. Since a fairly complex division of labor has not been rejected (although it is generally below that of the preutopian industrialized world, and although runaway economic development *has* been repudiated), the recognized public realm is a large one, embracing, as we have seen, the introduction of technology and the overall direction of the economy.

Under such conditions, it is also assumed that deliberations about the public weal should be public. In the old days, as the utopians constantly remind themselves, politicians and people exempted many elements of deliberation about public affairs from public scrutiny: thus there was the area of so-called national security, a kind of sacred cow, many aspects of which could not be contaminated by public debate. In utopia, however, there are no such sacrosanct animals. Publicity about public matters is deemed absolutely essential, and the freest criticism of everything is encouraged. In preutopian days, even in so-called democracies, utopian historians are fond of pointing out, many legislative hearings were held behind closed doors. Whole nations could be pledged through secret treaties to expenditures and actions about which their citizens knew next to nothing. Utopia will have none of this.

The nature of the economic order in utopia is such, moreover, that citizens have not only the right but also the power to criticize public decisions and to exercise their freedom. The vast reduction of income differentiation and the expansion of the realm of free goods assure a relatively firm base in economic power for most citizens, who develop confidence that there can be no serious economic retaliation simply because of what they say. Where distribution of free goods, including bread, is a first charge on the economy — and bread is indeed distributed free in much of utopia — larger numbers of bold souls are willing, if necessary, to live on free goods for a time if this is essential for them to be independent critics. They can no longer be intimidated by threat of starvation or undue deprivation.

Intimacy and Politics

In the neighborhood assembly members work together on various tasks of the neighborhood, and thus great personal knowledge of one another becomes a foundation stone of the political and social order. Involuntary personal isolation, so often characteristic of society in the old days, has sharply declined. The feasibility of consensus as a principle is encouraged by the somewhat lower-level division of labor, the people's direct experience of one another, the undermining of great income differentiations, and the expansion of public decision making. Utopian philosophers are fond of quoting Rousseau and believe that their system meets most of his conditions for genuine community: relatively small size of basic decision-making units, absence of serious factional rifts (except, perhaps, on some problems of introducing new technology), strong emotional ties, repudiation of luxury, and elimination of significant class distinctions. To be sure, the utopians are quite aware that consensus is unlikely to be attained on all occasions — hence the provisions, under certain circumstances, for a majority vote. They are quite aware that if no deliberate decision is reached within a reasonable period of time, then the decision is in effect made by events or "fortune" — and, according to their priorities, this is an extremely undesirable outcome.

To be sure, some of these advantages are not present, or present only to a limited degree, at assemblies above the level of the neighborhood. At division and city levels, they are no doubt still present in considerable extent, however, given the restricted size of cities, the possibility for commingling of citizens, and the decline in mobility. Drastically limited income differentiation, moreover, is the same at both neighborhood and higher levels. The intensity of emotional rapport would really decline at provincial, regional, national cultural, and world levels. Utopian philosophers do not think that some of this emotional dilution can be prevented. On the other hand, they point out that decisions at the higher levels affect citizens less directly, given limitations on technological growth, reduction in division of labor, elimination of war, and much decentralization. To be sure, national-culture and world assemblies have very important economic functions: the assurance of equity as between and among parts of the world; basic decisions about technology; development of principles for exchange of commodities, and so on. But they are the kinds of decisions that involve establishment of general frameworks rather than, with some exceptions, direct administration, which is primarily a task for the city.

Executive and Administration

At each level, any executive authority is chosen and dismissable by the assembly involved. The executives take a full part in debates of the assembly, often accompanied by their experts. At neighborhood and divisional levels, most of the administrative work is done by laymen, technical full-time experts being very few.

In the permanent administrative service at all levels, the principle of rotation among the higher offices is observed, and there is also a rotation from higher to lower and vice versa. Although the utopians recognize the need for experience and expertise, they are also keenly aware of the perils involved in developing vested interests, and often they are willing to sacrifice some presumed efficiency in favor of other values. The system of rotation, both horizontal and vertical, is applied to industrial as well as to general coordinating positions. The specific adaptations of the principle of rotation vary from national culture to national culture, or even from city to city, but a term of three to five years is generally thought to be about right for high-level bureaucrats, after which they are transferred to lower-level work, either in their own departments or in another agency.

Role of Law

Although the utopians have not yet attained a state of affairs in which pure equity, faithfully administered, has taken the place of law, many aspects of law and its administration have changed. The law of property, for example, is less involved and less entangling for the individual than it was in the old days; for in utopia private property chiefly consists of consumer rather than capital goods. Although contractual relations have expanded in some respects (for example, in developing cooperative relations between and among cities), they have, generally speaking, been simplified. Since private inheritance has virtually disappeared, except for family mementos and a modicum of personal possessions, the law of inheritance also has been largely denuded of its former complexity.

The criminal law, too, has been profoundly affected. Although there are still crimes against persons, particularly of passion (the utopians are under no illusions about the characteristics even of somewhat developed human nature), crimes against property rights are virtually nonexistent. The establishment of a minimal economic standard, the decline in institutional encouragement of acquisitiveness, the considerable change in operative values, the vast flexibility of the family system — all these have been factors in leading to the almost complete elimination of crimes against property and to a diminution of crimes against the person.

In sum, a relatively simpler society with public deliberation about public matters has led to a more understandable and effective legal system. As might be expected, the number of lawyers per thousand souls has rather sharply declined.

Stability and Change

It should be noted, too, that the principles involved in public deliberation about technology and in publicly limited economic development have served to slow down the furious pace of change so characteristic of the old, highly industrialized societies; and this has had its effect on all aspects of the law — public, private, civil, and criminal. The slowdown provides time for legal concepts to take account of social and technological alterations, and it is a boon for those who cherish that dimension of the law which values stability. Change simply for the sake of change is no longer valued at all.

Yet change is accepted if it has a legitimate purpose and contributes to the rational discussion utopians so value and which is integral to true politics. This can be illustrated by the utopian attitude to what in preutopian days were called political parties. In utopia there are no long-term political alignments and hence no permanent political parties. The supposed stability of preutopian days gives way to constantly shifting combinations directed to specific issues. "Political parties," if they can be said to exist at all, are not rigid and, indeed, they are simply temporary consciousness-raising groups, rarely flourishing for more than three or four years. The utopians hold, of course, that freedom of political alignments is crucial in their type of polity. At the same time, the emphasis on consensus-making decisions and the elimination of social and political classes in the traditional sense provide a context within which parties and "factions" alike are in effect strongly discouraged. The tenuous, tentative alignments which do exist soon fade away into others. At the time of writing a group is advocating revolution in utopia, citing as precedent the movement which brought about utopia itself. But this group is very loosely organized, and even if it succeeds in basically transforming utopian society, which is highly unlikely, it will probably dissolve, as did the movement which produced the utopian order. Thus changes in political advocacy groupings, as we may call them, are constant. Any organizations resembling the old Conservative and Labour Parties of Britain, for example, are unthinkable.

In general, the ancient problem of permanence and change is seen in a somewhat new light. Whereas in previous times, according to utopian historians, the idea of stability was often associated with a return to Nature and to the simplicity supposedly characteristic of Nature, now, in utopia, there is a conscious effort to balance a large measure of stability in civilization against social changes which are deliberately chosen by the collectivities. Access to primitive Nature on a large scale is insisted on and is combined with a technology and economy consciously shaped by the polity. Shifting political alignments signify that politics is no longer conceived to be the "conquest of power" by highly organized and rigid groups but rather the development of genuine authority through free debate and exchange of ethical and aesthetic experiences. There is no belief in inevitable progress through technological and economic change. At the same time, there is both a commitment to some technological and economic development and an acute realization of the difficulties in making change less blind. Both Gandhi, to whom we have already referred, and the late Norbert Wiener[29] are admired, for each is seen as embodying aspects of the utopian vision. However, if the utopians had to choose between the two, they would undoubtedly lean heavily in favor of Gandhi.

Coercion and Freedom

The question of coercion and freedom is, of course, a central one. In many respects and in terms of the several definitions of freedom, the utopians are freer than were men and women in the old days of blind industrialism and the idolization of technology. Thus they are liberated from the coercions of economic want and, at the same time, from the impulsions of limitless material desires. They are released from the illusion of inevitable progress and from the equally great illusion that they can completely transcend Nature and become like gods. In being aware of certain inevitable constraints — of scarce resources, for example, and of living in the community, which is so essential for free personality — they internalize these constraints and no longer see them as restrictions on essential freedom. Of three sanctions for law — force of habit, threat of physical coercion, or appeal to conscience and reason — the third has become by far the most important, due to the growth of awareness, to expanded education, and to altered institutions.

Tensions continue to remain, however, between individual and group and between group and group; the utopians, in fact, do not yet envision a day in which these strains will be entirely removed. Some of their philosophers argue, in fact, that it is both futile and undesirable to remove all these tensions, since, if only they are kept under some control, they may be a source of spiritual growth and insight.

Negative-freedom aspects of the utopian situation have their parallels in positive-freedom conditions. Freedom from economic want and from limitless desires liberates utopians for rational decisions, the contemplation of Nature, and personal development. Freedom from the illusion that they are gods enables them to make choices within the realistic limits of their human nature, and it stimulates an awareness that their own creations, including their tools, can enslave them. Liberation from the illusion that violent coercion is an answer to crime releases them to discover methods that can deal constructively with socially injurious conduct.

The general movement of utopian society is in the direction of indirect rather than direct constraints on human beings. Equitable distribution of scarce goods, communal ownership and administration of basic resources, the policy of the economic minimum — all these involve direct control of material goods and therefore only indirect control of human beings. One of the effects of the wide prevalence of the neighborhood structure, combined with ample provision for privacy and retreat, is to substitute informal, gentle, and indirect constraints on human conduct for the often brutal and violent constraints of the period before the utopian revolution.

Wherever possible, criminal offenses are dealt with at the neighborhood level. A neighborhood court handles minor disputes and juries of six (drawn, of course, from the extended family that is the neighborhood) pass on the facts. The judge resides in the neighborhood and has had legal training, even though his primary work may not be in the legal area. There is usually not enough work for a full-time judge. More serious offenses are considered at the division or city level, under similar principles. In the neighborhood, penalties may include apologies, exclusion for a time from certain of the amenities of the neighborhood, or a period of what is called "compulsory meditation" underneath the neighborhood plaza. More serious offenses might involve a fairly long period of probation, with reports to trained probation officials. At the city level, there may be a few isolation centers where serious offenders are kept under carefully controlled conditions before being released on probation. But nothing like the old prison exists — indeed, it was on the way out, even before the utopian revolution.

The decline in mobility has also contributed to the considerable reduction in crime. Too much mobility is associated with a sense of rootlessness and hence of hostility. An individual who has roots in a nuclear family as well as in an extended one is much less likely to commit serious offenses.

Since one of the first decisions about technology was to abolish the manufacture and sale of all arms, the tasks of the police are easier. The police themselves have never had arms. Sometimes, to be sure, they will have to utilize physical force in breaking up conflicts which promise to lead to violence; but since they lack guns, this force is based on unusual but nonviolent physical skills. It may be surprising that utopia still has a police force, but the utopians do not consider this extraordinary: freedom, they hold, entails the possibility of some wrongdoing and some irrationality, and the physical presence of the police on patrol is a constant reminder to men and women that, while they may will the good in all sincerity, they sometimes revolt against what they know to be right. The police are a visible embodiment of the general will of most human beings to do justice, even though at times they depart from that way. In utopia, too, the police are in no way agents of class rule, given the economic and social structure; far more than in the old days, they stand for the community as a whole. The neighborhood structure, moreover, by building ties of close community from the beginning, facilitates through positive means the development of rational personalities; and the decline in mobility reduces both the possibility of runaway crime and the temptation, so ubiquitous in preutopian days, to centralize police administration.

Accountability

A problem which utopians recognize as crucial is that of how to hold rulers accountable. In the old days, they remark, much was said about this issue, but often its ramifications were not explored in depth. It was often assumed that merely mechanical devices — "checks" and "balances" in formal organization, for instance — would be enough. And many naively believed that the notion of accountability was somehow reconcilable with an economic system that led inevitably to conflicts of interest for those who held office.

In utopia, the question of accountability is seen as a many-faceted one. Complete publicity for all public decisions — with no exceptions — is, of course, one effective method for promoting accountability and responsibility. So, too, rotation of higher administrators contributes much. Another feature of utopian life which tends to promote accountability is the effort to combine a measure of central planning with decentralism. This makes for a general sense of responsibility and for the consciousness that holding officials accountable is the task of the citizens themselves.

Centralization and Decentralization

The ramifications of the centralism-decentralism issue are many: for example, the existence both of vertical governance and of horizontal negotiations between and among cities, provinces, regions, and national cultures; and controlled general economic interdependence, along with the possibility in emergencies of relative economic self-sufficiency for cities and other units. As we have seen, general frameworks are established centrally, but in such a way that the various units of utopia, whether geographic or functional, will determine for themselves the ways in which to act within those frameworks. Market socialism itself can be looked upon as an element in this decentralism, as can the general decline in mobility. Within the general frameworks, too — whether world, national culture, regional, or provincial — many arrangements are established through horizontal negotiations rather than through the command-obey model. Thus neighborhoods may make informal cooperative arrangements for the exchange of nursery school teachers, or cities for the exchange of resources. Within the general framework, there may actually be some competition between types of socialized institutions — between, let us say, cooperatively administered enterprise and municipally run stores.

The utopians do not believe that the various segments of mankind should be economically self-sufficient in any kind of absolute sense or in the long run. They do think it desirable, as we have seen, to have sufficient diversification so that in essentials they could stand alone for a period of time, either by themselves or in combination with a few other units. Politically, this relative economic diversification would enable the cities and provinces to resist any tendencies to tyranny at the center. While the utopians believe that their institutions in general will reduce the possibilities of despotism, still they are so impressed by the bloody history of tyranny in human affairs that they wish to ensure as much as possible the viability of nonviolent resistance. Without some considerable measure of local control of economic resources, the practical possibility of such resistance would be reduced. Campaigns of noncooperation with central authorities would be undergirded by the capacity of the resisters for remaining alive.

Here, as elsewhere, utopian philosophers do not expect the impossible of human nature. They consider themselves political "realists" who, while impressed by man's enormous capacity for benevolence and rationality, are also conscious of his very real potentiality for destruction. From a purely economic point of view, they maintain, it might be possible to argue for an extreme degree of integration in social and political life, but political institutions must have in mind more than economic desiderata. They must also consider the fact that man is much more than an economic being, and that it is precisely in his noneconomic dimensions that he is perhaps most distinctively "human," for good or for ill.

All this is recognized, too, in their attitudes to law. Whereas in many other utopias an effort was made to eliminate law and lawyers, these utopians retain legal institutions. Earlier we pointed out that the concept of due process of law has been extended to include administration of the economic sphere, so that the worker, in his capacity as worker, is no longer subjected to the arbitrary actions of preutopian days. But while the utopians have retained law, since they believe that man cannot be trusted to act justly without the guidance of previously established legal norms, they endeavor to make sure that, in sharp contrast to the old days, legal principles are clearly and simply stated and that legal services are available to everyone through "communization" of distribution by means of legal clinics.

But it is impossible to understand the spirit of the polity or, indeed, of the other ramifications of utopia, without a concluding word about the strategy and tactics used to bring it about.

Strategies and Tactics

In the old days before the utopian revolution, much discussion was devoted to the problem of strategies and tactics for desirable social change. In Marxism particularly, strategic issues constituted the central theme, since Marxists were notoriously loath to prescribe what the new world ought to be; instead, they seemed to think that one could somehow rely on "history" to throw up and formulate its own ends. The movement that gave rise to utopia, however, thought that it was essential to prescribe in some detail the ends and goals of all its activity and to give careful attention as well to the means.

The movement was impressed by the fact that every utopia draws for its ends on suggestions present in the nonutopian society. Not everything in a given order is to be repudiated: Some features, indeed, are to be expanded. Thus the leaders of the movement saw that in existing society certain goods and services were distributed free, and they concluded that it would be desirable to extend this particular characteristic. They agreed with Arthur Morgan that "nowhere was somewhere."[30]

But just as there were things to be applauded in the preutopian world, so were some institutions and operative values to be utterly repudiated. The existing society taught the future utopians what to avoid as well as what to sanction. Hence the movement had as one of its goals the destruction of monarchical and aristocratic proclivities in executive authority — tendencies so well illustrated in the Presidency of the United States, which, far from being the simple, republican magistracy that at least some of its founders had envisioned, had become a monarchy far more powerful than that against which the Americans of 1776 had struggled. The movement, too, was utterly disillusioned by the subjection of human beings to the whims of either corporate capitalism or of a highly centralized alleged socialism — both of which accepted the mystique associated with commitment to technological progress.

In terms of means, the utopian movement was impressed by the futility of violence as a strategy of fundamental desirable change. Not only was violence against persons morally wrong, it was also politically impractical: it did not achieve the ends it set out to attain. The leaders of the movement were profoundly aware that the so-called revolutions of modern times went wrong and were frustrated in considerable measure because they turned to violence. Violence in attempted revolutions led almost inevitably to dictatorship, destruction of personal rights, disrespect for human life, and a kind of ethical nihilism. All this had been true of the French, Russian, Spanish, and Cuban revolutions. Violence was always counterrevolutionary, leaders of the movement concluded, even if the stated ends of the revolutionaries might be applauded as noble. Thus in terms of their means, men like Lenin, Trotsky, Che Guevara, Mao, and Ho Chi Minh were counterrevolutionaries; and because they were counterrevolutionaries in means, their ends would tend to be counterrevolutionary in fact. Stalinism was a result to be expected of Leninism, and the fatal flaw of Leninism was that it did not sharply distinguish its means from those of the old imperial regime.[31] To be sure, there is about life a kind of healing tendency which sets in after the wounds of violence have been inflicted. This is reflected in those passages of the Bible which suggest that God permits men to have new beginnings, or at least partial new beginnings: "He will not always chide, neither will He keep his anger forever." Or: "He forgave their iniquity . . . remembered that they were but flesh."[32] But this notion of a new beginning, far from undermining the notion of the organic connection between ends and means, confirms it: If somehow the cycle of violence and more violence were not broken into (and theologians might say that this is in part a matter of grace), the condition of mankind would be hopeless.

Those who helped bring in the new age were impressed, too, by what they took to be the political experience of the past: that there was no one simple method of producing revolution. The ancient debate between those who pled for a "revolution within" and those who argued for a revolution in institutions revealed an element of validity in both positions. Revolutions certainly could not be made without the existence of many individuals determined to transform themselves into the selves or souls they ought to be; but equally, there was a greater probability that this consciousness would arise in a context of institutions moving in the utopian direction. Operative as well as professed value transformations were absolutely essential, but their permanence depended in some considerable measure on transformations in institutions as well.

Although it was important to realize emotionally as well as intellectually that men were neither beasts nor gods, without social and political action to implement and reinforce this realization fully — including institutions and practices which would discourage human beings from returning to the illusions — the consciousness would tend often to fade. While legislation by accident had been central in modern life and the design of utopia was to reduce the sphere of accident, the future utopians came to realize that the attempt to legislate deliberately also created its own perils. Hence they insisted that utopia must not succumb to the notion that any degree of complexity in the economic and technological orders could be subjected to legislation by deliberation: Beyond a point, human capacity to direct and control would break down. Therefore the only alternative was to impose timely limits on the extent of complexity, specialization, and technical change before they overwhelmed mankind.

With these principles in mind, those who organized the Movement for the Peaceful Overthrow of War, Brutality, and Exploitation (often abbreviated simply MPO) sought in the beginning to establish small cells of committed individuals in every office, school, and industrial plant. At the outset, the cells were primarily educational and existed for raising the level of political consciousness of their members. In the preutopian days, political consciousness in general was abysmally low, and most men and women were only dimly aware of the vast ramifications of the political problem. The movement began to raise the level of consciousness. It appealed to a wide variety of individuals and, unlike many other revolutionary causes, did not believe that there was any particular class or group in the community which could be regarded as the chosen vehicle for desirable change.

The growth of the cells was, of course, assisted greatly by the objective situations. The expansion of the movement took place in a world divided into competing national sovereignties, which was spending well over a quarter of a trillion dollars annually to kill human beings. It was a world in which the income and power gulf between developed and developing nations was growing; a world where ruling classes everywhere sought to clothe their designs in secrecy, and pious appeals to a "national security" which few could define recalled Samuel Johnson's "Patriotism is the last refuge of the scoundrel." In such a world, even the obtuse began to see that there was something fundamentally wrong with human polities everywhere. The MPO began to have cells all over the world, and a spirit of solidarity gradually developed between and among the cells. Where they were not permitted to exist openly, they flourished secretly and covertly. Under these circumstances, thousands of members were frequently thrown into prison, but their morale was sustained by the international movement.

Where there was a relatively great degree of freedom of expression and opportunity for legislative work, the movement was active in the legislative field. Everywhere it was antimilitarist and voted against all military appropriations in every country. In some portions of the preutopian society, of course, the secrecy, repression, and lack of the rule of law were such that the movement went underground and regarded itself as in a "revolutionary" situation. Here it did not feel morally obliged to publicize its stands, but it vowed never to resort to violence.

As the movement grew and its international solidarity increased, it felt more and more able to successfully erode the war-making powers of the national governments. Thus when a world war threatened to break out in 2045, members of the cells in the countries involved called for a general strike; and with the assistance of sympathetic labor unions and even of business associations, the strike halted the war machine in its tracks. The tendency for organization to develop ends of its own and to run roughshod over human beings was now counteracted by a movement which, basing its principles on the idea of nonviolent power, could shock ruling groups into a realization of their weaknesses. Meanwhile, where this was possible, MPO members were being elected to legislative bodies and appointed to administrative positions at an increasing rate. Those with higher incomes contributed a sizable percentage of them to MPO causes — to succor those who were imprisoned, to pay fines, and to provide for dependents.

As the movement generated more power, it was, of course subjected to many internal perils; in fact, the dangers within were always greater than those from without. Thus some members were tempted to become simply careerists and many others not in leadership positions tended to follow the leaders rather blindly. These tendencies had to be constantly counteracted by rotation in leaders, expanded political education, and commitment of leaders to relative personal poverty.

As many aspects of the existing order began to crumble, MPO members came to be predominant, and they began to put into effect the ends set up for the utopia. Generals were pensioned off, for example, and corporation executives strongly unsympathetic to the rising alternative government were reassigned or retired. In the more repressive parts of the world, thousands of movement members were killed or tortured; but they were replaced by other thousands, many of them from the repressive police and army forces. Eventually, even in nations characterized by the most repression, the philosophy of nonviolent resistance steadily adhered to led to a crumbling of the ruling orders: Soldiers refused to shoot, policemen flatly declined to arrest nonviolent protestors, and well-disciplined strikes made it impossible for dictators to rule. In seeking precedents for its own nonviolence, the movement was strongly impressed by such historical successes as the nonviolent revolution of the Roman plebs against the patricians in 494 B.C.; the activities of Francis Deak in securing the autonomy of Hungary during the 19th century; the Russian Revolution of 1905; and the very early phases of the Russian Revolution of 1917.[33]

As these events gained momentum, "alternative government" — to use Gandhi's expressive term — generally grew up on the basis of the movement's ends-and-means framework. From one point of view, the movement was an "open conspiracy" of human beings across national and class lines — a conspiracy against the forces irrationally dividing mankind and impairing the liberation of personality.[34] It developed its own economy and its members, in the event of conflict, obeyed its laws rather than the claimed laws of the surrounding society. The conspiracy was "disarming" because it was committed to the ethic of nonviolence. Yet it was also firm in the propositions for which it stood.

Of course, things did not always run smoothly, and the time involved was often very long. It was two generations from the first beginnings of the movement to the time when it was generally recognized that it had become central to politics. But when one puts this time span up against the Thirty Years War or the Cold War or the French Revolution, it does not seem outrageously long, particularly in view of the fact that those conflicts were so notably unsuccessful in advancing the interests of humanity: Their enormous costs outweighed any incidental gains.

In some respects, the movement represented a force rather like that which Christianity might have been, had it not succumbed to the temptations of violence. There was the same dedication, the same awareness of mission, and the same consciousness of solidarity.

Through its long development, the MPO had constantly to struggle against the oligarchical tendencies and the inertia that affect all large organizations. One of its slogans was based on this enslaving tendency of all organized effort: "The Devil does not have to crush Truth; he simply relies on men to do so when they organize it." Perhaps the movement was somewhat unique in that awareness of the perils of organization, oligarchy, and overdependence on leadership was extraordinarily broad and deep. Although leadership was valued as indispensable for formulating alternative policy options, there was always an underlying suspicion of it. Noncharismatic or dull leaders were preferred, for the MPO correctly saw that if directions were shaped primarily by charisma rather than rational discussion and deliberation, the movement could easily become counterrevolutionary.

Periodically, the movement was reorganized in order to check tendencies to inertia, ossification, or reliance on traditional leadership. Its constitution and bylaws automatically expired at the end of every seven-year period, so that the membership was faced with the necessity of either reconstituting it or allowing it to dissolve. Precedents of this kind were to be important in developing the structure of utopia. For the spirit to flourish, the future utopians held, they must be willing to sacrifice organizations and not to be too attached to given leaders.

The movement was particularly adamant in rejecting the stated objective of so many ostensibly revolutionary movements — "the conquest of power." Too often that simply had meant emulating the methods of the status quo while hoping, somehow, to come out with ends that were radically different. Thus to many Marxist groups, "the conquest of power," appeared to mean getting control of the army, the police, and the civil service and imposing the revolution on the great bulk of the population. To the future utopians, this was unthinkable. For them, lasting "power" developed basically out of widespread convictions and ideas; and many institutions of the old society represented not power — the ability to accomplish desirable objectives — but rather violence. Above all, the movement insisted on openness and constant self-criticism, holding as it did that unless these qualities were built into its ethos, the revolution would be still-born. The movement did not desire the kind of power built primarily on the sheer manipulation of symbols, without a widespread understanding and voluntary acceptance of the goals and principles of the proposed revolution.

Struggle and adherence to a few definite principles helped build the community of the movement which became the community of utopia. Struggle also sharpened the wits of future utopians, particularly because it had to be nonviolent. A saying grew up which was constantly repeated both in the preutopian movement and in utopia: "The less the mind, the greater the violence; the less the violence, the greater the mind."

The Nature of the Transformation

Thus utopia emerged out of the practices and institutions developed by the movement, and the transition to the new order, while not without its difficulties, was not as traumatic as many old-style revolutionists might have supposed. In the old preutopian days, "revolution" was often associated with the sword or with the image of the surgeon's knife cutting out a serious cancer. But the utopian revolutionists preferred the image of the mustard seed. Just as the Kingdom of Heaven in Scripture is analogized to a mustard seed which has achieved its natural and full growth, so was the movement the experimental seed from which utopia arose.

Since utopia represents the achievement of the movement's goals, the movement itself ceased to exist, just as the day-old child is no longer thought of as an embryo, even though it is the result of the embryo's growth. The movement dissolved into the larger whole partly by design; for one of its principles was that once an objective of any political grouping has been attained, it is desirable that the organization disappear altogether. As we have seen, this notion is still reflected in the absence of permanent political parties.

Yet the elimination of long-term political parties and the tendency to greater fluidity in political alignments does not signify absence of rootedness and stability in utopian civilization as a whole. Families may cling to their neighborhoods over several generations, for example; the decline of mobility both makes for and reflects the greater value placed on relatively permanent aspects of human existence; the individual, no longer beset by unprincipled and blind social change, feels freer in the several senses of that term. Utopia is neither the regime of rigid custom nor the reign of an almost constant turbulence engendered by a more and more complex, undirected, unlimited, and accidental technological civilization.

Many utopians are fond of portraying their civilization as a blending of the Garden, which in much myth was the birthplace of man, and the City, which emerged with his sophistication. But utopia has neither the innocence of the primitive Garden nor the arrogance so often characteristic of the historical City. It seeks to combine closeness to beasts, and flowers, and the earth, with reason, deliberate planning, and strictly limited economic development.

In this marriage of the new Garden and the new City, humanity truly discovers and realizes its nature.

Notes

1   This has been notably true in the writings of Sir Karl Popper. In works like *The Open Society and Its Enemies,* he reflects a whole generation which became so disillusioned by the near achievement of a kind of permanent dystopia — fascism and national socialism — that it tended to repudiate all holistic visions.

2   Marie Louise Berneri, in *Journey through Utopia* (London: Routledge & Kegan Paul, 1950), is among those who seem to espouse this position or one very similar to it. She writes from an anarchist point of view.

3   J. B. Bury, in his great work *The Idea of Progress* (New York: Dover Publications, 1955) correctly makes the notion of progress rather distinctive of the modern age. But already when he was writing, the conception was beginning to be undermined, at least in the eyes of many. It was never as ubiquitous as some have argued, even in the United States. Thus minds like those of Brooks and Henry Adams were hardly ever attracted to it.

4   On Karl Barth, see particularly Barth's *Evangelical Theology: An Introduction* (New York: Holt, Rinehart & Winston, 1963) and *God Here and Now* (New York: Harper & Row, 1964). Such studies as Gerrit C. Berkouwer, *The Triumph of Grace in the Theology of Karl Barth* (Grand Rapids, Mich.: William B. Eerdmans Publishing Co., 1956) and Robert W. Jenson, *Alpha and Omega: A Study in the Theology of Karl Barth* (New York: Thomas Nelson, 1963), bring out Barth's emphasis on the transcendence of God and the vast gulf between man and God. Utopists are sometimes said to stress the divine qualities of human nature and, in their implicit theology, to reduce the role of divine grace, which to Barth is central.

5   Emil Brunner, *Justice and the Social Order,* trans. Mary Hottinger (New York: Harper, 1945). Theologically, Brunner did not go nearly as far as Barth in emphasizing the utter transcendence of God. Nevertheless, he stressed in modified form the many difficulties in defining justice and in deliberately constructing a social order built on its norms.

6   *The Nature and Destiny of Man,* 2 vols. (New York: Scribner's, 1940 and 1941), may be said to summarize Niebuhr's political philosophy and his criticism of the notion of inevitable progress. His criticism of "utopian" approaches will be found also in such works as *Christianity and Power Politics* (New York: Scribner's, 1940), *Children of Light and Children of Darkness* (New York: Scribner's 1944), and *Beyond Tragedy* (New York: Scribner's, 1937).

7   But G. H. C. Macgregor, in *The Relevance of an Impossible Ideal* (New York: Fellowship Publications, 1940), did endeavor to answer the contentions of Niebuhr, arguing that "impossible ideals," even though never attained, were important for the fate of mankind and for the achievement of desirable social change. See Mulford Q. Sibley, "Apology for Utopia: Professor Sait's Excogitated Ideas," *Journal of Politics,* February 1940, pp. 57-74, and "Apology for Utopia: Utopia and Politics," *Journal of Politics,* April 1940, pp. 165-88. Andrew Hacker's "In Defense of Utopia," *Ethics,* Spring 1954, pp. 135-38, is also relevant.

George Kateb, in *Utopia and Its Enemies* (Glencoe: Free Press, 1963), seems to suggest that utopia is connected with the notion of violent wholesale change but nevertheless defends it.

8   In the *History of Utopian Thought* (New York: Macmillan, 1926), J. O. Hertzler seeks to differentiate between "anticipations" of future events and utopian thought proper, the former being attempted *forecasts* of future events. "Nowadays," he remarks, "with our ideas of evolution we can have the same idealism as the utopists proper, but it does not take such unreal form, because we have come to feel that amelioration may go on even if the ultimate goal is not in sight." "Modern" utopias are "anticipations," whereas "classical" utopias did not necessarily suggest "forthcoming attainment" (p. 225).

9   See, for example, Sidney and Beatrice Webb, *Soviet Communism: A New Civilization?* 2 vols. (London: Longmans, Green, 1935). This work, written squarely in the midst of the brutal Stalinist epoch, illustrates how easy it is for even great minds trained in the social sciences to see what they wish to see.

10   In the *Gorgias*.

11   Romans, VII:15-24, which Goodspeed translates as follows:

I do not understand what I am doing, for I do not do what I want to do; I do things that I hate. But if I do what I do not want to do, I acknowledge that the Law is right. In reality, it is not I that do these things; it is sin, which has possession of me. For I know that nothing good resides in me, that is, in my physical self; I can will, but I cannot do what is right. I do not do the good things that I want to do; I do the wrong things that I do not want to do. But if I do the things that I do not want to do, it is not I that am acting, it is sin, which has possession of me. I find the law to be that I who want to do right am dogged by what is wrong. My inner nature agrees with the divine law, but all through my body I see another principle in conflict with the law of my reason, which makes me a prisoner to that law of sin that runs through my body.

12   Eugene Zamiatin, *We* (New York: E. P. Dutton & Co., 1952). Here nonhuman Nature as well as primitive human nature are looked upon as ragged, dirty, and uncouth. But they are characterized above all by the fact that they embody the element of spontaneity, which is anathema to those who wish everything to be highly organized.

13   Henry Adams, *Mont Saint-Michel and Chartres* (Cambridge: Houghton Mifflin, 1904), p. 299.

14   Hebrews, XI:1. Or, as Goodspeed translates it: "Faith means the assurance of what we hope for; it is our conviction about the things that we cannot see."

15   That is to say, both prescriptive and descriptive statements can be defended only within paradigms which themselves are taken for granted. When and if these general paradigms or frameworks change, then the context within which the statements are made also changes, and the very meaning of "validity" and "proof" will be affected by the frameworks.

16   Dante Alighieri, *De Monarchia*, ed. E. Moore (Oxford: Clarendon, 1916).

17   Sir Alister Hardy, the biologist, maintains that telepathic communication between and among members of animal species may have played an important role in biological evolution. See his *The Living Stream: Evolution and Man* (New York: Meridian Books, 1968), pp. 234-61. In utopia, of course, this telepathy has a far different status, reflecting the movement from primitive to civilized nature. If telepathy was a vital factor in biological evolution, as Hardy maintains, it was presumably a kind of instinctive faculty at the unconscious level. In utopia, human beings have learned its secrets and raised it to the level of a highly sensitive consciousness, and they use it selectively for their own purposes.

18   On the ethical and legal dimensions of abortion, see, for example, Daniel Callahan, *Abortion: Law, Choice and Morality* (New York: Macmillan Co., 1970); American Friends Service Committee, *Who Shall Live?* (New York: Hill & Wang, 1970); and John Finnis et al., *The Rights and Wrongs of Abortion* (Princeton, N.J.: Princeton University Press, 1974). All applied morality, of course, entails the drawing of lines, and the question in the case of abortion and infanticide is precisely where and under what circumstances the lines are to be drawn. The utopians obviously think that physical life begins with the fertilization of the ovum and that thereafter one is dealing with a potential human being. Just as the child is "father to the man" or to the developed human being, so the embryo is "father to the child," who in turn is father to the fully developed human. And the existential human being foreshadows the teleological human being, who may never be achieved.

19   In Zamiatin's *We*, sex relations take place only under strictly regulated conditions, and reproduction is the privilege of a very few; in George Orwell's *1984* (New York: Harcourt, Brace, 1949), sex relations, except for purposes of reproduction, are discouraged for party members. Explains Orwell: "It was not merely that the sex instinct created a world of its own which was outside the Party's control and which therefore had to be destroyed if possible. What was more important was that sexual privation induced hysteria, which was desirable because it could be transformed into war fever and leader worship" (p. 134). Implicit in both Zamiatin's and Orwell's portrayals of extremely repressed sexual expression would appear to be Wilhelm Reich's notion that sexual repression is always associated with the repression of freedom (at least negative freedom) in general, or with "fascism." See Wilhelm Reich, *The Mass Psychology of Fascism*, trans. Vincent R. Carfagno (New York: Farrar, Straus & Giroux, 1970).

20   William James, "The Moral Equivalent of War," in *Pragmatism and Other Essays* (New York: Washington Square Press, 1970), pp. 289-301.

21   William Wordsworth, "Ode on Intimations of Immortality from Recollections of Early Childhood."

22   The whole idea of the city-country region in utopia is reminiscent of Ebenezer Howard's conception of the "garden city." The Garden Cities and Town Planning Association, in conjunction with Howard, defined a garden city as "a town designed for healthy living and industry; of a size that makes possible a full

measure of social life, but not larger; surrounded by a rural belt; the whole of the land being in public ownership or held in trust for the community." F. J. Osborn in Ebenezer Howard, *Garden Cities of Tomorrow* (Cambridge: M.I.T. Press, 1965), p. 26.

23 *Laws*, Bk. II, where Egypt is commended for allegedly instituting forms of music (and the other arts) conducing to virtue and then allowing no innovations. Innovations in music and the arts may portend undesirable social and political changes.

24 F. H. Bormann, "Growing, Going, Gone," *Not Man Apart* (Friends of the Earth Newsletter), April 1973.

25 From an article by Shri Mahadev Desai in *Harijan*. This article was subsequently reprinted as a preface to the new edition of Ghandhi's *Hind Swaraj* in 1938.

26 *Young India*, October 13, 1921.

27 Henry George, in *Progress and Poverty* (New York: D. Appleton, 1879) had asked why involuntary poverty often seemed to accompany "progress" in science, technology, and the arts. He found the answer in the private ownership of land. The utopians obviously think that, while his answer was too simple to account for the manifest injustices of the old days, the public ownership and administration of land is nevertheless an essential ingredient for the just society.

28 Many utopias in the past, of course, have seen rotation of occupations as an answer to the problem of boredom with work. This was true of John Humphrey Noyes's Oneida Community, for example, where each person performed a given task for only a relatively brief period of time. In the HEW study, *Work in America* (Cambridge, Mass.: M.I.T. Press, 1973), cited in Chapter 6, a similar answer is suggested. But this would involve radically different ways of training and of life expectations — changes in occupation perhaps three, four, or more times during a lifetime. For American utopian experiments and their attempts to deal with issues of this type, see Mark Holloway, *Heavens on Earth* (New York: Library Publishers, 1951).

29 Wiener is admired for his imaginative and creative statements about technology. Norbert Wiener in *The Human Use of Human Beings* (Boston: Houghton Mifflin, 1950) emphasized the need for a more humane use of the newer forms of technology. Earlier, in *Cybernetics* (Cambridge, Mass.: Technology Press of Massachusetts Institute of Technology, 1948), he had pioneered in the study of "thinking machines."

More recently, E. F. Schumacher, in *Small Is Beautiful: Economics as if People Mattered* (New York: Harper & Row, 1973), has restated many of the Gandhian claims for decentralization, small scope and size, and restraint on acquisition. Observes Schumacher: "In the excitement over the unfolding of his scientific and technical powers, modern man has built a system of production that ravishes nature and a type of society that mutilates man." According to this system, "if only there were more and more wealth, everything else . . . would fall into place." Within its scale of values "money is considered to be all-powerful; if it could not actually buy non-material values, such as justice, harmony, beauty, or even health, it could circumvent the need for them or compensate for their loss." In this system, therefore, "the development of production and the acquisition of wealth have . . . become the highest goals of the modern world in relation to which all other goals, no matter how much lip-service may still be paid to them, have come to take second place." These primary goals are self-justifying, and all other goals "have finally to justify themselves in terms of the services their attainment renders to the attainment of the highest." See particularly pp. 52, 54, 55, 70, 110, 227.

30   Arthur Morgan, in *Nowhere Was Somewhere* (Chapel Hill: University of North Carolina Press, 1946), contends that many utopian visions were built on the suggestions of actual historical examples.

31   Thus after the Russian Revolution, the old secret-police structure — under a different name, of course — was simply used against a new set of political dissidents; and the centralized structure of the Communist Party took the place of the inner circle of the czarist regime. Stalinist (and post-Stalinist) structures of repression, far from constituting a reversal of Leninist conceptions and practices, were the logical outcome of them. See Barrington Moore, Jr., *Terror and Progress in the USSR* (Cambridge, Mass.: Harvard University Press, 1954) and Nicolas Berdyaev, *The Origin of Russian Communism* (London: Centenary Press, 1937). Alexander Solzhenitsyn, in *The Gulag Archipelago*, trans. P. Whitney (New York: Harper & Row, 1974), is not essentially wrong in seeing a direct link between Lenin and the existence of Soviet concentration camps.

32   Psalms, CIII:9. The Goodspeed translation puts it: "He will not always chide,/Nor hold his anger forever." In Psalms LXXVIII, 38–39, the Goodspeed version puts it: "But he is merciful; He pardons guilt and does not destroy. And frequently he restrains his anger,/And does not arouse all his rage. So he remembered that they were flesh,/A breath that passes and does not come back."

33   For these and other examples, see Mulford Q. Sibley, *The Quiet Battle: Writings in the Theory and Practice of Non-Violent Resistance* (Boston: Beacon Press, 1969). See also Gene Sharp, *The Politics of Non-Violent Action* (Boston: Porter Sargent, 1973). The possibilities of nonviolent power of various kinds — from pure persuasion to nonviolent coercion — are vast and have only just begun to be studied systematically.

34   Cf. H. G. Wells, *The Open Conspiracy* (London: V. Gollancz, 1928).

Name Index

NAME INDEX

Subject Index

THE BOOK MANUFACTURE

Nature and Civilization was set at Fox Valley Typesetting, Menasha, Wisconsin, and was printed and bound at Kingsport Press. Internal design by the F. E. Peacock Publishers, Inc., art department. The type is Baskerville.